D1547679

WITHDRAWN

The Social Life of Language

The
Social Life
of
Language

GILLIAN SANKOFF

UNIVERSITY OF PENNSYLVANIA PRESS

1980

Library of Congress Cataloging in Publication Data

Sankoff, Gillian.
  The social life of language.

  Bibliography: p. 347
  Includes index.
    1. Language and culture.   2.   Papua New Guinea—Languages   3.   French
language in Montréal, Québec.
I. Title.
P35.S2   401'.9   79-5048
ISBN 0-8122-7771-6

For my parents, Tom and Marjorie Topham

Contents

Contents

Foreword

DELL HYMES

This book might have as its subtitle "Counting in Context." I had best leave the counting to the author, but I can comment on context in ways that may help to highlight the significance of the contents.

Some highlighting, indeed, is needed. The first thing to say about the significance of this book is that the author takes its work so much for granted. The social study of language abounds with brand names and claims for special significance, and the author of this book cites many names associated with public pronouncement, but primarily as helpful colleagues. For her the field is not composed of "conversational analysis," "ethnomethodology," "ethnography of speaking," "sociolinguistics," "sociology of language," and the like, so much as of colleagues whose ideas can help to make sense of Papua New Guinea and French Montréal. There is a need to defend the use of elementary scientific operations (counting) against those who somehow think of them as inappropriate to the science of language, but the greater need is to bring reliable evidence to bear on language situations charged with a priori attitudes.

Such modesty conceals much. True, the systematic quantitative study of on-going linguistic change was initiated by another; a critique of general ideas about language from the standpoint of cultural functions was there to read; but where else can one find systematic quantitative study of on-going linguistic change in a newly independent Third World society, addressing the emergence of a former pidgin as a national language? Or in regard to a subordinated New World immigrant group whose struggle for equality suggests to some the dissolution of a major nation? Is it to be taken for granted that a woman from English-speaking Canada would become a professor at the French-language Université de Montréal? Organize one of the major sociolinguistic research teams of the world? Conduct anthropological field work in New Guinea? Contribute to the limited store of quantitatively based accounts of social and cognitive categorization in non-Western cultures? Work that presupposes everyday fluency in at least four languages? And intensive ethnographic experience across an ocean, and, perhaps farther, across an ethnic boundary in one's home town? Many have cut a dramatic public figure out of far less.

Foreword

The striking thing, then, is that the studies collected in this book take themselves so much for granted, yet are collectively unique. An integration of linguistics and anthropology, of urban ethnography and cross-cultural ethnology, is taken for granted; yet this book is the first to treat such an integration as if it were "normal science." In its silence on the point lies much of its importance. The congeries of interests that coalesced in the 1960s around the goal of a sustained social study of language have tended to separate out again. In arguing for the social study of language, each had its specific opponent, its specific disciplinary world to conquer. For some, it was conventional sociology, for some conventional linguistics, for others philosophy, for still others anthropology, or some combination of these. The impulse to band together depended on a sense of marginality in a home discipline. Achieved legitimacy has weakened the impulse. Old methodological fault lines tend to prevail—logic, intuition, transcripts, cultural ethnography, survey and questionnaire, and the like. A shared interest in "how people do things with words" helps, but the scholar concerned to prove a point in the philosophy of language is not much concerned with whether or not his categories are "emic" among, let us say, the Navajo; someone concerned to argue a claim about "English" or "conversation" in general may not wonder about differences among classes.

Sankoff takes for granted the plurality of interests in the social study of language, as sources of relevant ideas. These studies take account of political oratory, discourse analysis, semantic and grammatical systems, dialect boundaries, language contact, changes in social and political status of a language. The world of the studies begins with actual speech communities, and the work invariably assumes variability: whatever one's question, the answer needs to be informed by evidence of actual occurrence, of what is done.

There are other configurations of activity that promise to develop the diverse tendencies of language study as "normal science," notably configurations within the rubrics of "discourse analysis" and "pragmatics." None has quite the importance of the configuration represented in this work—not, at least, if one wants to understand the world not only as structure, but also as change. One might call the implicit perspective of the work in this volume "micro-evolutionary." It is micro-evolutionary in both its model of the human actor and its contextualization of language.

As to the human actor: Sankoff escapes the limitations of both implicit determinism and anarchism in analysis of cultural behavior. Counting, as normal science, enables one to go beyond statements of the sort: "speakers of English, Canadians (whatever) do this, do that."

People are not tacitly reduced to what the phenomenological sociologist Harold Garfinkel has called "cultural dopes," actors who can do only what cultural rules provide. (Given our concern in linguistics and anthropology with structure, the phrase "structural dopes" might be appropriate.) Yet the existence of indeterminancy, the fact that behavior and meaning can be newly interpreted and constituted with each situation, does not lead to a view of actors whose action is an unchartable miasma. Cultural regularity is not dissolved into ad hoc and post hoc free creation. What people do is variable according to situation, interest, need, yet intelligible to themselves and others in terms of recurrent patterns.

So much may seem too obvious to belabor, but contemporary linguistics and social science have yet to find a unanimous balance between the two poles just sketched. Chapter 2 of this book seems to me to do an excellent job of integration. The distinction between situation-defining variables and marking variables is one that I think is general to the social study of language. Since one of Sankoff's concerns is to join quantitative study with the ethnography of speaking (see chapter 3), let me mention the generalization here. In order not to miss factors that may be relevant to a given rule, event, or way of speaking, one needs an adequate "etic" frame of reference (Hymes 1972a), but such a frame of reference does not indicate how to determine just which of its factors are relevant in a given case. Of course the general notion of contrast within a relevant frame applies, and there are well-known systematic methods of ethnography; but it is possible to suggest something specific to speaking. For a given case, it appears that some of the potential factors of speaking will be considered given, and hence can be treated as context. Just certain factors will be those focused upon as admitting of choice. The choices constitute style, and the reasons or import of the choices can be considered an intended or imputed strategy. The range of potential factors, in other words, can be seen in terms of the relations among style, strategy, and context. These terms are simply appropriate names at the level of discourse and interaction for the values of a relationship fundamental to linguistics, the relationship of form and meaning in context. Sankoff's situation-defining variables are equivalent to context, and her marking variables are equivalent to a style in service of a strategy.[1]

1. I first formulated this in response to the manuscript of Keith Basso's *Portraits of Whitemen* (New York: Cambridge University Press, 1979). Let me thank Basso and Joel Sherzer for their comments on that formulation, and Martin Steinmann for inviting me to speak at a conference on rhetoric at the University of Minnesota in May 1978, where the formulation was presented.

Such a formulation is essentially rhetorical, as is Sankoff's own analysis of cognitive variability with respect to the Buang notion of *dgwa* (chapter 8). Insofar as integrated perspective on the social study of language in terms of interaction is concerned, I believe it must indeed be rhetorical along the lines indicated by Sankoff's chapters and the comments just made. The classical concern of rhetoric for persuasion, amplified by Kenneth Burke in terms of identification (Burke 1950), is the same as the concern of all who would link structure and strategy in the study of language today.

There is a second dimension to an integrated perspective on the social study of language, and the one to which the chapters of this book contribute most. If we wish to understand language in history, we find that linguistics has developed considerable precision in the analysis of processes and products of change that reflect a period of human history that is largely at an end. The precision addresses the differentiation of languages from a common ancestor. It addresses the peopling of the planet, the movements and migrations of peoples, under conditions that sever communicative contact, so that intrinsic variability and cumulative change inevitably result in mutual unintelligibility. In our era, however, the major processes are not of that kind. A "New World" that had thousands of distinct languages in 1492 now is dominated by English, French, Portuguese, and Spanish over most of its terrain. The languages that survive or have immigrated are largely subordinate. Instead of differentiation of English, say, into mutually unintelligible languages every so many miles (as was the aboriginal situation in much of the present United States), one has *reintegration* of diverse languages within areas of political hegemony; specializations in functional domain, as to the home, religion, certain tasks.

Of course there was always more differentiation of personal and social linguistic repertoire than summary maps and the assigning of one name, color, and language to people suggest. Still it was possible in the past to imagine the anthropological world as if languages came one to a culture. Some scholars and citizens may wish that were the case today, but, as Sankoff shows vividly for New Guinea, it is not. Yet, as scholars, we are best equipped to trace a language back to a reconstructed ancestor, or to trace an ancestor through differentiation into its descendants. We are ill equipped to make sense out of the adaptation of a subordinated language to a rise of national feeling, or to use as a national *lingua franca*; to trace the consequences of ebb and flow in communicative status and prestige; to recognize recurrent patterns in the adaptation of a language to a certain kind of niche in a personal, community, national repertoire. In short, we are best equipped to look at languages

xii

as evolving isolates, most poorly equipped to look at languages as instruments of evolving populations.

The first model (genetic differentiation) has its badges—regularity of sound change, and regularity of sound correspondence. Variable rules bid fair to become a badge of the second model, which might be dubbed "functional integration." Regular sound change and variable rules are both phenomena within a single line of linguistic development (and of course have an intimate connection). What might correspond to sound correspondences, as a badge of the second model, that would have to do with relations between languages? Regular sound correspondence deals with the results of regular sound change in languages having a common ancestor; it reflects a unity preceding separation. Can variable rules imply a unity subsequent to integration? A regularity due to convergence and interinfluence? Or, more generally, can regularities in linguistic features be found among languages that are connected, not as descendants of a common ancestor, but as varieties having a common niche?

Sankoff's seventh chapter contributes to the first possibility. It helps to make the foundations of historical linguistics a field for investigation, not something simply handed on as received truth. Her first chapter concludes by suggesting a regularity of the more general sort, linking linguistic niche and linguistic attitudes. Like the classical precedent in contemporary work, Ferguson (1959) on diglossia, the passage shows the importance of this kind of contribution. The sense of worth and the opportunities open to millions upon millions of people are involved. As Ferguson's pioneering study shows, such a contribution is difficult. A parallel niche may give rise to similarity, not only of attitude (social meaning), but also of form. If languages are indeed means of adaptation, then adaptation cannot be assumed to be without consequence. A linguistic variety adapted to some purposes and not others is likely to become better suited to serving those purposes and not others. A language integrated within one set of norms of interaction, cognitive styles, literary genres, is not necessarily as effective within another. Stereotypes and prejudices about languages because of their secondary associations are indeed so great a problem that the kind of attack Sankoff launches at the end of her first chapter no doubt is the primary need.

And the careful depiction of variation and on-going change in Montréal French has as its implicit context a social order that does not think of French in Montréal as like that at all. Sankoff once recorded a man and woman speaking alternately in the Montréal standard, then in the colloquial called "Joual," and played their speech to a respectable luncheon audience. The audience could not accept that what it heard was spoken by one and the same couple. There is a further parallel here to the history of the model of genetic differentiation. When developed in the nineteenth century, the regularities of the model were thought by many not to apply to "lesser" languages, such as those indigenous to the New World. The thesis that regular sound change and sound correspondence are universal, applicable to Algonquian and Athapaskan just as to Indo-European, was a liberal as well as a scientific cause for Edward Sapir and Leonard Bloomfield. Just so today, the thesis that systematic variability is inherently true of all languages, including the standards of elites in urban centers such as Montréal, may be a liberal as well as a scientific cause. One should think of the Montréal studies in this book as documents in a struggle against prejudice and disdain.

From the standpoint of scientific understanding, and social change based on scientific understanding, the treacherous facts of interdependence between linguistic means and the social ends they have evolved to serve must also be addressed. Our discipline is somewhat schizophrenic in this regard. When differences are presented as favorable to the underdog, as in Whorf's comparison of Hopi to "Standard Average European," we can rejoice. The private conversations of linguists often enough contain remarks about the wonderful things that "my" language has and others do not. When differences might reflect unfavorably on the underdog, we retreat to the equality of all languages in the eyes of science. Yet it is inconsistent to approve of Hopi being "rapierlike" (Whorf's word) in some respects in comparison to English, yet not to recognize the opposite of "rapierlike" as a fact of languages as well. The marvelous accounts of the continuity of expansion in content and function of Tok Pisin in this book have as their implicit counterpart contraction in content and function of other language varieties in other situations.

The kind of modeling developed in chapter 6, as to "language limit" in a given social context, could perhaps be elaborated from questions of mutual intelligibility between languages to questions of relative effectiveness of varieties for purposes other than information transfer. Clearly any adequate analysis of such questions will have to make use of the quantitative approach to linguistic change across cultural contexts, as does Sankoff. Indeed, the ingredients that are required for an adequate analysis of the social life of language in the modern world are all here—technical linguistics, quantitative and mathematical technique, ethnographic inquiry, ethnohistorical perspective. Just the fact that all are needed may militate against success—the author is almost alone in having such a combination of talents—but if the modern world should finally come to have the modern linguistics that it needs, this modest book will be seen as a landmark.[2]

2. Let me claim personal privilege for a note on recent history. In her preface Sankoff presents an honest account of the climate of opinion of a decade. The sequence is correct, I believe, as to the prevailing climate, but not perhaps as to every niche. Ecology teaches that a small difference in altitude, declivity, shade, can cause a distinct micro-climate, and so also in scholarship. Where the preface speaks of "consensus" and "the discipline as a whole," the expressions should be taken to allow for variation. If taken in absolute terms, then they would not allow my work to have been part of "sociolinguistics."

The explanation no doubt lies in personal experience. Each of us has a working conception of the development of the field based in that; different contexts of training, research, employment, association give rise to different contours and landmarks. My 1970a paper may appear a turning point (Sankoff's introduction, fn. 1) partly because we both attended the conference at which it was presented. To me, looking back, the paper appears a thoroughgoing presentation of a perspective that informs previous writing, beginning with two papers of 1961 ("Functions of speech: an evolutionary approach," and "Linguistic aspects of cross-cultural personality study"). The first argues that existing languages differ in degree of evolutionary advance as a consequence of sociocultural adaptation, and the second that language and speech are relative to sociocultural values and practices. I would think of papers of 1964 ("Introduction: Toward ethnographies of communication"; "A perspective for linguistic anthropology"; "Directions in (ethno-)linguistics") as based on the priority and relativity of functions of speech. The analysis of the language and culture of the Wishram-Wasco Chinook as rooted in common cognitive orientations (1961, 1966) seem to me to have the same basis, as does the general interpretation given the Whorfian hypothesis in the latter paper. Again, papers of 1967 ("Models of the interaction of language and social setting"; "On communicative competence"; and "Why linguistics needs the sociologist") seem to elaborate such a perspective. The theme of an expanded conception of linguistics, in terms of description of speaking, pervades these papers, but so does the theme that discovery of structure depends on description of speaking as something socially constituted and relative. So, at least, it seemed to me, looking back in the introduction to my own book in this series (1974).

It is not that I should claim credit for the general point. Years earlier Greenberg (cited at the end of 1964c) had observed that the relation between levels of language structure was such that from the structure, one could not predict the function. I inverted this. I had learned from Kenneth Burke (while we were at the Center for Advanced Study in the Behavioral Sciences in 1957–58) that a descriptive framework not including purpose always failed in his experience to be adequate. He ascribed the lesson himself to Aristotle.

Obviously the history of a discipline is not a history of the origin of ideas but a history of their use. It may well be right to single out 1970 as a date when my personal history and the history of sociolinguistics, as an aspect of linguistics, began effectively to coincide. Sankoff is in a better position to judge. The only difference would be that I would see it as a date in the history, not of the author, but of the audience.

Introduction

The papers in this collection were written over a span of ten years: 1968–78. During this period many scholars addressed the problem of how language is molded by the social world in which it lives. The view of the relationship between society and language that this phrasing reflects is not, however, one that prevailed in the sixties. At that time, the goals of sociolinguistics were thought to be more modest, i.e., the investigation of the social circumstances of the *use* of language.[1] During most of the decade after the appearance of Chomsky's *Syntactic Structures* in 1957, consensus had it that the locus of language was the mind.[2] Thus anything theoretically interesting about language was thought to derive either from its internal logic as an autonomous system, or from properties of the mind. Certainly the contributions of people who viewed language in this way taught us that it would be foolish to neglect the extent to which language is shaped by the universals of human cognition, memory, logic. But by the late sixties, sociolinguists were beginning to show that language structure is also importantly a product of the social world: the only world in which speakers' internalized language systems can be actualized, the only place where the word can be made flesh.

There occurred, then, over the period when these papers were written, a transition between studying the social context of language use (language structure presumed to be a separate matter, attended to

1. Though Hymes's early papers had prepared the way for a reconception of the relationship between language structure and language use, it was only in 1970 that he made this reconception explicit. Arguing for "the priority, plurality, and problematic (empirical) status of the functions of speech" (1970a: 113), he stated that a sociolinguistic critique of linguistic theory must be "functional, in that the discovery of new structural relationships depends on the recognition of the functions that they serve" (1970a: 112). Similarly, Labov's early papers were often misinterpreted as seeking to correlate social ("extralinguistic") factors with autonomous linguistic rules—a misinterpretation completely in line with the then prevalent view of language as an autonomous system.
2. This was, of course, not a new idea. Weinreich, Labov, and Herzog (1968) trace it back to the Neogrammarians of the nineteenth century, through Saussure and the American structuralists.

by autonomous linguistics) and studying how the social nature of language use may constrain, influence, and shape language structure. This transition is reflected in the papers collected here as it is in the writing of other sociolinguists working at this time. The papers in this volume that were published between 1969 and 1973 did not explicitly challenge the assumption that social factors served merely to provide a setting or context for language use. These papers (e.g., chapter 2, published in 1972) investigated the social conditions of language use without making the further claim that such conditions—or that language use itself— impinged in any significant way on language structure. The distribution of language use across categories of participants and situations constituted the problem to be explained.

Somewhat later papers (e.g., chapter 3, published in 1974) claimed that "performance" (actualized, performed speech) could be properly treated as a sample of what could be generated by speakers' internalized rules, and as such provided a better basis for the writing of abstract grammars than did linguists' intuitions. Here, the distribution of linguistic features across speakers was taken to reflect differences among their grammars, differences that could be accounted for in terms of the different social experience of various categories of speakers.[3] Similar arguments were developed in Labov (1970) and in Cedergren and D. Sankoff (1974).

More recent papers propose a yet stronger influence for social phenomena in accounting for linguistic facts. Chapter 11, for example, published in 1976, suggests that social-interactional considerations specific to verbal exchange among a small number of co-present participants have been central in shaping the syntax used for relativization in New Guinea Tok Pisin.

The papers assembled here do, then, reflect the transition that characterizes the discipline as a whole—a transition towards a view that language is structurally stamped by the fact of its use in social life. The papers have nevertheless been organized otherwise than as a linear series.

The first part of the book includes papers that situate language within social and historical space. Few of them discuss details of language structure. Rather, they examine various models for understand-

---

3. Different social experience of course includes growing up and acquiring language at different times. Cf. Labov's (1963, 1965, 1972a) demonstration that systematic age differences in the distribution of particular linguistic features as observed at one point in time could reflect ongoing language change. This theoretical reintegration of diachrony and synchrony was perhaps his most important contribution to linguistic theory.

ing particular kinds of language distribution. They also deal with how people in different kinds of language environments understand the place of language in their lives, and how people use language in talking about the social world.

The second part consists of papers that deal with the structure of language as such. The approach is uniformly quantitative and historical, and in every case there is an attempt to understand how, and to what extent, social facts are necessary in explaining the linguistic patterns. These social facts can be usefully divided into two types, corresponding to two levels that can be discerned in the social world in which language lives.

The first level consists of the political, social, and economic events that affect the place of a language or language variety in social life, e.g., the conquest of people speaking one language by people speaking another; the importation for relatively short periods of time of "guest workers" or indentured laborers who do not know the language of the place to which they come; legislation about which language(s) will be legitimated by the institutions of the modern state.[4] A surprising amount of information about relevant events can be found in the "external histories" of various European languages.

The second level consists of the social situations of language use. Over most of human history language has evolved in situations of face-to-face interaction, which makes this the first place to look for influences that may contribute to *general* properties of language.[5] Aspects of face-to-face interaction that would seem to bear on language include the management of order (the allocation and internal organization of turns; openings and closings of occasions of speaking; sequence structures including two-part pairs such as questions and answers, greeting exchanges, apologies and acceptances, and so on), and also include the expression of relationships among participants.[6]

Many linguists still find it difficult to see how either one of the levels of the "social world" is relevant to the internal structure of language. A close reading of the sociolinguistic literature of the past decade, however, indicates that it *is* possible to make significant generalizations about how both human interaction and general sociohistorical processes contribute to giving language its particular struc-

4. Cf. Bourdieu and Boltanski 1975.
5. Other, special types of communication situations (e.g., speechmaking, whether in the Roman forum or on television) may be responsible for some less general properties.
6. In many ways, the forms that seem to "express" relationships are in fact creating, building up, and maintaining the understanding among participants that "relationships" exist.

ture.[7] And about how particular aspects of particular social systems, resulting from particular historical forces, have shaped particular languages.

As a student, I was puzzled to learn that although events like conquests and revolutions could control the life and death of a language, they were thought to have nothing to do with the internal workings of the language; at least nothing of any theoretical interest could be said about the topic. "Macro"-sociolinguistics was considered to be a theoretically irrelevant field. I think this was caused partly by the antihistorical bias that pervaded the social sciences in this period (the idea that structure exists only in a synchronic slice), and partly by the strength and attractiveness of the thesis of language autonomy.[8] In 1980, however, it is clear that some theoretically interesting things *can* be said about this area. For example, concerning the linguistic consequences of the social marginalization of languages, compare the social situation of the Celtic languages in western Europe, Albanian in Greece, and many native American languages in the United States, and the types of grammatical changes they are undergoing, as studied respectively by Dorian (1973, 1978), Trudgill (1976–77), and Hill (1973). Many other examples could be adduced, including the case of pidginization and creolization discussed in several of the present papers.

The social-interactional level was perhaps accepted as theoretically relevant to language somewhat earlier than was the social-historical. Nevertheless, even classic studies like those of Brown and Gilman (1960) and Geertz (1960) could be dismissed as dealing with matters like pronouns or address systems that were not part of the "grammatical core" of language.[9] Recent work like that of Brown and

7. Sankoff (1979) and Levinson (1978) go so far as to talk of "universals" in this context. Certainly on the level of the structure of interaction it seems reasonable to talk of "universals" in the way that they are currently being discussed in linguistics. (Indeed, as Levinson points out, this is in part the domain of pragmatics, conceived in terms of the participant-language relationship—though it is more difficult to see how pragmatics covers the "management of order" aspects of interaction). In terms of social history, though, one cannot conceive of "universals" in at all the same way. "The plantation context," for example, is not a social type, but rather a result of specific historical forces that produced one social (and linguistic) result at one time and place; another at another.

8. Hymes (1975) argues convincingly that having an autonomous object of study was important in legitimating linguistics as an academic discipline within the American university system.

9. Sherzer (1973) describes a number of aspects of language structure to which linguists appear to have systematically avoided relating relevant social facts.

Levinson (1978), however, has shown that the influence of social relationships, of "politeness," can penetrate much more deeply into the
internal organs of language than had previously been suspected. And
questions of the sequential organization of turn taking have been shown
(Duranti and Ochs 1979) to bear on matters like word order (a topic
than which it would be difficult to find a more syntactic). Several of the
papers included here (notably chapters 11 and 12) also attempt to show
how social-interactional properties relate to language structure.

I have spoken of language as "living in a social world." This is
not an idle figure of speech. It is meant to convey my conviction that in
the long term language is more dependent on the social world than the
other way around. It is true that linguistic interchange facilitates social
intercourse, and that language can be used to create structures of understanding that define and redefine the world for speakers. Despite the
reasonableness of this view, however, the world, in a pinch, turns out
to be able to force its reality on language.[10] Language *does* facilitate
social intercourse, but if the social situation is sufficiently compelling,
language will bend. Someone learns someone else's language, or a compromise is reached. As argued in the first paper in this collection, the
existence of language is totally dependent on the maintenance of social
possibilities for its use, as the value speakers attribute to it depends on
the quality and nature of these possibilities.

This could, of course, all be true without implying the truth of
the further claim, that the social world is to some degree responsible for
the structure of language. My interpretation of the studies cited above,
and others along similar lines, is that they indicate the likelihood of our
discovering further properties of language that are attributable to its
social underpinnings. In 1968, Gumperz distinguished between referential and social functions of language. Referential refers to the informa-
tional structure of discourse, to truth-values and propositional logic.
Certainly language as a code is specialized for this purpose. But language is also designed to convey other ("social") information, expressing speaker orientation to the message content as well as to other
participants, and expressing social divisions through the variable use of
optional features in the grammar.[11]

I take it as demonstrated that language is sensitive to all of these
things, and that language use, subject to all of these influences, does

10. Certainly the realities of things like physical situation show up in
verb deixis (Fillmore 1972), as does temporal situation in tense and aspect
systems (Givón 1973; Traugott in press).

11. Labov's as yet unpublished exploration of grammatical elaboration
as a response to the expression of social meaning (ms., 1971) has stimulated
much of my thinking about this problem.

mold language structure. To my mind, the most challenging problems in contemporary sociolinguistics involve putting together the two levels in the society-language relationship. It is almost a truism that within language use, one can locate practices that mark the speaker socially. Indeed, any relevant social distinction will be marked linguistically.

But how does this come to pass? If social change creates new social categories and classes, how do these social distinctions come to be reflected in linguistic practice? We can, for example, relate the rise of the bourgeoisie in Western Europe to the industrial revolution and the expansion of capitalism, and we can learn how the concept of a uniform national language was supported by the institutions of the emergent nation-states.[12] We can understand how the establishment of standard languages was in the interest of the developing bourgeoisie. And we can see that social class differences today are marked by differences in language. But the creation, development, and maintenance of these linguistic distinctions are located within verbal interaction. And we do not really know how this works. How does the norm of the standard language come to carry the weight that it does, able to create embarrassment and shame on the part of those who do not possess it, able even to exclude them from domains where its use is obligatory? This is more than a matter of a slip between language legislation and the lips of speakers, for there are many aspects of the legitimate language, of the standard or ideal model, that never find their way into language legislation. And indeed the issue is more general, not at all specific to societies with language legislation and mass education. How are macrohistorical processes realized through interaction such that the (usually minor) linguistic differences that mark the (often major) social differences come to carry the symbolic weight that they do?

These questions have emerged as a kind of long term project, out of work to which many people have contributed. Six of the papers in this book have coauthors, because the work from which they derive (especially the Montréal French project) has been team work. Words are not enough to acknowledge the very great intellectual debt I owe to all the people who have worked with me over the decade during which the papers in this book were written. Very special thanks to Henrietta, Suzanne, Pierrette, and Didi. Thanks also to the Center for Advanced Studies in the Behavioral Sciences, Stanford, California, where a number of these papers were written.

G.S.

12. Cf., for example, Balibar and Laporte (1974).

I. Language in Social and Historical Space

In speaking of languages that are not buttressed by the institutions of the modern state, linguists have come to treat their abstraction (some might say reification) of a "language" as some kind of naturally-occurring entity ("language x has such-and-such rule of grammar"), neglecting the fact that unwritten as well as written languages have the underpinnings of their existence in social processes. The papers in this section take the very definition of "a language" as problematic, exploring questions of differences among speakers and among speech varieties, questions of the social processes underlying the creation of language boundaries, questions of how to model language variation at several levels.

At the most macrohistorical level, the problems have to do with how the distribution of languages and language varieties "on the ground" affects the way they are used. Languages certainly can be said to have a geographical distribution, but the geographical space they occupy is also social space. Chapter 5 discusses the distribution of the languages of Papua New Guinea, with particular attention to the consequences of this distribution for multilingualism. Chapter 2 explores models for analyzing code switching among multilingual speakers, and chapter 1 takes up the political consequences of the inequality of access to particular languages.

Several of the papers discuss the social processes underlying particular types of language distribution. Chapter 7, in comparing models of the relationship among languages, makes the point that the social model underlying the Stammbaum model is one of the split-and-divergence of populations, whereas the wave model assumes social communication across language boundaries. Chapter 6 discusses how the "mutual intelligibility" criterion for deciding on language and dialect boundaries can come to be affected by the acquisition of passive competence in other language varieties, typical of speakers in a chain-dialect situation. Chapter 1 discusses the differences between the relationships obtaining among languages whose speakers are on an equal social footing, as compared with those obtaining under situations of inequality of various kinds.

3

The four remaining papers deal more specifically with how to analyze variability among speakers. Chapters 8 and 9 treat the issue of mapping from how people talk about particular areas of social organization onto how they conceive of those aspects of social organization. Chapters 3 and 4 are concerned with quantitative methods in grammatical analysis. These four were published between 1971 and 1974, a time that in current terms is almost prehistoric in view of the tremendous developments in quantitative linguistic methods of the mid-seventies (cf., for example, D. Sankoff, ed., 1978). Since I believe the points they make are still relevant, I have chosen to leave them pretty much as is, only warning the reader that the quantitative methods therein are not the most modern vintage.

I.

Political Power and Linguistic Inequality in Papua New Guinea

I. INTRODUCTION

Perhaps the major task of sociolinguistics is to reconcile the essentially neutral, or arbitrary, nature of linguistic difference and linguistic change with the social stratification of languages and levels of speech unmistakable in any complex speech community. Indulging in personification, we might term this the study of how social processes seize upon linguistic disparities that are intrinsically symmetric, and upon innocuous linguistic processes constantly operating in any language, and systematically manipulate them into a highly structured system of speech varieties which mirrors and reinforces social class and power distinctions. My object here is to focus upon some of these transformations as I have studied them in Papua New Guinea.[1] The theme is general, though I will draw most heavily on my own experience in Lae, in the Buang area near Mumeng, Morobe Province, and in Morobe Province in general.[2]

In the next section I will review some notions of linguistic relativity and show how and to what extent these are exemplified by the socially symmetric relationship of languages and dialects in the pre-

This paper originally appeared in William and Jean O'Barr, eds., *Language and Politics* (Mouton, 1976), pp. 283–310. The present version has been revised by updating the Papua New Guinea census statistics, by eliminating one table that contained material found elsewhere in this volume, and by making a few minor textual alterations.

1. Papua New Guinea is a newly self-governing nation of some 2.5 million people, situated north of Australia and east of Indonesia (see Map 1). New Guinea was a former German colony which came under Australian rule in 1914; Papua was a former British colony which passed to Australian rule in 1906. They were jointly administered by Australia from 1946–1973 under United Nations supervision. Papua New Guinea gained self government in late 1973 and full independence in 1975.

2. I wish to thank the many New Guineans without whose generosity and hospitality during my three visits to New Guinea (July 1966–August 1967; July–August 1968; June–September 1971) this essay would not have been possible. I also thank the Canada Council for sponsoring the first two visits.

colonial situation, or, at present, among local languages. In the third section I will briefly summarize the state of sociolinguistic knowledge about the other extreme: the class structure of language in present-day urban North America. In the fourth section I will sketch typical political organization at the village level in New Guinea, and the changes that have occurred in the power structure since the colonial period. The fifth section will discuss rhetorical aspects of political behavior and will trace the integration of the dichotomy between local languages (Tok Ples) and the colonial *lingua franca* (Tok Pisin) into relationships of power and authority.[3] Finally, in the last section, I will discuss the deepening of linguistic stratification accompanying the current spread of English.

Studies of "language and politics" frequently focus their attention on the use of language in political action at the local level—what happens in village meetings, village courts, and so on. It seems to me misleading, however, to concentrate on this level, as such a focus all too often contains the implicit assumptions (1) that the ultimate or at least major political decisions are made within local level institutions, and (2) that such institutions are recognized by all participants as the legitimate structures in which political problems are concentrated. My concern here is to try to understand the larger social and political forces that shape and constrain the place language comes to occupy in people's everyday lives.

2. LINGUISTIC RELATIVITY AND VILLAGE NEW GUINEA

The basic tenet of linguistic relativity is that all natural languages are on an equal footing in terms of their capacities for human communication. There is no denying, of course, that some languages are used in cultural contexts and for purposes for which other languages are not, and that they are to some extent adapted or specialized to these purposes and contexts. This adaptation is, however, largely a matter of lexical proliferation and stylistic elaboration; there is no evidence that in terms of the basic machinery of a language considered as a code for transmitting messages, i.e., the phonology, morphology, syntax, or even the overall semantic organization, any one language is inherently superior, more logical, accurate or efficient, or in any way preferable to any other language. Thus stereotypes such as that French is a particularly beauti-

---

3. Tok Pisin is variously referred to in the literature as Melanesian Pidgin (Hall 1943; Mihalic 1971; Brash 1971), Neo-Melanesian (Mihalic 1957), and New Guinea Pidgin (Wurm 1971b; Laycock 1970a). I follow the usage of its speakers in referring to it as Tok Pisin.

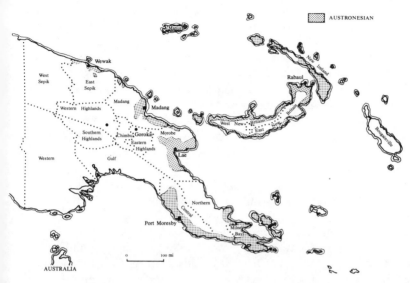

Figure 1-1. Linguistic divisions of Papua New Guinea.

ful or precise language, that English is inherently better suited to scientific thinking, that nonstandard English is illogical, etc., have no basis in linguistic science. No language, by virtue of its inherent structure, bestows any general cognitive advantage on its speakers.

Extreme linguistic relativism needs a good deal of qualification, such as is provided by the evolutionary perspective of Berlin and Kay (1969), Kay (1977), Berlin (1972), or the functionally adaptive and ethnographic perspectives of Hymes (1961a, 1966, 1972a). Situations of prolonged bilingualism (Gumperz and Wilson 1971), situations of language contact, of the use of *lingue franche* and especially of pidgins seem to lead to certain types of reduction in surface complexities of the languages used (Ferguson 1971; Kay and Sankoff 1974; Hymes 1971; Traugott 1973). Nevertheless it is important to stress the great consensus among linguists regarding the scientific validity of the relativist position on grammar, viewed as a code or instrument for communication—a point that few nonlinguists realize.

Anyone familiar with western speech communities knows that in various periods and in various regions, people have been willing to accept the superiority of Greek, Latin, French, German, English, or Russian over their own language as being linguistically justified. Even more widespread are opinions that Parisian French, Oxford English, High German, etc., are inherently more comprehensible, more logical, and more beautiful than provincial or nonstandard varieties and dialects. The historical record incontrovertibly shows that these languages and varieties have spread because of the political and economic dominance of their speakers, and one would be hard put to argue that, for example, the Germanic dialects were better adapted to warfare and thus helped their speakers to dominate the Celts. But those who came to accept these various languages were convinced not only that it would be more practical to use a common standard for wider communication purposes, but also that these languages were inherently superior instruments as compared to the local languages or dialects they had previously spoken. Indeed it has become common to attribute the political and economic inferiority of speakers of nonstandard varieties to mental and communicative incapabilities deriving from sloppy or illogical language, as the abundant literature on compensatory language education programs alone would attest.

The linguistic situation in Papua New Guinea, including attitudes towards language, has been strikingly different from the picture I have just painted. There has always been a great deal of linguistic diversity in Papua New Guinea, but in precolonial times this diversity was accompanied by very little inequality—egalitarian relationships among language groups had not been altered by imperialism, social stratification, or nationalism. The linguistic diversity and the great differences in even major grammatical features between languages whose speakers are in geographical proximity have been noted by numerous authors (Capell 1971; Hooley and McElhanon 1970; Wurm 1971a). These major language differences, it should be noted, occur among groups having very similar cultures. Wurm (1960: 129) estimates approximately 700 separate languages for Papua New Guinea. With a total population of approximately 2,600,000 (Papua New Guinea Population Census 1971), this averages out to about one language per 3,500 people. This distribution is, however, fairly uneven (Wurm 1960: 132; chapter 5 below). The approximately 80 largest language groups include over a million speakers, whereas at the other end of the spectrum, the 200 smallest languages total fewer than 50,000 speakers.

The languages of Papua New Guinea belong to two large families: the Austronesian languages, which are distributed throughout the Pacific; and the non-Austronesian or Papuan languages, unrelated to any other known language family. The largest language groups are mainly Papuan, found predominantly in the center of the Papua New Guinea mainland as well as in the centers of many of the smaller islands. Though not all languages in the coastal areas are Austronesian, this is where they are concentrated, the only large inland groups of Austronesian speakers being in the Markham Valley and the subcoastal areas of southern Morobe Province. Many Austronesian groups are very small pockets on the coast, surrounded by Papuan speakers. This distribution tends to suggest that Austronesian speaking peoples arrived in Melanesia after the Papuan speakers, occupying many of the coastal areas and forcing Papuan speakers inland. The large size of many of the interior Papuan speaking groups in the Highlands would also suggest a relatively recent and rapid expansion.

In most areas other than the wide valleys of the Highlands, then, linguistic groups tend to be relatively small, and even within the Highlands, dialect differentiation is such that neighboring groups often speak perceptibly different dialects. Thus it is a reasonable assumption that most New Guineans living before the colonial period had personal experience of linguistic diversity, without having ventured very far from their home villages. We may well ask, however, what this linguistic diversity implied in social terms, i.e., what were the social parameters that made for a considerable degree of linguistic diversity, coupled with a fair degree of knowledge of other varieties on the part of many people.

Haudricourt (1961) has described a state of what he called "egalitarian bilingualism" in precolonial New Caledonia, resulting from social contacts such as intermarriage between small groups. Hollyman (1962) sees this type of bilingualism as responsible for a tendency he has noted in some Melanesian languages toward extensive borrowing, particularly at the phonological and lexical levels. Certainly neighboring groups in Papua New Guinea had contact through intermarriage, trade, and warfare, leading to a certain amount of bilingualism or competence in other dialects, depending on the degree of linguistic difference among neighboring groups. Clearly women who married into other language or other dialect villages would have this competence, as might their children, particularly if visiting of affines were kept up. And the fact that linguistic differentiation exists even on the level of neighboring villages speaking the same "dialect" has been pointed to in several studies of disparate geographical areas and language groups including the Eastern Highlands Kainantu area (McKaughan 1964, 1973), the Dani in West Irian (Bromley 1967), both Papuan speaking groups, and the Austronesian Buang of the Huon Gulf hinterland (Sankoff 1968; chapter 6 below). On bilingualism in the Highlands, see Wurm and Laycock (1961). Thus it is quite possible that a sizeable minority of New Guinean women have had the experience of being at least to some degree linguistic "foreigners" in the village into which they have married.

Given this general situation, we might well ask why such contacts did not lead to a *lessening* of linguistic differences, through dialect or language leveling. A partial explanation probably lies in the fact that New Guineans often make use of other-language and other-dialect knowledge in rhetoric and verbal art (Sankoff 1977a), highlighting the known differences between their own and neighboring speech varieties. Salisbury (1962), for example, describes the importance the Siane attach to the distinctiveness of their own language from neighboring languages. Given the degree of bilingualism Salisbury describes for the Siane, it appears that contacts with and awareness of other languages have led not to leveling but to heightened consciousness of and pride in difference.[4]

This type of situation also prevails among speakers of Buang, as described in chapter 6 below. Among the Buang, knowledge of these related language varieties fades out with distance, but of the varieties that they recognize, speakers will insist that their own variety is the best, that it is the easiest and clearest to understand, that it is in fact understood by people from miles around, that it is the easiest to learn, and so on. Other varieties are judged to be some kind of corruption or aberration from the speaker's own, and imitations occasion much mirth on the part of any local audience. The point is that each village feels its own dialect to be the best, and accentuates its particular features especially in contrast with those other varieties it is most familiar with, i.e., the closest ones, geographically and usually also in terms of degree of similarity.

In precolonial Papua New Guinea, then, language diversity was at least as marked as in Europe, for example, but lacking stratified societies, far-reaching empires, and nationalist consciousness, this horizontal diversity was not accompanied by any linguistic stratification. Each group was ethnocentric about its own variety, but since such groups were all very small, since people knew that other people thought their own was the best, and since within a region there was no consensus that a particular variety was the best, the situation was certainly an egalitarian one.

The question of whether in precolonial times there existed any nonegalitarian situations with respect to language use and attitudes brings forth three possible affirmative answers, all of which revolve around the idea of language as a resource. The language of ritual, of sorcery, and of spells has been discussed in several of the classic ethnographies on Papua and New Guinea, the best known being Malinowski's *Coral Gardens and their Magic,* volume 2 (1935).

4. On language as a symbol of identity in bilingual situations, cf. Gumperz (1969); Gumperz and Hernández-Chavez (1972); Jackson (1972: Ch. 6).

Malinowski's analysis of the language of Trobriand magic stresses the importance of what he calls "weirdness" in giving language its power. He notes that "a great deal of the vocabulary of magic, its grammar and its prosody, falls into line with the deeply ingrained belief that magical speech must be cast in another mould, because it is derived from other sources and produces different effects from ordinary speech" (p. 218).

Nevertheless, his analysis of the magical formulae shows that magical language is based on ordinary language, but involves lexical, phonological, and grammatical elaboration, including literary devices such as "use of metaphor, opposition, repetition, negative comparison, imperative and question with answer" (p. 222). There is, to my knowledge, no other description, for any other language of Papua New Guinea, of the exact nature of a ritual speech variety and of its differences from everyday speech as detailed as Malinowski's Trobriand analysis. Various authors mention "esoteric formulae" or "nonsense syllables" when discussing spells; the language used may be supposed to be that of the gods or ghosts, but not that of other groups. Fortune, for example, in *Sorcerers of Dobu,* states that: "The words of Dobuan magic are not words of ordinary speech. They form a secret esoteric language, a language of power" (1963: 130).

Differential access to magical language and the power it brings may be determined by sex, as well as by social position and personality, attributes which have to do with whether or not, or to what extent, an individual is taught such language by local experts. In any case, such language appears not to constitute an entirely separate code, but to be either limited in scope (sets of nonsense syllables) or some sort of elaboration or alteration of normal speech as in the Trobriand case.

The second case of a nonegalitarian situation with respect to language concerns the linguistic skills of political and economic leaders in precolonial Papua New Guinea. It appears that many such men may have possessed extraordinary linguistic resources, both in terms of rhetorical skills and in terms of bilingualism. Salisbury (1962) mentions bilingualism as a high-status characteristic among Siane, and biographical material on some contemporary leaders in New Guinea also tends to give supporting evidence. Handabe Tiabe (Member of the House of Assembly, Tari Open Electorate, 1964–67) would appear to fit into the category of a "traditional leader" (Hughes and Van der Veur 1965: 408). He cannot speak any of the national *lingue franche,* but his multilingualism in Tari area languages is probably a mark of local big man status, and may well have helped to increase his vote among linguistic groups other than his own. Another contemporary politician noted for his linguistic skills in local languages is Stoi Umut, former Rai Coast Open Member of the House of Assembly. Harding (1965: 199) notes that Umut's trilinguality in Komba, Selepet, and Timbe is an important aspect of the ethnic base of his popularity. The multilingualism of these current politicians in local languages offers some indication that the traditional leaders of the past also outstripped their fellows in such skills. The Gahuku leader Makis (Read 1965) would appear to be one example.

Bilingualism was useful to traditional big men in at least two ways: most obviously as a means of talking with politicians and others away from home, and second as one in a battery of rhetorical skills used in speechmaking in their own villages or areas. Skill in oratory has long been recognized as a crucial attribute of Melanesian big men (Oliver 1949; Reay 1959, 1964). Big men must know when to speak in public (optimally after consensus has been reached so as not to lose face by taking an unpopular position), how to harangue and convince an audience, how to hold the floor without being interrupted (speaking forcefully, articulately, retaining the audience's interest), how to use allusion and metaphor (Strathern 1975), and so on.

A third situation of linguistic inequality could be seen in the realm of commerce. Knowledge of the *lingua franca* of the traders in the coastal areas where long distance trading circuits were in operation was obviously an advantage and probably formed the only clear case where a particular language was commonly agreed to be in ascension or to have higher status than others.[5] It is important to note, however, that this case remains within the entirely practical realm of language as a resource. Trading visits were often of fairly long duration, and of considerable economic and social importance. To be able to communicate with the traders was advantageous, but learning "their" language (generally a pidginized version thereof) did not carry the added connotations that "their" language was in any way inherently better. Even magical language could be seen in this light and probably was, since spells had commercial value in many areas of Papua New Guinea, and were a means or resource to be applied to a particular end.

In summary, it would appear that the best reconstruction we can make of the precolonial sociolinguistic situation is one in which the basic relationship of languages and dialects was a socially symmetric one. Language was viewed as being essentially pragmatic, a means to communicate with natural or supernatural beings, whether local or

---

5. For further details on bilingualism in trade languages, see chapter 5, section 1.1.2 below.

foreign. People learned and used languages as a function of their personal exposure and interest. Differential size of the various language groups can be seen therefore not as a result of the general prestige and/or economic utility of these languages, but rather as a result of the differential rate of expansion of the populations speaking them and of their success in competing with other populations for material resources such as land.

In the few situations where linguistic differences within a community displayed a nascent correlation with power differentials, it is clear that the language disparities must be considered to be the dependent variable. Aggressive and intelligent individuals would learn ritual languages, *lingue franche,* neighboring languages, etc., as just one aspect of their economic and political striving. Moreover, whereas rhetorical skills are directly observable, power must be inferred rather indirectly. Hence it is difficult to know whether rhetorical talents lead to political power, or whether, as is more likely, the oratorical behavior of leaders is in part a result of the deliberate development of rhetorical skills by aspirants to leadership positions, and in part a reflection of the self-confidence of leaders and of the respect they enjoy within their communities as a result of their political or economic position. This does not, I believe, contradict Reay's (1959: chapter 5; 1964) observations about the importance of rhetorical skills as a prerequisite for Kuma leadership. Reay notes that Kuma rhetoric is a highly developed art, and that "a man who makes accomplished speeches is likely to be sought as a leader in public affairs" (1964: 244). She also gives evidence, however, that men who seek positions of leadership work hard to practice their rhetorical skills (cf. the case cited in 1964: 251); the Kuma "Rhetoric Thumper" was thus not only in important ways an achieved position, but the linguistic skills it demanded were also consciously developed by aspiring politicians.

3. THE SOCIAL STRATIFICATION OF LANGUAGE

The New Guinea case described in the preceding section showed that language is not only a resource but also a symbol of identity. The question we now wish to ask is under what circumstances does the identity function become inverted in such a way that a particular group becomes alienated from its own language or language variety and begins to regard it as inferior to some other language or language variety. I argue that these tend to be circumstances in which it is quite clear that some other group, speaking some other language or language variety, is economically and politically dominant. A corollary of this is that there are circumstances in which access to a particular language or language variety works to create and maintain real differences in power and wealth.

In the same way that even slight speech differences in Papua New Guinea serve to place an individual in terms of his/her geographical origin, language is a sensitive indicator of social position (and to some extent geographical origin) in contemporary North America. Particular varieties of or features in English are associated with various ethnic and racial groups, and there are some marked regional differences. Even holding constant race, geography, and ethnic groups, linguistic differences have also been found to correlate with class in several studies of large urban centers (e.g., Labov 1966a; Cedergren 1972; Sankoff and Cedergren 1971). The linguistic features that differentiate the population in this way often seem to be arbitrary and quite inconsequential from the point of view of communication. Thus pronunciation of /r/ in preconsonantal and final position (e.g., "cart" and "car," respectively) has been at various times a low and a high prestige feature in American English (McDavid 1948).

A phenomenon that regularly co-occurs with class-based differentiation of speech is an attitude of linguistic insecurity and linguistic alienation on the part of many of those who speak nonprestige varieties. The well known hypercorrection of some segments of the "middle" class and of people who have undergone rapid social mobility without adequate opportunity to learn the linguistic behavior appropriate to their new station is evidence of such insecurity. People recognize that they have stigmatized features in their speech, but in lamenting this state of affairs, the way they talk about it tends to show that they *accept* a standard external to their own behavior; that is, they acquiesce in another group's definition of features in their speech or of the whole code itself as being inherently inferior (Labov 1966b; Laberge and Chiasson-Lavoie 1971). This is a type of "mystification" in which a symbol (language, or particular features of language) takes on *in its own right* the negative evaluation of the object (in this case a group of people) with which it has become associated. Acceptance of such mystification is self-defeating, since other symbols can always be found if and when the group in question manages to alter the present set of offending behaviors.[6]

There are two mutually reinforcing phenomena here: first, the extent to which lack of knowledge of a particular language or language variety blocks access to other resources or goods within a society—

6. Cf. Weinreich, Labov, and Herzog (1968) on change in status of features.

education, jobs, wealth, political positions, and so on; and second, the extent to which the inferior political and economic position of a particular group results in a devaluing of its language or language variety, and in feelings of inferiority and worthlessness on the part of its speakers. In its extreme form, this set of attitudes is similar to the "complexe de colonisé" described by Fanon (1961). A quotation from a volume published by the Académie canadienne-française illustrates this syndrome with respect to Quebec or Canadian French:

> J'affirme que la langue n'est pas d'abord un moyen de communication mais bien l'outil de la pensée. La pauvreté d'expression que l'on constate chez les nôtres, leurs lacunes dans les domaines culturels, leur impuissance à créer, proviennent d'une incapacité de concevoir. Une langue amoindrie, rapetissée, déformée, tronquée et méconnaissable, ne produira jamais que des cerveaux incultes (Roy 1960: 112).
>
> (*Translation:* I maintain that language is not principally a means of communication, but in fact the vehicle of thought. The poverty of expression which we note among our own people, their cultural gaps, their lack of creativity, come from a conceptual incapacity. A language which is diminished, shrunken, deformed, truncated, and unrecognizable will never produce anything but uncultivated minds.)[7]

It seems clear that the latter phenomenon, the devaluation of a speech variety to reflect the socioeconomic position of its speakers, is primary, and that the converse, the negative consequences of speaking a given variety, is but a derivative effect. Historically, the changing political and economic fortunes of nations and of groups within them have been followed, with a certain lag, by a reevaluation of their languages. However, it would be difficult to find a clear case where the change in status of a language variety led to a change in the socioeconomic status of its speakers.

Many other factors are of course involved, including whether the situation is one of different dialects or different languages. When it is necessary for a group of people to learn another language for the practical reasons mentioned earlier, this may or may not lead to language loss, and the variable tenacity of different linguistic groups in maintaining their languages is difficult to explain in terms of purely economic criteria (cf. Hymes 1966 on two Amerindian groups). In the single language situation, the characteristics of "good" or "correct" speech can be broadly or narrowly defined to broaden or reduce accep-

---

7. I am grateful to Suzanne Laberge for bringing this citation to my attention.

tance of those whose speech is more or less divergent from the prestige form. Entrance examinations can be deliberately manipulated to exclude all "non-U" (Ross 1954) applicants, who are bound to give themselves away sooner or later.[8] And of course the prestige features themselves can be changed when the wrong people acquire them, or simply as a result of a new geographical or social center of prestige.

It is also the case that when differential linguistic knowledge becomes important in providing access to other goods and resources, social structure also determines differential access to the resource of language itself. Thus language is at once a symbol of an individual's place in the society, since it represents the opportunities she/he has had for learning language varieties, the people she/he has been in contact with, and so on; and a resource providing access to particular activities and opportunities, and blocking access to others.

4. THE CHANGING POWER STRUCTURE IN PAPUA NEW GUINEA

Having briefly reviewed some of the characteristics of a highly stratified sociolinguistic situation, let us return to a consideration in greater detail of politics in Papua New Guinea, beginning with a closer look at traditional political organization.

As mentioned in the second section of this chapter and as is widely recognized, the "big man" system was the pivotal political institution over much of Papua New Guinea. Becoming a big man entailed political manipulation of lending and borrowing relationships involved in trade, whether local (e.g., bridewealth) or foreign (e.g., the Enga *Moka* or the Trobriand *Kula*). It also involved being a war leader (this is obviously the skill about which least is known), and being able to attract and hold a loyal following who would accept one's leadership and not defect to another leader. Community activities requiring leadership included decision-making regarding large communal gardens, especially in preparation for feasts (whose timetable and other associated planning also had to be decided), trading and warfare expeditions, settling of local disputes, arranging marriages, and so forth. The men's house was a key institution here, and the men's house group (under the leadership of a particular big man) could presumably be relied on for economic assistance and moral backing in time of need. The system has been described as a highly competitive one involving

8. Michener's epic novel *Hawaii* describes in a moving historical vignette the application of such entrance tests to keep Chinese children out of white schools.

considerable rivalry among actual and potential big men. Big man status in most of Papua New Guinea was not hereditary though having an influential backer (usually a father or uncle) was a decided advantage for any young man.

What were the traditional sources of power in Papua New Guinea, and what resources could a powerful man draw on? In Buang society, probably the most important were land and labor. Yam growing was the prestigious activity, and large and well tended yam gardens required both. Land was managed by the kin group, but individual inheritance of particular fields or portions of fields meant that some people found themselves with more and better land than others. Labor was more difficult, as it depended not only upon the demographic vagaries of one's close family, but even more upon clever manipulation of available kin, trade, and friendship ties. The rich and powerful man who had successfully managed his marriage(s) and his inherited resources could always count on finding a ready work force when he needed a roof thatched or a large garden cleared. He could entertain such work parties in style, with pork from his own herd or hunted in the forest, and he could also entertain distant trade friends, having the time and resources to cultivate such contacts.

Thus in any community there were influential and powerful men (Tok Pisin *bigpela man*) with large and well tended gardens, possibly more than one wife, many pigs, the authority to direct community activities and command a large labor force, likely having a better command of foreign languages than their fellows as well as a larger collection of traded goods, particularly the highly visible clay pots from the coast. Big men could, through a combination of seniority and astute political behavior, become managers of the garden and forest land of their descent group. There were also the men referred to in Tok Pisin as *rabis man* 'inconsequential men', people whose gardens were more modest, who more often found themselves clearing other people's gardens than vice versa. These people were not poor, or in a condition of servitude to the more powerful—they simply did not command the resources and authority that the *bigpela man* could.

The coming of colonial rule immediately began to transform the configuration of power. The localized and unstable community influence wielded by individual big men was dwarfed by the (relatively) unified and absolute power of the colonial authority. How did this affect the big man system? Since colonial authority, including missionary influence and the power brought to bear by commercial interests, was exercised only in connection with certain matters, such as warfare, taxation, religion, paid labor, and relations with non-New Guineans, and was only sporadically viable except in towns and government stations, the big man tradition was able to continue, albeit in a somewhat modified fashion. Indeed, the cessation of warfare permitted a certain expansion of the influence of particular big men from the local to the regional level, as discussed for example by Salisbury (1964) and as has been noted in the case of several cargo cult leaders (e.g., Lawrence 1964; Schwartz 1962).

Nevertheless, power with respect to all matters of a nonlocal nature was clearly vested in the colonial triumvirate of government, mission, and business. This was understood by all concerned from the earliest stages of colonization. It was most apparent and most significant in towns, government stations, missionary outposts, and commercial enterprises such as plantations and mines.

Despite the clear stratification between Europeans and New Guineans, correlated with exaggerated power disparities, there were some possibilities for vertical movement for New Guineans within the colonial power structure. *Bosboi* 'foremen', *blak misin* 'evangelists', and *plis man* (*plis boi*) 'police sergeants' are examples of some of the positions whose incumbents often had a great deal of influence and control over other New Guineans within colonial institutions. These distinctions entailed prestige and authority through their closer association with the true power holders, not only within town and station communities, but extending back to their home rural populations.

Today, skills such as literacy, accounting, the ability to drive a truck, and knowledge of the language(s) of the wider arena(s) can be of immense benefit to those who possess them, and can lead to much larger differences among villagers than could possibly have existed in the precolonial society. These differences may even be measurable in traditional resources such as land, as when a local entrepreneur gains permanent control of large tracts of good gardening land for cash crop production. Differences also come to exist among areas rich in resources usable by the colonial system and/or close to the new centers of power and those not so endowed.

Today, young Buang men in their twenties who cultivate the traditional virtues and take pride in their yam gardens refer to themselves as *rabis* men, in contrast to their peers who decide to go away to work and earn money. The sophistication of the retired policeman or other ex-official in the workings of the colonial society, his fluent Tok Pisin in dealing with representatives of this society, his well educated children who return home only for brief visits on vacation from "good" jobs in the city, have not failed to impress those who stayed at home. Indeed, political astuteness has become synonymous with the ability to further big man status locally, using achievements and associations within the colonial world while simultaneously improving one's situation within the urban or station community by using the economic resources or political support of the people from one's local area (Sankoff 1968: 52–54).

The changes brought by the colonial society have made for some fundamental alterations in village level politics, though a number of formal aspects have remained the same. In some Buang villages the men's house has fallen into disuse, but there are still "big men" in the sense of influential leaders whose opinions carry weight in meetings, who can recommend courses of political or economic action that others will follow, and who can organize a large labor force for community work of various sorts. But both political issues and the resources used in deciding them have undergone fundamental changes. First, the scope of decision-making at the village level has had to expand to take in issues of wider arenas—the regional and national levels and the questions which their agents raise. These include questions like the support of local Lutheran religious officials and of Buang Lutheran officials in other areas of New Guinea, preparation for a visit by the health inspection team of the Local Government Council, members of which include one representative from each one or two villages, participation in the agricultural cooperative, work on roads or airstrip, and response to questions about national policies raised by the travelling Member of the House of Assembly, as well as traditional matters such as settling marital or other family disputes, deciding where and when to carry out communal garden plantings, and so on.

Second, decisions emanating from these wider arenas can have important effects at the local level in ways which completely surpass any possible input from the local level. Geography alone has had a huge effect on access to markets for local producers, as well as on access to schools, jobs, and the like. Thus distance from the town of Mumeng and a major road to the coast is inversely proportional to emigration to urban centers from Buang villages. In 1967, 47 percent of the Manga Buang population was living elsewhere compared with 39 percent in central Buang and only 20 percent in headwaters Buang. By 1971 there was one Buang university student—from Manga Buang. Economic decisions made internationally (e.g., the World Coffee Agreement) or in another country (e.g., Australian decisions regarding imports of sugar) or even at other levels or in other areas of New Guinea (e.g., the decision about where to put a road or a bridge or a factory) can have effects whose magnitude at the local level is greater than that of decisions taken at the local level.

5. Tok Pisin in Colonial New Guinea

The birth of Tok Pisin coincided more or less with the beginning of the colonial period in New Guinea. It gained a foothold in the Rabaul area of New Britain, later the site of the German colonial capital, in the 1880s (Laycock 1970b; Mühlhäusler 1975a, 1976a; Salisbury 1967). It has been from this earliest period the language of colonization. It has always been spoken principally in what is referred to as the "New Guinea side," i.e., the ex-German territory: current island provinces of Manus, New Ireland, East and West New Britain, and Bougainville, and mainland provinces of East and West Sepik, Madang, Morobe, Chimbu, and Eastern and Western Highlands (see Map 1). Papua, the ex-British territory that was administered jointly with New Guinea since the Second World War (present Western, Gulf, Central, Northern, Milne Bay and Southern Highlands provinces), has used Hiri Motu[9] as a *lingua franca*. In 1971, of the approximately 1,631,000 Papuans and New Guineans age 10 and over, 45.0 percent spoke Tok Pisin and 9.4 percent spoke Hiri Motu (Papua New Guinea Population Census 1971, Bulletin No. 1, Table 8).

The first Buang men to learn Tok Pisin acquired it in what has now become the classic tradition—as indentured laborers on a plantation.[10] The plantations at this stage, just before the First World War, were German, and the men were taken by ship to New Britain[11] where they worked for seven years before being returned home. Buang men also worked as carriers on "patrols" of various sorts—including trips of exploration for minerals and police patrols, sometimes in reprisal for an incident in which other villagers had harmed or killed someone in the former "patrol" category. The most important source of learning Tok Pisin was the Bulolo gold rush in the early 1930s. Because of its relative proximity to Buang territory, it attracted dozens of Buang men to their first opportunity to earn money and the things it could buy.

In retrospect, men who had worked for Europeans during that time had almost nothing good to say about the experience. They com-

---

9. On the *lingua franca* Hiri Motu (formerly known as Police Motu) see chapter 5 below.

10. In some areas of New Guinea, the missions were important agents in the spread and use of Tok Pisin, e.g., the Roman Catholics in the Sepik area (1966 and 1971 census figures showed the East Sepik District [now Province] counting more Tok Pisin speakers in terms of absolute numbers than any other). Nevertheless Tok Pisin was always predominantly a language learned in the world of work.

11. Cf. Salisbury 1969: 157 on the relations between the Tolai of New Britain and the plantation laborers brought in to work on what was formerly Tolai land.

plained of long hours, hard masters whose whims were difficult to understand or comply with, and low rates of pay. Some of them escaped and came home; others stayed in order to be able to earn more money, or out of fear of reprisals, and learned more about how the colonial society worked.

We can only extrapolate as to the effects on local level politics of these early returnees, with their goods and their knowledge. Men who were part of this group say that they gave many of their goods away; like more recent returnees in areas of Papua New Guinea where the first return of indentured laborers has occurred when an anthropologist was there to observe it, probably they found their goods rapidly integrated into the distribution system controlled by older men who had not been away (cf. also, Corris 1973, chapter 7, on Solomon Islands returnees). But knowledge was another matter, and especially valuable was the knowledge of Tok Pisin, referred to as *bubum ayez* 'the white men's language', the language which permitted access to the colonial society. Indeed, knowledge of Tok Pisin was originally the criterion for appointment as a *luluai* or *tultul* (village officials given military caps and expected to translate the words of visiting government officials, to assemble the population for censuses and tax collection—in other words to be the official brokers between the village and the secular colonial society).

The regimented character of the contacts between villagers and visiting whites in the early colonial period, added to the highly disciplinary tone of contacts between master and servant (the primary work relationship known to Buang workers up to and including the present, though the style of most current masters probably differs considerably from the earlier ones we are discussing here), made for a strong association between Tok Pisin and authoritarian behavior. Tok Pisin was demonstrably a language in which one could give orders and expect to be obeyed, even if the persons to whom the orders were given displayed little comprehension (as was the case for most workers during the early phases of their indenture). Though as we shall see below, Tok Pisin is now a common denominator, even a language of equality, among urban New Guineans from diverse linguistic groups, it has retained its associations with and connotations of power and authority at the village level, learned by each new generation in the context of giving orders and shouting at people, as well as in playful imitation of such contexts.

The extent to which returned laborers used Tok Pisin in the village context during this early period remains unknown, but it is likely that they at least repeated common expressions of the *kiap* (patrol officer) or other visiting dignitary, explaining to the others what they meant. Certainly the high degree of comprehension of Tok Pisin among people under fifty in Buang villages today (including women and people who have not been away or to school) would attest to the early use of Tok Pisin locally, at least to some extent. There is some sex difference in comprehension of Tok Pisin, though this is not extreme, but education makes for very little difference in competence in Tok Pisin. Tok Pisin is definitely not a school language, but a language introduced in the sphere of outside work which has been integrated to some extent into village life. Hearing a father instructing his daughter who can barely toddle, '*Yu kam!*' 'come on!', is not at all uncommon, and children's games include epithets such as *bladi* 'bloody' and *yupela klia* 'you guys get out of the way'.

Village meetings are, however, the most common context for the use of Tok Pisin, particularly the *lain* morning meetings where people (particularly women) are supposed to line up and receive orders about the work they are to do later in the day; and the "special events" meetings often called to discuss economic (cash economy) matters. The forced regimentation of the *lain* borrows the symbolism of "lining up" (as indeed have a number of millenarian religious movements in Papua New Guinea) as well as the language of the prototype: village visits or "patrols" by government officers. Men will get up and harangue the crowd alternately in Tok Pisin and tok ples (in this case Buang) regarding issues like absenteeism at the *lain,* work not properly done, orders not followed, and so forth.

The literary rhetorical devices used in the oratory at this and other kinds of village meetings are many. Synonymy through borrowing is particularly frequent. One device is code switching (chapter 2, this volume), where whole passages are spoken in one language, then followed by making the same point in a slightly different way in another. (In the present context, the two languages are always Buang and Tok Pisin.[12]) Or the dire consequences to befall someone who violates a condition stated in an if-clause in one language are explained in the other, as in sentence 1 below.

(1) ŋau ti ŋəmədo (Buang), bai ol ikot stret long yu (Tok Pisin).
'If you're the only one sitting down (i.e., doing nothing), they'll take you straight to court.'

Though people being shouted at, harangued, or sworn at in Tok Pisin do not necessarily take this behavior very seriously on all occasions, neither can it be completely disregarded, since its use reflects the village power structure. Table 1-1 compares language use in eight village

12. Laycock (1966) provides texts showing switching between Tok Pisin and Abelam.

22

Political Power and Linguistic Inequality in Papua New Guinea

| | Language used | | |
Speakers	Buang	Tok Pisin	Total Speeches
The "government" leader	9	9	13
The "economic" leader	12	11	17
Others	75	17	86
Total	96	37	116

TABLE 1-1. Language used in speeches in eight village meetings.[a]
[a] From Sankoff (1968: 191).

meetings of the *lain* and "special event" type. We see that the two most influential men in the village used Tok Pisin more frequently than all the others combined, and that they frequently switched codes during a speech. "Special events" meetings sometimes use a device clearly borrowed from the "officer on patrol" situation, i.e., the formal use of an interpreter. Formal interpreters may even be used when the "visiting dignitary" is himself a Buang. In such a case the "visting dignitary" speaks Tok Pisin throughout the meeting, the translator repeating at short intervals in Buang.

The meetings discussed above are "political" in the sense that they are held in order to make decisions regarding future action which will affect a number of people. And some participants are more powerful or influential than others in that their opinions are more likely to hold sway, and in that the decisions taken at the group level are more likely to favor their personal interests. It is not principally a man's behavior at public meetings which *creates* this kind of power for him, though it is important in providing justifications, assuaging those who might be against the course of action, and validating support in terms of agreement by other speakers.

For the past thirty years or so, Buang parents have seen the acquisition of Tok Pisin as perhaps *the* chief resource which will gain their children access to the riches of the colonial society, and have been anxious that they learn it. Its obvious usefulness and the relative ease with which it could be learned, however, made it the type of practical resource which was readily within the grasp of almost anyone. The last four or five years have shown a growing awareness that, on the contrary, Tok Pisin does not get you far enough in the new society, that it is not the white man's language after all. It is English that must be known.

The introduction of English, to be discussed in the next section, has put the position of Tok Pisin into clearer relief. Thus though Tok Pisin has indeed been the language of colonization, it has, been far more. From its earliest usage, it has been the *lingua franca* of New Guineans of diverse ethnic backgrounds. It is the language of much everyday life in towns such as Lae, Rabaul, Madang, Goroka, Wewak, and Mount Hagen, in most of which over 85 percent of the people speak it (see Table 5-4, p. 126), and it is increasingly used in Port Moresby and other Papuan centers. Though from the village perspective it may have been considered the white man's language, its integrating and solidarity functions in the activities of multiethnic New Guinean urban and commercial life have been increasing.

6. ENGLISH AND THE DEEPENING LINGUISTIC STRATIFICATION OF PAPUA NEW GUINEA

The dramatic introduction of English in the past ten years has again symbolized, or perhaps even fostered, the changing social structure of Papua New Guinea. It is a scarce resource—to have your children learn it, you must send them to school early and pay for them to stay there for many years.

Though in the past Tok Pisin was conceived at the village level as an important resource for getting on in the colonial society, its accessibility made its integration into village life relatively undisruptive. Big men could use it as an added resource in rhetoric; signs could be posted on competitive festive occasions stating the cost of the food being distributed; its acquisition by virtually everyone within a reasonably short time span meant that it could be more useful than symbolic.

Permanent or relatively permanent urban living is also a novel phenomenon in Papua New Guinea. It is here that the resource of learning English is chiefly possible. But accompanying the spread of English as an elite language is also the spread of Tok Pisin as a general language of solidarity among the urban population. It is the language in which a growing minority of urban children and adolescents are most fluent and it has become the native language of many (Sankoff 1975). Many highly educated New Guineans who are perfectly fluent in English use Tok Pisin in relaxed, informal situations with friends. Some of its proponents whom I talked to about it in 1971 waxed very enthusiastic about its communicative usefulness, its solidarity function, and the fluency of their children in it, as indicated in the following quotations:

> (2) Em, long Pisin olsem tok ples bilong yumi yet. 'That's right, Tok Pisin is like our real language.'

> (3) Ol i no harim Tok Ples na ol i Tok Pisin tasol olsem na, Tok Pisin bilong ol i no inap ron o mekim wonem; em i klia. 'They (the children) don't understand Tok Ples, just Tok Pisin, you

know, and their Tok Pisin doesn't wander or go off the mark; it's clear.'

(4) Ating bihain bai Tok Ples bai inogat ia. Bai i Pisin na Inglis tasol. 'Maybe after a long time there won't be any more Tok Ples. Just Pisin and English.'

Nevertheless, the current situation is one in which English is reinforcing and clarifying urban social stratification. Already in 1966, over 30 percent of the Papua New Guinean population of most major towns spoke English. During the five year period between 1966 and 1971, there was a massive influx of migrants into towns. The increase in both English and Tok Pisin speakers can be observed in Figure 1-2. Thus in Port Moresby, the capital, there were 14,880 English speakers in 1966, representing 64.4 percent of the city's population age 10 and over at that time. By 1971, there were almost double the absolute number of English speakers in Port Moresby (26,580), still representing about the same percentage of the population (64.6 percent). Nevertheless, English made greater proportional strides than Tok Pisin in every major town. Whereas in most towns the proportion of Tok Pisin speakers remained about the same, the proportion of English speakers was up in every case (see Table 5-4, p. 126).

Currently, in every town, there are always new migrants or transients (e.g., market vendors or village people visiting urban relatives) who speak only tok ples, with little or halting Tok Pisin or none at all. These are the *bus kanaka* 'bush natives', the country bumpkins

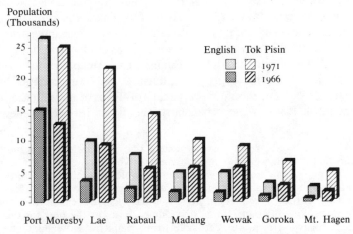

Figure 1-2. Speakers of Tok Pisin and English in seven major towns of Papua New Guinea, 1966 and 1971.

who are increasingly ashamed of their tok ples. Next is the bulk of the urban proletariat—mostly Tok Pisin speaking, and working at service jobs or as manual laborers. They may resent being spoken to in Tok Pisin by a white person or a Chinese, or sometimes even by a Papuan, regarding it as an insult even if they do not speak English. Then there are the English speakers, who tend to be fairly young and who work in stores or offices, or in technically skilled jobs, or as teachers. Among these people, it is recognized that there are many degrees of fluency in speaking English, and that speaking it "well" is a difficult but worthwhile task.

What appears to have happened is that the original tok ples/Tok Pisin dichotomy has been largely replaced by Tok Pisin/English as a symbolic marker of power and status in the urban society. In every town except Port Moresby,[13] Tok Pisin speakers vastly outnumber English speakers, both in 1966 and in 1971. English speakers are by definition educated, and most of them also speak Tok Pisin. This means that the urban proletariat (mainly uneducated) is linguistically symbolized by the feature [−English], the learning of any English at all being a scarce resource. But as English instruction spreads, Standard 6 educated speakers will increasingly find that [+English] is not a useful resource. Speaking English "well" (i.e., having the amount of schooling that fluency in English can symbolize) will increasingly come to mark the elite.

Though the distinction between Tok Pisin and English is still very clear, there are some signs that the urban New Guinea linguistic situation is moving toward what has been characterized as a "post-creole continuum" (De Camp 1971) in other colonial and ex-colonial situations. As educated and powerful New Guineans replace Europeans in high government posts, as aggressive rural migrants succeed in setting up profitable enterprises, as school-leavers from various levels enter the public service, Standard English, English spoken as a second language with varying degrees of fluency and correctness, highly anglicized Tok Pisin, the more classical Tok Pisin of migrants, and the creolized Tok Pisin of the urban born coexist and loosely reflect the

13. Port Moresby and to some extent Lae are different from the other towns in that their hinterlands are more extensive than simply their adjacent areas. As the capital, Port Moresby draws people from all over Papua New Guinea. Though it is located in an area where few people speak Tok Pisin—the Central District (now Province) of Papua—it has received tens of thousands of Tok Pisin-speaking migrants from New Guinea. Lae, as the port for the busy Highlands highway, is more accessible to migrants from the populous (and largely non-English, non-Tok Pisin-speaking) Highlands, than are other major towns located outside of the Highlands.

emerging social stratification of urban New Guineans (cf., Bickerton 1975a; Mühlhäusler 1977a).

To return briefly to formal institutions, it is likely that education, speaking English, office holding at every level, and urban residence will become even more strongly correlated. Even now, English speakers are increasingly concentrated in the towns. The gap between the proportion of English speakers in urban and rural areas widened in the 1966–71 period, as the proportion of English speakers in the countryside grew much more slowly than it did in the towns. On the other hand, the corresponding gap for Tok Pisin lessened considerably, as there was a dramatic increase in the number of Tok Pisin speakers in rural areas. The concentration of English speakers in the towns is probably due in part to the concentration of educational opportunities there, and in part to the in-migration of English speakers from rural areas.

Prolonged exposure to a situation where a knowledge of English is a clear advantage will probably not lead to the loss of many local languages, since there is every indication that a majority of people will continue to use tok ples or Tok Pisin in family and informal contexts. But the symmetrically egalitarian relationship that existed among local languages—tok ples—has already been irrevocably altered by the spread of Tok Pisin and of English. That some speakers are more equal than others will probably lead many to the antirelativist position that some languages, and particularly some language varieties ("good" English), are more equal than others. And will lay the way open to the classic, erroneous, but treacherously seductive argument that it is this unfortunate "linguistic inferiority" (symbolizing, for some, even *cognitive* inferiority) that is the *cause* of poverty and powerlessness.

2.

Language Use in Multilingual Societies: Some Alternate Approaches

The behavior of multilinguals in communities where multilingualism is the norm, and communication regularly takes place in two or more codes, has received a considerable amount of attention in recent years. Rather than concentrating on the historical linguistic consequences of such heterogeneous situations, scholars have dealt instead with the network of communications itself, trying to elucidate, on the synchronic level, the systematic aspects of people's use of the various codes available to them. In this chapter I intend to review some of the major trends in the analytical approaches that have been proposed, and to illustrate with data I collected on the behavior of multilinguals in New Guinea during 1966–67 and 1968.[1] It is not my intention to provide an exhaustive review of even the recent literature on multilingualism; rather, I wish to discuss several currents of thought within sociolinguistics, and to show their relevance to the study of speech behavior in multilingual communities. The three main trends with which I shall deal can be summarized as: (1) attention to the functions of speech; (2) attempts to specify the configuration of nonlinguistic variables that result in the choice of particular linguistic options on the part of individual speakers; and (3) detailed examination of linguistic variation per se, and its correlation with nonlinguistic variables.

Though the data with which I shall be dealing are drawn from a multilingual community, it is clear that the kind of linguistic behavior involved (e.g., shifting, or switching, among the various codes available) is not specific or limited to multilinguals, that is, it does not differ

This chapter was originally published in John Pride and Janet Holmes, eds., *Sociolinguistics* (Harmondsworth, Middlesex, England: Penguin, 1971), pp. 33–51. I thank Regna Darnell, Norman Denison, John Gumperz, Dell Hymes, and Elli Köngäs Maranda for comments on an earlier draft, read at the Canadian Sociology and Anthropology Association meetings, Winnipeg, Manitoba, May 1970.

1. I wish to thank the Canada Council for support during both fieldwork periods.

qualitatively from the behavior of monolinguals (shifting of style or level). Hymes, discussing bilingualism, puts it this way:

> Cases of bilingualism par excellence . . . are salient, special cases of the general phenomena of variety in code repertoire and switching among codes. No normal person, and no normal community, is limited in repertoire to a single variety of code. (1967: 9)

And according to Gumperz:

> In many multilingual societies the choice of one language over another has the same signification as the selection among lexical alternates in linguistically homogeneous societies. (1968: 381)

Both authors make the point that in every speech community there exist a variety of repertoires, of alternate means of expression. They go on to note that this fact has social implications, i.e., that in choosing among the various codes available to them, speakers indicate what might be called social meaning. A corollary of this is that speakers in any community share rules regarding language usage which allow them to interpret the social meaning of alternate linguistic choices. Multilingual speech communities are, however, unique in one way: the fact that the alternates in question are (theoretically) discrete and easily identifiable (as separate languages) makes them particularly prone to certain types of sociolinguistic study.

1. FUNCTIONS OF SPEECH

That speech has functions other than referential, and that stylistic and other shifts in the linguistic content of discourse often serve to mark off shifts in function is not a new idea in linguistics (see Firth 1935; Malinowski 1935). The centrality of the question of linguistic function to linguistic theory was not dealt with in depth, however, until the more recent work of Jakobson (1960) and, more specifically, of Hymes (1962, 1970a). In his most recent work on linguistic functions, Hymes (1970a) notes that functions have often been treated in the linguistic and an-thropological literature in a piecemeal way. Anthropologists, for example, have noted special code varieties in the repertoires of some com-munities, such as differences in men's and women's speech (mainly North America) and in everyday versus respectful speech (mainly Oceania), and have then tried to discover and describe the social func-tion served by the use of these varieties. Hymes proposes that a more balanced, global approach would proceed in the reverse direction, starting with social function (e.g., that respect will be expressed in every society) and seeking the linguistic means by which various functions are expressed. Ervin-Tripp (1972: 231) notes that this is also the approach adopted by Geoghegan (1971) and Goodenough (1965).

It is easy to see the appeal of functional analysis to students of language behavior in multilingual communities. Shift in function appears a natural and highly useful way of explaining speech variation including code switching. Conversely, to those interested in demonstrating function, multilingual societies often provide the most obvious or salient examples.

The perspective of examining the linguistic data in terms of the function of what is said implies that function be defined, in general, as the social effect of given forms or usages, and that the unit of analysis be defined in social terms—hence the importance of the concept of speech event as a basic analytical unit. Taking the speech event as a starting point, one can either study how the choice of language affects ongoing social interaction (an approach we shall later discuss as "interpretive" in its analysis of the social meaning of language use), or one can take the reverse point of view and attempt to see to what extent the (broadly social) *factors* present in the communication situation influence what is expressed linguistically. It was those authors concerned primarily with linguistic function (Jakobson 1960; Hymes 1962, 1964a, 1967a) who first presented systematic discussion of the components or factors in communicative events.

2. FACTORS AND COMPONENTS

Taking now the alternation among various codes as a point of departure, we can point to a large number of studies that have attempted (at least implicitly) to predict language choices from a knowledge of the factors or components present in the communication situation. Summarizing her own discussion of types of formal statements or rules that could be made in sociolinguistics, Ervin-Tripp could well be speaking for numerous authors who have had the same general goals without necessarily attempting such a formal approach when she says that her description of "alternation rules" was "primarily made from the standpoint of predicting a speaker's choice of alternatives in some frame" (1972: 233).

Various lists of types of factors that influence speech behavior have been proposed, based broadly on those factors suggested by Jakobson (1960) and Hymes (1962). These lists usually include such factors as participants, topic, setting or context, channel, message form, mood or tone, and intentions and effects. "Code" is generally also listed in theoretical discussions of the components of speech events

31

(see also Hymes 1967a), but in descriptive and analytical work it is most often treated as the dependent variable, where certain combinations or configurations of the other factors are treated as independent. Of these, the three that have been discussed most widely, and that appear to be the most powerful in predicting language choice, are those involving participants, setting, and topic (possibly in that order). This does not of course imply that the other factors can be neglected, and cases can readily be cited where factors such as speaker's intent or message form are clearly dominant.

With regard to the participants in a communicative event, a knowledge of their individual characteristics (extent of personal repertoires and competence in the various codes and speech varieties in question; class and ethnic identification) and of the relationships between participants can go a long way towards predicting their choices among alternate speech varieties, always *given a knowledge of the cultural definitions of appropriateness*. And particularly in situations where verbal repertoires are highly compartmentalized (see Gumperz 1968: 386), codes are often topic- and/or setting-specific.

Despite the hope expressed by some authors that careful, thorough, and prolonged study of the factors involved in speech events might at some future date lead to the ability to completely predict, or state rules specifying "who speaks what language to whom and when" (Fishman 1965), it now appears that such hopes are somewhat overambitious. This has become obvious through a number of detailed studies that, motivated at least in part by such a hope, have run into difficulty in two major ways: (1) Multi-code situations often appear to be marked by extremely frequent and rapid switching that, to put it bluntly, defies explanation, if by explanation one means accounting for every switch. (Texts cited by Gumperz and Hernández-Chavez (1972) on Spanish-English bilinguals show this type of frequent switching very clearly.) (2) In many cases, analysts have experienced difficulty in attributing segments to one code or the other. This is especially true in cases involving diglossia, e.g., a creole and the standard European language from which the bulk of its lexicon is drawn. Such linguistic situations have recently been recognized as displaying the characteristics of a continuum (DeCamp 1971; St-Pierre 1969: 110–11). Labov (1970: 35) cites a six-line text involving eighteen "switches" to show the futility and arbitrariness of trying to identify segments as being one or other dialect of English. There may also be some cases where this problem arises in multilingual speech communities (e.g., Denison 1970). Thus in any multi-code situation, it is important to remember not only that the codes in question often do not approximate to the monolingual standard (Gumperz 1969), but also that they may not display the property of discreteness. It is clear, however, that this second difficulty is more problematic in situations of diglossia than in cases of multilingualism.

3. LINGUISTIC VARIATION

The third major trend I wish to outline is best exemplified in the quantitative work of Labov (1966a, 1971, 1972b, 1972c).[2] Labov takes the variability of linguistic data as a starting point, but instead of examining linguistic variants that can readily be identified as belonging to one speech variety or another, he has studied, in detail, specific linguistic variables, first in terms of their linguistic context, then in terms of their distribution within the speech community, correlating them mainly with characteristics of the speakers and of the situation (examining in particular the property of formality). In studying situations in which the salient linguistic variables form a continuum, he has argued, for example, that "idiolects" show less system (internal consistency) than does the speech community taken as a whole, because individuals occupy or control particular ranges of variables whose total distribution (in social terms) must be known in order to understand the speech community as a system. Labov (1970, 1971) argues against postulating the existence of a number of speech varieties or codes within a community if it cannot be shown that these constitute separate systems:

> We have the problem of deciding the place of this variation in linguistic structure. Current formal analysis provides us with only two clear options: (1) the variants are said to belong to different systems, and the alternation is an example of "dialect mixture" or "code switching." (2) the variants are said to be in "free variation" within the same system, and the selection lies below the level of linguistic structure. Both approaches place the variation outside of the system being studied. There are of course many cases which fall appropriately under one or the other of these labels. But to demonstrate that we have a true case of code-switching, it is necessary to show that the speaker moves from one consistent set of co-occurring rules to another. (1970: 34)

Labov has shown that certain types of variation previously conceived as "free variation" (New York City case) and "code switching" (Black English case) are better analyzed in terms of a single system, within which variation correlates highly with social and situational as well as

---

2. Since the original publication of this paper, quantitative studies of code switching have begun to appear, e.g., Di Sciullo et al. 1976; Gal 1978; Poplack 1978.

linguistic constraints. But it is clear that similar types of constraints are also operative when linguistic behavior involves choice among alternatives belonging to what we can safely identify as more than one code or speech variety. Further, there is another problem of considerable ethnographic interest which appears to be relatively intractable to Labov's methodology, i.e., the question of how the various speech variables combine to form clusters having particular social meaning as defined by members of the speech community (e.g., questions of styles, genres, appropriateness to particular social circumstances, etc.)

Labov himself specifies the two possible approaches (1966a: 209): one can either start with speech variables and examine their social distribution, or one can start with particular people and/or particular situations and examine the linguistic behavior relevant to them. He prefers the former as giving a better idea of the linguistic system as a whole; if one is interested in the latter, however, it cannot be totally deduced from data collected within the framework of the former. This point will be raised again below in connection with the recent work of Gumperz, whose approach is more ethnographic in that he stresses this second line of inquiry.

4. MULTILINGUAL SPEECH COMMUNITIES: THE BUANG CASE

To illustrate the analytical points I wish to discuss, I shall present a brief description of the language situation among the Buang of New Guinea. The main analytical questions to which I shall subsequently address myself are:

(1) What are the relative merits of the various approaches I have presented and discussed in the first part of this chapter in the analysis of speech variation in multilingual communities?

(2) Is the assignment of segments to one or other speech variety or code an important problem, i.e., does it matter whether speech varieties are seen as one or several systems?

(3) Independent of the type of approach chosen, how far can we reasonably go in accounting for code switching on the part of multilinguals?

The approximately two thousand people who live in the seven villages of the headwaters region of the Snake River (Morobe Province, New Guinea) identify themselves as being one of the three Buang dialect groups. Informants explained that all the Buang speak one language, but that there are three dialects, of which one (lower or ''Manga'' Buang) is not well understood by them, although they communicate easily with speakers of the central dialect (for detailed discussion, including measures of language similarity and mutual intelligibility, see chapter 6, this volume, and Sankoff 1968: chapters 4, 9, 10).

Headwaters Buang is the native language of virtually all of these people (exceptions being a small number of foreign-born wives, mainly from central Buang). Almost everyone is fluent as well in Tok Pisin (New Guinea Pidgin English). A few Buang men were exposed to Tok Pisin beginning in about 1910, as indentured laborers conscripted to work on plantations in New Britain, and as carriers for various (mainly German) explorers. During the 1930s, knowledge of Tok Pisin became almost universal among Buang men as they migrated in large numbers to work on the Bulolo goldfields. Subsequent generations have continued this trend of working away from home, so that at present virtually everyone under forty is fluent in Tok Pisin, as are most men over this age. Tests indicate that over 80 percent of the population resident in the Headwaters in 1967 had at least a good working knowledge of Tok Pisin, a proportion which would probably rise to 90 percent if we were to consider the large numbers of Buang residing in towns.

A third language for many Buang is Yabem, also introduced during the 1930s by evangelists from the coast, themselves mainly native speakers of Bukaua, a language closely related to Yabem. Yabem, a language native to the Finschhafen area of the Huon peninsula, was used by the Lutheran mission as a language of evangelization throughout the Huon Gulf area. Evangelists to the Buang were closely followed by teachers and pastors, and it appears that the first mission school was set up in the headwaters area in 1936. Since then (except for a brief interruption during the Second World War, when the Japanese occupied the Huon coastal area), most Buang have attended village school for at least a couple of years, where, until the 1960s, instruction was carried out entirely in Yabem. Knowledge of Yabem is largely restricted to those who have been to school, although in most villages there are two or three people with special relationships to the mission who have picked up a fair amount of Yabem on their own. In the 1960s, probably about 80 percent of the population between ages ten and forty-five could speak and understand Yabem.

Although there are some people with a knowledge of other languages (including languages of various neighboring groups; English; and Hiri Motu, the *lingua franca* of the Port Moresby area), communication within the headwaters Buang area is restricted to Buang, Tok Pisin, and Yabem.

In collecting data on language usage, my first approach was simply to accumulate examples, in as exhaustive a manner as possible, and my data include notes, tapes, and transcriptions of a large number of communication situations, both informal and formal, as well as normative statements about language use. I rapidly became alert to any instance where a language other than headwaters Buang was being used. This, in turn, led to a number of obvious generalizations about the contexts of use of Yabem and Tok Pisin and the search became one of looking for refinements and counter examples to these generalizations.

In carrying out this work I was, in essence, trying to use a predictive model in which language choice on the part of individual speakers was taken as the dependent variable, and to account for choices in terms of social and situational variables. This attempt is summarized in Figure 2-1, which gives the major or gross constraints on code choice. Starting with the top of the diagram, "Decision to speak," the model allows for choice between or among alternates having to do with various factors in speech events, so that, for example, the first factor has to do with the status of the interlocutor—is he/she a Buang or not? If yes, we examine the type of situation; if no, we check whether he/she is a stranger or not, and so on.

Notice, however, that the model does not present conditions that allow complete prediction of code choices. That is, more than one code possibility is listed as "outcome" at the bottom of several branches. This is due to my rejection, during analysis of the material (see Sankoff 1968, chapter 11) of the "predictive" approach as outlined in the section on "factors and components" above. I realized that such

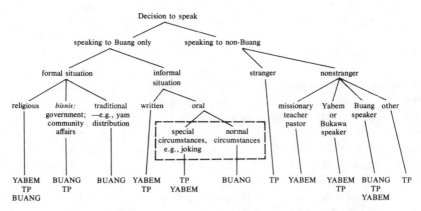

Figure 2-1. Factors constraining code choice for the Buang. (TP = Tok Pisin;—indicates optional distinction discussed on p. 40).

factors could not be taken as predictive in the strict sense, and that they served rather to define certain types of situations in which particular code choices were normally acceptable, appropriate, and even likely. In this sense, they bear a certain resemblance to grammatical constraints.

Grammatical rules for any one language describe the structure of possible strings in that language but do not predict any particular surface realization of these rules by any particular speaker at any particular time. Rather, the rules enable us to parse such surface realizations (i.e., to account for them in terms of the rules), as well as to identify some sentences as being ungrammatical. Similarly, sociolinguistic rules should enable us to interpret the social meaning or significance of choices or decisions (not necessarily conscious) on the part of speakers among alternates or variants carrying other than strictly referential meaning; they tell us which choices are acceptable ("grammatical"), which are inappropriate or unacceptable ("ungrammatical"), and may even give us gradations between these two (cf. Labov's "variable constraints" [1970: 61ff], which state probabilities of occurrence for certain linguistic forms given social as well as linguistic environment). To say that sociolinguistic rules are weak because they do not entirely predict which code a speaker will choose is analogous to saying that feature-specifying vocabulary selection rules are weak because they do not predict which word a speaker will choose.

Sociolinguistic rules can and do specify conditions under which certain kinds of choices are appropriate, whether the domain of choice be relatively restricted (use of honorifics or not; choice of terms of address in general [see Geoghegan 1969]) or very broad (choice of code over all occurring communication situations). In addition, they can be ordered in terms of generality or applicability. In the Buang case, for example, it would not have made sense to start with the variable "tone" (e.g., joking) as the first factor to be considered in accounting for code choices, as it does not apply equally over all situations. Rather, I considered that facts having to do with the interlocutors were of primary importance and, as they apply in every case, placed this variable near the top of the tree for greater economy in the model. Next came situation-defining variables having to do mainly with setting and topic, followed by variables involving tone, channel, etc.

Notice also that the use of Buang constitutes what could be called the "unmarked"[3] case. Thus unless the situation is specially

3. For recent discussions of marking, see Geoghegan (1969) and (for an application to the language use of bilinguals) Gumperz and Hernández-Chavez (1972) and Gumperz (1970).

marked as having a non-Buang interlocutor, or being formal, or containing special characteristics of tone, Buang is the language used. The fact that the use of Buang is unmarked also implies that when another factor not indicated in the diagram is added, the language used is still Buang. For example, we might consider "channel"—the Buang are proficient yodellers, often calling across valleys to each other from distant ridges, and the only language they ever use for this is Buang. Nevertheless it is not necessary for the model to take yodelling into account, unless this channel must be marked for the use of other-than-Buang as is, for example, the written channel. Letters are written in Tok Pisin or Yabem.

To recapitulate the general argument: the model presented in Figure 2-1 defines certain general types of speech situation in which particular code usage is felt to be appropriate by the Buang. It does not predict which code will be used in any particular case. In fact, it defines certain situations in which *alternation* among the various codes is felt to be appropriate—formal meetings having to do with government affairs or economic development, for example.

One factor of great importance, particularly in formal situations where a speaker is addressing an audience is that which Hymes calls "goals" or "ends" (1967: 22). Skill in oratory has often been described as one of the defining criteria of the Melanesian big man (e.g., Oliver 1949), and I would contend that in a situation where several codes are available to a speaker, he manipulates them in many subtle ways in trying to harangue or convince his audience, choosing a particular turn of phrase in a particular language to drive home one point, switching languages and turning to another portion of his audience to make another. Use of code switching as a creative rhetorical device by skilled orators was a marked feature of all formal public meetings among the Buang except those dealing with purely traditional topics. This behavior was predictable in the sense that there existed a situational definition of when rapid code alternation would or could take place; one could not, however, predict what language a speaker would choose at any point in time. One could be fairly certain that the powerful, influential men in the community would use code switching more than most of the other speakers. Nevertheless, for them, variation would occur no matter how closely one specified the environment. It is more important to understand that speech variation is a crucial aspect of the position of these men than to attempt to construct an elaborate deterministic model covering every possible instance of language choice.

Gumperz and Hernández-Chavez take a similar position when they say:

38

It would be futile to predict the occurrence of either English or Spanish in the above utterances by attempting to isolate social variables which correlate with linguistic form. Topic, speaker, setting are common in each. Yet the code changes sometimes in the middle of a sentence. (Gumperz and Hernández-Chavez 1972: 88)

Most students of multilingual code switching situations would probably agree on the futility of attempting to construct a complete predictive or deterministic model of code switching. What kind of analytical procedures can we then follow? Gumperz and Hernández-Chavez, in their perceptive analysis of code switching on the part of Spanish-English bilinguals, follow an approach also used in Blom and Gumperz (1972). They propose that despite the unpredictability of code switching, code usage by multilinguals still carries social meaning. They suggest that cognitively oriented studies can indicate such social meaning, and propose that, following the cultural or social definitions of which language constitutes the unmarked usage in a particular situation, we can identify a speaker's strategies in using a language that is "marked" in that situation to convey particular social meaning. Thus instead of trying to predict switches, they feel that it is more important to try to account for or interpret them in terms of social function.

Though I agree entirely with the thrust of their argument, and have used such an "interpretive" approach myself (see Sankoff 1968: 194–200), I have some reservations about whether it is always possible to identify one of the codes in question as being unmarked, and about whether in fact it is possible or feasible to attempt to interpret *every* switch. To justify these reservations, I shall summarize the material I have presented on the Buang in terms corresponding to those which they have used. Earlier, I noted that the use of Buang could be taken as the unmarked case. Rethinking in terms of Gumperz and Hernández-Chavez's discussion, however, it would seem more reasonable to attempt to specify which code is felt to be unmarked in the relevant, culturally defined situations. We can, however, see the diagram presented in Figure 2-1 as defining such situations, and each of the linguistic "outcomes" as being unmarked for that particular situation. Thus, for example, to use Buang or Yabem in addressing a complete stranger would be marked as distinctly peculiar; to use Tok Pisin or Yabem to another Buang, in an informal situation, under "normal circumstances" would imply a change in these "normal circumstances," generally marking a joke, or a game or put-on. In this sense, language choice is constitutive of social meaning.

Analyzing the Buang material, I suggest that the various factors in speech events can be ordered in accounting for code choices. Some of these factors (in the Buang case, participants, setting and topic, in that order) serve to define a number of situations in terms of appropriate (or unmarked) code usage. The model could be made more complicated by adding branches representing the influence of other factors (such as tone, ends, etc.), and I have illustrated this by the optional addition of "joking" as a separate branch. It could, on the other hand, be made less complicated by removing, say, topic, from the situation-defining variables, treating foreign languages as unmarked for formal situations except when such situations are marked, by topic, as being [+ traditional]. Heuristically, however, it seems more satisfying to consider variables or factors having to do with individual speech strategies as constituting a marking of situations defined by the other variables. Thus the cutoff point between the situation-defining variables and the marking variables, which have to do with individual speech strategies, is not entirely arbitrary (see Figure 2-2). In terms of the first two approaches discussed in this chapter, we would thus be using the factors near the top of the list as in some sense predictive (in defining appropriateness or unmarked forms). Variation beyond this point would be analyzed in terms of the "functions" of using forms defined as marked, which in turn could be analyzed, post hoc, as reflecting factors having to do with speakers' intentions.

"Receiver" or "interlocutor" has to do with whether the receiver is a Buang, stranger, missionary, etc. "Situation" can be either formal or informal, defined in terms of "setting" (e.g., village square,

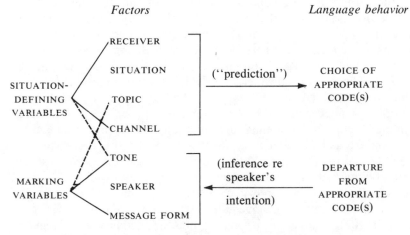

Figure 2-2. Tentative schematization ordering factors in speech events for code choices by the Buang.

church, etc.) and "ends" or reason for speech event (e.g., report of local councilor). "Topic" is qualified as being traditional, having to do with mission affairs or government business, etc. "Channel" is either written or oral. "Tone" refers to the speaker's intent to be serious, jocular, etc. "Speaker" has to do not only with the individual speaker's linguistic competence in the various codes, but also with the impression the speaker wishes to convey about himself/herself. "Message form" refers to the use of prayer, rhetoric, ordinary conversation, etc.

As well as being a tentative formulation, Figure 2-2 is also a generalization and thus a simplification of reality. I have already noted that the choice of which variables to call "situation-defining variables" and which to call "marking variables" has been made in order to best account for a large number of cases. This is not to say that for some speech events, the factors cannot be ordered differently. With regard to the "language behavior," it is also true that a choice from among the codes regarded as appropriate can carry social meaning (not indicated in the diagram), that code choice including departures from the appropriate can alter the definition of the situation (as well as constituting a "marking" of already defined situations), and so on. The schematization is presented as a convenient way of looking at a complicated situation.

Turning to my contention that, at least for the Buang case, there are situations that define alternation as appropriate (i.e., no one code can be analyzed as unmarked), I present excerpts from a speech recorded at a village meeting. The topic was *bisnis* (see Sankoff 1969), more specifically, a village store for which the original capital had been contributed by several hundred people from several villages, some of whom now wanted their money back. The main village entrepreneur (and "big man") was trying to convince people that he was running things properly and that people should leave their money in the enterprise.

(Tok Pisin is italicized and Buang is not; ". . ." indicates a very short portion of the speech not hearable on the tape; "#" indicates what I have analyzed below as alternations, *not* any material omitted or break in the tape).

	Buang/Tok Pisin *transcription*	*English translation*
B	Olo ba kena, *trovel* ti vu Buweyew.	Next, there is a problem in Buweyew.
	#Orait, man bilong com-paun, inoken ripot long 5 *husat pepul bilong*	#Now, men away at work shouldn't bring grievances to just anyone from Ayayok,

Ayayok, Mambump, wonem hap. I mas ripot long olgeta long ples
TP *stret* (continuing entirely
10 in TP for 15 lines)
ikamap trovel o wonem, mi ken stretim olgeta toktok, Orait.

Mambump, anywhere at all. They must report to people from their *own* villages (omitted) If any problem comes up, I will be able to settle all the arguments. O.K.

#Pasin ke ken be, *moni* ti
15 ken nyep la, su lok lam *memba* re, olo ba *miting autim olgeta tok . . .*
B *moni* ti ken nyep ega, rek mu su rek ogoko
20 nam be, ong *moni* rek, *. . . moni* ti ken *bak stua* lam vu Mambump re, m nzom ayon.

#This is the way—the money that is there can't go back to the shareholders, and the meeting brought up all these arguments . . . the money that's there you won't take back, your money will . . . this money from the bulk store will come back to Mambump, and we'll hold on to it.

#Orait, bihain, bihainim
25 *bilong wok long bisnis, orait, moni bilong stua bai ibekim olgeta ples, Husat igat moni paul na istap long buk bilong mi*
TP 30 *yet, orait mi yet mi gat plantesin kopi, mi ken bekim dinau bilong ol. Orait disfela tok em bilong pepul na ol ikirap*
35 *gen orait pastaim kirap.*

#Now later, if we continue these business activities, then the store money will be repaid to everyone. Whoever's money has gone astray, and it's registered in my book, very well, I have a coffee plantation of my own—I can pay the debts owing to them. Now this talk has to do with the people, and if they want to bring it up again, let them bring it up.

#Orait, nga ti ken be, vu, vu *as ples. Orait,* su rek be *winim* ke, be *winim olgeta direkta,* ga be
B 40 *winim ol pepul,* olo ba *kamap* vu bumbum re.

#Now, this has to do with us, in the villages. And it's not too much to handle for me, or for the directors, or for the people, that it has to be taken to the white man.

#Ino samting bilong masta na samting bi-
TP *long kiap, em i samting*
45 *bilong mipela yet!*

#It's not something to do with the white man or the government officer—it's our thing!

If we count the actual number of switches, including isolated words, in this text (which goes on in the same vein for about an hour), we arrive at a total of twenty-nine, which does not tell us much. Looking more closely, we can perhaps separate two kinds of tendencies. First, there is an alternation between sections of the speech which are basically Tok Pisin and sections which are basically Buang. Line 1 is basically Buang, then starting with *orait* on line 3 and continuing to *orait* on line 13 is Tok Pisin. Continuing from there through line 23 is again basically Buang, with another entirely Tok Pisin section beginning on line 24 and continuing to *kirap* on line 35. From *orait* on line 36 to *re* on line 41 is again basically Buang, with another Tok Pisin section starting on line 42.

Thus in gross terms, we might say that in this text, there are only five alternations: Buang—TP—Buang—TP—Buang—TP. It is this gross kind of alternation I am referring to when I say that both codes are acceptable in the situation. It may be partly explicable as a stylistic, rhetorical feature having to do with the importance of repetition and translation in Melanesian oratory (Salisbury 1962). This speech, and others like it, is certainly repetitive, but the speaker does not "translate" what he has just said into the other language as he goes along. Rather, he makes one point in one language, then switches to the other to bring out a different aspect of the argument.

The second tendency evident in this speech involves the very great admixture of Tok Pisin words and phrases into sections of it which are basically Buang (the reverse never occurs).[4] The most blatant example of this is the negative construction, which in Buang involves *su* + predicate + *re*, starting with *su* on line 37 and finishing, after an almost entirely Tok Pisin vocabulary in the predicate, with *re* on line 41 (other Buang elements in the predicate include conjunctions, the future marker *rek,* and the pronoun "I"). Although some of the words in question (e.g., *moni*) might be classed as loan words,[5] representing items or concepts for which there is no analogue in Buang, this is certainly not true for all, and there are many Tok Pisin words which could easily have been replaced (referentially) by Buang equivalents. Close examination of these suggests tentative interpretations for some of them. For example, it seems that the Tok Pisin conjunction *orait* is being used stylistically, for greater emphasis, in place of the Buang

4. Norman Denison's study of Sauris, a trilingual community in Italy (see Denison, 1968, 1971) also shows directionality in interference, and Denison (personal communication) has suggested that interference from 'H' to 'L' may be a "near universal." In the present case, however, I would hesitate to classify the two speech varieties in question as representing the type of 'H' vs. 'L' distinction found in sociolinguistic situations of diglossia as classically defined by Ferguson (1959).

5. For an interesting comparison with the Buang case, see texts presented in Laycock (1966), involving heavy Tok Pisin borrowings into the Wosera dialect of Abelam.

conjunctions *olo ba* or *olo ga*. But for many other segments, there appears to be no very satisfying explanation in terms of the social meaning of *that particular element*. I would argue that what carries weight in this "marking" of Buang sections of the speech with extensive use of Tok Pisin is best analyzed as a matter of degree, not in terms of what each element contributes. In addition, we are still faced with the problem that there does not appear to be any obvious way in which the larger segments in Tok Pisin differ from the basically Buang segments.

It is clear that this speaker's use of the two languages does carry social meaning. The use of Buang represents an identification with the people, shows that the speaker considers himself a part of the local community and is accepted as such. But he is also a valuable link with the modern, outside world, and his authority in this domain, his claim to understand *bisnis* (how modern economics works), to have outside contacts with urban businessmen (in this case, a Chinese merchant) and government officials are all substantiated by his use of Tok Pisin. That the speaker use both languages in this context is important—he keeps in touch with all segments of his audience by constant alternation. But exactly what he says in one language or the other is not in itself important.

For the headwaters Buang, use of Tok Pisin is regarded as appropriate for people of power and authority, in contexts having a relationship to the broader colonial society, especially the domains of business and government. Its use in this context is not marked for leaders, or for people recognized as having had extensive contact with the outside world. But it easily becomes a joke when used by others. For example, Tok Pisin is often used, seriously, to give orders, as by a man at the village meeting assigning a work detail to a group of women, and in this context is perfectly acceptable (not necessarily to the women in question, who frequently disregard the orders). But for a child to tell her/his mother, in Tok Pisin, to do something is definitely marked.

So far, I have discussed both the predictive and the interpretive approaches in the analysis of language use in terms of the Buang data. I believe that the third type of analysis discussed at the beginning of this paper is also applicable. That is, it is possible to show that the extent of use of Tok Pisin (or of Yabem) forms a continuum that could be correlated with various social and situational variables, simply in terms of the relative proportion of Tok Pisin used. In terms of social stratification, for example, it seems clear that high status correlates with high frequency of use of Tok Pisin. One very gross comparison I did along these lines in analyzing eight village meetings showed that in thirty speeches by the two most eminent community leaders, Tok Pisin occurred twenty times, whereas it occurred only seventeen times in eighty-six speeches by all others present (Table 1-1 above). (It might also be possible in such small communities to make status ratings in terms of folk categories, e.g., TP *bikpela man* ('big man') versus *rabis man* (< Eng. 'rubbish', 'low status man').)

5. DISCUSSION

To summarize, I would like to return to the three questions posed at the beginning of this chapter. First, I think that each type of approach discussed has something to contribute to an understanding of the Buang case. With respect to *predicting,* i.e., the specifying of appropriateness in social-situational terms, I have suggested that the factors influencing speech events can be hierarchically arranged in terms of their relative weight in defining speech situations for the Buang, and that a good cutoff point would seem to be at the level where a speaker's intentions come into play. Again to illustrate with the example of a joke, I can think of no a priori way to predict when a speaker is about to make a joke or otherwise change the tone of the conversation. Thus it seems more reasonable, with this kind of factor, to do a post hoc, interpretive analysis, given that a joke has occurred, of its function and social meaning within the context of the conversation, and to state the linguistic means by which the utterance was marked as a joke (e.g., code switch).

An interpretive analysis of the social meaning of code choice would obviously give a great deal more depth to our understanding of language use by the Buang. I have made several suggestions as to the functions of some kinds of code choices. These interpretations could be deepened and expanded through the use of methods pioneered by Gumperz, i.e., working closely with Buang speakers in analyzing recordings of speech events in which they actually participated.

Further evidence of the systematic aspects of code usage could be given by using the third approach, that is, the demonstration that it is possible to specify social and situational constraints according to which the relative frequency of code usage forms a continuum.

This brings us to the second question, i.e., whether it is necessary, given that the language behavior demonstrates at least to some extent the properties of a continuum, to conduct the analysis in terms of one system. That code choice demonstrates systematic properties does not necessarily imply that there is only one code present. That is, in sociolinguistic terms, code choice is one aspect of a coherent sociolinguistic system; it is clear that, in the Buang case, each of the three codes in question is analytically separable from the others as a language.

Regarding the third question (how well code-switching can be accounted for), it would appear that each of the three approaches has different goals. The last discussed approach is concerned rather with demonstrating tendencies than with the prediction of separate cases, and the predictive approach is, in my estimation, more useful in defining conditions of appropriateness. The interpretive approach would appear to be the most concerned with accounting for individual cases, although Gumperz and associates too seem to be interested at least as much in making general statements about the kinds of social functions indicated by code choices.

It would appear that the general focus of studies of code switching and code choice has been shifting towards an appreciation of the complexity of this behavior as part of a sociolinguistic system. Ethnographies of speaking in multilingual communities can only profit by continued attempts to apply a variety of methodological and analytical approaches.

3.

A Quantitative Paradigm for the Study of Communicative Competence

1. INTRODUCTION

The past decade has seen a great increase in scholarly efforts directed to exploring the systematicity of the relationships between sociocultural organization and language use. A basic assumption behind this search has been that speakers functioning as members of a particular society in terms of a particular culture have internalized not only rules of grammar, but also rules of appropriate speech usage that are widely shared and widely employed by other members of their society. Thus *competence* has been extended from the notion of the mastery of a set of grammatical rules to the mastery of a set of cultural rules that include the appropriate ways to apply grammatical rules in all speech situations possible for that society (Hymes 1972b). The notion of context has been extended to apply not only to linguistic context or environment, but to the social-situational circumstances of the speech event, even to the intent or ends of the speaker.

Many important concepts were developed during the 1960s for dealing with systematic sociolinguistic variability, as it came to be generally recognized that no community or individual is limited to a single variety of code (Hymes 1967a). Such concepts include the idea of

This paper was originally published in R. Bauman and J. Sherzer, eds., *Explorations in the Ethnography of Speaking* (Cambridge, Eng.: Cambridge University Press, 1974), pp. 18–49. It is reprinted here with only minor editorial changes. I wish to thank the Canada Council and the Ministère de l'Education, Québec, for their support for the Montréal French project. I am grateful to the following people who contributed to the analysis of examples discussed in this paper: Suzanne Laberge, for her work on the collection and analysis of the Tok Pisin material; Eleanor Herasimchuk Wynn, for further help with the Tok Pisin data; Dorothée Bertrand-Mineau, Henrietta J. Cedergren, Michèle Chiasson-Lavoie, Suzanne Laberge, Monique Dumont, Jean-Jacques Gagné, Robert Sarrasin, David Sankoff, and Marjorie Topham for their work on the Montréal French project. I wish to thank Henrietta Cedergren, John Gumperz, Eugene Hammel, Dell Hymes, Paul Kay, William Labov, Marc Leduc, Claire Lefebvre, Paul Pupier, and Madeleine St-Pierre for helpful discussion of some of the specific issues discussed in the paper, though the opinions expressed are my own.

47

a *linguistic repertoire* (Gumperz 1964, 1965, 1968) of a community or of an individual, the *code matrix* of a community, consisting of all of its codes and subcodes, including languages, dialects, styles (Gumperz 1962), or registers (Halliday 1964) in their functional relationships; the idea that speech events can be characterized in terms of a set of *components,* such as channel, setting, participants, etc. (cf. Ervin-Tripp 1972; Hymes 1967a, 1972a), each of which may be factored into a number of relevant *features.* "Relevant" is used here in a functional sense, i.e., the components interact with each other in terms of covariation of features. A related idea was that variation in language use could be dealt with in terms of the variable *functions* of speech (cf. Jakobson 1960; Hymes 1962, 1970a), the basic notion here being that what might be referentially "synonymous" could at the same time be a socially meaningful distinction.

Within this broad framework, there is a general recognition both of the heterogeneity of all known speech communities, and of the extent to which variation in use carries sociostylistic meaning, i.e., of the *structure* of linguistic variation within speech communities. Given this general agreement, however, there are several possible approaches to the study of speech use within its sociocultural context, approaches that are not, in my view, mutually incompatible. Many of those who work within the "ethnography of speaking" tradition take as a starting point the examination of the sociocultural matrix of language use (defined in terms of interpersonal interaction or in terms of culturally specified situations of speech use) and investigate in some detail their linguistic concomitants. Most of the research reported in this chapter starts from the other side of the same coin, trying to demonstrate that the distribution of linguistic features cannot be understood solely in terms of their internal relationships within grammar, but must be seen as part of the broader sociocultural context in which they occur. Despite this apparent difference, however, I will argue that the theoretical and methodological issues I raise are of direct relevance for both approaches.

At the most general level, the basic problem is that of the accountability of a description of any behavior to some data base, a problem that can also be seen as the quite straightforward matter of how to generalize from a set of observations. In any analysis, one searches for structure, pattern, and relationships; I contend that in speech behavior as in many other kinds of behavior there is a great deal of statistical variability. This does not imply that such variability is unstructured, nor does it imply that there do not exist categorical (nonvariable) rules and relationships in language and in language use. However, in attempting to find patterns that are expressible other than as categorical rules, it may be possible to pioneer techniques that will prove useful to sociolinguists of various persuasions. Many sociolinguists are now working with situations in which rules appear to be more categorical than variable, situations of highly marked speech use including rituals, greetings, games, insults, and the like. In dealing with such cases, it appears convenient and indeed logical to borrow models and formalisms from linguistics, and to attempt to formulate the types of rules suggested in Ervin-Tripp (1972). But most models originating from modern linguistics have no way of treating variability, and tend to carry with them idealistic postulates of homogeneity and determinacy that I believe will prove unsuitable for sociolinguistics in the long run, as they have proven unsuitable in the field of ethnosemantics (cf. chapters 8 and 9, this volume) and as scholars working on purely grammatical problems have begun to find in this area as well (Elliot, Legum, and Thompson 1969; Ross 1972, 1973; Sag 1973).

The variability of speech as people actually use it has been only too painfully obvious to anyone attempting to work with large bodies of recorded speech of any sort. It is my contention in this chapter that quantitative techniques can be fruitfully used in demonstrating not only the general patterns existing within a speech community, but also the individually internalized subtle distinctions that are based on the human ability to deal with differences of degree, both in producing speech and in interpreting the speech of others. A meaningful and realistic framework need not imply that if only the analyst could exercise enough ingenuity, all variation could be accounted for, deterministically, by specifying long enough lists of constraints.

One might well ask why it is necessary at all to talk about behavior when dealing with questions of internalized ability to use speech grammatically and appropriately, i.e., with questions of competence. Whether we assume such competence to be a property of the individual or of the community (in the sense of shared rule systems), and whether we understand it to mean linguistic or sociolinguistic competence, we are faced with the problem of what kind of evidence we can use as a basis for our analysis. Since all evidence (with the possible exception of introspection by the analyst herself/himself, but including elicited grammaticality judgments) consists of behavior, and generally verbal behavior (performance), of some sort, it is virtually impossible to escape the problem of making inferences from behavior. (On the perils of introspection, see DeCamp 1973; Labov 1970.) It is my view that performance consists essentially of *samples* of competence (see also Cedergren and D. Sankoff 1974). In any attempt to abstract from performance the kinds of patterns we would expect in competence, it is important to recognize the problems that result from the statistical fluctuation inherent in all probabilistically generated behavior. Most of the issues here hinge on the nature of similarity and difference. What degree or extent of difference in performance would lead us to infer difference in competence?

The analytic goals different sociolinguists set for themselves are many and varied. In the work I describe here, the goal is not to start afresh and write whole grammars; I think it is essential in dealing with the details of language to build on the work of scholars concerned with narrowly linguistic rather than sociolinguistic competence. But a clearer understanding of those particular areas of grammar that are intimately intertwined with social and cultural domains, and of the detailed nature of these interconnections, is one of the most clearly definable and attainable goals of sociolinguists.

2. THE NATURE OF THE QUANTITATIVE PARADIGM

A number of proposals have been made by linguists and sociolinguists in the past few years for dealing with some of the aspects of linguistic variation discussed in the previous section. The quantitative approach advocated here implies a number of procedures for data collection and analysis that are shared to some extent with other approaches, but which nevertheless form a unique and coherent system (cf. D. Sankoff 1978). Not only are such procedures necessary for the adequate formulation of variable rules, they also provide crucial data for verifying categorical rules of grammar or of speech use.

Many of the properties of the approach I am proposing are shared by what Bailey (1970, 1973) has referred to as the "dynamic paradigm." The existence of structured variability, however, is not necessarily a sign of linguistic change in progress (Fasold 1973). A linguistic change once begun can be halted or even reversed (Weinreich 1958; Labov et al. 1979), and the ensuing variation may come to characterize various kinds of linguistic subcodes, systems, or varieties, whether these be defined in terms of particular sociolinguistic events (genres, routines, etc.), or in terms of types of speakers.

Quantitative studies of speech behavior within a speech community perspective depend on good data. This means that it is essential to have sufficient types and amounts of clearly recorded speech data on individuals or communities whose social properties are taken into account. Accordingly, section 2.1 deals with the nature of the data base, and particularly with the question of the representativity of recorded speech data. Sections 2.2 and 2.3 deal with subsequent steps in data processing and analysis, and 2.4 shows how such data can be used in the writing of variable rules.

2.1. The Data Base

Grounded in the notion of a speech community, the quantitative approach involves the collection and analysis of a corpus that adequately represents the speech performance of members of that community. A systematic set of recordings must be made that will represent the various dimensions of variability existing within the community. Thus sampling is important, as is the problem of how to control for the presence of the observer in altering "normal" performance. Both of these problems are common to other behavioral investigations, and here the sociolinguist has much to learn from other social sciences, though the fact that speech behavior is the object of study causes special problems.

In sampling, there are three types of decision that must be made:

(a) The first is to delineate, at least roughly, the geographic, social, etc., boundaries of the speech community or subcommunity of interest; i.e., to define the sampling universe.

(b) The second is to assess the possibly relevant geographic, social, and sociolinguistic dimensions of variation within the community; i.e., to construct a stratification for the sample. As the goal of sampling is to tap the existing linguistic variation in a community, it is important for the investigator to consider carefully all types of existing variation. Are there ethnic groups that display different speech variants (e.g., Laferriere 1979)? Might age (Labov, Yaeger, and Steiner 1972), sex (Shuy 1970; Trudgill 1972), social class (Labov 1966b) make a difference? How may migration alter community speech patterns (Payne 1979)? Do individuals speak differently in different social circumstances? (Labov 1966a, chapter 4). Sampling should take account of at least these dimensions, as well as any others that might be relevant to a particular situation.

(c) The third type of decision is to settle on the number of informants and the amount of material to be collected from each; i.e., to fix the sample size.

A speech community sample need not include the large number of individuals usually required for other kinds of behavioral surveys. If people within a speech community indeed understand each other with a high degree of efficiency, this tends to place a limit on the extent of possible variation, and imposes a regularity (necessary for effective communication) not found to the same extent in other kinds of social behavior. The literature as well as our own experience would suggest that, even for quite complex speech communities, samples of more than about 150 individuals tend to be redundant, bringing increasing data handling problems with diminishing analytical returns. (Cf. Labov 1972d on the homogeneity of peer group speech behavior). It is crucial, however, that the sample be well chosen, and representative of all social subsegments about which one wishes to generalize.

Once these decisions are made, sampling can proceed, either by formally random methods, or through a social network approach. In the latter approach, one must rely on the stratification scheme, and on deliberate attempts to diversify, in order to ensure a degree of representativity of the sample and to avoid sampling just a small circle of personal friends.

The nature of these procedures can best be understood through examples. For our study of Montréal French, we defined our universe as consisting of all native French speakers resident in predominantly French areas of Montréal since early childhood. We stratified according to age, sex, socioeconomic level of residence area, and geographic area. The sample of 120 was picked using formal methods involving random choices in a street directory, and a strict protocol for selecting informants. (For further methodological details on this study, cf. D. Sankoff and G. Sankoff 1973.)

In Labov's study of Black English (Labov et al. 1968) he concentrated on the male adolescent subculture in Harlem and stratified mainly by age, choosing to focus on peer groups at each of several age levels. His work on the Lower East Side is based on a more formally produced sample of 122 speakers, which he culled according to linguistic origin and residential criteria from the Lower East Side survey carried out by sociologists.

For her investigation of Spanish in Panama, Cedergren (1972) chose 79 native Spanish-speaking informants stratified according to age, sex, socioeconomic level, and age at arrival in the city.

In our work on New Guinea Tok Pisin (cf. chapters 10, 11, and 12, this volume), Laberge and I searched for some subsection of the New Guinea urban community in which there would be a concentration of first-language speakers. We found such a situation in the town of Lae, in neighborhoods where there were numerous interlanguage marriages. We were then able to construct a carefully matched sample of about 25 adolescents and children, all of whom spoke Tok Pisin as a first language, and an equal number of their parents, who spoke it as a second language.

Ma and Herasimchuk (1968: 666) describe the selection of 45 informants chosen for a study of Spanish-English bilingualism in Jersey City, on the basis of residence within the two-block predominantly Puerto Rican area being studied, sex, and occupational and educational characteristics.

A Quantitative Paradigm

Shuy et al. (1968) based their Detroit sample on families having children in elementary school, in ten geographical areas of the city. Though a total of 702 interviews from over 250 families were completed, only 48 of these were actually used in analysis in the most detailed study of the Detroit material to appear (Wolfram 1969).

There is often a conflict between the goals of representing in a systematic series of recordings both inter- and intra-individual variation. That is, in systematically sampling for different types of individuals, it is impossible not to deal with strangers, but the very fact of not knowing people makes it difficult to record them in more than one kind of situation, usually that of an interview, in which they exhibit only a particular segment of their linguistic repertoire. The resulting data may be limited grammatically as well as stylistically. For example, people being interviewed are not likely to use many interrogatives. It also often happens that the more informal (natural) the situation, the more difficult it is to record, as background noise seems to increase exponentially with informality. The closer the microphone is to the mouth of the speaker, the better the recording quality (technically) and the more likely it is to intimidate the speaker into a more formal style; the farther away from the speaker, the greater the informality but with a general drop in technical quality. Hidden microphones tend to be inefficacious as well as unethical.

In our Montréal French study, we decided to approach some of these problems by working with two different samples of people. The 120 carefully sampled subjects were interviewed as a "one shot" study, by individual interviewers, who tried to encourage informal speech by various means: urging other members of the subjects' families to remain in the room during the interview and participate in the conversation; using Lavaliere microphones, which are less obtrusive than a visible microphone held or on a stand in front of the speaker; discovering through a pretest the topics on which Montrealers appeared to enjoy talking freely, etc. Interviewers also attempted to tap more formal styles toward the end of the interview, where we thought the topic of language attitudes would encourage greater self-monitoring and editing. Lastly, subjects were asked to read a short text both to elicit careful style and to guarantee comparability through the use of the same measuring instrument for all subjects. Particularly important for phonology, the text included minimal pairs on which we wanted data. Tape recorders were left running throughout the interviewers' visits, including before and after the interview proper and during interruptions of various sorts.

Despite all of these measures, we could not hope in the space of an hour or so to tap the whole range of subjects' linguistic repertoires, especially those specific to situations and activities other than those typically occurring within the home. Thus a second part of the Montréal study includes making a series of recordings of individuals and groups over a wide range of interaction situations. This, of course, involves the cooperation of the people chosen, as well as a period of becoming accustomed to the presence of the field worker and recording instruments. Studies in which similar procedures have been carried out include Gumperz (1964), Labov et al. (1968), Lefebvre (1974), Mitchell-Kernan (1971), Sankoff (1968), and chapter 2 above.

It should be remembered that we are primarily interested in describing "everyday" speech, that is, the kind of speech that Labov (1972e: 256–57) has termed the "vernacular." Vernacular speech is, from the participants' point of view, *least* marked for special features, whether linguistic or social. It differs in several respects from the highly marked genres of ritual speech, linguistic games, oral literature, public speaking, and so on. Our approach can, however, be extended for describing the specific linguistic nature of many other kinds of speech that are of social significance in the communities being studied. Such speech varieties may differ from the vernacular by being "marked" with one or more categorical features, or may differ simply in terms of proportions or degree, some feature(s) being more or less frequent.

2.2. The Handling of Data and the Choice of Variables

Methods developed for dealing with variability stem from an appreciation of the fact that a particular underlying element in language may have two or more surface realizations that are not completely determined by environmental constraints. A first step involves the extraction of all (or a systematic sample judged to be sufficiently large) examples of the variants of one or other of the variables in the corpus. This implies that recordings be in accessible form, at least as well-documented tapes, and at best accompanied by complete, detailed transcriptions in a standardized orthography. Usually some compromise is made between these two extremes. In order to automate some parts of the analysis, we have developed procedures for putting our Montréal corpus on computer cards and tapes. The resulting data includes a three thousand-page computer printed transcription, as well as a fifteen thousand-page microfiche concordance of all occurring lexical items (each item listed with one eighty-character line of context). For further details, cf. D. Sankoff, Lessard, and Nguyen (1978).

It is rare that one knows in advance of the analysis exactly which variables are to be studied. This means that many "passes" have to be made over the complete corpus. This is not inefficient, however, since it is confusing to try to extract several unrelated variables during

54

the same pass; more importantly, each search inevitably leads to a better "feeling" for the material, to unsuspected discoveries of patterns and of further variables to investigate.

The basic principle in extracting information on variation is that of noting not only each instance of a particular variant, but also the number of instances in which it could have occurred, but did not. As Labov says, "Any variable form (a member of a set of alternative ways of 'saying the same thing') should be reported with the proportion of cases in which the form did occur in the relevant environment, compared to the total number of cases in which it might have occurred" (1969: 738). Other types of statistics may also be interesting, but if the ultimate goal is an assessment of competence in terms of grammatical rules, then proportions, or relative frequencies, are essential.

2.3. Analysis: How to Expand Environments

In analyzing variable linguistic data according to the quantitative paradigm being proposed in this chapter, extralinguistic as well as linguistic constraints are examined. That is, the notion of environment is expanded both to include different kinds of constraints and to deal with questions of proportion or degree.

An example from out study of Montréal French will illustrate both points. Underlying /l/[1] in the pronoun *il* in Montréal French exhibits a variable surface realization, being uttered as either [l] or Ø. Thus we have

(1) il fait [i fɛ]—'he does'

(2) il est [y e]—'he is'

We also, however, find the forms 3 and 4.

(3) il fait [il fɛ]—'he does'

(4) il est [il e]—'he is'

According to any kind of conventional linguistic analysis, therefore, we have not discovered a rule which handles the alternate realizations of /l/ as [l] on the one hand, or as Ø on the other. We have to treat it as an unconstrained optional rule or as "free variation," unless we can find some other constraint that will categorically handle the alternate realizations.

In looking at a large number of cases of *il* in the speech of six Montrealers, however, we found that the distribution of the various

---

1. The / / notation is not meant to represent phonemic brackets, but simply an abstract phonological representation.

alternate realizations of /l/ is phonologically conditioned, and that the succeeding phonological environment has a very definite effect on the deletion of /l/. Where it is followed by a consonant or glide [−syll], it is much more likely to be realized as Ø (93.7 percent of 648 cases) than when it is followed by a vowel [+syll] (57.1 percent of 196 cases). In addition, the phonological realization of /l/ is conditioned by the grammatical function of the pronoun in which it occurs. As we see in Table 3-1 (from Sankoff and Cedergren 1971: 74), where *il* is impersonal, as in *il pleut* "it is raining," or *il y a* "there is/are," /l/ is realized as Ø almost 100 percent of the time in a [−syll] environment; the personal pronoun is realized as Ø only 80 percent of the time in the same environment. The distinction is maintained before vowels, the personal pronoun undergoing less frequent /l/-deletion.

Thus though each of these speakers demonstrated variability in their realization of /l/, their behavior was nonetheless constrained by phonological and grammatical factors. It could be argued that if we were clever enough to think of a few other factors it might be possible to explain away the remaining variation. I would counter that in this case and in many others like it, variability is inherent, and speakers alternate in their use of the two or several alternate forms.

Understanding that, on the one hand, such variability may be maintained even in the most closely and carefully specified phonological and syntactic environments, and that, on the other, it is to some extent constrained by these environments, as shown in the percentages, is central to an understanding of how the "quantitative paradigm" can be used in the more difficult (when attempted deterministically) case involving nonlinguistic environments. Thus, though such variability, for some particular linguistic variable, may be characteristic of even a single speaker in a stable situation, within a small segment of connected discourse, it is in fact the case that variation is constrained, again to varying degrees, by social and stylistic factors. With an "all-or-nothing" mental set, the linguist can be caught in a never ending search

Forms	Environments	
	/ __[−syll]	/ __[+syll]
il impersonal	% 97.2 (516)	% 69.9 (13)
il personal	80.6 (139)	56.3 (183)

TABLE 3-1. Deletion of /l/ in *il* for six Montrealers according to grammatical category and succeeding phonological environment.

for an ever vanishing determinacy. The realization that "languages" are not homogeneous led to an unsuccessful search for homogeneity at the "dialect," then the "idiolect" level (cf. Bloch 1948, and discussion in Weinreich, Labov, and Herzog 1968). If, however, we accept a quantitative analytical method for its demonstrated ability to locate systematicity in terms of purely linguistic environments, its extension to non-linguistic environments becomes a powerful tool for sociolinguistic analysis.

The "proof" that variable use of a given feature carries social or stylistic meaning need not be in terms of all-or-nothing rules. In fact, since Fischer's (1958) early study showing quantitative variation in the use of -in versus -ing in the English present participle by a group of New England school children, it has been clear that by aggregating performance data in various ways, it is possible to determine regularities and relationships that, though not categorical, are surely part of the competence of normal native speakers.

A further example from our data on /l/-deletion by Montrealers indicates how non-linguistic features can be treated as part of the environment within a quantitative paradigm. Table 3-2 (from Sankoff and Cedergren 1971: 82) shows that people differ in systematic ways with respect to their surface deletion of underlying /l/. /l/ deleted in initial position produces examples like:

(5) [dæ: rü]—'dans la rue'—(in the street)

(6) [ʃe: sœr]—'chez les soeurs'—(at the nuns' place)

The table contains a total of 6,844 cases for 16 speakers, subdivided into four groups.

Forms	Professionals		Working Class	
	Women	Men	Women	Men
	%	%	%	%
il (impersonal)	94.7 (249)	98.5 (340)	100.0 (351)	99.4 (314)
ils	67.7 (242)	88.4 (139)	100.0 (358)	100.0 (330)
il (personal)	54.0 (187)	90.0 (180)	100.0 (353)	100.0 (397)
elle	29.8 (77)	29.7 (47)	74.6 (225)	96.4 (114)
les (pronoun)	16.0 (50)	25.0 (28)	50.0 (46)	78.1 (32)
la (article)	3.8 (314)	15.7 (414)	44.7 (440)	49.2 (378)
la (pronoun)	0.0 (8)	28.5 (7)	33.3 (24)	50.0 (8)
les (article)	5.4 (315)	13.1 (297)	21.7 (326)	34.6 (254)

TABLE 3-2. Deletion of /l/ by occupation and sex, for 16 individuals (4 per subgroup) and for eight forms. In general, percentages increase from left to right and from bottom to top.

For each form *il*, . . . , *les*, we find that /l/-deletion follows the order: women professionals < men professionals < women workers < men workers, with only one exception to this for the eight forms considered, women workers > men workers for *il* (impersonal). Again, reading vertically, we see that each subgroup of four individuals maintains a regular order in terms of deletion rates for individual forms. Thus *il* (impersonal) > . . . > *les* (article), with only five figures "out of order." In fact, this is the same order we obtain from aggregating and averaging the deletion percentages for all sixteen individuals.

This is not to imply, however, that we presume to be discussing four "dialects," or that because individuals can be subdivided into groups showing different mean scores for particular speech behavior, their speech constitutes linguistically valid subgroupings of any sort (see 4.2). What Table 3-2 shows is that higher rates of /l/-deletion are a tendency characteristic of men and of working class people.

2.4. Variable Rules

While tabular displays such as Tables 3-1 and 3-2 are illuminating and useful, a true integration of information into competence models has only been achieved through Labov's development of variable rules. Ordinary generative grammars, where deep structure strings and phrase markers are successively transformed by a series of rules into a surface string, allow for some rules to be optional. If a string satisfies the structural conditions of an optional rule, then both application and nonapplication of the rule are permitted at this stage in the generation of the sentence.

Labov noted that, in a large corpus, the frequency of application of a given optional rule might depend strongly on details of the linguistic context. Thus, of two contexts, both of which satisfy the structural description of an optional rule, one might favor application 80 percent of the time and the other only 10 percent of the time. Labov proposed that such tendencies be incorporated into the formal statement of the rule. Thus for any optional rule in the grammar for which this information is available, there should be associated with each linguistic context satisfying the structural description of the rule a number between zero and one, specifying the probability that the rule will apply in this context.

Because of the potentially enormous number of different contexts which might satisfy a given structural description, associating a probability with each one could well be unfeasible. Labov suggested that it suffices to examine a limited number of components of each linguistic context, and calculate a probability based on the independent contributions from each of these components. This would greatly simplify the notation, and if it predicted behavior well, then it would tell us something about the interaction of syntactic, phonological, etc., contexts in influencing rule probabilities. Labov proposed one way of doing this and applied it to his rules for contraction and deletion of the copula and other phonological rules in Black English. The details of his method have been improved by Cedergren and D. Sankoff (1974), and I will briefly sketch their procedure.

Consider Labov's data on contraction in the twelve different contexts of Table 3-3.

Preceding environments	Succeeding environments			
	__NP	__PA-Loc	__Vb	__gn
Pro__ [−cons]	2/32	1/65	1/34	0/23
Other NP__ [+cons]	22/35	24/32	5/14	1/9
[−cons]	13/64	7/23	2/14	0/6

TABLE 3-3. Frequency of noncontracted copula by preceding and following environment. Abstracted from Labov (1969) by Cedergren and D. Sankoff (1974).

The variable rule is written:

$$\begin{bmatrix} +voc \\ -str \\ +cen \end{bmatrix} \rightarrow \langle \emptyset \rangle \bigg/ \begin{array}{c} \langle Pro \rangle \\ \langle -cons \rangle \end{array} \#\# \underset{[+T]}{\quad} C_0^1 \#\# \left\langle \begin{array}{c} Vb \\ gn \\ NP \\ PA\text{-}Loc \end{array} \right\rangle$$

and the probability of contraction in an environment

$$A \#\# \underset{[+T]}{\quad} C_0^1 \#\# B$$

is given by the formula

$$1 - (1 - p_0)(1 - \alpha(A))(1 - \beta(A))(1 - \gamma(B))$$

where p_0 is an "input probability" common to all environments, α depends on whether A is a pronoun or not, β depends on whether the final segment in A is [−cons] or not, and γ depends on the grammatical nature of the constituent B.

The statistical method of maximum likelihood produces the estimates:

59

$$p_0 = 0.25$$
$$\alpha(\text{Pro}) = 0.86; \ \alpha(-\text{Pro}) = 0$$
$$\beta(+\text{cons}) = 0; \ \beta(-\text{cons}) = 0.65$$
$$\gamma(\_\text{NP}) = 0.16; \ \gamma(\_\text{PA-Loc}) = 0; \ \gamma(\_\text{Vb}) = 0.49; \ \gamma(\_\text{gn}) = 0.89$$

These estimates predict, instead of the figures in Table 3-3 above, performance as presented in Table 3-4.

The correspondence between Tables 3-3 and 3-4 is extremely good, by visual inspection and when measured by chi-square. In this small example, Cedergren and D. Sankoff estimated six parameters (the three zero parameters do not count, since the method always requires one feature in each position to have a zero parameter) instead of twelve separate parameters for twelve contexts. This is not much of a saving, but for more complicated conditioning, the economy of this procedure increases geometrically. In addition, the multiplicative formula which in general is:

$$1 - (1 - p_0)(1 - \alpha(A))(1 - \beta(B)) \ldots (1 - \omega(Z))$$

where $A, B, \ldots, Z$ are the relevant features present in an environment, implies that these features act independently on the rule probability (cf. Cedergren and D. Sankoff for further details). Finally, this procedure extends without any amendment to incorporate features in the nonlinguistic environment.

2.5. Differences from the Standard Generative Paradigm
Though the ultimate product of the quantitative paradigm is similar to that of generative grammar, i.e., a set of grammatical rules describing competence, the similarity does not go much farther. The quantitative paradigm requires data of a radically different type, involving a deliberate selection of various kinds of informants speaking in a variety of

Preceding environments	Succeeding environments			
	_NP	_PA-Loc	_Vb	_gn
Pro_ [−cons]	1/32	2.3/65	0.6/34	0.1/23
Other NP_ [+cons]	21.9/35	24/32	5.3/14	0.8/9
[−cons]	14/64	6/23	1.9/14	0.2/6

TABLE 3-4. Predictions of noncontracted copula according to estimates of p_0, α, β, and γ.

social contexts. There is much less reliance on the major tools of much linguistic analysis, such as introspection and judgments of grammaticality and paraphrase. Labov (1970) and particularly Bailey (1971) discuss a number of ways in which an approach to linguistic analysis based on the regular structures of variation imbedded in speech communities differs from standard linguistic analysis, and for further details, cf. also chapter 4, this volume.

3. THE SCOPE OF THE PARADIGM

Several characteristics of the paradigm need clarification, especially in the light of some recent discussion by scholars who recognize the importance and extent of variability, but who have not incorporated all of the implications of variability into their analyses. One important point has to do with the existence of different *kinds* of linguistic variables. These variables are articulated in different ways with the social structure and the sociolinguistic system of language use of the community, and with the complex processes of linguistic change. A further important issue has to do with the psychological and social reality of variable rules.

3.1. Types of Linguistic Variables

In his early studies of a number of different phonological variables both in Martha's Vineyard and in New York City, Labov (1965, 1966a) pointed out that the variables in question exhibited very different behavior with respect to their distribution both socially (among different groups of people) and stylistically (on the intraindividual level). He distinguished between *stereotypes, markers,* and *indicators.* On a synchronic level, these distinctions have to do mainly with the categorical versus variable nature of the social and stylistic marking involved. Both markers and indicators are variables that seem to be largely outside of conscious awareness, but whereas indicators are categorical for a particular group of speakers and do not show stylistic variation, markers are involved in stylistic variation (Labov 1965: 110–11). Stereotypes are highly stigmatized variables which can "become the overt topic of social comment, and . . . eventually disappear" (ibid.: 112). Differential awareness of linguistic variables in Montréal French was found by Laberge and Chiasson-Lavoie (1971).

3.2. Structure of Variation Within a Speech Community

Some linguistic variables appear to be maintained over long periods of time as a stable system of alternates which may, at one extreme, not be "noticed" by the community at all (i.e., they do not serve any purpose of social or stylistic differentiation), or which may, at the other extreme, serve to categorically mark social or stylistic difference. Between these extremes there is, of course, a range of possibilities, and though some of the particular structures we find may be related to change processes (cf. section 3.4), synchronic data can tell us much about the nature of the linguistic marking of social and stylistic differences within a community.

A particular rule may be categorical for one person, optional for another. If we are prepared to admit that the *nature* of distributions is important, we will see that for some variables, speakers are clustered around a relatively small range of values, whereas for others, the distribution is much more spread. This may also be the case with respect to particular environments for a single rule. In one environment, speakers may be clustered about a relatively small range of values (not necessarily 0 or 1, for a variable with two alternatives); in another environment, they may display a much greater range of values.

Further data from our work on /l/-deletion in Montréal will illustrate the point that real, socially meaningful differences between individuals or groups of individuals are very often differences of degree, rather than categorical differences. In this regard, let us examine individually the speech of the sixteen Montrealers of Table 3-2 with respect to their deletion of /l/ in the personal pronouns *il* 'he' and *elle* 'she' and in the definite articles *la* (fem. sing.) and *les* (pl.). (The masculine singular article *le* does not undergo /l/-deletion; it is the schwa which is lost in rapid speech (Picard 1972)). Figure 3-1 shows that ten of the sixteen individuals had a categorical deletion rule for *il* (these were the people not included in Table 3-1), that two people had a categorical rule for *elle,* showing 100 percent deletion, and that one had a categorical rule for *les,* showing no deletion. Everyone exhibited variable /l/-deletion for *la,* as did most people for *elle* and *les.* It is abundantly clear, however, that despite the relative lack of all-or-nothing behavior, people do differ in systematic ways with respect to their *proportion* of deletion. Working class people show generally higher deletion proportions for each form, yet there appears no clear break between them and the professionals;[2] it is evident that there are not two (or sixteen!) "dialects" with respect to this variable. For all forms except *il,* people are distributed very evenly along the continuum, and most individuals tend to follow the order *il* >

2. The 16 individuals chosen for this analysis were selected before our Montréal corpus had even been completely transcribed, and certainly before any social analysis had been done of the 120 people in the total interview sample. It is interesting to note that the 8 working class people of this subsample have a mean "linguistic market" index (D. Sankoff and Laberge 1978b) of .08; the 8 professionals have a mean index value of .83.

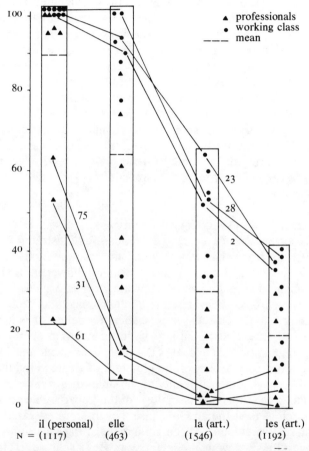

Percentage
of deletion

Figure 3-1. /l/-deletion percentages for sixteen subjects on four
forms. Percentages for subjects 2, 23, 28, 75, 31, 61 on each
form are linked by straight lines. Other subjects are not joined
because crossing of lines obscures the patterns for each form.

elle > *la* > *les* in terms of their relative proportions of deletion. Though
the few people at the top and at the bottom of the continuum for each
form tend to be the same ones (linked by straight lines in Figure 3-1),
some crossing over is already evident (e.g., number 61 exhibits the

63

lowest deletion for *il, elle,* and *la,* but is only the third lowest for *les*), and more crossing over would be shown were all individuals indicated.

/l/-deletion is a complex phenomenon and we are unable to say for sure at present what is happening with respect to change. There has been a tendency historically in French toward loss of /l/ in a number of environments, with deletion of final /l/ in *il* documented several centuries ago, and in *elle* indicated for the early twentieth century in France. It appears possible that the rule has gone to completion for *il* in Montréal, and that the minority of speakers who do not delete 100 percent result from a long standing hypercorrective tendency. It also appears that the rule has been extended to apply to *elle,* categorically for some speakers, and to initial environments for *la* and *les.* Though the fate of this change is presently unclear, it is obvious that varying /l/-deletion rates are of current social significance in differentiating speakers. The regularity in the relative frequencies for each form, as well as the ordering of individuals, indicates that relative proportions can be structured in an orderly way, imbedded in the social structure of the community.

3.3. Variability and Psychological Reality

Relative proportions of rule application can, as illustrated in 3.2, be incorporated into social as well as linguistic structure, and distinctions need not be categorical to carry social meaning. Powerful use has been made of this notion in studies of linguistic change, especially in interpreting a synchronic slice in terms of "apparent time" (cf. Hockett 1950; Labov 1965), as discussed in section 3.4 below. It is important, therefore, to show that variability is not *merely* a property of communities, or an important aspect of the way change operates, but that it exists as an ordinary aspect of the grammar of single individuals, i.e., to clarify the psychological reality of variable rules.

Bickerton (1971), in his analysis of the "post-creole continuum" in the speech of East Indian Guyanese, has interpreted variability in a particular rule as evidence of on-going change in that rule over time, according to Bailey's wave model (cf. 4.4). He has, however, taken the option left open by Bailey in any particular analysis, and set out to demonstrate what appears to be an a priori assumption on his part that variability is in general infelicitous. Thus though variability must be admitted in the data, Bickerton, in seeking to limit it as much as possible, attempts to prove that for any particular speaker, variability in a particular rule can exist only in one environment at a time, that after a rule has become categorical for a speaker in one environment, it can begin to be optionally applied in another environment, and so on. Thus Bickerton's basic mistrust is not of variability per se, but of variable *rules,* and he states in the first part of his article (p. 460) his belief that the human mind essentially operates in terms of categorical, rather than variable, rules.

Bickerton characterizes a variable rule as involving a statement such as: "When you recognize environment *X*, use feature *Y Z* percent of the time," and goes on to state that those who believe there can be such rules should demonstrate the mental processes that must exist to mediate such rules. He states that children, in acquiring language, tend to generalize rules for things like English past tenses and plurals, noting the "exceptions" later. In fact it may well be that part of becoming a normal native speaker, rather than continuing to sound like a child or a foreigner, consists of learning how to use variable rules, thereby replacing some of an earlier set of categorical rules by the more usual and normal variable rules. Slobin, for example, has noted (personal communication) that children tend to use full forms much more frequently than do adults in utterances that can be realized as either full or contracted forms. The argument really depends on whether or not one believes that degrees of variability can be processed by the human brain, and in the absence of evidence that it can only work in all-or-nothing terms, I do not see why we would want to assume that this is the case. In the light of abundant evidence given in Labov (1965, 1966a) about the different kinds of variables that can exist, in terms of their perception by hearers as well as their production by speakers, it appears that human beings can indeed process and deal with this kind of variation.

Bickerton interestingly and convincingly analyzes change in the "preinfinitival complementizers *fu* (or *fi*) and *tu*" in the "creole speech continuum of Guyana" (p. 462). Rather than halting the search for relevant environments on the phonological or lexical-morphological levels, he finds that a semantic-syntactic distinction provides an important environment for constraining the choice of F (*fu* or *fi*) or T (*tu*) by the speakers he studied. Thus he establishes three categories: I-inceptives; II-desideratives and other "psychological" verbs; III-noninceptives/nondesideratives. His analysis that replacement of T by F proceeds from environment III, through II, to I for any given speaker, is convincing. But to insist that variation can only occur for a particular speaker in one environment at a time seems unnecessary, and unwarranted by his data, especially if the implication is that this result casts serious doubt on variable rules as a principle.

To argue that the normal, natural use of human language involves inherent variability, and that the human mind is perfectly capable of handling this, does not mean that the linguist should abandon the search to locate relevant environments that will further clarify the way a rule operates. Such a search is as applicable to a variable rule model as to any other model. Indeed, within the framework proposed by Cedergren and D. Sankoff (1974) for dealing with variable rules, not only is it possible to further specify environments without altering the fundamental nature of a particular rule, but the predictions may provide a check on whether relevant environments have been excluded (Cedergren 1973).

A complementizer example from Montréal French demonstrates that while variability can indeed occur in more than one environment (even for one speaker), this does not necessarily detract from the systematicity of the processes involved. It will be apparent that a further objection of Bickerton, which I will call the "grouping problem" (4.2 below), can be dealt with appropriately in terms of the kind of variable rule model I have adopted.

The case in point has to do with the deletion of complementizer *que* by the same sixteen speakers as were discussed with respect to /l/-deletion (Sankoff, Sarrasin, and Cedergren 1971). Here again, it is the phonological environment which is important, and the dominant process seems to be one of consonant cluster simplification. (Grammatical and phonological features interact in the deletion of *que* as a relative marker; cf. chapter 4 below.) Two examples of complementizer *que* present and deleted, taken from our taped interviews, are as follows:

(7) *A l'école on nous enseignait* que *les protestants c'est des pas bons.* 'At school they taught us that the Protestants are no good': 75.

(8) *Le séparatisme. Au début je pense Ø ça a été plutôt un snobisme.* 'Separatism. At the beginning I think it was more a kind of snobbery': 70.

A series of phonological environments relevant to the deletion of *que* are displayed as Figure 3-2. It is clear that though more than half of the individuals display variability in more than one environment, deletion decreases fairly regularly for all the individuals from environments 1 through 9, with only one person exhibiting no deletion in any environment. Of the nine people who exhibit variability in more than one environment, virtually all show greater proportions of deletion in the environments closer to the left side of the figure. Deletion proportions tend to follow the order of environments such that $1 > 2 > \ldots > 9$. Environments scale in more or less the same order when we average all sixteen individuals' deletion proportions for each environment (except for fluctuation due to low numbers in environments 4 and 8). Individ-

Phonological environments

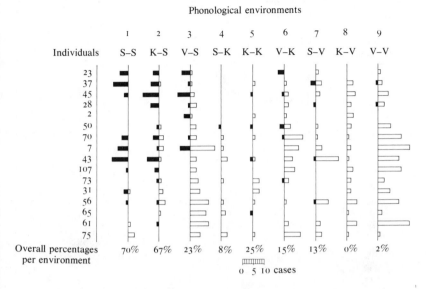

Figure 3-2. Deletion of *que* for 16 subjects in 9 phonological environments. Black bars on the left represent *que* absent; white bars on the right represent *que* present.
S = [+sib]; K = $\begin{bmatrix} +\text{cons} \\ -\text{sib} \end{bmatrix}$; V = [−cons]

uals are ordered in Figure 3-2 according to their overall deletion frequencies, which range from 0 to 82.4 percent.

Table 3-5 regroups the data of Figure 3-2 in terms of proportions. In all cases where individuals had variable *que* in environments I and II, their proportion of deletion was much higher in environment I than in environment II. There were only four individuals who had any deletion at all in environment III (three cases for number 37; two cases for number 28; and one case each for numbers 43 and 56), and though three of them had slightly higher percentages in environment III than in environment II, this can be seen in terms of statistical fluctuation in a variable rule model.

The fact that more than half of the speakers in our sample exhibited variable *que* deletion in more than one of the nine closely distinguished environments of Figure 3-2, and that these environments can be ordered in terms of *proportions* of deletion, proportions that hold up remarkably well for individual speakers as well as on the average, would appear to indicate that these speakers have no trouble in consistently producing regularly variable behavior in specific environments. In the absence of any sound psychological evidence as to why people

Individuals	Environments				
	I (1 and 2 of Fig. 2)	II (3–6 of Fig. 2)	III (7–9 of Fig. 2)	Overall deletion	N
	%	%	%	%	
23	100	87.5	0	82.4	17
37	91.7	25.0	27.5	55.5	27
45	100	66.7	0	53.1	32
28	100	16.7	28.5	41.2	17
2	–	50.0	0	33.3	9
50	50.0	40.0	0	23.3	21
70	75.0	12.5	0	21.6	37
7	75.0	25.0	0	21.0	53
43	44.4	8.3	4.4	18.9	53
107	100	0	0	12.0	25
73	50.0	9.1	0	11.1	18
31	40.0	0	0	9.5	21
56	40.0	0	4.6	7.7	39
65	0	9.1	0	6.7	15
61	50.0	0	0	2.9	35
75	0	0	0	0	25
Overall deletion	68.5%	19.2%	4.0%	23.0%	
N	89	177	178		444

TABLE 3-5. Percentage of deleted *que* in three environments for sixteen individuals.

should *not* be able to produce such behavior, I suggest that it be accepted as it stands.

3.4. Variability and Linguistic Change

Since most of our data on communities so far studied in great detail (i.e., taking account of the structure of linguistic variability within the social and cultural structure of the community) is synchronic rather than diachronic (a few exceptions are noted in Weinreich, Labov, and Herzog 1968), inferences with respect to change must generally be based on the distribution of the value of particular variables within the population sampled at one particular point in time. In the simplest case, the proportion of occurrence of some variant of a particular variable is correlated with age. More often the age distribution is complicated by the fact that changes follow more complex sorts of social boundaries within a community or society. A change may originate in a particular class, ethnic, or occupational group, and spread from there to other groups in one subgroup of a population, whereas it has barely begun in another segment. In most communities it appears that almost any division existing within the population which has any kind of social significance is somehow reflected in the linguistic behavior of that community, and changes in progress do not operate without regard for these existing differences.

Cedergren (1972) has quantitatively documented in detail a number of phonological changes in the Spanish of Panama City, changes originating in various subsegments of the population and being differentially involved with, and at present at different stages of, the change process. Labov's work in both Martha's Vineyard and New York also contains several examples of the complex quantitative interrelationships between social groups and subgroups and phonological changes in progress. Labov (1965) and Weinreich, Labov, and Herzog (1968) set forth a series of possible stages for the interrelationships of ongoing changes to social groups and processes.

Bailey (1969–70, 1970, 1973) has produced a dynamic, or wave model for linguistic change (diffusion) that incorporates a number of the kinds of variation mentioned above. Of particular importance in his work is the idea that a rule, which may change "from variable to categorical or from one environment to the next . . . initially operates variably . . . in each successive environment or situation in which [it] operates" (1970: 178). There are, however, two possibilities in the further changes to the rule, according to Bailey. Either "variability ceases in one environment before going on to another" or the rule is variable in more than one environment at a time, with the proportion of application of the rule in the two or more environments in question indicating the progression of the rule.

An example that demonstrates the significance of proportions in the analysis of linguistic change in progress is drawn from data on New Guinea Tok Pisin collected by Suzanne Laberge and myself during June–August 1971. A guiding hypothesis of this study was that native speakers (most of whom are under age twenty) would show different competence in the language than even fluent nonnative speakers. We made a number of tape recordings of families who use Tok Pisin in everyday communication, but for whom Tok Pisin is the native language of the children only. The decade of the 1960s was probably the first to see significant numbers of native speakers, though Tok Pisin has existed for a hundred years or so as a second language *lingua franca* in New Guinea.

In a study of some of the speakers in this corpus (chapter 10 below), we found evidence to support the hypothesis that the adverb *baimbai* has been reduced to *bai,* and that it is being increasingly treated like an obligatory future tense marker rather than an optional adverbial indicator of future time. Of a total of 395 cases for 18 speakers (nine children between the ages of 5 and 17; nine adults, parents of seven of the children, between the ages of approximately 25 and 45, and all of whom use Tok Pisin as the normal medium of communication in the family), there are only 5 instances of *baimbai,* pronounced [bə′mbai] or [bə′bai]. *Baimbai* occurred in the speech of three of the nine adults in our sample; there were no instances in the speech of any of the nine children.

Table 3-6 shows the results of tabulating the stress level for all cases of *baimbai* and *bai* in our sample. *(Bai) mbai* never receives primary stress in a sentence, but it frequently receives secondary stress (analogous to stressed syllables in nouns or pronouns), and tertiary stress, equivalent to "unstressed" syllables in nouns or adjectives, or to most prepositions. The fourth stress level involves a reduction of the vowel nucleus to [ə], or even its disappearance, so that *bai* is barely, if at all, distinguishable as a syllable, the only audible indication of its presence being [b]. Examples of each of these levels are as follows:

(9) *Em bai yu kam, bai yu dai.* 'You come; you'll die'
     (Mrs. T.)

(10) *Ating bai klostu belo.* 'It must be nearly noon'
      (Mrs. D.)

(11) *Suga bilong mi klostu bai* [bə] *finis nau.* 'My sugar cane is nearly finished now' (C. W.)

The cases of stress level 4, though not exhibited by every speaker, are interesting in that stress level 4 was found for six of the nine children, but for only two of the nine adults. Plotting individual

Stress level	Children	Adults
	%	%
2	29.1	51.7
3	60.4	47.3
4	10.4	1.0
N	(192)	(203)

TABLE 3-6. Differential stress on *bai* for nine children (native speakers) and nine adults (nonnative speakers).

speakers' values on a graph (Figure 10-1, p. 204) shows that the differences between children and adults are not mere artifacts of aggregating cases; when we calculate the percentage of level 2 stress for each speaker, we find that there is minimal overlap between children's and adults' ranges. Thus four of the nine children and two of the nine adults have between 35 percent and 43 percent of *bai* in their speech receiving secondary stress. The five other children fall below 35 percent; the seven other adults above 43 percent. Figure 10-1 also indicates some correlation of the percentage of secondary stress with age for these speakers, and it is probable that native speakers are simply carrying further a trend in the reduction of (*bai*) *mbai*. Although all speakers vary the stress they give to *bai,* it is clear that for the children in the sample, there is a tendency to place a lesser stress on *bai.* As we have argued, this is partial evidence for a change from adverb to tense marker for *baimbai.*

Though not many languages are presently undergoing a change toward being, for the first time, native languages, the kinds of intergenerational differences observable among these speakers can be seen in other speech communities, and differences among groups need not be categorical to be significant. Even in this case, where change would be expected to be more rapid and dramatic than in most situations, change occurs by degree, and intelligibility is preserved among the different groups of speakers. Native speakers of Tok Pisin exhibit more morphophonological reduction than nonnative speakers, yet this does not mean that the two groups cannot understand one another.

It is probably completely out of the awareness of members of the Tok Pisin speech community today that its younger members exhibit less stress in their pronunciation of *bai,* and that they no longer seem to use *baimbai* at all. Yet adults do say that children speak the language very fluently and rapidly. They also freely admit that there are differences in competence among speakers of Tok Pisin, that rural people who have not been exposed to Tok Pisin at home, and who have recently arrived in town, do not speak as fluently as the urbanites. Town dwellers said that for their children Tok Pisin was a native language. They do not need to be aware of, and able to state, precise features that vary, to be able to observe that there are differences between the way they and their children speak, or between the way they and the newly-arrived speak. Nor do people need to be assumed to have some kind of a mechanical device clicking away in their heads keeping track of percentages in order to exhibit regularly variable behavior. It appears (cf., for example, Labov 1966a, part III) that people may often perceive behavior in ways that are more categorical than the behavior itself.

This is one reason why the validity of linguists' judgments of unrecorded speech behavior, as well as the unsystematic citing of examples, is so open to question.

4. APPROACHES TO HETEROGENEITY

4.1. Scaling

Since the insightful paper of Elliot, Legum, and Thompson (1969), it has become fashionable to describe variability in terms of Guttman scales. Not only grammars of individual community members, but also styles, regional dialects, and historical stages of the same dialect can be scaled. De Camp, as one of the first to experiment extensively with scaling, has pointed out their theoretical power in dealing with problems of rule ordering (1971).

There is no doubt that such scales, where they exist, are interesting and useful (cf. Bickerton 1971; Day 1973; Labov 1971; Bailey 1973; Ross 1972, 1973 in addition to De Camp 1971). It is, however, important to notice that in its strong form, scaling can be used as a last-ditch, wheels-within-wheels attempt to account for variation without changing the deterministic assumptions of the traditional generative paradigm. The underlying hypothesis here is that the heterogeneity in a community is due to the fact that it comprises a whole range of individual grammars that can be linearly arranged so that each one differs slightly, but categorically from its neighbors on either side.

My critique of an over-reliance on scaling as the main way of "explaining" (away) variability is both theoretical and methodological. On the theoretical level, there is no reason for whole individual grammars to be scaleable except for special cases where political, geographical, and social factors all affect language in a coincidental way over time. This would be confined to certain highly polarized social systems, perhaps including the post-creole continuum, or to a chain of dialects along a river valley or some other linear configuration, or to a pattern of change emanating for a long historical period from a single metropolitan focus, each change affecting distant points in order of their proximity to the center.

This type of special configuration is only *necessary* for scaling; it is not sufficient. Other conditions are also required, such as that all changes, innovations, pressures, etc. must emanate from one or other end of the linear configuration. When a non-endpoint becomes the focus of a change, this tends to destroy scaling. In general, as in Bailey's wave model, where the geography offers more than one dimension of change and influence, where the social stratification is not necessarily correlated with geography, where historical change may be reversible, there is no reason to expect one-dimensional scaling. Well-known phenomena such as middle class hypercorrection of conscious variables, multiple geographic foci of innovations, and age-group-specific usages are all incompatible with simple scaling.

Cedergren's (1972) analysis of the complex of linguistic constraints and social factors affecting a series of phonological variables in Panamanian Spanish is instructive here. Different phonological variables are differently affected by the factors of age, sex, class, and rural versus urban origin, as well as being differently involved in stylistic marking. For example, a rule involving velarization of (n) is favored by younger speakers in formal styles within Panama City, but appears to have originated with non–city-born speakers. A lenition rule for (č), also favored by younger speakers in formal styles, is especially characteristic of women, and originated with city-born speakers. It is clear that though speakers may be scaleable in one way for a particular variable, scaling on another variable will not always result in the same ordering of speakers.

On the methodological side, as mentioned in 3.3 above, the strong categorical view of scaling almost inevitably produces some amount of "error" which it seems preferable to regard as normal statistical fluctuation. The more data are added, the more likely one is to run into "exceptions" to categorical scale types. On the other hand, a somewhat weaker view of scaling such as that proposed by De Camp (1972) may be able to nicely incorporate "more or less" notions to replace "all or nothing" postulates, with consequent benefit to the analysis. (See also D. Sankoff and Cedergren 1976.) Otherwise we may be lost in a never-ending cycle of finding variability in previously categorical environments, and of searching for categorical environments to explain away variability.

4.2. The Grouping Problem
Once we have accepted that people's speech differs both from the speech of others and from their own speech at other times, and that the ways in which they differ may be more a question of relative presence of some feature, rather than its total presence or absence, we must face the grouping problem. That is, how do we decide on the status of variants, whether social (groups of people; "styles") or linguistic (groups of speech variables).

For grouping to be other than arbitrary, especially in a situation of extreme variability, it is essential to attempt to follow procedures of description and analysis that will clearly indicate the kinds of system which obtain. There are basically two ways of doing this. One way is to define a grid of some sort beforehand, whether in terms of groups of people defined on the basis of social characteristics, or of particular occasions on which people would generally be likely to exhibit more or less formal behavior, or even in terms of categorical grammars of two or three speech varieties, gradations between which will be seen as some sort of mixture. An alternate method is to examine the linguistic variation as the main object of study and try to use its internal structure as discovered, to map or group the nonlinguistic variables. There are some obvious advantages and disadvantages to both methods, and in dealing with each of these in turn, I will attempt to clarify these as precisely as possible. Essentially, the difference is between trying to fit linguistic data to nonlinguistic data, or vice versa.

The methods developed by Labov to deal with variability grew out of a realization that at no level, whether that of the language, the dialect, the idiolect, the style or register, or whatever, could homogeneity be found in speech. Most of his published work demonstrates a particular way of dealing with this problem, involving the selection of a number of nonlinguistic variables that can be shown to influence speech, the segmentation of each variable (or sometimes an index derived from combining variables), and the demonstration that grouping nonlinguistic variables according to this segmentation results in different configurations of speech (usually means or averages) for each defined segment.

Examples of this technique can be found in the New York City study (1966b) where a combination of socioeconomic variables was used in the construction of a nine-segment index for "class," and individuals grouped according to it could be shown to display different speech behavior; if performance was averaged for a particular variable, the different subgroups of people showed different behavior that was, nevertheless, regular. Groups tended to show progressively higher or lower scores on a particular variable according to a well-defined pattern, deviant groups (the "hypercorrecting" lower middle class) could be defined, etc. Similarly for five (mainly) nonlinguistically defined points on a stylistic continuum of "formality," Labov was able to show systematic differences in behavior. In other cases, he has used more "emically" valid grouping procedures, and given mean scores for actually existing groups on particular variables, for example, in the studies of various peer groups in Harlem (Labov et al. 1968; Labov 1972).

In working within this framework, Labov has made the same choice as a number of other sociolinguists, that of using socially or culturally valid units as a basic framework for analysis, and attempting to investigate the way the linguistic behavior patterns according to such categories. In somewhat the same vein, Gumperz chooses to work within the general framework of the "speech community"[3] rather than the "language," partly because local varieties and "dialects" can often be linguistically quite far from "standards" (cf. also Hymes 1968; chapter 6, below on boundaries). Many other scholars have attempted to define the kinds of linguistic behavior appropriate to (or usually observed in) named (by the community in question) linguistic varieties or speech events (cf. B. Bailey 1971).

There remains the objection that groupings of linguistic behavior based on nonlinguistic criteria will be in some sense arbitrary. DeCamp for example states (1971: 355) that:

> A linguistic geographer would be properly horrified at the following suggestion: let us use state boundaries as preconceived pigeonholes for sorting the data from an American linguistic atlas, and then merely indicate the percentage of New York informants who say *pail* as opposed to *bucket*, the equivalent percentage for Pennsylvanians, for Virginians, etc. . . . Why, then, have sociolinguists so often correlated their linguistic data to preconceived categories of age, income, education, etc., instead of correlating these nonlinguistic variables *to* the linguistic data?

The reason, I think, lies on the one hand in the desire of sociolinguists for their results to have some sociocultural validity, and to attempt to define categories that are socially meaningful to the people whose linguistic behavior is being investigated, and on the other in the realization that variation will not be eliminated completely, no matter what categories are defined. In other words, sociolinguists who start by defining categories based on social or cultural criteria are not doing so to be arbitrary, but so that their results will correspond to socially or culturally meaningful categories. There are, of course, two principal ways one can do this: proceeding by either "etic" or "emic" categories. With the variable "age," for example, one could, in adopting the view that age might be important as a variable differentiating speech, proceed by cutting the sample into regular age categories: 0–9; 10–19; . . . ; 90–99 ("etic" procedure), or one could find out how the people themselves define various age groups; e.g., "infants" might be from 0–2; "children" from 3 to 11; "adolescents" from 12 to 17; "young adults" from 18 to 30; and so on. Similarly one could group people

3. Gumperz's work presents a major difference from most of the studies cited in this chapter, since he generally treats social categories as emergent from patterns of language use. A more detailed account of some of his work on code switching is presented in chapter 2, this volume.

according to years of formal education, or according to labeled categories with presumably some cultural meaning (e.g., one can be a "high school dropout" having completed anywhere from seven to twelve years of schooling). Another example involving grouping kinds of behavior rather than people would involve the difference between the analyst creating an index of formality using a number of criteria defined by her/him versus examining the differences between behavior according to labeled speech events, e.g., "telephone call," "seminar," "lecture." The difference between using one or the other kind of nonlinguistic category can be debated; it is often necessary to use both kinds.

I submit, however, that the dialect geographer would not be horrified, properly or otherwise, at the suggestion that one use the political boundary between Italy and France as a convenient location for the dialect atlas of Italy to stop and that of France to begin, nor at the suggestion that one can find speech patterns specific to "estate laborers" by investigating the population of Jamaicans who work as employees of sugar estates, as opposed, for example, to "peasant farmers" (DeCamp 1971). The fact that ten-year-olds may share a feature or rule with fifty-year-olds (or shopkeepers with estate laborers, or high school dropouts with lawyers, or the "telephone call" situation with the "formal lecture" situation) does not necessarily invalidate using such criteria to investigate speech differences. If it is the case that a particular nonlinguistic variable has no relevance—no effect—in defining the distribution of a linguistic variable, then one of course discards it. Certainly anyone would object to the use of arbitrary criteria (as well as to gross or infelicitous ones), especially when it can be shown that there are much better ones available (a mountain range may be a more effective boundary than a state boundary, except for cases like the Berlin wall), and anyone trying to use extralinguistic criteria must display intelligence, sensitivity, and intuition in experimenting with such criteria, as well as an awareness of the importance of linguistic criteria.

One further basically cultural category is that of labeled languages or language varieties. What the community refers to as different speech varieties (particularly in the case of nonstandard varieties) may show some rules in common with each other, some rules categorically different, some rules variably different, and so on.

The second major kind of approach one can use is to try to match the nonlinguistic behavior to the linguistic behavior. For example, in the case of a variable discussed earlier, rather than trying to see how /l/ behaves according to various sociocultural categories, we might take all the realizations as /l/ and observe where they occur, similarly with all the realizations as Ø. But unless we are prepared to look at proportions, we will find no constraints for forms like *elle* and *la*. If we examine all the cases where /l/ appears as [l], we will find that higher proportions of them occur after consonants, before vowels, and out of the mouths of women and professionals.

It appears that with either approach, one is involved methodologically in a process of testing, of going back and forth between linguistic and nonlinguistic features, retaining in one's analysis those that best account for the linguistic data under consideration.

In a new mathematical framework for dealing with variable rules, Cedergren and D. Sankoff (see also Rousseau and D. Sankoff 1978b) have made a number of proposals that make it possible to eliminate some of the problems associated with grouping and with the choice of constraints. Rather than seeing nonlinguistic variables as necessarily defining different discrete groupings, it is possible to see them as environments that define continua. It is thus possible to deal separately with individuals if it seems advisable to do so, and to follow the kinds of groupings that come most naturally out of the linguistic data. The variable parameters attached to rules can apply to communities or to individuals, and can also take account of situational variability.

5. Discussion

The object of this chapter has been to describe and illustrate a theoretical standpoint and a set of procedures for the study of communicative competence within a speech community perspective, and as part of a quantitative paradigm. A central motivation has been the attempt to systematically and rigorously relate linguistic performance to competence. Performance data consist, in the studies considered here, of large bodies of recorded speech of samples of the members of particular communities in a variety of speech situations. The problem is to infer the competence of these people, given the fact that, like any other behavioral data, speech performance data will contain statistical fluctuation. My position has been that statistically fluctuating performance data need not be interpreted as reflecting underlying competence that is categorical in nature, and that a paradigm representing competence as containing some probabilistic and nondeterministic components is a better approximation to linguistic reality than one that insists on categoriality and determinacy. Note that this does *not* imply the nonexistence of categorical rules, but simply the existence as well of probabilistic rules.

Such an assumption does not counter the principle that (socio)linguistic competence is what exists in people's heads; rather, it takes the position that people can internalize rules that are not categorical.

The first kind of situation in which this principle can be seen to operate is the case of purely linguistic constraints on the operation of a rule for a particular speaker. Thus we saw in Figure 3-2 that subject number 7 deletes *que* categorically in environment S–S, deletes approximately 50 percent in environment K–S, approximately 30 percent in environment V–S, and 0 percent in all other environments. This statistically variable performance we interpret as reflecting an underlying different *probability* of deletion for the various environments for this particular speaker which ranges from 100 percent in one environment to 0 percent in another set of environments, and which differs *in terms of degree* in intervening environments. Speaker number 7 may have a probability of, say, 0.4 or 0.6 in environment K–S that was realized in behavior in the cases we observed as 0.5; similarly, in environment V–S her probability may be 0.25 or 0.36. The important point is that when we observe a sufficient number of cases for a particular speaker, we can assume that relative differences count for something, that competence need not fall into only three boxes: "0," "variable," and "1."

I have tried to refute a frequent criticism of the early work on variable rules: that statistical tendencies on the level of the community reflect only a mixture of different categorical grammars for different speakers. Our *que* example, the /l/ example, the *bai* example, and a number of examples studied by Cedergren (1972) show that statistical tendencies on the community level are reflections of statistical tendencies at the level of each individual.

If we accept that there can be significant differences of degree in particular linguistic environments, we can extend this principle in two important ways: (1) to apply to extralinguistic environments, including things like degrees of formality, particular speech situations or topics, or emotive or expressive marking (few examples of this have been cited in this chapter as we have not yet completed the analysis of any such cases in our own data; however examples can be found in Labov 1966, 1969; Brunel 1970); and (2) to say something about the differences between speakers or groups of speakers. Whereas the first aspect of difference (nonlinguistic constraints on a rule) can be built into a rule as part of the conditioning on that rule (cf. Cedergren and D. Sankoff 1974), the second (difference between speakers) is of course *not* part of a speaker's competence, though it can still be incorporated into a variable rule model in terms of different *input probabilities* for different kinds of speakers. Several examples have been cited from our own work in New Guinea and Montréal of how differences between individuals or groups of speakers can be significant in terms of proportions of occurrences of particular rules (e.g., applying less than secondary stress to *bai* in New Guinea Tok Pisin), rather than total presence or absence of a particular rule.

If we look at sociolinguistics from the broad perspective sketched by Hymes in 1962, where the linguistic resources of a community were viewed as means, articulated within its total communicative structure, the work outlined in this paper can be seen as an attempt to investigate the nature and distribution of these means within particular communities. Indeed, as soon as we stop talking about "a language" in an abstract and ill-defined way and begin looking at what actually goes on in the speech community, we find that the distribution of these means, of features and rules, across situations and across individuals, is structured in nontrivial and investigable ways.

4.

Above and Beyond Phonology in Variable Rules

My principal goal in this chapter is to extend the scope of an analytical framework that treats variation in linguistic behavior as being entirely natural, rather than anomalous, error-laden, or otherwise unmanageably messy. Perhaps the very success of such a framework in dealing with phonological data and with morphophonemic reduction rules has led many to believe that concepts of variation are applicable only in these domains, and that strict application of all-or-nothing principles is still defensible at other levels of grammar. I will argue that this is a misconception based in large part on an overly mechanistic view of language, which in turn stems from the traditional deterministic postulates underlying most of modern linguistics, including both structuralist and generative schools of various persuasions. Thus I think that work on systematic variability has often been misperceived by those who react to numbers and tables as being boring, trivial, or alarming, as being simply a detailed *description* of *performance*. My view is quite the opposite: I think that from the beginning, and I refer principally to the continuing ground-breaking research of Labov and associates, the attempt has been to find more adequate ways of dealing with the great subtleties of competence in some of its most complex and interesting, i.e., noncategorical, aspects.

This is not to argue for chaos; quite the reverse. Perception of a set of observations as chaotic or otherwise disorderly may well stem from the inadequacy of the analyst's model to account for the kinds of diversity represented in the observations. Some recent work provides grounds for the fear that the renewed interest of linguists in the study of language in context stems from a desire to widen the field in which it is permissible to search for categorical constraints on linguistic behavior,

This chapter was originally presented as a paper at the First NWAVE Conference, Georgetown University, October 1972, and published in C.-J. N. Bailey and Roger Shuy, eds., *New Ways of Analyzing Variation in English* (Washington, D.C.: Georgetown University Press, 1973), pp. 44–61. Discussion of two of the three major examples has been revised as a result of further work on these problems, but the conclusions remain the same.

e.g., to disambiguate referentially synonymous expressions *categorically* by reference to social context. There is, in my view, mounting evidence that such semantic, discourse, or cultural constraints will be no more (or less) categorical than the type of linguistic constraints now agreed to be allowable. Both Hymes (1962, 1972a) and Labov, (1966a, 1969, 1972d) from somewhat different traditions of enquiry, have for some years supported this point of view. Sherzer (1973) has recently provided some very cogent arguments as to why it is inadequate to deal with cultural and interactional context only in an ad hoc way and only when strictly "necessary" (i.e., when all else appears to fail), that is, why a systematic study of the latter is indicated. Careful work by Gumperz (e.g., Gumperz and Wilson 1971; Blom and Gumperz 1972) and others has shown the complexity of the two-way interactions between language behavior and its context. In brief, the study of the context of language use as an integral part of linguistic description is necessary on a number of grounds, but there is no reason to suppose that it will in any way simplify the linguist's task or provide easy, categorical solutions to current linguistic problems. The futility of the search for complete determinacy in language was not found at the level of the so-called idiolect, and it is difficult to imagine why it might be found to any greater degree at the level of speech act context.

Briefly, I posit that linguistic behavior, like other behavior, is subject to statistical variation that can best be accounted for by an underlying model that is probabilistic rather than deterministic in nature. This position has been argued recently by a number of researchers, and I will not go into any details here except to state one salient point: such a model contains no implication that any or all rules will be variable, i.e., it can deal with the kinds of structures involved in both variable and categorical rules.

In order to demonstrate that variability occurs and can be dealt with at levels of grammar above (or beyond) the phonological, I have chosen some examples from syntax and semantics, drawn from the current work of myself and coworkers on two linguistic communities: native, French-speaking Montrealers, and urban New Guineans who speak Tok Pisin, formerly a pidgin language which now boasts a first generation of native speakers.

1. New Guinea Tok Pisin: The Placement of the Future Marker

The first example has to do with the placement of the future marker in New Guinea Tok Pisin (cf. chapter 10, this volume). This was a study in which we did an extensive series of recordings of members of about a dozen families in the town of Lae, as well as a considerable number of other recordings of individuals, groups, public gatherings, and the like. There was no formal sample: families were chosen for intensive study on the basis of their having children of at least seven or eight years old who spoke Tok Pisin as a first language. The families were members of a close-knit, multi-linguistic neighborhood. Few of the adults had a native language in common, and this included most spouses: all were fluent second-language speakers of Tok Pisin.

One of the results of an investigation of the syntactic marking of futures in the speech of nine adults and nine children in seven of the families was that *bai,* the marker, is variably placed before or after the subject NP. This has historical implications, as it seems that fifty or sixty years ago the standard order was to place *baimbai* or *bai* (now reduced to [ba] or [bə] by fluent speakers in informal conversation) *before* the subject NP. Though generational differences between our speakers appear in reduction of stress on *bai,* there appears to be no generational difference, nor a difference between individual speakers, with respect to order. Rather, there are a series of syntactic constraints, some of them categorical and others variable. Table 4-1 indicates the influence of the various pronominal subjects as well as nonpronominal noun phrases.

We see that all pronouns except the third person singular characteristically follow *bai,* whereas *em* and nonpronominal NPs generally precede, though with considerable variation. Further examination of the structure of nonpronominal subject NPs shows (Table 4-2) that there is a categorical rule which inserts *bai* after the NP when the latter contains an embedding whether the embedding contains a surface verb or not.

Subject NP		Position of *bai*	
Definition	Form	___NP	___VP
1st sing.	mi	78	7
2nd sing.	yu	52	1
3rd pl.	ol	31	1
1st pl. incl.; $\left\{ \begin{array}{l} \text{1st pl. excl.} \\ \text{2nd pl.} \end{array} \right\}$	yumi; $\left\{ \begin{array}{l} \text{mi} \\ \text{yu} \end{array} \right\}$ pela	22	6
3rd sing.	em	11	47
other NP		22	36
Ø subject		—	53

TABLE 4-1. *Bai* placement in terms of subject NP.

Structure of NP	Position of *bai*		
	_NP	NP_	_NP_
NP containing *bilong* (possessive)	–	8	2
NP containing embedding (with surface verb)	–	6	1
Other NP	17	17	2
Total	17	31	5

TABLE 4-2. *Bai* placement in terms of structure of non-pronominal subject NP.

Thus a sentence like 1, with a simple NP subject, applies the same *bai*-movement rule as a sentence like 2, with a complex S subject, though only in the second case is the rule categorical:

(1) Na meri bilong en *bai* igo bek. 'And his wife will go back.' (Speaker 7)

(2) Igat planti man *bai* igo. 'There are lots of people who'll go.' (Speaker 7)

The transformation for *bai*-movement is given as Rule 1.

$$\text{RULE } 1. \quad \text{bai} + \left\langle \begin{matrix} \text{NP} \\ \text{N–S} \end{matrix} \right\rangle + \text{VP}$$

				2:	NP	N–S
1		2	3 $\Rightarrow \langle 2 + 1 + 3 \rangle$	p='	0.5	1.0

In the case where the subject NP is nonpronominal and contains no embedding, the *bai*-movement rule operates with a probability of approximately 0.5, no further grammatical, social, or contextual constraints being evident. Thus the same speaker will use sentences like 3 and 4:

(3) Dispela kot ating *bai* i pinis nau. 'That court case probably will soon be finished.' (Speaker 8)

(4) *Bai* wara igo insait. 'The water will get into it.' (Speaker 8)

There is one further point of interest, and that is the existence of sentences containing a *bai* both preceding and following the subject NP, as shown in the far right-hand column of Table 4-2. Thus there seems to be a "copying" alternative to the *bai*-movement rule based on the length of the subject NP, as this pattern seldom appears with NPs of less than three phonological words. A rather long example is the following:

(5) *Bai* man i wok gaden o mikim wonem istap long bus, *bai*
tingting. 'The people working in the fields or whatever they
may be doing in the forest, will be thinking.' (Speaker 14)

In summary, we can say that the *bai*-movement rule is found to be quite
stable in some syntactic environments, operating always (in the case of
subject NPs containing embeddings) or almost never (in the case of
most NPs consisting of a single pronoun other than *em*). Interestingly,
most of the exceptions to the latter applied the *bai*-movement rule to
indicate particular emphasis on the pronoun subject to the exclusion of
other people, as in 6:

(6) *Mi* bai kisim! '*I* [not you guys] will get it.' (Speaker 3)

In the case of the pronoun *em*, however, *bai*-movement applies with a
probability of approximately 0.85, and in the case of an NP consisting
of more than a single pronoun, it applies with a probability of 0.5.

2. MORE ON MONTRÉAL *que*

A preliminary analysis of the deletion of complementizer *que* in the
speech of sixteen Montrealers (Sankoff, Sarrasin, and Cedergren 1971)
indicated a structure of variable phonological deletion constraints. Further work on other constructions containing *que* has shown that not
only is *que* absent in a great many places where there is every indication that it is present as an underlying form, but also that it is present on
the surface in co-occurrence with *wh*-forms like *quand* 'when', *comment* 'how', and *où* 'where', a co-occurrence that standard French
grammar would label "expletive" presence of *que* (Cedergren and
Laberge 1972). Examples 7 and 8 show the alternation of *que* after
quand for speaker 109; and examples 9 and 10 show the same kind of
alternation with *comment:*

(7) *Quand qu'* on sort, bien on va pas loin. 'When you leave, you
don't go far.' (Speaker 109.145)

(8) *Quand* tu as tout en main puis ça va bien, bien là tu te
décourages moins. 'When you have everything in hand and
things are going well, you don't get so discouraged.' (Speaker
109)

(9) Tu sais *comment qu'* ça se passe. 'You know how it happens.'
(6.101)

(10) Je sais pas *comment* ça se fait. 'I don't know how it works.'
(6.400)

Insertion of *que* results in a grammatically different structure, as the subordinator *quand* or *comment* appears to lose its subordinating function and act like an adverb, the subordinating function being taken over by an attached *que*.

Not all speakers use *que* variably in co-occurrence with *wh*-subordinators. Of the 23 speakers analyzed here, 5 used no *que* with any of their *wh*-subordinators. These included speaker 30, a fifty-seven-year-old foreman in a print shop; speaker 25, a twenty-seven-year-old intern; speaker 20, a seventy-six-year-old retired civil servant; speaker 68, a fifty-one-year-old veterinarian, and speaker 87, an eighteen-year-old student. One speaker, number 22, a nineteen-year-old manual worker, used *que* categorically with all his *wh*-subordinators. Table 4-3 presents the data for these and the other seventeen speakers,

Speakers	*comme*	*quand*	*comment* *combien* *pourquoi* *où*
30	1.00	1.00	1.00
25	1.00	1.00	1.00
20	1.00	1.00	1.00
68	1.00	1.00	1.00
87	1.00	1.00	1.00
75	1.00	1.00	.71
89	1.00	1.00	.71
98	1.00	1.00	.50
13	1.00	1.00	.57
97	1.00	.89	.56
83	1.00	.83	.50
24	1.00	.98	.12
2	1.00	1.00	.33
36	1.00	.89	.33
14	1.00	.75	.33
6	.57	.57	.14
40	.33	.33	.66
52	.25	.68	.36
23	.50	.50	.08
105	.50	.36	.70
94	0	.23	0
17	–	.38	0
22	0	0	0

TABLE 4-3. Ordering of speakers according to their percentages of use of subordinators without *que*-attachment. The forms in the far right-hand column have been grouped together because of the paucity of data relative to *quand* and *comment*.

all of whom varied their use of *que*-attachment in at least one environment. These data scale quite well. Speakers tend to use *que*-attachment most with the *wh*-forms *comment, combien* 'how much', *pourquoi* 'why', and *où* 'where', and least with *comme* 'like, as' (the only one of the set that is not also an interrogative), with *quand* falling somewhere in the middle.

I have sketched a variable rule (Rule 2) involving *que*-attachment that takes into account only the syntactic constraints (i.e., the differences among the various subordinators, without regard to the differences among speakers). This shows that *parce* 'because' is a very favorable (i.e., categorical) environment for *que*, whereas *comme* is a distinctly unfavorable environment.

RULE 2.   *wh*-raising rule.
$$VP + [NP + V + Adv. Pro]$$
$$1 \quad {}^s \ 2 \quad 3 \qquad\quad 4 \quad {}^s \Rightarrow 1 + 4 + \langle que \rangle + 2 + 3$$

Approximate probability values for variable *que* are:

term 4:	*comme*	*quand*	*où* *comment* *combien* *pourquoi*	*parce*
p=	.1	.3	.4	1.0

At this point, however, we encounter a major problem. Presence of *que* added as an adjunct with *wh*-raising appears in Table 4-4 to be highly unlikely in anything but a succeeding vocalic environment, in

	Succeeding phonological environments					
	[+sib]		$\begin{bmatrix} +\text{cons} \\ -\text{sib} \end{bmatrix}$		[−cons]	
	quand *comme*	*où* etc.	*quand* *comme*	*où* etc.	*quand* *comme*	*où* etc.
que present *que* absent	2 113	2 41	1 56	3 16	96 50	26 54
Total	115	43	57	19	146	80

TABLE 4-4. Presence of *que* according to phonological environment for speakers who vary in terms of *que*- attachment.

which its surface representation is generally the consonant [k]. The question immediately arises as to whether this [k] represents simply a phonological insertion, a liaison-like phenomenon where speakers replace [kɑ̃tɔ̃] with [kɑ̃kɔ̃] (for *quand on*). I reject this hypothesis not only because of the infrequent, but well-attested, existence of full-form *que* [kə] before consonants (a total of 8 cases in Table 4-4), but also because another type of embedding is also limited almost entirely to the succeeding vocalic context. This type of embedding inserts some form of *est-ce* between the *wh*-form and *que,* as in example sentences 11 and 12:

> (11) Je trouvais ça formidable *comment c'que c'est.* 'I thought it was great, how it is.' (Speaker 89)

> (12) Je sais pas *comment c'est qu'*ils la faisaient dans ce temps-là. 'I don't know how they did it in those days.' (24.429)

This insertion may take the form of *c'est,* or (inverted) *est-ce.* Thus sentence 11 has *est-ce* (reduced to [s]) inserted between the *wh*-form *comment* and *que;* sentence 12 inserts *c'est.* As in 11, the *est-ce* form often becomes [s], so that we have [sk] representing *est-ce que.* These *est-ce/c'est* embeddings are, in our data, entirely limited to the forms *où, combien, comment,* and *pourquoi,* and almost entirely limited to the vocalic context (of 54 cases, only 1 occurs prior to a [+sib] segment; all the others precede [−cons] segments). The fact that these forms can occur in prevocalic contexts is, I think, due to the same low-level phonological rule that deletes *que* in constructions such as complements where it is in the underlying form (Cedergren and Laberge 1972). This rule appears as Rule 3. *Est-ce* would be added as an optional complication of Rule 2, but would then be virtually always removed as a further consequence of Rule 3 in the favored environments. But if, as we have shown, presence of *que* is a result of an optional attachment rule followed by an optional deletion rule, it be-

RULE 3: *que*-deletion rule

$$que \rightarrow \emptyset \ \Big/ \ \left\langle \begin{matrix} [+\text{sib}] \\ \begin{bmatrix} +\text{cons} \\ -\text{sib} \end{bmatrix} \\ [-\text{cons}] \end{matrix} \right\rangle \ - \ \left\langle \begin{matrix} [+\text{sib}] \\ \begin{bmatrix} +\text{cons} \\ -\text{sib} \end{bmatrix} \\ [-\text{cons}] \end{matrix} \right\rangle$$

Effects:	[+sib]	$\begin{bmatrix} +\text{cons} \\ -\text{sib} \end{bmatrix}$	[−cons]
pre. seg.	.13	.02	0
fol. seg.	.36	.09	0

(1 − deletion prob.) = [1 − effect (pre. seg.)] × [1 − effect (fol. seg.)]

comes difficult to state the conditions under which attachment applies, since absence of *que* may result from its never having been attached in the first place, or from its having been attached and later deleted. It would seem at best inappropriate to postulate both attachment and deletion for those individuals and those forms where *que* never appears on the surface.

Perhaps here we can look at some of the probabilities attached to various constraints in clear deletion cases (e.g., *parce que*, complements, relatives) and, comparing them to the observed data on possible attached, then deleted cases, infer what such frequencies might represent in terms of cases originally attached. For even if, turning back to the figures in Table 4-3, the phonological rule sweeps across surface *que*s of every grammatical stripe, it is clear that some of the forms are simply less amenable to *que*-attachment. It seems, for example, that *que* is what some might call "less good" with *comme* ('like') than it is with *quand* ('when'). Again, compare *quand*, which occurs only by itself and with *que*, but does not take any *est-ce* in between. Informants questioned about the acceptability of a construction like *quand est-ce que*, or *quand c'est que* all said this would be fine, but *not* with *comme*, thus **comme c'est que*, **comme est-ce que*, etc. This difference may stem in part from the fact that *comme* can never be used in a surface direct question, whereas *quand* can. Referring back to the table under Rule 2, which shows very approximate probabilities of *que*-attachment for the various forms in the tables as well as for *parce*, we might also note that in comparing *que* deletion in complements versus relatives, we have found the latter to be a much more conservative environment—though the phonological constraints pattern in the same way. All speakers would be less likely to say a sentence like 13 than a sentence like 14:

> (13) C'est la fille 0 j'ai vue. ('That's the girl I saw' instead of 'That's the girl that I saw.')

> (14) Je pense 0 ça a été plutôt un snobisme. (70.175) ('I think it was more a kind of snobbery' instead of 'I think that it was more a kind of snobbery.')

We have not yet investigated distinctions in the way a grammatical difference like restrictive versus nonrestrictive relatives would affect presence or absence of *que*, or, to turn the thing on its head, what *que*-attachment can tell us about the nature of the NP which follows it, in terms of being more or less like other NPs. But we can already see that presence or absence of *que* is differentially allowable for different grammatical constructions in a way that is clearly important to an understanding of the grammar of French. This would seem to be the kind of area one might also investigate from the perspective of universals. (Cf. Wolfram 1973 on variable rules and universals; Keenan and Hull 1973 on universals in relatives and indirect questions; Kemp 1977 on universals in various rules of movement in *wh*-embeddings.)

Before passing to the last example, which is taken from the area of semantics, I would like to say a little more about the relationship between variability studies and the work of linguists who do not explicitly base their formulations on systematic studies of speech production. It is clear that Chomsky was correct in pointing out that there is no necessary connection between frequency of occurrence and grammaticality. Yet it is also clear that the questions of degrees of grammaticality or acceptability discussed so elegantly by Ross (1973) and by Sag (1973) fit very naturally into the overall framework of variability that we base our work on. The problem comes back to a question of the interpretation one would be able to give to a table like Table 4-3. What does it mean to note that speaker 97, say, was never observed to use *comme que,* though he did use *quand que* a little, and made considerable use of constructions like *comment que?* Is *comme que* disallowed by his grammar? Would he react to its use by others as being "funny?" Could we say that *comme que* would be more likely to be grammatical for him in some sense, even though he does not use it, than it would be for speaker 20, who also does not use it, but does not use any of the others either? Here we get into the problems of production versus reception, the fact that we can receive correctly, and without thought that they are "peculiar," messages in forms that we would never ourselves use, and so on, as Trudgill (1973) has pointed out. Further, questioning people about whether they find nonstandard forms "grammatical" poses a number of special difficulties (cf. Labov 1970 on this general point).

3. PRONOUN SEMANTICS IN MONTRÉAL FRENCH

My last example, dealing with pronoun semantics in Montréal French, is drawn from Laberge (1977). I am presenting only one small part of the system: the variation Laberge found in the indefinite pronoun which can be conveyed by *on, tu,* or *vous.* This is the indefinite *par excellence,* traditionally represented as *on* on the surface in French grammar, and containing no features indicating inclusion or exclusion of the speaker (ego) or hearer, nor the singular/plural distinction. Some examples taken from our recordings are listed here:

> (15) *J'*aime mieux boire une bonne brosse, c'est mieux que fumer de la drogue, *je* trouve. Le lendemain matin *tu* as un

gros mal de tête mais ça fait rien, *tu* es tout là. Tandis qu'avec la drogue, *tu* sais pas si *tu* vas être là le lendemain. *Tu* peux *te* prendre pour Batman ou Superman puis *tu te* pitch dans les poubelles. 'I'd rather have a good drink, it's better than smoking drugs, I find. The next morning *you* have a terrible headache but it doesn't matter, *you're* all there. But with drugs, *you* don't know if *you're* going to be there the next day. *You* might think *you* were Batman or Superman and throw *yourself* into the garbage pail.' (62.224)

(16) *Tu* as beau parler de l'éléphant, du serpent, mais si *on* peut pas le décrire, hein? 'It's all very well to talk about elephants, about snakes, but if *you* can't describe them, eh?' (99.320)

(17) Quand *une personne* élevait une famille à ce temps-là, *vous* étiez pas capable d'avoir de luxe. 'When *a person* was bringing up a family at that time, *you* couldn't afford luxuries.' (37.16)

Often what the speaker appears to be doing is talking about an experience of his/her own, but he/she is actually generalizing to apply as a general rule (cf. chapter 13, this volume). In sentence 17 the speaker does not imply that the twenty-two-year-old addressee has herself raised a family during the Depression; this is the indefinite *vous,* which is distinguished clearly from personal *vous* in its underlying representation. Further evidence for this distinction (*tu* and *vous* personal versus *tu* and *vous* indefinite) comes from a comparison of speakers' address terms with their indefinite usage. Several older speakers consistently used the *vous* politeness form in addressing young interviewers, yet used *tu* (alternating with *on*) as an indefinite. An example is given as sentence 18, from a fifty-five-year-old unemployed laborer:

(18) Aussi, vous savez, quand *tu* as tout à la main puis ça va bien, bien là le courage vient. 'So, you know, when you have everything and things are going well, it's then that you get courage.' (Speaker 109).

Laberge calculated individual probabilities of *on* use for each of the 120 speakers of the Montréal French corpus, and found the dramatic age and sex differences demonstrated in Table 4-5. We see that the majority of speakers of both sexes who were over forty in 1971, the year the recordings were made, show a preference for *on*. Of the 28 men over forty, 65.8 percent had a probability of *on* use greater than or equal to 0.5, and this was also the case for 68.7 percent of the 23 women. Among younger speakers, however, there was a great sex difference. Only 28.1 percent of the younger men preferred *on,* whereas among younger

Probability of *on* use	age over 40		age 40 and younger	
	men	women	men	women
	%	%	%	%
≥.5	65.8	68.7	28.1	75.6
<.5	34.2	31.3	71.9	24.4
N =	(28)	(23)	(32)	(37)

TABLE 4-5. Proportion of older and younger men and women preferring *on* (p ≥ .5) versus *tu* or *vous* (p < .5). Based on Laberge 1977, Table 10, p. 233.

women, there was an even higher proportion preferring *on* (75.6 percent) than among the older women.

For the great majority of Montréal French speakers of both sexes, *on* has become the usual surface form for 'we'—in standard French, *nous* (Laberge 1977, chapter 3). It appears that the younger men, having moved *on* into the traditional *nous* slot, have filled the *on* slot with *tu* and *vous,* creating a potential ambiguity with "personal" *tu* and *vous.* For younger women, however, the potential ambiguity is with the two uses of *on.* (These are of course tendencies in the data. Almost all speakers in fact show variable use of *on, tu,* and *vous* as indefinites.) The fact that younger men show decreasing input probabilities for *on* as an indefinite indicates a change in progress among this segment of the population. It does not, however, suggest that younger male speakers have difficulty understanding women and older men when they use *on* as in 16, or that these people cannot in turn correctly decode uses of indefinite *tu* or *vous* as in 15, 17, and 18.

4. Concluding Observations

The extension of probabilistic considerations from phonology to syntax is not a conceptually difficult jump. Whenever there are options open to a speaker, we can infer from his or her behavior an underlying set of probabilities. It seems clear to us that in the increasing number of situations that have been studied in depth, this inference is more than an exercise in data organization, since the underlying probabilities are consistently and systematically patterned according to internal (linguistic) and external (social and stylistic) constraints. There is no reason not to expect similar patterning elsewhere in grammar, aside from the phonological rules and syntactic transformations we have been discussing. Indeed, though there has been relatively little of the type of systematic data collection associated with variable rule studies, a certain amount of linguistic and probabilistic theorizing has been taking place with respect to other components of grammar.

On the level of phrase structure grammar, for example, considerable work has been done. The choice of one of a number of possible rules to rewrite a nonterminal node in a phrase marker is not strictly comparable to the application or nonapplication choice of a meaning-preserving transformation; nonetheless it frequently involves a certain freedom in the way a speaker organizes what he/she is saying. Furthermore, in the base component of many grammars, rewrite choices in phrase structure rules involve a strong stylistic component. The extension of phrase structure grammar to include probabilistic considerations has been suggested, largely independently and in ways that are mathematically almost identical, by Klein (1965), and by the mathematicians Grenander (1967), Horning (1969), Suppes (1970) working with Roger Brown's acquisition data, and D. Sankoff (1971a, 1972a); see also Peizer and Olmsted (1969).

Without going too far into problems of lexical choice and lexical insertion, it is not difficult to see how phenomena such as synonymy, overlapping meanings, specificity versus generality, and referents that are marginal or on the border between two semantic domains could all lead to probabilistic considerations of the lexicon. In this connection we can point particularly to the work of Lehrer (1970) on probabilistic weights of features in the semantic domain of "containers." The mathematical and probabilistic implications of this approach were investigated by D. Sankoff (1971b). Finally we may cite Labov (1973), showing the role of probabilistic choice near the boundaries between semantic domains, and D. Sankoff, Thibault, and Bérubé, showing partial overlapping among words relating to the domains of "work," "residence," and "things" (1978).

Much of the work done thus far, including our own, is fragmentary. Nevertheless it seems readily discernible that there is a natural and behaviorally motivated trend to extend grammatical theory, which is primarily discrete and algebraic in character, by the introduction of well-defined probabilistic notions.

5.

Multilingualism in Papua New Guinea

Bilingualism, indeed multilingualism,[1] is a resource many contemporary Papua New Guineans have in common. Yet it is not the case that this is a phenomenon unique to the colonial and independence periods of Papua New Guinea history. In order to better understand multilingualism in the present day, it is necessary to attempt the best possible reconstruction of the degree and nature of multilingualism in the precolonial period.

I. MULTILINGUALISM IN THE PRECOLONIAL PERIOD

1.1. Language Distribution: Implications for Multilingualism

Papua New Guinea is well known as a country with a multitude of languages. The approximate number of languages, the relative distribution of Austronesian and non-Austronesian (Papuan) languages, and the implications of this distribution in reflecting prehistoric relationships and migrations have been dealt with extensively in works such as Capell 1969, 1971; Chowning 1970; Dutton 1969; Healey 1964; Hooley and McElhanon 1970; Laycock 1965; Wurm 1960, 1971a; Wurm and

This chapter originally appeared in S. A. Wurm, ed., 1977, New Guinea Area Languages and Language Study, volume 3: Language, culture, society and the modern world. *Pacific Linguistics,* C–40, Fascicle 1, pp. 265–307. Because of the availability, since the original writing, of extensive new materials on Austronesian languages (in Wurm, ed., 1976), on mission *lingue franche* (in Wurm, ed., 1977), and the Papua New Guinea 1971 census statistics, sections dealing with these materials have been revised accordingly. I wish to express my thanks to the Buang people of Mambump Village, Papua New Guinea, who initiated me into the subtleties of multilingualism in that country. I also wish to thank Pierrette Thibault and Marjorie Topham for their help in preparing the manuscript.

1. I will use the terms "multilingual" and "multilingualism" in the generic sense throughout, to refer to speakers having competence in more than one language. "Bilingual," "trilingual," etc., will be used to refer more specifically to particular groups or individuals having competence in two, three, etc., languages.

Laycock 1961; Z'graggen 1971; and the many detailed studies in McKaughan, ed., 1973, and Wurm, ed., 1975, 1976. Various kinds of language contacts in the New Guinea area, with particular reference to contacts between speakers of Austronesian and Papuan languages, have been described by Laycock (1973). Our main concern here, however, is the implication of such diversity for multilingualism.

1.1.1. *Very Small Languages*

Of the probably 700 or more languages of Papua New Guinea, it is likely that over a third have (and have had for some time) an extremely small number of speakers. "Extremely small" here means less than 500 speakers. This approximation is based (for Papuan languages) on data presented by Wurm (1971a).[2] Eliminating several of his groupings that fall largely in Irian Jaya, we are left with approximately 449 languages, of which 169 have fewer than 500 speakers, as shown in Table 5-1. We have no such complete statistics, analogous to Wurm's, for the Austronesian languages of Papua New Guinea. Data were culled from Hooley and McElhanon (1970) on 37 Austronesian languages of Morobe Province, from Beaumont (1972) on 20 New Ireland languages as well as Kuanua (the Tolai language of New Britain), and from several of the articles in Wurm's (1976) collection: Dutton (1976) and Pawley (1976) on 19 Central Province languages; Healey (1976) on 26 languages of the Admiralty Islands area; Laycock (1976) on the 10 Austronesian languages of the two Sepik Provinces; Lincoln (1976) on 13 languages of Bougainville; Lithgow (1976) on 40 Milne Bay languages; and Z'graggen (1976) on 15 Madang Province languages. These 181 Austronesian languages—probably about 80 percent of the Austronesian languages of Papua New Guinea[3]—show a pattern similar to that of the Papuan languages in terms of the proportion of speakers of "very small" languages: 50 of these Austronesian languages have fewer than 500 speakers. Thus of the 629 languages of Papua New Guinea for which statistics have been compiled in Table 5-1, we find that 219, or 34.8 percent, have fewer than 500 speakers.

2. Since this source was fairly complete, and the job would have been extremely time-consuming for very little change in the results, I have not revised my statistics for the Papuan languages with material published in Wurm, ed., 1975, which became available only after the original version of this article had gone to press.

3. The 37 other Austronesian languages of New Britain discussed in Chowning (1969; 1976) have not been included because she does not cite population figures. Adding these 37 to the 181 for which we have at least population estimates would make a total of about 220 Austronesian languages for Papua New Guinea as a whole.

Speakers per language	PAPUAN LANGUAGES		AUSTRONESIAN LANGUAGES		TOTAL	
	No. of languages	Approx. total population	No. of languages	Approx. total population	No. of languages	Approx. total population
30,000 +	9* (2.2%)	460,000 (31.4%)	1** (0.6%)	63,200 (14.4%)	10 (1.6%)	523,000 (27.5%)
10,000–29,999	22 (4.9%)	385,000 (26.3%)	6 (3.3%)	80,385 (18.3%)	28 (4.5%)	465,385 (24.4%)
5,000–9,999	38 (8.5%)	265,000 (18.1%)	15 (8.3%)	104,047 (23.7%)	53 (8.4%)	369,047 (19.4%)
1,000–4,999	135 (30.1%)	274,000 (18.7%)	76 (42.0%)	155,580 (35.4%)	211 (33.5%)	429,580 (22.6%)
500–999	76 (16.9%)	48,500 (3.3%)	33 (18.2%)	22,971 (5.2%)	109 (17.3%)	71,471 (3.8%)
less than 500	169 (37.6%)	33,500 (2.3%)	50 (27.6%)	12,771 (2.9%)	219 (34.8%)	46,271 (2.4%)
TOTAL	449	1,466,000	181	438,954	629	1,904,954

TABLE 5-1. Distribution of the number of speakers of 629 Papuan and Austronesian languages in Papua New Guinea. See text for data sources.

* The 9 languages are Enga—110,000; Melpa—60,000; Chimbu—60,000; Huli—54,000; Kewa—39,500; Kamano—38,500; Wahgi—37,000; Gawigl—31,000; Mendi—30,000.

** The Austronesian language in question is Tolai.

Most of the speakers of these very small languages are (and probably were in the past) bilingual or multilingual, according to evidence from recent language surveys. Laycock (1965), for example, discussing the two smallest members of the Ndu language family of the East and West Sepik Provinces, has this to say (p. 131):

> Ngala is spoken by the 134 inhabitants of a single village, Swagup, [which] . . . lies off the Sepik River, several hours' travel up a narrow tributary stream. The nearest speakers of an Ndu-family language are the Iatmul-speaking inhabitants of Brugnowi, with whom however the people of Swagup have till recently had a long-standing feud. . . . It is with the Wogamusin-speaking inhabitants of Washkuk that the Swagup natives have most of their trading contacts . . . a large number of adult males in Swagup speak Wogamusin.

(It should be noted that Wogamusin, a non-Ndu Papuan language, itself has only 336 speakers, which is, however, more than double the number of Ngala speakers.) Laycock continues:

> Yelogu is spoken by the inhabitants of a single village. . . . All 63 inhabitants appear to be bilingual, speaking the unrelated Kwoma language as well as Yelogu. (Laycock 1965: 139)

No such bilingualism is reported for the four other languages of the Ndu Family, all of which number well over one thousand speakers.

In a study of the languages of the Finisterre Range, Claassen and McElhanon (1970) make similar observations concerning a number of the very small languages of that area. For example, discussing the Erap Family of Morobe Province, they state (p. 56):

> The Mamaa language is spoken in the village of Mamaa (pop. 200) on the east bank of the lower Irumu River. With the exception of the Finungwan language, this language shows no lexico-statistical relationship greater than 35% with the other languages in the family. The 46% relationship with Finungwan may reflect borrowings since the people are being assimilated by the Finungwan people and most of them are bilingual.

In a close parallel with the Ngala speakers of Wogamusin cited by Laycock, we note that the Finungwan language, like Wogamusin, is itself very small, numbering only four hundred speakers, but again double the number of speakers of Mamaa.

A further case cited by Claassen and McElhanon (1970) is that of speakers of the Yabong language of the Yaganon Family in Madang Province (p. 61):

The Yabong language (pop. 370) is spoken in five villages west of the Yangda River. . . . Many of the people are reported to be fluent in the Rawa language.

(Note that Rawa is an only very distantly related, fairly large language of six thousand speakers belonging to the Finisterre Stock, whereas Yabong belongs to the Rai Coast Stock.)

Parallel evidence is presented in studies of other very small languages, many of which tend to occur in border areas between larger language groups, often as a result of the drastic reduction of a population through warfare or disease. Such a situation is discussed for the Binumarien (three small villages in the Kainantu Sub-District of the Eastern Highlands Province, very near the Morobe Province border, and containing a total of 117 people) by Oatridge and Oatridge (1973: 517):

> The Binumarien are a very small group. Within the memory of the older men, they were more numerous, but because of tribal fighting resulting in prolonged residence in the Markham Valley and resultant malaria, their numbers have been greatly reduced. Their neighbors to the west and south are the Gadsup, and to the north the Azera in the Markham Valley. The closely related language of Kambaira is in the southeast. The Binumarien are most closely related to the Tairora though some of the men speak Azera and Gadsup while others speak Gadsup and Tairora as well as their own language.

Though I have rather conservatively restricted the "very small" language category to those numbering less than 500 speakers, it is quite likely that many speakers of slightly larger languages, numbering, say, up to 1,000, were also bilingual. Bee (1965: 39–40) describes such a situation for the Usarufa:

> Usarufa [is] a language spoken by approximately 850 persons in the Eastern Highlands District. . . . The Usarufa-speaking area is located in a pocket surrounded by Kamano, Kanite, Fore, and a small segment of Auyana speakers. All of these languages except the Auyana have been classified by Wurm as members of language families distinct from Usarufa. Nevertheless most adult Usarufa speakers speak at least one of the three more distantly related languages and many speak all three. Contrariwise very few Fore, Kamano or Kanite speakers are able to speak Usarufa. Also of note is the fact that . . . few Usarufa speakers admit to speaking or understanding Auyana which is so closely related that the two may be dialects of one language.

This is confirmed by Berndt (1954: 291), who notes also that "nearly all" of the Usarufa "seem to have some knowledge of Jate." The Jate (or Yate, according to Wurm (1971a), who have a population of 3,988) lie immediately to the west of the Usarufa, "in some cases only 15–20 minutes' walk away" (Berndt 1954: 291).

The quotation from Laycock (1965) cited above states one reason for speakers of such small languages to be bilingual, i.e., trading contacts, necessarily (especially when the language is confined to a single village or hamlet) with speakers of other languages. Another type of contact, even more important for fostering bilingualism in such cases, was intermarriage, again a virtual necessity for members of very small language groups. This meant that a large number of women brought up in such a small language group would, upon marrying outside of it, find themselves to be in a linguistically foreign environment for their married lives; and that men brought up in such groups would very likely bring in wives who did not initially speak the group's language, which in turn would expose their children to more than one language.

Note that in all of the citations above, either no sex difference in bilingualism is noted or else special note is taken that men are bilingual. It is unlikely that this reflects a real sex difference in bilingualism; rather, given that in such small language groups a large proportion of the adult women will be married in from other language groups and therefore not be native speakers of the language groups in which they now live, they are of little or no interest to a linguist whose main job is finding out about the language of the group in question, and therefore will not perhaps notice that these women are also bilingual.[4]

1.1.2. *Trade Languages in Coastal Areas*

Though, as is indicated in Table 5-1, speakers of somewhat over a third of the languages of Papua New Guinea were probably obliged by demography alone to become bilingual, it is also clear from this table that such speakers never constituted more than a tiny minority of the total population. Even if we include the next smallest group of languages, those having between 500 and 1,000 speakers, only just over 6 percent of the population would be in this category (though the two groups constitute just over half the languages!).

We now turn to an examination of the case of the great majority of Papua New Guineans, that 94 percent of the population not living in

---

4. It may also reflect the fact that since the majority of linguists are men and therefore also speak mainly with men in the language groups they visit (often for reasons of social acceptability, as noted in Laycock 1965: 13), they have incomplete information on the language competence of women.

language isolates, and whose language groups consist of over 1,000 speakers. Though data relevant to multilingualism are very incomplete for these larger language groups, we can, I feel, piece together a general picture with respect to multilingualism among speakers of many such languages. The larger the number of speakers of any particular language, the less likely are contacts such as trade and intermarriage with speakers of other languages. There is still considerable evidence, however, indicating varying degrees and types of competence in other languages and dialects among many speakers of such languages.

First, note in Table 5-1 that the distribution of speakers differs between Papuan and Austronesian languages. The largest concentration of Austronesian speakers (35.4 percent) is concentrated in languages having between 1,000 and 5,000 speakers. As is well known, most of these languages (as well as a number of Papuan languages of similar medium size) are located in coastal areas, where there were a number of trade circuits spanning considerable distances.

In many coastal areas, the language of one of the trading groups, sometimes in a somewhat simplified version, was used as a *lingua franca* throughout the trade circuit in question. A very famous case is that of Hiri Motu (also known as Police Motu), the language

> which came into being as a trade language used by the Motu people of the Port Moresby area during their annual trading expeditions to parts of the coastal area of what is today the Gulf District. . . . The language is a pidginized Motu which shows marked influence of the Papuan language type which is attributable to the fact that the coastal people in the Gulf District are speakers of Papuan languages. (Wurm 1969: 35)

As early as the beginning of the twentieth century, "the fact that the Motu and the various Gulf tribes visited by them make use of a common trading dialect which is in some measure distinct from the very widely divergent languages of either" (Barton 1910: 96)[5] was cited as

---

5. Barton (1910: 119–20) gives a wordlist of over 100 words in what he calls the "lakatoi language" used as a trading language between the Elema and the visiting Motu traders. Checking this list against the dictionary in Wurm and Harris's Police Motu manual (1963), I found that of the 105 lexical items I could locate in both lists, only 21 were obviously the same words. Whether this means that Barton's list is aberrant or that Hiri Motu has changed very drastically in the intervening fifty years, is impossible for me to judge. (Note that in an article published in the same volume as the original version of the present paper, Dutton and Brown 1977 confirm this discrepancy and provide the most complete and informative account to date of the possible transition between the language of the Motu traders and the "Police Motu" later used by the Papuan constabulary.)

evidence that such trade had "existed for a very considerable period" (p. 96). Thus bilingualism in their own language and Hiri Motu existed among members of those groups who traded with the Motu speakers well before the beginning of the colonial period. This language was used by the Motuans and their trade partners both on the Motuans' visits to the Papuan Gulf, and on return visits by the peoples of the Gulf, as described by Eri (1970: 35). Speakers of Koita have also been bilingual in Motu for a very long time:

> The Koita are a tribe speaking a Papuan language who have for generations intermarried with the Motu and whose villages are usually built near, or even in direct contiguity with those of the Motu. Although the Koita still speak a Papuan language the majority of the males speak Motu, a Melanesian language. (Seligman 1910: 16)

Later Seligman goes on to say that "practically all the Koita speak Motu" (p. 45).

In another well-known trade circuit, that of the Kula, it appears that Dobuan was the *lingua franca*. Writing of the period between 1914 and 1918, Malinowski states:

> It is characteristic of the international position of the Dobuans that their language is spoken as a lingua franca all over the d'Entrecasteaux Archipelago, in the Amphletts, and as far north as the Trobriands. In the southern part of these latter islands, almost everyone speaks Dobuan, although in Dobu the language of the Trobriands or Kiriwinian is hardly spoken by anyone. (Malinowski 1966: 39–40)

Malinowski mentions this fact mainly because he finds it a curious one, his feeling being that Kiriwinian, as the language of the more numerous and equally prestigious Trobrianders, would have been a more likely choice for a *lingua franca*. In describing the trade visits of the Trobrianders in Dobu, Malinowski again remarks on the use of Dobuan. He says:

> In the villages, they are entertained by their male friends, the language spoken by both parties being that of Dobu, which differs completely from Kiriwinian, but which the Sinaketans learn in early youth. (Malinowski 1966: 364)

Despite the widespread use of Dobuan, it appears that the Trobrianders did use their own language on visits to certain other islands. The fact that "the natives of the eastern islands, from Kitava to Woodlark, . . . speak the same language with dialectical differences only" (Malinowski 1966: 478) is said by Malinowski to have facilitated trade between the

Trobrianders and the people of these islands. He also describes (p. 270) a trade visit in the Amphletts in which Kiriwinian was the language used.

Farther west along the northern coast of Papua New Guinea, bilingualism in the language of traders appears to have existed in two other areas: the northern coast of the Huon Peninsula, and the Huon Gulf area. According to Harding (1967: 203):

> Sio informants say that communication was based on a pidgin form of the Siassi language (*tok Siassi haphap*), a trade lingo with a Siassi vocabulary which was useful not only in meetings with the Siassis themselves, but with other island and coastal peoples.

Slightly farther south, in the Huon Gulf area,

> It seems that in the past the pot makers from the south, the basket weavers from Labu, and the Tami Islanders all made a practice of learning Gawa (or Kawa), the vernacular spoken on the North Coast and around Busama. (Hogbin 1947: 247)

This sample of four regional trading languages certainly does not exhaust the total coastal area of Papua New Guinea; nevertheless, these four alone were spoken as a second language by thousands of people speaking many languages, both Papuan and Austronesian, along hundreds of miles of coastline. In addition, similar situations probably existed in many other coastal areas on which I have not been able to locate any data.[6] Unlike the bilingual speakers of the very small languages discussed in section 1.1.1 above, people bilingual in their own language and one of the coastal trade languages appear not to have been so likely to intermarry with speakers of these languages.[7] Trading voyages involved the traders' being entertained, each by his own trade friend in a foreign port, for fairly short periods on any one trip, i.e., not more than a couple of weeks at a time. The traders were men, and were on their trips apparently engaged in talk principally with other men in the language groups they visited. This probably means that unlike the situation in very small languages, there was a sex bias in favor of men with respect to bilingualism in the villages visited by traders. It also seems likely that few men or women who were native speakers of the

6. Another case that came to my attention during revision of this paper was the use of Suau as a trade language by Mailu traders in southeast Papua (Abel 1977).

7. The only exception to this in the four examples discussed appears to be the Koita, bilingual in Motu. As very close neighbors of the Motu speakers, however, they had relations other than trade with the Motuans, specifically a great deal of intermarriage.

lingua franca were themselves bilingual, as Malinowski specifically states for the Dobuans. (If Barton is correct in his statement that the Motu spoken as a contact language was indeed quite different from Motu, then the Motuan traders could be said to have been "bilingual" and form an exception to the pattern of speakers of languages like Dobuan.)

In an article Don Laycock kindly brought to my attention after this chapter was completed, Schlesier (1961) discusses the impact of "trade friend" relationships on bilingualism in various parts of New Guinea, citing missionary and other sources dating from the 1890s. He stresses the often lengthy period of time spent by youths in their fathers' trade friends' villages, during which visits language learning was a major goal.

1.1.3. *Inland Middle-Range Languages*

Section 1.1.2 has dealt with the middle-range languages of the coast, mainly Austronesian though including some Papuan languages. (It is of note that the four trade languages discussed in section 1.1.2 in which both Austronesian and Papuan speakers were bilingual, are all themselves Austronesian.) But the bulk of speakers of the middle-range Papuan languages are to be found inland.

Here again, the situation appears to be a result of the interaction between demography (itself a result of the nature of the terrain and of historical forces in shaping migration patterns) and socially regulated patterns of trade and intermarriage. But even more than in preceding sections, we are severely hampered by lack of information; very few ethnographies or linguistic surveys have paid much attention to bilingualism. Very roughly, it appears that there has existed a fair amount of bilingualism in border areas and among the smaller or more isolated segments of any linguistic group, but that multilingualism is unlikely in the central areas of large linguistic groups.

The most detailed account of multilingualism in a middle-range Papuan language is Salisbury's (1962) description of the Siane, located in the border areas of the Chimbu and Eastern Highlands Provinces southeast of Chuave. Siane, which according to Wurm (1971a: 549) numbers approximately 15,336 speakers, is the westernmost member of the East-Central Family of the East New Guinea Highlands Stock. Salisbury documents a very high degree of bilingualism on the part of Siane speakers in "various of the Dene dialects" (Salisbury 1962: 2). (Note that "Dene" is regarded by Wurm (1971a) as two languages: Chuave [population 5,639] and Nomane [population 2,502], belonging to the Central Family of the East New Guinea Highlands Stock.) Salisbury, who lived in a village where the language spoken was the Komunku dialect of Siane, states that

> Conversations among the residents could often be trilingual, a Ramfau [note: Ramfau is another dialect of Siane] wife speaking Ramfau to her son who replied in Komunku and who was supported by his wife speaking in Dene. (Salisbury 1962: 2)

Salisbury (1962) reports that in informal situations among groups of bilinguals, each would speak "whatever language was easiest for them" (p. 3) with no translation occurring, whereas in formal situations, "each formal speech would be followed immediately by a translation of it into the other language" (p. 3). Some Komunku speakers would use Dene on formal occasions, speaking Komunku on informal ones, an indication of the high prestige of multilingualism among the Siane (pp. 4–5). Salisbury also mentions that whereas Komunku dialect speakers in the western area tended to be fluent in Dene, many of those in the east also knew Gahuku.

Salisbury's interesting and provocative account raises a number of questions about bilingualism from a qualitative point of view, questions involving such difficult problems as active versus passive bilingualism (in conversations where each speaks his "easiest" language and listeners appear to understand), the issue of whether a linguistic boundary constitutes a language or dialect difference, and the relative prestige (or lack of it) of bilingualism. As these issues will be discussed in section 1.2 below, let it suffice to mention here that the relatively large size of the Siane language does not appear to have impeded a fair amount of bilingualism among its speakers, at least those in border areas. The fact that the Siane live in a very densely populated area and are surrounded on all sides by other language groups is probably one of the reasons for this; another very important reason is that the Siane traditionally did not appear to regard speaking Siane as a basis for any type of political identity. Salisbury is quite explicit that (as of 1952–53) they had:

> no consciousness of an overriding political unity. . . . The same general culture . . . continues both to east and west of the Siane, with no sharp discontinuities, with non-Siane attending Siane ceremonies and vice-versa. Interaction between Siane and non-Siane is also the rule, and a statistical analysis of the marriage pattern indicates that marriages are random as between Siane and non-Siane. (Salisbury 1962: 1)

Other ethnographers working in various inland areas of Papua New Guinea have also noticed multilingualism in border areas between middle-range languages. Harding, discussing the interior of the Huon Peninsula in Morobe Province, speaks of:

> an area of intergrading, . . . known by the indigenous people as the 'head' of the Komba, Selepet and Timbe peoples. Linguistically, the area is mainly Komba, but the Timbe and Selepet are close at hand and there is a marked degree of multilingualism. (Harding 1965: 199)

It should be noted that the population figures given for these three Papuan languages of the Huon Stock are ten thousand speakers each for Komba and Timbe, and fifty-five hundred for Selepet (Hooley and McElhanon 1970: 1082).

Rappaport, discussing the Maring (population forty-five hundred according to Wurm 1971a: 550), states that four of the fifty married women and widows living in the Maring local group of two hundred which he studied in 1962–63 "came from nearby Karam-speaking groups" (Rappaport 1967: 102). Karam (population ten to fourteen thousand) belongs to a family quite distant from Maring, with which it shares only "19% basic vocabulary cognates" (Wurm 1971a: 553). Rappaport (1967: 102, n.2) also states that:

> marriage between Jimi Valley Maring and Narak speakers is frequent. It may be that propinquity, rather than linguistic affiliation, is the decisive factor in intergroup marriage.

Though the status of Narak has been somewhat disputed in the literature, Cook (1966: 442) affirms that both according to its degree of cognation with Maring (only 57 percent) and according to the views of Maring and Narak speakers, Maring and Narak are separate languages. Wurm (1971a: 550) concurs with this view, listing Narak as a separate language with approximately forty-five hundred speakers. Though Rappaport does not draw any conclusion on bilingualism from his intermarriage data, we can conclude that wives from both Karam and Narak would probably have become bilingual in Maring upon marrying into that language group, and that maintaining affinal relations among the various groups probably also made for a certain amount of bilingualism among the men as well.

Taking one further example of a middle-range Papuan-speaking group in the Highlands, Wagner (1969) has this to say about the Daribi, of the extreme south of Chimbu Province:

> Approximately 3000 Daribi live on the volcanic plateau north of Mt. Karimui and in the adjacent limestone country to the west; they have intermarried extensively with a pocket of 1000 Tudawe [= Pawaia] speakers living northeast of the mountain. (Wagner 1969: 56)

According to Wurm (1971a), the Mikaru-speaking Daribi number approximately four thousand, and the Pawaia, who belong to a different family, somewhat under two thousand (Wurm 1971a: 551).

There is a certain amount of evidence that where large and small groups were in contact, it was generally the members of the small group or isolate who became bilingual, though some of the members of the larger linguistic groups also found it advantageous (or necessary) to learn the others' language. Among the larger groups neighboring the Usarufa discussed in section 1.1.1, Berndt (1954: 291) remarks that:

> bilingualism . . . is much more common in the border districts than in those which have rather less frequent contact with people speaking languages other than their own. . . . Members of the three larger language units rarely trouble to learn Uturupa [= Usarufa], except in matters involving continued personal contact—such as, especially, alien women married to Uturupa men.

Nevertheless it seems that a considerable number of foreign women did marry into Usarufa, as is shown in the following quotation:

> Kemiju (Yate), Moiife (Usarufa), Ofafina and Asafina (Fore) are bitter enemies of Kogu (Usarufa), but they are also its main source of wives as well as its guests for certain festivals, ceremonies, and so on. They comprise the principal units in the zone of most intensive interaction centering on Kogu . . . they are engaged jointly in so many transactions, . . . they come in contact with one another fairly regularly and are dependent on one another, and . . . their territories adjoin. (Berndt 1962: 234)

It also appears that in this border area, the larger groups also knew each other's languages to some extent. Berndt mentions that in three border villages of the Fore, "the Fore language predominates, with some Jate" (Berndt 1962: 8).

The five multilingual situations discussed in this section have all involved linguistic groups of the middle range, numbering between about twenty-five hundred (Nomane, in the Siane example), and fifteen thousand (Siane itself). In addition, all five have involved border areas, in four of which intermarriage has been specifically mentioned. Both Salisbury and Rappaport stress the lack of political unity or common identity within the language group, and the fact that linguistic differences do not seem to constitute a barrier to intermarriage. One is left with the distinct impression that this is a situation common to many, if not most, linguistic border areas in the Highlands. As we shall see below in section 1.1.4, this situation can indeed be generalized to at least three of the nine "large languages" of the Highlands.

1.1.4. *Large Languages of the Highlands*

Though people in the central areas of the large language groups (those numbering over 30,000 in Table 5-1) are likely to be much more numerous than those living in the central areas of the smaller language groups we have so far been discussing, the phenomenon of multilingualism in border areas appears to be just as common in these groups as in the smaller ones. Brookfield and Brown have this to say about the Chimbu, which with sixty thousand speakers is probably the second or third largest language group in Papua New Guinea:

> The high mountains which enclose the Chimbus to the east, north, and north-west have not proved a barrier to trade, migration, and marriage. To the east are Asaro-speaking people, . . . in another language family. For the last three generations at least, the Chimbus have intermarried with Asaro people near Mirima and Korfena, and about 350 have established villages on land which they acquired from their affines. Yonggamugl Chimbus have migrated eastward to establish villages among Siane-speaking people, . . . with whom they intermarry. To the north-east, the Chimbus have similar relations with the Bundi (Gende) people. In these cases visiting and ceremonial activities continue with the people of the Chimbu Valley. (Brookfield and Brown 1963: 78)

Not only Asaro (population 11,597) but also Gende (population 8,000) and Siane (population 15,336) are in a family different from that of Chimbu. And the situation (intermarriage, visiting for ceremonials) sounds very similar to that described by Salisbury. On this basis, we are justified in postulating a certain amount of multilingualism, at least (conservatively) among those who are actually intermarried with members of other language groups, and probably extending to a majority of those in border villages.

Brookfield and Brown (1963) go on to discuss relationships with the Chimbu's neighbors to the southeast, south, and west, with whom linguistic and cultural ties are "much closer" (p. 78) than those with the Asaro, Gende, and Siane. On the Wahgi, to the west of Chimbu, they say:

> At the border of Chimbu and Wahgi, territories have interpenetrated, intermarriage is common, and languages, which belong to different sub-families, are mutually understood by the frontier groups. (Brookfield and Brown 1963: 78)

According to Wurm (1964), such cases of bilingualism at the borders of large languages were not at all uncommon. He says:

The spreading of large languages is progressing at the present day, and the widespread bilingualism is one of the means by which one language gradually supersedes another. . . . This may lead to the gradual extinction of small languages. (Wurm 1964: 97)

Our second case of language contact in the border area of a large language group is that of the Huli, as discussed by Glasse (1968). In describing Huli relationships with their neighbors, Glasse does not appear to feel there is much contact. He states that the Huli (population fifty-four thousand according to Wurm 1971a: 551) "exchange visits and occasionally intermarry" (Glasse 1968: 20) with the Waga, the Dugube, the Ipili (population forty-five hundred according to Wurm 1971a: 550) and the Duna (population six thousand according to Wurm 1971a: 551). Nevertheless he comments in discussing the geographical extension of Huli that "just where the dividing line—or zone of transition—between Huli and Duna culture is to be found, was still uncertain in 1959" (Glasse 1968: 18). The reason for construing the border area as a "zone of transition" appears in a chance remark regarding the location of the patrol post at Koroba, "in a bilingual area where Huli and Duna are both spoken" (p. 18). It is of note that Duna is the most distantly related language of any of the Huli's neighbors, being in a different family and showing only 25 percent cognates with Huli according to Wurm (1971a: 557). The Huli-Duna border area is one of the very few areas where two languages are shown as overlapping on Wurm's (1961) map of the Highlands languages.

Lastly, Strathern (1972) gives some evidence regarding the Melpa (the second largest Papuan language, at sixty thousand) of the Mount Hagen area in the Western Highlands. She says (pp. 3–4):

North of the Gumant [River] people speak Melpa . . . almost exclusively, while to the south many understand both Melpa and the closely related Temboka (a dialect of Gawigl . . .). Warfare, group expansions and migrations in the recent past had led to the intermingling of Temboka and Melpa groups in the immediate vicinity of the present town.

Summarizing very briefly, it is clear that though only a minority of the speakers of the large Highlands languages had occasion to become bi- or multilingual, this was a common phenomenon whose incidence was principally dictated by demography. Language differences were not in and of themselves considered as barriers to communication.

1.2. Qualitative Aspects of Multilingualism in the Languages of Papua New Guinea

1.2.1. *Languages, Dialects, Intelligibility, and Passive Bilingualism*

Finishing our discussion of language distribution with the "large" languages of the Highlands has perhaps given a false impression of less linguistic diversity than actually exists. For even in these large languages, there was no linguistic homogeneity across all thirty thousand or fifty thousand speakers, and as has been attested to in 1.1 above, speakers did not recognize or often even know of the existence of such large linguistic groups. Instead, the situation was, and is, one of a multiplicity of speech varieties, many of which are very difficult to classify as between languages and dialects. From the point of view of linguistic identity of a particular speaker or group of speakers, and even sometimes from the point of view of intelligibility, two speech varieties which seem to diverge only at the "dialect" level will count as separate languages. Conversely, two neighboring speech varieties that differ at the "language" level may have sufficient contacts to allow everyone to become passively bilingual, a situation that superficially resembles mutual intelligibility.

The Buang dialects described in chapter 6 constitute an example of the language-dialect problem. The three main Buang speech varieties, located along the Snake River Valley in Morobe Province south of Lae, are related in the chain-dialect form common throughout Papua New Guinea. Lexicostatistic results (chapter 7, this volume, as well as Hooley and McElhanon 1970) indicate that "Headwaters" and "Mapos" Buang are two dialects of one language ("Central Buang," according to Hooley and McElhanon), while the third, "Manga Buang," is to be classified as a separate language. Nevertheless, in one Mapos-dialect village near the Manga border, people had more trouble understanding the closely related Headwaters dialect (which they rarely had an opportunity to hear) than the more distantly related Manga language (which they heard often). Headwaters, Mapos, and Manga speakers, when meeting anyone from one of the other two groups, always use their native variety, as does their interlocutor. The only people to become actively rather than passively bilingual in one of the speech varieties other than their native variety were in-married other-dialect (or other-language) women. However these constituted a very small proportion of the population. In seven villages where there were approximately 670 married women, only 27 were from other speech varieties, i.e., approximately 4 percent of the married women. Most of the Buang people with whom I spoke did not recognize that

Manga was more different from Headwaters, and Mapos, though they all recognized the three major divisions.

Though Buang is unusual in being one of the few relatively large inland Austronesian language groups, the sociolinguistic situation involving chain dialects and languages, more intelligibility and heightened cognate percentages at dialect or language borders, and much passive bilingualism, is found all over Papua New Guinea in the distribution particularly of the Papuan languages. The most detailed and comprehensive study of chain relationships is Dutton 1969. Dutton uses the complex relationships among the languages and dialects of the Koiarian language family as an aid in reconstructing the history and patterns of migration of the Koiarian-speaking peoples. Dutton's careful work shows that five of the six Koiarian languages[8] have numerous dialects, and in all six of the languages, virtually every village is to some extent distinguishable in its speech from others sharing the same "dialect." For example, Mountain Koiari, with a population of approximately 3,700, is divided into six dialects, of which Dutton's remarks on the Southern Dialect (population 347, spread among six villages) are illustrative of the general state of relationships in language-dialect chains (Dutton 1969: 49):

> This is a small dialect . . . markedly different from its northern and western counterparts sharing only an average of 68–76% basic vocabulary with its nearest neighbour, the Central Dialect. Normally this degree of lexical relationship would be considered too low for a dialect-level relationship. However, since the grammatical structure of the Southern Dialect is very much akin to the rest of Mountain Koiari it is here regarded as merely a divergent dialect of this language rather than a separate, though very closely related, language. Part of the reason for its low lexical relationship with the Central Dialect probably lies in the fact that it is in close contact with Koiari and Barai to the south and east.
>
> Lexically and phonologically the Southern Dialect is also divergent within itself. Thus, at Naoro, villagers living on opposite sides of the village 'street' speak quite differently from one another.

That this situation is also typical of the large languages of the Highlands has been recognized since Wurm and Laycock's classic article on language and dialect (1961), in which they discussed speech varieties of

8. In the sixth, Koita, the complexity of the linguistic situation is due to a great deal of bilingualism in Motu, as discussed in section 1.1.2, rather than to dialect diversity.

the East New Guinea Highlands Phylum sharing cognate percentages of between 60 and 80 percent. They noted a tendency towards greater mutual intelligibility among speech varieties in the 70-80 percent range, but also warned that such "intelligibility" can be due in part to such "speaker-related" factors as passive bilingualism and the subject of the discourse.

As an illustration of the "dialect" diversity that exists even in the very largest Papuan languages, we shall consider the case of Kewa, on which we are fortunate in having a detailed dialect study (Franklin 1968). Franklin gives 39,453 as a conservative population estimate for Kewa (p. 9), making it the fifth largest of the Papuan languages listed in Table 5-1. Franklin (1968: 9) distinguishes three major dialects of Kewa: West (population 17,921), East (population 17,758), and South (population 3,774). These can, however, be further subdivided, as the West dialect contains a subdialect referred to as Northwestern (population 6,864), and the South dialect contains a subdialect called Southeastern (population 404). In addition,

> There are 3,652 speakers located on the putative boundary of the East and South, all of which are classed as East Dialect speakers. This line actually represents an imagined transition zone between the two dialects. (Franklin 1968: 9)

Counting the two subdialects and the transition zone, we now have Kewa divided into six speech varieties. But Franklin (1968: 1) also notes that:

> there is a great deal of regionalism within the language so that few clans ever speak exactly the same as their neighbours. . . . This is often reflected in their mimicry of how a group nearby speaks. . . . For example, if such a nearby group has vowel nasalisation and the focal group does not, the latter will deliberately nasalise all vowels, showing their recognition (in some sense) of one point of difference.

Maps showing isoglosses and distribution of particular lexical items confirm this picture of ordered, but marked, diversity.

Many other authors confirm the fact that virtually all over Papua New Guinea, people pay very great attention to small linguistic differences in differentiating themselves from their neighbors. In addition to Franklin's observations for the Kewa of the Southern Highlands, we have similar statements from Cook (1966), discussing the relationships of Narak (Western Highlands) with its neighbors. He says:

> Many natives of these small speech communities are extremely sensitive to even the most minor of dialect differences and,

within a limited spatial range, a perceptive informant can tell you almost precisely in which village an individual was raised as a child. Dialect variations constitute one source of humour, and the speech of natives from slightly or greatly varying speech communities is often the subject of exaggerated mimicry by local inhabitants. (Cook 1966: 442)

Z'graggen (1971: passim) frequently mentions the accuracy of speakers' identification of differences, in his survey of Madang Province languages. For example, regarding the inhabitants of Gumalu village, he says, "Informants insisted on having their own distinct language, although a high degree of mutual intelligibility was admitted" (Z'graggen 1971: 26). Further on (p. 27), he continues:

> All my informants insisted, even after repeated inquiries, that there was a considerable difference between Yoidik and its neighbours, but they admitted that there was a high degree of mutual intelligibility.

As a last example, my own work on Buang dialects again confirms the great importance speakers place on recognizing the small linguistic details that differentiate one village from the next. In Mambump village (a village located near the middle of the Headwaters dialect) where I lived, people distinguished not only among Headwaters, Mapos, and Manga, but also among three subvarieties of Headwaters, citing lexical and phonological correspondences, though exactly what features differentiated Mapos from Manga most were unable to say. The following quotation shows the close parallel with the Kewa and Narak cases cited above:

> That people are interested in other languages and dialects is evident in linguistic play, particularly in mimicry, where it is possible to observe the stereotypes people hold about the phonology of other languages. Mambump people, mimicking [Mapos people] . . . pretended to speak like toothless old people, making [s]'s into [š]'s. (Sankoff 1968: 104)

In addition to the detailed evidence from Kewa, Narak, and Buang, the very existence of small differences (e.g., in cognate percentages) reported from one village to the next, in situations where people were stated to be in close contact, in a number of studies (especially Dutton 1969, who has paid more attention to documenting such differences), bears witness to the fact that Papuans and New Guineans were often very much aware of the linguistic details, great or small, differentiating them from their neighbors.

Some readers may feel that this discussion of dialect difference has little to do with bilingualism, except in the case that the "dialect" in question is really sufficiently distinct to be considered a separate language (and we have seen that there are many such marginal cases). However, from the point of view of a speaker who does not know of the existence of, or recognize any affiliation with, local groups speaking other "dialects" of his own language, but who has through contact with near neighbors learned to recognize and understand (and perhaps also produce, sometimes only in a stereotyped form) their dialect or language, be the differences from his/her own great or small, perhaps the distinction is of secondary importance. This is not to say that people were unable to distinguish degrees of difference, as well as qualitative differences (as between language and dialect). The Buang device for measuring differences of degree was the length of time a person from one's home village would need to stay in village X in order to be able to "hear" (i.e., understand) the speech variety spoken there. This model was applied to speech varieties within their own language family. For unrelated languages, this model was not applied, they being regarded as qualitatively different.

Knowledge of foreign speech varieties, whether active or passive, varied enormously in precolonial New Guinea, but we do have evidence that where it did exist, it was socially valued. The next section attempts to set this differential knowledge and use within a social matrix.

1.2.2. *Multilingualism (Knowledge of Foreign Speech Varieties) and Its Social Uses*

The reasons for the existence of multilingualism in precolonial Papua New Guinea have been cited as involving a combination of demographic considerations (especially population density and size of language groupings) and the socially necessary contacts of trade and intermarriage. It has been clear that even in isolates, in communities visited by foreign-language traders, and in border areas, knowledge (whether active or passive) of foreign speech varieties has not been uniformly distributed among all members of the population. Differential knowledge by sex has been discussed with respect to each of the three types of multilingual situation presented in section 1.1. Here we shall briefly consider three other aspects of multilingualism: its prestige value, its role in oral literature and verbal art, and its possible relationship to language differentiation.

Salisbury's view that bilingualism "is treated as a desirable accomplishment" (Salisbury 1962: 4) among the Siane has been mentioned in section 1.1.3 above. Discussing the fact that men of high status often made speeches in Dene, he says:

It seems likely that there is a relationship between high status and observed bilingualism, but such a relationship may well be due to high status (or nearness to me) giving more opportunity to display linguistic ability. (Salisbury 1962: 8)

It is well known that traditional leaders in Papua New Guinea were highly skilled in rhetoric, and it may well be that in areas where the learning of foreign languages was possible, aspiring politicians added such foreign speech varieties to their battery of rhetorical skills, as suggested in chapter 1, this volume.

The use of foreign languages in oral literature and verbal art is also mentioned by Salisbury for the Siane, who generally sing songs in languages other than Siane. In Buang poetry, other-dialect synonyms are often used to make up semantic pairs necessary to the parallel structure of the poems. In Kewa, where the initiation cult puts a taboo on the use of certain words, other-dialect equivalents are often used in their place (Franklin 1968: 27–28). Though in other areas verbal art and sacred language appear to differ from the everyday language more in terms of various systematic ways of altering everyday forms (cf. Laycock 1969 on Buin songs, as well as Malinowski's classic work on the language of Trobriand gardening magic, 1935), certainly for Kewa and Buang, knowledge of foreign forms is part of the repertoire for verbal art and elaboration. In Buang, puns based on foreign synonyms constitute a commonly heard form of joke. This is one reason for the existence of the "multiple cognates" discussed by Wurm and Laycock (1961: 134) as being present

> in a situation in which the speakers of one form of speech use only one of a pair of items with the same meaning, but recognize the other member of a pair when it is used by the speakers of another form of speech.

Based on Buang data, I would further specify "use only one of a pair of items with the same meaning in their everyday speech, but use the other member of the pair in various marked usages, including poetry, irony, puns, etc." This "other member" may or may not be known to be the commonly used term for that meaning by neighboring or distant groups (Sankoff 1977a).

As with the other two themes in this section, I begin this paragraph with a suggestion from Salisbury, who seeks to relate the prestige of bilingualism to a more rapid rate of language differentiation. Quoting him at length, he states:

> If to know a foreign language is prestigeful, and situations exist where interpretation is a ceremonial device for the individual to show his knowledge, while at the same time stressing the impor-

tance of the occasion, then interpretation will be used more than is necessary to ensure communication. It is clearly pointless to interpret speeches to people of the same speech community, but if differences of speech are magnified so that it is possible to deny that the neighboring group speaks the same language, point is added to the making of interpretations. Innovations may be added to language with no fear of the language ceasing to be understandable, as one's own village are all aware of the innovation and can translate for strangers. In short, the counterpart of an emphasis on bilingualism and interpretation is an added intensity of local patriotism and ethnocentrism regarding the local dialect. Linguistic differentiation and change would then be given added impetus by political rivalries between groups, while existing speech barriers are encouraged by individuals wishing to prove their ability to learn difficult, exotic languages. (Salisbury 1962: 11–12)

It seems possible and indeed quite apt to extend Salisbury's argument to the situation of local pride in difference, coupled with a rather thorough knowledge of the nature of the differences, even where such emphasis is not placed on translation. In fact this is a situation that appears to be extremely widespread in Papua New Guinea. Whether or not it really does cause more rapid differentiation of neighboring speech varieties, or even more rapid overall change of all the speech varieties together is, however, not an easy question. It may be a situation in which lexical and phonological diffusion is favored, coupled with many basic similarities in syntax and semantics that would allow for more communication with "lower than usual" cognate percentages, as again has been observed all over Papua New Guinea. Areal features aiding communication may indeed be diffused across language family boundaries, creating a Sprachbund-like situation.

Here we are venturing, but only very tentatively, into a consideration of the possible linguistic effects of a situation (language contact and bilingualism) that is itself only very imperfectly known. In order to go any further, a much better knowledge of the situation would be required. Nevertheless, it is clear that the way people use languages is of great importance in understanding the structure and relationships of those languages.

1.3. Summary

The attempt in section 1 of this chapter to reconstruct the extent and nature of multilingualism in precolonial Papua New Guinea would appear to lead to a conclusion very different from the view expressed by Laycock, who states that, given the linguistic diversity of Papua New Guinea, one would expect a fair amount of bilingualism, but in fact in pre-European times native knowledge of other languages was apparently not as extensive as was, for example, the knowledge of other languages on the part of Australian aboriginals. There are a number of reasons for this: (1) there was often extreme dissimilarity between neighbouring languages; (2) the major language groups in New Guinea are relatively large, larger than in Australia, so that it was possible to travel a fair distance without encountering very different tongues; (3) many factors operate against contact between different linguistic groups. In the Sepik area the main social unit was the village, and even trading with other villages of the same linguistic community was fraught with suspicion. Trading was carried on across linguistic groups— often in the form of "silent trading," where, for example, hills natives would lay down their yams and sweet potato against the fish from the river, until an agreement was reached—but the more normal social interaction was warfare, where a knowledge of the other language was not necessary. (Laycock 1966: 44)

In my attempt to seek out cases of multilingualism and generalize from them, I did not mean to deny the existence, as well, of the type of situation Laycock describes. In sparsely populated areas, in areas where there were awesome natural barriers like swamps or high mountains, in areas where there were great cultural differences or a state of warfare that impeded amicable communication, people would not speak or understand their neighbors' languages.

Indeed, cases of "silent trade" are attested for areas other than the Sepik. Harding, describing trade encounters between the "bush" and coastal peoples on the Rai Coast, says:

At the old-time markets the two groups of men and women, one to three dozen people on each side, sat down in two rows facing each other. The bush people normally initiated the transaction by pushing forward a net bag of food and taking back the goods—fish, coconuts, and pots—which the Sio had in front of him. . . . The exchanges were conducted largely in silence, without haggling or bargaining. (Harding 1967: 63–64)

Hogbin makes a similar comment about trade between coastal and interior peoples on the southern side of the Huon Gulf:

The peoples of the coast and the interior . . . had no common tongue and had to conduct their barter either through a few interpreters or by means of signs. (Hogbin 1947: 24)

Such cases seem to have occurred where a combination of geographical and cultural barriers made communication difficult, the prototypical case being where the people of the last mountain village in an inland trade circuit came down to the coast to trade with the coastal dwellers. (Though in other areas, despite very great linguistic differences, e.g., in the case of Koita-Motu, the mountain people came down to the coast and integrated with the coastal people.)

For reasons explained in various parts of section 1 above, I do not feel that the first two of the reasons adduced by Laycock were in fact operative to any great degree. The third factor, as he himself admits, was variable and depended very much on local circumstances. And Laycock himself does admit some bilingualism, as he goes on to say:

> Nevertheless, many natives did pick up at least smatterings of languages, sometimes of several different languages, and there existed in native communities . . . a small proportion of people with an interest in foreign cultures and languages. In complex linguistic areas like the Sepik it was customary for young boys to be exchanged between villages at the age of about ten, so that they could grow up bilingual and mediate in disputes. But the knowledge of foreign languages was individual and restricted. (Laycock 1966: 44)

In looking at the cases of multilingualism that have been described, and in attempting to draw inferences from them to those situations on which I have no information, I have come to a set of conclusions which must, however, differ from Laycock's. First, I believe that there has probably been in Papua New Guinea a great deal more multilingualism than is usually admitted. For various reasons, the subject has been very much neglected. Most of the ethnographic sources I consulted mentioned marriage and/or trade with neighboring groups at least in a footnote, and these neighboring groups often turned out upon further checking to speak a different language, sometimes very different, but few ethnographers devoted any attention to the linguistic consequences. Conversely, many of the linguistic surveys explained the heightened proportion of cognates in certain unlikely speech varieties by postulating borrowing between the two, but did not state what type of bilingual situation might have produced the borrowing. There is a general lack of attention to boundary problems, a tacit acceptance of the "one language = one culture" assumption, and a concentration on phenomena internal to the language or culture in question, with a consequent neglect, even underrating, of boundary problems of all sorts. This focus is maintained despite the considerable evidence that linguistic identity was generally highly local, as one further quotation, this time for Kewa, indicates:

Socially, the Kewa language does not represent any political or national group. In fact, many speakers from separate dialects will deny that they speak the same language. (Franklin 1968: 1)

Glasse is the only author to state otherwise, remarking that:

Unlike many highland peoples, the Huli are conscious of their cultural homogeneity and they are aware of the differences between their own social institutions and those of their neighbors. This cultural self-consciousness may be partly attributed to the mobility of the population. With no high mountain ranges to cross, travel is comparatively easy, and people often maintain two or three homesteads in different places. (Glasse 1968: 20)

At least on one of their borders, however, the Huli are not at all clearly demarcated from their (linguistically) most different neighbors, the Duna, and there is a sizable area of bilingualism, as described in section 1.1.4 above.

Second, over much of Papua New Guinea, though people had a great deal of pride in, and derived some of their identity from, their own local speech variety, often exaggerating its differences from the speech of their neighbors, this went hand-in-hand with an openness of attitude and an interest in the learning of other speech varieties.

Third, language boundaries were not necessarily considered barriers to trade, intermarriage, and other types of communication.

Fourth, inasmuch as the learning of other speech varieties, in border areas, coastal areas visited by traders, and language isolates, was conditioned by social roles and relationships, multilingualism was differentially distributed among members of any given population.

Fifth, where multilingualism did exist, it was a resource that formed part of the set of rhetorical devices put to use by politicians and other orators.

The above account is necessarily lacking in some details, given the paucity of information available on multilingualism in precoionial Papua New Guinea. Many readers with personal experience of one or another of the types of situations described may find some of the details to be in error, and perhaps this will urge them to make available more information. The wealth of material published since approximately 1965, particularly the many language surveys of a large number of areas, has made possible this attempt at reconstruction, and it is hoped that, by the end of another decade, the picture may be more complete.

Clearly, the hundred years or so of colonial rule in Papua New Guinea has wrought enormous changes of many kinds, not least in the area of multilingualism. In section 2, we turn to a consideration of multilingualism directly related to the presence of Europeans in Papua New Guinea.

2. MULTILINGUALISM IN THE COLONIAL PERIOD

With the postindependence period of Papua New Guinea history just beginning, the time is opportune for an assessment of the multilingual situation at the end of almost a century of colonial rule. Section 2.1 below will be devoted to a brief examination of the spread of regional *lingue franche,* mainly by the various Christian missions, and in section 2.2, we shall consider the use of the three official languages of Papua New Guinea: Hiri Motu, Tok Pisin, and English.

2.1. Regional Languages in Papua New Guinea

Many of the missions in Papua New Guinea found it difficult or impossible to use all of the languages of a region in their schools and churches, especially in areas of extreme linguistic diversity. The result was often the spread of a particular language to neighboring populations, for whom it became a "church language." In some cases, missionaries used a language which was already spoken extensively as a second language. Thus Dobuan, an Austronesian language widely known by participants in the Kula trade (as we saw in section 1.1.2 above) was used by the Methodists in the Milne Bay area (Lawton 1977). Similarly, the London Missionary Society used Motu in the Central District (now Province) of Papua (Taylor 1977). A third Austronesian trade language, Suau, was used by the London Missionary Society along the southeast coast of Papua, where Mailu traders had already spread it extensively (Abel 1977).

Another Austronesian language which has become a regional *lingua franca* is Kuanua, or Tolai, already the language with by far the largest number of speakers in the New Ireland–New Britain area. Wurm (1971c: 1018) explains that Kuanua

> has been adopted as the mission language by the Methodist Mission throughout the New Britain–New Ireland region, and it is also used by the Catholic Mission, but only for the Tolai area itself. The language is now a quite widespread *lingua franca* in these areas.

Fry (1977: 867) states that at the height of its use as a second language, during the period 1950–60, as many as fifteen thousand people may have known and used Kuanua as a second language. Though Kuanua, like other mission languages, has declined since about 1960, when government policy made English the language of education, its use on

Rabaul radio may have helped maintain knowledge of it as a second language.

Two other Austronesian languages widely used by the Lutheran mission are Gedaged (Graged, Bel) in Madang Province and Yabem in the Huon Gulf area of Morobe Province. Yabem, which according to Hooley and McElhanon (1970: 1086) has 2,900 first-language speakers, probably numbers at least 25,000 second-language speakers,[9] and is used to some extent at least as a regional *lingua franca* in nonmission contexts.[10] (This generalization is based on my own observations of situations in which Buang speakers communicated with other Morobe Province Lutherans in Yabem, despite the fact that both parties to the interaction could have used Tok Pisin. Such languages may be of preferred usage in some cases in order to stress regional or religious solidarity.)

The number of Papuan languages which mission use has promoted to regional *lingua franca* status is somewhat smaller. They include Orokolo and Toaripi in the Gulf Province (Wurm 1971c: 1018; Brown 1976), and Kiwai, in the Fly Delta area of the Western Province (Wurm 1966: 141).

The Papuan language with the greatest second-language use has also been the most successful of the *lingue franche* of the Lutherans in Papua New Guinea. Originally spoken by only about 600 people, Kâte has been used by the Lutheran mission in the populous Huon Peninsula of Morobe Province for the past seventy years. This has resulted in an estimated 75,000 speakers of Kâte as a second language, with perhaps another 40,000 who have a passive knowledge (Renck 1977b: 844).

It appears that the heyday of mission-propagated regional *lingue franche* has passed. At one time, people wishing to send their children to school had no choice but to have them educated (at least at the primary level, which was the only schooling available for almost everyone until recent times) in one of these *lingue franche*. But "since 1960 it has been government policy not to register or recognize mission schools which use such languages" (Rowley 1965: 146), which means lack of subsidy for these schools. With no institutional support, re-

---

9. This figure, given by Renck (1977a: 852) agrees with my own estimate, drawn from observations of Lutheran Church activities in the Huon Gulf area. It is interesting to note that the close similarities between Yabem and Bukaua (Capell 1949), said by Hogbin to have served as a *lingua franca* in the Huon Gulf area, may have aided in the dissemination of Yabem.

10. Based on field research in coastal areas of Morobe Province almost a decade after my own, Bradshaw (in press) came to the conclusion that the use of Yabem as a second language was becoming increasingly restricted to church contexts.

gional *lingue franche* are losing ground to English, Tok Pisin, or Hiri Motu, though to the extent to which they continue to be used as religious languages, they may continue to be spoken as second languages by many people for some time to come. Though the regional *lingue franche* propagated by the various missions number many thousands of speakers, none of them surpasses the largest of the Papuan languages discussed in section 1 above, and in terms of their numbers of speakers, they are no match for the national *lingue franche* to be discussed below in section 2.2.

2.2. Official Languages in Papua New Guinea

2.2.1. *Hiri Motu*

Of the *lingue franche* discussed earlier in this chapter, only one has acceded to the status of one of Papua New Guinea's official languages. This is the language today called Hiri Motu, formerly known as "Police Motu." Though doubt has recently been cast on the relationship today's Hiri Motu may actually have with the language of the *hiri* trade voyages (cf. fn. 5 above), the accepted view has run somewhat as follows. After a good start as one of the most widely used precolonial trade languages,

> this lingua franca was later adopted by the administration of British New Guinea for use by the native police force, the Royal Papuan Constabulary—hence its name "Police Motu"—and as the unofficial administrative language for native affairs. (Wurm 1969: 35)

Hiri Motu is an official language in that it is one of the three languages in which members may speak in the House of Assembly, and in which simultaneous translation is provided. Official government documents, notices, etc., are printed in three languages, and the radio stations daily broadcast the news in all three. But very rarely is a speech in Hiri Motu actually heard in the House of Assembly. Of the three official languages, it is Hiri Motu that has the fewest speakers overall, and that is the most restricted regionally.

Table 5-2 shows the overall proportion of speakers of Hiri Motu and of the other two official languages, Tok Pisin and English. Figures are from the 1966 and 1971 population censuses of Papua New Guinea. Though all three have increased considerably in numbers of speakers in the five year period, it is clear that even in 1966, each of them had more speakers than any of the large Highlands languages. (In comparing the figures given for the three official languages with those cited for the large languages of the Highlands, it should be remembered that popula-

Language		Male	Female	Total	Percentage of total population 10 yrs. and older
English	1971	211,651	112,115	323,766	20.4
	1966	130,429	62,908	193,337	13.3
Tok Pisin	1971	469,770	237,355	707,125	44.5
	1966	369,855	161,835	531,690	36.5
Hiri Motu	1971	103,016	47,636	150,652	9.5
	1966	86,665	31,910	118,575	8.3

TABLE 5-2. Population ten years of age and over speaking each of the official languages in 1966 and 1971 (expatriates excluded). Data abstracted from Papua New Guinea census bulletins.

tion estimates for the latter included all speakers, whereas these are based on speakers over age ten only.)

The regional character of Hiri Motu becomes more evident on examining Table 5-3, which shows the number and proportion of speakers of the three languages by District. (Districts have become Provinces since 1971.)[11] It is readily observable that second-language speakers of Hiri Motu are almost entirely confined to the five Districts of coastal Papua, and that in all five, Hiri Motu speakers greatly outnumber Tok Pisin speakers. Comparing English and Hiri Motu speakers, however, we see that English is coming to be almost as widely known as Hiri Motu in Papua. Census data on the number of people speaking various combinations of the official languages showed that in 1966 many thousands more people in these five Districts could speak "only Hiri Motu" than "only English" (approximately 53,300 versus 24,900). By 1971, however, "only English" had grown to 38,400 whereas "only Hiri Motu" had remained about the same (approx. 54,700). In Milne Bay District, English had even become the best-known of the three official languages (the only District where this is the case, though Northern looks like a likely candidate for the next census, with only one more person speaking Hiri Motu than speaking English in 1971!) Hiri Motu was, in 1971, still the most practical *lingua franca* in the Central, Gulf, and Western Districts.

11. This chapter, written in 1974, conserves the then current political subdivisions of Papua New Guinea, i.e., the Districts whose titles appear in Table 5-3 and elsewhere, principally because these are the categories of the 1966 and 1971 census data upon which this section is largely based. The current Provinces retain the old District boundaries.

	Districts	Tok Pisin		English		Hiri Motu	
		No.	%	No.	%	No.	%
Papuan Coastal	Central	41,772	36.0	52,778	45.5	70,570	60.8
	Northern	11,991	28.6	18,683	44.5	18,684	44.5
	Gulf	4,446	12.5	8,490	23.9	12,701	35.7
	Milne Bay	5,742	8.1	25,061	35.3	17,665	24.9
	Western	4,198	9.5	10,628	24.0	13,730	31.0
New Guinea Islands	New Ireland	37,443	93.1	14,013	34.8	509	1.3
	Manus	14,232	93.1	7,031	46.0	236	1.5
	West New Britain	34,090	89.4	11,377	29.8	623	1.6
	East New Britain	54,208	73.4	29,758	40.3	2,008	2.7
	Bougainville	45,575	76.1	21,569	36.0	1,596	2.7
New Guinea Coastal	East Sepik	91,031	82.1	19,861	17.9	1,127	1.0
	West Sepik	39,223	63.9	7,457	12.3	422	0.7
	Madang	74,950	68.9	21,522	19.8	1,215	1.1
	Morobe	93,175	59.3	25,941	16.5	4,333	2.8
Highlands	Eastern Highlands	50,863	33.5	13,589	8.9	1,570	1.0
	Chimbu	27,604	26.4	6,909	6.6	537	0.5
	Western Highlands	56,228	24.3	19,900	8.6	1,460	0.6
	Southern Highlands	20,356	15.9	9,109	7.1	1,566	1.2

TABLE 5-3. The number and proportion of Papuans and New Guineas age ten and over speaking Tok Pisin, English, and Hiri Motu in each District in 1971.

Note: For each language, italicized percentages are those that exceed the national average for that language. (Data abstracted from Table 8 of the 1971 Census Bulletins for each District.) Note that the (now abolished) political division between Papua and New Guinea is entirely unrelated to the distinction between Papuan and Austronesian languages.

2.2.2. *Tok Pisin*

Useful materials on the linguistic aspects of Tok Pisin (otherwise known as New Guinea Pidgin, Pidgin (in the census reports), Melanesian Pidgin, and Neo-Melanesian) exist in abundance, e.g., Dutton 1973; Hall 1943; Laycock 1970a; Mühlhäusler 1976b; Sankoff 1977b; Woolford 1977; Wurm 1971b; chapters 10, 11, and 12, this volume. There is also considerable literature available on the history and use of Tok Pisin, several of the most informative treatments being Laycock 1970b, Salisbury 1967, Wurm 1966–67, and Mühlhäusler (1975; 1976a).

We can see from Tables 5-2 and 5-3 that Tok Pisin is currently the most important language in Papua New Guinea as far as bilingualism is concerned. Not only does it have numerically more than twice as many speakers as either of the other two official languages; it also has a very impressive regional spread. As indicated in Table 5-3, Tok Pisin is the most widely spoken official language in all but the five Papuan Coastal Districts: Central, Northern, Gulf, Milne Bay, and Western.[12] In all of the New Guinea Coastal and Islands Districts, Tok Pisin is spoken by a proportion of people considerably higher than the national average of 44.5 percent. And even in the New Guinea Islands Districts, where the proportion of English speakers is far ahead of the national average of 20.4 percent, the number of Tok Pisin speakers in every case greatly exceeds the number of English speakers, and there are very few "English only" speakers. Tok Pisin currently dominates as the language of widest currency in the largest proportion of Districts.

2.2.3. *English*

As mentioned above, in 1971 English was numerically dominant in only one of the Districts of Papua New Guinea: the Milne Bay District. In the other Papuan Coastal Districts it ran second, often a

12. Landtman (1927) discusses the "pidgin-English" spoken by the Kiwai of the Fly River Delta during the period 1910–12, claiming that "many men in the coast villages" knew it:

> The explanation is that the men were commonly recruited to work on the pearl-fishing boats in Torres Straits and on the plantations in Central and Eastern Divisions, and their own languages and dialects being so different that they could not understand each other, pidgin-English became a sort of *lingua-franca* among themselves which they learnt from each other and spoke fairly well on returning to their villages after a period of three to six months of work. (Landtman 1927: v)

Though this variety is probably more akin to that spoken in the Torres Straits (cf. Dutton 1970), I do not know how many Kiwai still speak it, and whether they consider it to qualify as Tok Pisin and would report themselves as speakers of it in the census. I am indebted to Ann Chowning for bringing Landtman's discussion to my attention.

close second, to Hiri Motu. In all the other Districts it ran a rather poor second to Tok Pisin.

Quite expectedly, the Districts where English speakers exceed the national average are those which were earliest colonized and where the early missionaries set up schools—the New Guinea Islands and all of the Papuan Coastal Districts with the exception of the Western District. English speakers tend to be young, as English has been a school language and English schools in any numbers are largely a phenomenon of the 1960s and 1970s.

The gain in English during the years 1966–71 was quite remarkable—from 13.3 percent to 20.4 percent in the country as a whole. This is probably due to the great increase in school enrollments, especially with the phenomenal growth of towns in the period (cf. Table 5-4 below; Fig. 1-1, p. 7). This increase of 7 percentage points

Major towns of Papua New Guinea	% of Tok Pisin speakers 1966	1971	% of English speakers 1966	1971	% of Hiri Motu speakers 1966	1971	Total population (expatriates excluded) 1966	1971
Port Moresby (Central)	54.9	61.0	64.4	64.6	77.8	71.1	31,983	59,563
Lae (Morobe)	94.2	95.1	36.1	43.8	14.8	12.9	13,341	32,076
Rabaul (East New Britain)	97.1	94.0	37.4	51.4	11.9	7.3	6,925	22,292
Madang (Madang)	96.2	97.4	30.8	47.4	8.0	7.2	7,398	14,696
Wewak (East Sepik)	96.2	97.0	27.8	52.8	5.2	6.9	7,967	13,837
Goroka (E. Highlands)	89.6	85.9	31.6	41.4	14.3	9.1	3,890	10,509
Mt. Hagen (W. Highlands)	82.7	76.8	27.0	37.3	13.5	7.1	2,764	9,257
Total							74,268	162,230

TABLE 5-4. Language distribution in the seven largest towns of Papua New Guinea. Note that percentages are calculated on the population over ten years old, whereas the total population includes all age groups.

was still surpassed by Tok Pisin, which gained 8 percentage points over the same period, from 36.5 percent to 44.5 percent.

2.3. Qualitative Aspects of Multilingualism in Papua New Guinea's Official Languages

From many points of view, Hiri Motu, Tok Pisin, and English occupy very different roles from those served by the large languages of the Highlands and even the regional *lingue franche*. Most importantly, they are essentially second languages, learned by the people of Papua New Guinea in addition to their native languages, and having very few if any native speakers. In theory at least, none of these is identified as the *tok ples* 'native language' of a particular, geographically located group. Hiri Motu, however, is very closely identified with Motu, with Port Moresby, and with Papua generally. In the minds of the majority of non-Hiri Motu speakers, "Hiri Motu" and "Motu" are indistinguishable, being the *tok ples* of the Motu people of the Port Moresby area. This close regional identification detracts somewhat from one of the usual advantages of a *lingua franca* that is no one's native language—its neutrality.

For most New Guineans, Tok Pisin is such a neutral language. Being, in the view of most New Guineans, no one's *tok ples,* it is thereby in the public domain and can be learned with impunity. That is, learning it will not succeed in improving the fortunes of some other (its native) group. On the other hand to many Papuans, this is exactly the connotation of Tok Pisin, which, as the *lingua franca* of New Guinea, is viewed as a threat to the use and status of Hiri Motu. Despite the antagonism of Papuan nationalists, however, Tok Pisin appears to be making definite inroads. Though many of the 41,772 Tok Pisin speakers in the Central District are New Guinean migrants resident in the Port Moresby area, an increasing number of Papuans are also learning Tok Pisin. On a visit to Port Moresby in 1973, I was surprised to note the increase in the use of Tok Pisin by Papuans conversing with New Guineans, a situation which had changed considerably since my last visit in 1971.

With the continuing spread of Tok Pisin, in conjunction with very rapid urban growth, various urban communities in New Guinea now have small but growing communities of people for whom Tok Pisin has become a *tok ples,* i.e., who speak it as a native language. These are mainly young people, children whose parents regularly communicate with each other in Tok Pisin, often because they have no other language in common. Though many of these children are learning English at school, any type of "continuum" situation between Tok Pisin and English is still virtually nonexistent. The variety of Tok Pisin most heavily larded with English loans is that spoken by national politicians, who have incorporated a great deal of English parliamentary vocabulary into their discussions of government affairs. Outside of this very restricted group, one hears virtually no speech that is in any way "in between" Tok Pisin and English. The two languages as spoken at present are too far apart in structure for any mutual intelligibility beyond the understanding of the occasional vocabulary item, as I discovered in testing fluent Tok Pisin speakers whose native language is Buang for their comprehension of simple stories in English (Sankoff 1968, chapters 9 and 10). Most New Guineans who speak both English and Tok Pisin use very little English outside of contexts where it is obligatory, such as school or work.

Of the three official languages, it is clearly English that is regarded as the most neutral, the least related to any particular group. There are probably no more than a thousand Papuans and New Guineans at most who speak it as a native language. But in many ways it is regarded as almost too neutral, too foreign. There is no doubt that knowledge of English is a very great advantage, economically and politically, a fact not lost on the many thousands of parents whose central goal for their children is to learn English well (cf. chapter 1, this volume). Nevertheless, except among some very restricted groups, such as tertiary-level students, very little English is used outside of formal contexts.

A second commonality among the three official languages is that all of them are spoken by very many more men than women. In 1966, 67 percent of English speakers were male, as compared with 70 percent of Tok Pisin speakers and 73 percent of Hiri Motu speakers.[13] Women had caught up a little by 1971, the analogous figures being 65, 66, and 68 percent.

13. This skewing in favor of males strongly reflects the colonial history of Papua New Guinea, as it has always been men who were the more involved in the European spheres of work and, later, schools. It was, of course, the plantation system that fostered the spread of Tok Pisin. Writing in 1943, Reed made a "conservative estimate" of the number of Tok Pisin speakers as approximately 100,000, or about one-fifth of the total population of the Mandated Territory as of the 1936 census. This estimate is based, he says:

> first, on the assumption that all indentured natives learn to speak pidgin; second, on the native labor statistics since the inauguration of civil government by the Australians in 1921. The total number of contracts made between 1921 and 1936 has been 425,000, with five years as the average period of contract. Thus some 85,000 work boys have learned pidgin under the Australian regime alone. The number of natives who learned the speech during German times, together with the wives and children of work boys who have acquired the language and pupils of the mission schools, would certainly account for another 15,000. (Reed 1943: 284, n.39)

Thirdly, the proportion of speakers of all of these languages is much higher in urban than in rural areas. Note in Table 5-3 that the only non-Papuan Districts in which the number of Hiri Motu speakers exceeds two thousand are Morobe and East New Britain, because of the presence of Lae and Rabaul respectively. The location of Port Moresby in the Central District is responsible for the relatively high proportion of Tok Pisin speakers there. Table 5-4 shows the proportion of speakers of each of the three official languages in the seven major towns of Papua New Guinea. Every town has a higher proportion of speakers of each of the three official languages than does the District in which it is located. This is due to the presence in town of many Papuans and New Guineans from other areas and Districts, to the presence of most of the educated and highly skilled members of the labor force, and to the greater number of schools located in urban areas.

2.4. Regional Differences in Multilingualism

We are now in a position to characterize each of the four regions into which the Districts were grouped in Table 5-3 with respect to the prevalence and nature of multilingualism. In section 2.2 above, the New Guinea Islands and the Papuan Coastal Districts were characterized as "most multilingual." In all of them, the proportion of English speakers was higher than the national average. In addition, each of them was also higher than the national average for one of the other two languages, Hiri Motu for the Papuan Coastal Districts, and Tok Pisin for the New Guinea Islands Districts. But an examination of Table 5-5

New Guinea Islands			Papuan Coastal		
	No.	%		No.	%
New Ireland	2,299	5.7	Central	23,516	20.3
Manus	936	6.1	Northern	12,390	29.5
West New Britain	3,932	10.3	Gulf	18,042	50.7
East New Britain	15,076	20.4	Milne Bay	36,535	51.5
Bougainville	13,661	22.8	Western	25,008	56.5
New Guinea Coastal			Highlands		
	No.	%		No.	%
East Sepik	19,484	17.6	Eastern Highlands	100,607	66.2
West Sepik	22,069	35.9	Chimbu	76,584	73.3
Madang	33,464	30.8	Western Highlands	172,530	74.7
Morobe	63,018	40.1	Southern Highlands	105,960	82.9

TABLE 5-5. The number and percentage of Papua New Guineans age ten and over unable to speak any of the official languages, 1971. Italicizing represents figures up slightly from 1966. All others decreased.

shows that a far greater proportion of the population of the New Guinea Islands Districts is bilingual or multilingual in one or more of the official languages. In fact, the proportion of people who speak none of these three languages ranges from only 5.7 percent in New Ireland to 22.8 percent in Bougainville. In the Papuan Coastal Districts, by contrast, the proportion speaking none of the three official languages ranges from 20.3 percent in the Central District to 56.5 percent in the Western District. As the national average proportion of people who speak none of the three official languages is 46.9 percent, we see that the Milne Bay, Gulf, and Western Districts exceed this proportion. Though many people in these districts may be multilingual in local or regional languages, their multilingualism does not extend to the official languages of Papua New Guinea, as over half of them speak none of the three.

From this perspective, the New Guinea Coastal Districts appear to be characterized by much more multilingualism than the Papuan Coastal Districts. Though only one language dominates (Tok Pisin), the fact that large numbers of people speak it means that relatively few are unable to speak at least one of the three official languages. This figure ranges from 17.6 percent in the East Sepik District to 40.1 percent in the Morobe District, a figure below the national average in every case.

Lastly, it is clear that in the densely populated districts of the Central Highlands of Papua New Guinea, a very small proportion of people speak any of the three official languages. In all cases, the proportion of people who speak none of these languages is much higher than the national average, and is everywhere over 65 percent. These are the people who, along with a majority of the inhabitants of the Gulf, Milne Bay, and Western Districts, are the most cut off from communication on the national level.

There is, however, one very encouraging development. Between 1966 and 1971, despite a 9 percent growth in the total population over ten years of age (from 1,458,054 in 1966 to 1,589,593 in 1971), the total number of Papua New Guineans unable to communicate in at least one of the official languages actually *decreased*. From 805,742 persons in 1966 (55.3 percent), the number decreased to 745,112 (46.9 percent) in 1971, as shown in Table 5-6. The decrease was fairly regular in all Districts, even the Highlands. The District with the highest percentage of people speaking no official language, the Southern Highlands, decreased from 91.3 in 1966 to 82.9 in 1971. This is a remarkable change in only five years. It must be remembered that it is in the Highlands that the majority of the very large language groups are located, and thus the speakers of these large languages are at least ideally part of communication networks that include tens of thousands of people. But the fact

	1966		1971	
	No.	%	No.	%
Male	315,189	41.5	274,320	33.4
Female	490,553	70.2	470,792	61.2
Total	805,742	55.3	745,112	46.9
Population age ten and over	1,458,054		1,589,593	

TABLE 5-6. Number and percentage of people not speaking any official language, by sex, 1966 and 1971.

that the great majority of them do not know any of the three official languages probably implies little travel or contact with people outside of their own small local groups, not to mention their corresponding lack of access to national level news through the main medium of mass communication, the radio.

3. SUMMARY

Nowhere in section 1 did we attempt to estimate the number or proportion of people with some degree of competence in languages other than their own, except on a very local basis. It is even harder to combine the qualitative picture obtained from looking at types of multilingual situations with respect to local languages, with the quantitative data on knowledge of the official languages.

We know that 46.9 percent of the Papua New Guinean population does not speak any of the official languages. Only 3.0 percent claim to speak all three, and these would virtually all be people who also speak their own language, from which we can draw the conclusion that this tiny minority is quadrilingual at least. Similarly for the 12.2 percent claiming to speak both English and Tok Pisin, the 2.1 percent claiming English and Hiri Motu, and the 1.0 percent claiming Tok Pisin and Hiri Motu —most of these people would be at least trilingual. As for those who speak, of the three official languages, only English (3.1 percent), only Tok Pisin (28.3 percent), or only Hiri Motu (3.5 percent), most of them would be at least bilingual in one of the three and their own language.

In examining the two big subdivisions of the population, i.e., the 53 percent who speak at least one of the official languages and the 47 percent who do not, an educated guess is as far as we can go in estimating the multilingualism of these two groups in terms of local languages or regional *lingue franche*. It is very likely that there is a great deal more multilingualism in local and regional languages among the 53 percent than among the 47 percent, as these people tend to belong to smaller language groups (with consequently greater border area and thus more opportunity to learn neighboring languages) and to live in areas nearer the coast where there was greater chance of learning a trade language in the precolonial era, and greater chance of learning one of the mission-propagated *lingue franche* over the last several generations.

6.

Mutual Intelligibility, Bilingualism, and Linguistic Boundaries

When a Swede and an Italian succeed in communicating verbally with each other, it is obvious that at least one of them must be bilingual. In the case of a Swede talking to a Dane, however, it is possible that neither is bilingual (Haugen 1967). When the codes or speech varieties X and Y of two speech communities are closely related, it is often difficult to distinguish between *mutual intelligibility* of X and Y and *bilingualism* of speakers of X and/or Y. In this chapter I shall propose definitions for terms used in the study of this problem, illustrating with quantitative data I collected in New Guinea.

THEORETICAL ASPECTS

I assume there exists an index $e_Z(x, y)$ that measures the efficiency of information transfer from a speaker x to a hearer y when x is speaking code Z. If y understands nothing, $e_Z(x, y) = 0$; if y understands everything, $e_Z(x, y) = 1$. I will restrict the symbols x and y to native speakers of X and Y respectively, no matter which code is being used as the medium of communication.

I define the *intelligibility* of A to B, $I(A, B)$, as the theoretical expected value of $e_A(a, b)$ over all possible b who have no experience with A, and over all possible a. That is, the intelligibility of A to speakers of B would hypothetically be measured by doing a series of experiments in which all speakers of B who have never heard A, listen to each a speaking A. $I(A, B)$ would be the average efficiency of information transfer for the series of experiments. Note that it is not necessary that $e_A(a, b) = e_B(b, a)$, or even that $I(A, B) = I(B, A)$. The efficiency of

This chapter is based on field work done in Papua New Guinea in 1966–67 and in 1968. I thank the Canada Council for sponsoring both trips. The chapter first appeared in *International Days of Sociolinguistics* (Rome: Istituto Luigi Sturzo, 1970), pp. 839–48. It appears here with only minor editorial revisions.

133

information transfer from an a speaking A to a b is not necessarily the same as it would be for an a listening to a b speaking B, nor does this necessarily hold on the average (for I).

If in a given social context, $e_Z(x, y) \geq \alpha$ (greater than or equal to α) is regarded as a sufficient level of information transfer ("sufficient" here being socially defined as sufficient for communication), and $e_Z(x, y) < \alpha$ as insufficient, then I define α as the *language limit* for this context. If $I(A, B) \geq \alpha$, and $I(B, A) \geq \alpha$, then A and B are *mutually intelligible*, or are *dialects* of each other; otherwise they are *distinct languages*. Note that if A is intelligible to B but B is not intelligible to A, this definition classifies them as distinct languages.

If A is not *intelligible* to B (that is, $I(A, B) < \alpha$), but $e_A(a, b) \geq \alpha$ for a particular b and all or most a, then b is *passively bilingual* in A. Thus passive bilingualism means that a speaker of B can understand (at some adequate level) what is being said in A even though A is not intelligible to B. If $I(A, B) < \alpha$ and if $e_B(a, b)$ for all or most b, then a is *productively bilingual* in B.

Suppose for a certain b, $e_A(a, b)$ is only slightly less than α. Then b is *incipiently bilingual* in A (*passive*). If $e_B(a, b)$ is slightly less than α, then a is *incipiently bilingual* in B (*productive*).

These definitions are easily applicable to situations where A and B are very different and are the codes of well-defined speech communities. When speakers come from communities more closely related geographically and linguistically, it becomes difficult to determine, for example, whether $I(A, B) \geq \alpha$, or whether $I(A, B) < \alpha$ but almost all B are passively bilingual due to geographical proximity and language learning. It is clear that I(Swedish, Italian) $< \alpha$ in any context, i.e., the languages are not intelligible. The real task is to try to determine whether I is greater or less than α in borderline cases (such as that of Danish and Swedish), where the situation is almost always complicated by the existence of previous contact between speakers of the two codes in question, which leads to language learning and possibly bilingualism.

Intelligibility per se obviously depends to a great extent on the structural similarity between the two codes; yet no single index of similarity has yet been developed that satisfactorily predicts I, although measures of similarity involving lexical, phonological, and grammatical similarity have been investigated (e.g., Pike 1954; Dyen 1965; Wurm and Laycock 1961).

In situations involving structurally similar languages, the problem in investigating intelligibility is to attempt to separate two components in the observed data of comprehension: that which results from structural similarity of the codes in question, and that which results from learning.

ESTIMATION OF EFFICIENCY OF INFORMATION TRANSFER

On trips I made to study multilingualism in New Guinea between 1966 and 1968, I collected quantitative data on passive competence, in various languages and dialects, of the speakers of the Buang language.

The Buang live in twenty-four villages on mountain slopes along the length of the Snake River Valley in Morobe Province, of northeastern New Guinea. According to their own categorization and those of linguists (Hooley and McElhanon 1970), they may be divided into three speech communities: Headwaters Buang (eight villages); Central Buang (ten villages); and Manga Buang (six villages), which I will refer to as A, B, and C respectively. I will present data I collected in two A villages, three B villages, and two C villages.

In order to estimate passive competence of speakers of each variety of Buang in each other variety, I devised a test as follows (adapted from Hickerson et al. 1952). Six short stories dealing with everyday events in village life were translated and tape recorded in their own language by three young men, native speakers respectively of A, B, and C varieties of Buang. Subjects were tested in two parts. The first part consisted of listening to one of the tapes, and then answering three questions based on it, calculated to judge comprehension of events in the story. It was obviously impossible to test subjects on vocabulary in their native variety; they were, however, asked to answer questions on a story in their own variety in order to provide a control. I administered all the tests myself, to a total of eighty-eight subjects[1] from seven of the twenty-four villages, and asked the three questions in the variety of Buang native to the subject being tested. I have described the sample, the test, and its administration in greater detail elsewhere (Sankoff 1968, chapters 9 and 10).

The scores on the two parts of the test were used as independent assessments, $e_x^1(x, y)$ and $e_x^2(x, y)$, of efficiency of information transfer, where x is the story teller and y the subject being tested. Of course, these assessments are distorted by variation in memory and intelligence of the subjects, differences in clarity of the tapes, the relative difficulty of the test stories, etc. Nevertheless we might expect that these effects

---

1. The 1967 data from the village of Wins (Dawong), collected under poorly controlled testing conditions as reported in Sankoff (1968) have been replaced by data from a new sample, collected in 1968.

average out over the sample and do not distort the overall comparisons of efficiency of information transfer.

RESULTS

The average values of $e_X^1(x, y)$ and $e_X^2(x, y)$ over all y in the sample and for appropriate x (the three native speakers who recorded the text) are presented in Table 6-1.

It should be noted that on the first part of the test, the apparent efficiency of information transfer even for hearers of a speaker of their *own* speech variety was only about 0.70, due to a variety of factors, such as forgetfulness, mentioned earlier. As information transfer among native speakers of the same speech variety can be regarded as theoretically almost perfect, a score of approximately 0.70 on the first part of the test represents quite high information transfer. Scores on the second part of the test (vocabulary) are much higher, since subjects were tested at much smaller intervals (a phrase or sentence at a time, as opposed to the whole text), and on hearing the story for the second time.

Villages	Speech variety (Y) of hearer (y)	$e_X^1(x, y)$ (measured by questions) Speech variety (X) of speaker (x)			$e_X^2(x, y)$ (measured by vocabulary) Speech variety (X) of speaker (x)			Sample size
		A	B	C	A	B	C	
Buweyew	A	.67	.44	.14	—	.87	.40	6
Mambump		.73	.67	.25	—	.97	.61	48
Wins	B	.73	.60	.23	.98	—	.72	5
Chimbuluk		.43	.67	.52	.99	—	.94	7
Papekene		.53	.53	.53	.96	—	.98	5
Manga	C	.43	.43	.68	.86	.88	—	10
Kwasang		.50	.52	.57	.90	.91	—	7[a]

TABLE 6-1. Efficiency of information transfer as a function of native speech varieties of speaker and hearer. The blank entries represent hearers' knowledge of their own vocabulary, which can be assumed to be 1.0.

[a] Six complete tests and one test missing the part on speech variety A.

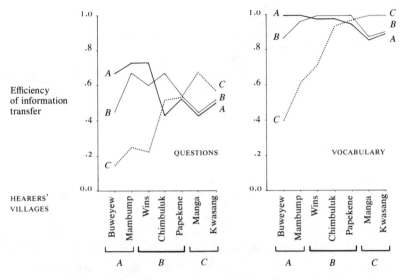

Figure 6-1. Passive competence of Buang villagers in 3 Buang speech varieties.

While the scores from individual villages are subject to statistical variation, there are clear overall trends. These are more apparent when the results are plotted in Figure 6-1, with the sequential position of the villages along the valley represented on the horizontal axis. The speakers of each variety tend to score better than others on hearing their own variety, and also tend to score better on their own variety than on other varieties. This trend is summarized in Table 6-2.

Speech variety of hearer (y)	$e_x{}^1(x, y)$ Speech variety of speaker			$e_x{}^2(x, y)$ Speech variety of speaker		
	A	B	C	A	B	C
A	.70	.56	.20	—	.92	.51
B	.56	.60	.43	.97	—	.88
C	.47	.48	.62	.88	.90	—

TABLE 6-2. Results of Table 6-1 averaged for villages in the same speech group.

137

A	B			C		
Mambump	Wins	Chimbuluk	Papekene	Manga	Kwasang	
.88	.82 .83	.78 .83	.77 .80	.65 .61	.62 .60	Buweyew Mambump A
		.88	.87 .93	.67 .66 .69	.66 .66 .67	Wins Chimbuluk B Papekene
					.94	Manga C

TABLE 6-3. Lexicostatistic comparisons among seven Buang villages. Proportion of meanings represented by cognate words in the speech varieties of any two villages.

The variations *within* each group of villages, however, indicate that for speakers of any one variety of Buang, competence in other varieties increases with proximity—this despite a relatively high degree of homogeneity among the codes of villages within any one of *A, B,* or *C.* For example, speech variety *B* of Wins, Chimbuluk, and Papekene villages is quite uniform, but inhabitants of the three villages display dramatically different competence patterns in *A* and *C* varieties, Wins being geographically closer to the *A*-speaking villages and the other two being closer to the *C*-speaking villages. The people of Mambump and Buweyew speak the same variety, but Mambump villagers, being closer to the *B*-speaking villages, understand *B* much better than do the Buweyew people.

Table 6-3 represents a lexicostatistic comparison[2] of the speech of the seven villages. This indicates, roughly, the uniformity in linguistic structure within each of the three speech groupings and the consistent differences between groupings. This, in conjunction with Table 6-1, is a quantitative demonstration that efficiency of information transfer is not simply a function of the degree of linguistic similarity.

An interesting feature of the graphs in Figure 6-1 is their asymmetry. For example, the *"A"* curves behave in the opposite way from the

2. The test list comprised 162 of the first 170 items on the Summer Institute of Linguistics Survey Word List, which includes Swadesh's 100-word list as well as a number of cultural items specific to New Guinea. The relationship between *A* and *B* is approximately the same as would be shown by lexicostatistic comparisons of Danish and Swedish, and that between *C* and either *A* or *B* is similar to that shown by lexicostatistic comparisons of Spanish and Italian or French and Italian.

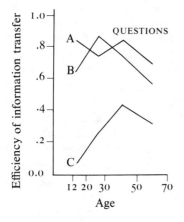
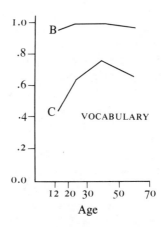

Figure 6-2. Competence of Buang *A* speakers as a function
of age.

"*C*" curves, but are much less steep. This is indicative of nonreciprocal intelligibility and/or different patterns of travel, contact, and hence learning experience. I will discuss this in the light of a final set of data. These data consist simply of fairly accurate age estimates for the forty-eight people in the Mambump Village sample. These data enable us to produce curves showing differential competence for the four age groups seen in Figure 6-2.

Figure 6-2 shows that the competence of Mambump villagers in *A* and *B* is relatively uniform with respect to age, except for a decline in later ages (probably a testing artifact due to older subjects' unfamiliarity with and discomfort in the test situation). The "*C*" curves, however, demonstrate a marked learning effect.

DISCUSSION

We are now in a position to discuss the status of speech varieties *A*, *B*, and *C* as dialects or as distinct languages. Using $e_x{}^1(x, y)$ as our measure of efficiency of information transfer ($e_x{}^2(x, y)$ would do as well), we note that if the language limit, α, is anywhere above, say, 0.3, then *C* is a distinct language with respect to *A* and *B*. This follows from the fact that $I(C, A)$ and $I(C, B)$ should be calculated on the basis of subjects *inexperienced* in *C*, and will thus be less than the average efficiency of

139

information transfer for *all* subjects (including bilinguals). Since the average efficiency is less than α for people from Buweyew (A), Mambump (A), and Wins (B) villages, $I(C, A)$ and $I(C, B)$ must be less than α. Note that the scores in C of people from Chimbuluk (B) and Papekene (B) are far higher than the scores of people from Wins (B), indicating a high incidence of passive bilingualism in C in these villages.

If α is set at 0.55 or higher (still using $e_X^1(x, y)$), then A and B must also be considered distinct languages. In contexts where α is lower, say 0.4, then A and B must be viewed as dialects of the same language. Irrespective of the definition of the language limit, it is clear that there is a high degree of passive competence in Mambump (A) in the B variety and in Wins (B) in the A variety. Evidence for this can be obtained by comparing Mambump's B score with Buweyew's B score, and Wins' A score with Chimbuluk's A score. This competence is acquired early (see Figure 6-2), at least on the part of Mambump people.

The asymmetry of the curves depicted in Figure 6-1 demands an explanation of why C speakers do so much better in A and B than vice versa. Is $I(A, C)$ much greater than $I(C, A)$, and is $I(B, C)$ much greater than $I(C, B)$, or do C speakers, for some reason, have a greater tendency to become bilingual? Exploring nonreciprocal intelligibility of C versus A and B on the basis of phonetic differences between the codes (Pike 1954; Wurm and Laycock 1961) gives equivocal results (Sankoff 1968: 183). In sociolinguistic terms, however, it is relatively easy to understand why C speakers should be more bilingual. The major route out of the Snake River Valley is downriver towards the government station, through which a road passes to the coast. C speakers, living downriver with respect to both A and B, are likely to be exposed to A- and B-speaking travelers (mostly adults) visiting in their villages, and become experienced with A and especially B from an early age. A and B speakers, on the other hand, are exposed to C only when they journey down the valley (infrequent, expecially for children), or when the occasional C speaker comes to visit kinsmen (also relatively infrequent for the A villages). That the acquisition of passive competence in C on the part of A speakers occurs during adulthood is illustrated in Figure 6-2, where we note that passive competence of the thirty to fifty age group in C is just over 0.40, a figure that approximates the mean comprehension of A on the part of C speakers, 0.47 (Table 6-2).

Another factor explaining the differences in linguistic abilities is the relative similarity between A and B contrasted to C. If people who reside near another speech group tend to become passively bilingual, and we have seen that they do, then both A and C speakers will become bilingual in B. Once a C speaker understands B, however, it is relatively easy for him/her to overcome the comparatively slight differences between A and B so that she/he understands A, i.e., she/he can extrapolate from B to the quite similar A. On the other hand, an A speaker's passive competence in B does little to help him/her in understanding the quite different variety, C.

In conclusion, I would suggest that in many cases, including that of the Buang, intelligibility phenomena are heavily masked by acquired passive competence. Casual observations or testimonials as to the mutual intelligibility of two speech varieties should not be taken as proof of such intelligibility. As we have seen in the case of Buang, it is important to control for the subtle action of the sociolinguistic variables of proximity, linguistic contact, and language learning.

7.

Wave Versus *Stammbaum* Explanations of Lexical Similarities

DAVID SANKOFF and GILLIAN SANKOFF

There are two "ideal types" of explanation for patterns of linguistic similarity within a geographical region. The *Stammbaum* (family-tree) explanation attributes similarities to shared evolution, so that languages or dialects with a recent common ancestor will share more retentions and innovations than either of them shares with a language that is more remotely related. In the *Stammbaum* model, the observation that linguistic similarity often correlates well with geographical proximity is seen as a consequence of the fact that speakers of recently diverged speech varieties will have had less time to migrate apart from each other. The alternative kind of explanation, the "wave theory," places much more emphasis on diffusion of innovations across language or dialect boundaries. Proponents of this theory argue that family-tree structures misrepresent the nature of linguistic relationships and that the branchings in the tree bear no necessary resemblance to historical fact (cf. Lehmann 1962: 138–40).

Both models treat as significant the fate of innovations, but they differ in their view of the permeability of boundaries, the family-tree model treating language boundaries as impermeable. A strong version of this theory would have it that once two speech varieties have diverged sufficiently to be called separate languages, there can be no further mixture, no language leveling. A weaker version would admit some borrowing, but not enough to obscure the genetic relationships, not enough to create a "mixed language."

Most lexicostatistic work has been carried out in the framework of the family-tree model despite the fact that extensions to take into account geographical diffusion have been proposed many times. As long ago as 1950, Swadesh spelled out the importance of geographical proximity in accounting for internal relationships of the Salishan languages.

This chapter originally appeared in the *Cahiers de l'Institut Linguistique de Louvain* 3:5–6 (1975–76), pp. 29–41. It is reprinted here with only minor revisions.

One of the difficulties in developing a lexicostatistic wave theory is the lack of any very natural mathematical model for the process of diffusion of words. The family-tree is compatible with a very simple and natural stochastic process of word replacement, namely a homogeneous Poisson process taking place along each evolutionary branch independently. The wave model, however, may be formalized in many different ways, each one involving arbitrary parameters and no one more obviously fundamental than another. In the present chapter we construct a simple diffusion model for which the parameters can be determined by certain empirical observations.

The object of this chapter is not primarily to discover degrees of relatedness among a group of languages (the languages on which we are working have already been studied from this point of view), but rather to compare the *Stammbaum* and diffusion models with respect to how well they account for the lexical relationships existing among these languages.

The Languages

Morobe Province, northeast Papua New Guinea, is characterized by extreme linguistic diversity. Over much of its area, each village of two to five hundred inhabitants can be identified by a speech variety perceptibly different from that of its neighbors (cf. chapters 5 and 6, this volume). A comprehensive linguistic survey has been undertaken by Hooley and McElhanon (1970) (cf. also Hooley 1964b, 1970; Sankoff 1968; Capell 1962, 1976), and the lexicostatistically determined relationships that we describe below are very similar to their results.

Two extended periods of sociolinguistic research in the Buang area of the Snake River headwaters enabled us to collect a number of word lists from Buang and surrounding groups. The relationships between the Austronesian languages spoken by these groups can be summarized as in Figure 7-1, which is interpretable either as a tentative family-tree or, more conservatively, as a simple synchronic summary of overall linguistic similarities. Of the five groups, two consist of mountain dwellers, Buang and Hotec, one (Coastal) lives along the Huon Gulf Coast of the Solomon Sea, one (Azera) is dispersed along the length of the Markham River Valley, while the Mumeng speakers inhabit the grassy plain and hill country around the small town of Mumeng (see Figure 7-2). Migration patterns in early times cannot be reconstructed with confidence but it is clear that trade, warfare, intermarriage, and migration all constituted considerable influences on language distributions.

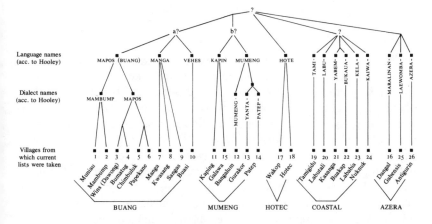

Figure 7-1. Linguistic relationships of Austronesian speech varieties represented by the twenty-six word lists collected in Morobe Province. This summarizes existing knowledge about these varieties and is not based on these word lists. The tree is in accord with Hooley's groupings except that he would perhaps collapse nodes *a* and *b*, calling both Buang and Mumeng the Buang family. (*?* indicates uncertain sequence of branching.)

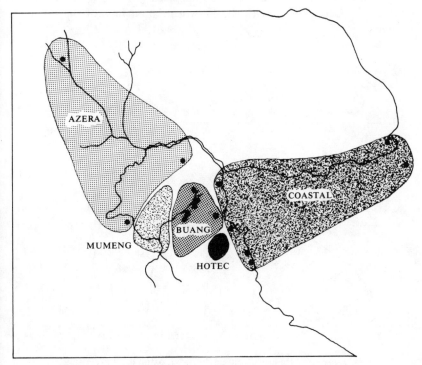

Figure 7-2. Geographical relationships of language groups.

145

STANDARD LEXICOSTATISTIC ANALYSIS

From twenty-six of our word lists, we selected the standard Swadesh 100 items. Cognation judgments were fairly liberal, to avoid any bias against remote relationships due to the obscuring effect of phonological change over very long periods of time. Despite our relative generosity in judging, many of the lexicostatistic percentages remained very low, corroborating Dyen's (1965) finding of extreme diversity among the Austronesian languages of this area. Lexicostatistic percentages, ranging from 10 to 95 percent, were calculated in the usual way, yielding a symmetric similarity matrix. To construct a tree we employed the following well-known hierarchical clustering procedure. At each step the maximum matrix element is selected; the languages or nodes it represents are connected to a new higher node; and the two rows corresponding to these two languages or nodes are replaced by rows of zeros, and similarly with the corresponding columns; a new row (and column), representing the new node, is added to the matrix, its elements being the weighted average of the corresponding elements in the two rows just deleted, weighted by the number of languages represented by each row. The result is depicted in Figure 7-3. As can be seen, this accords well with the known relationships of the language groups.

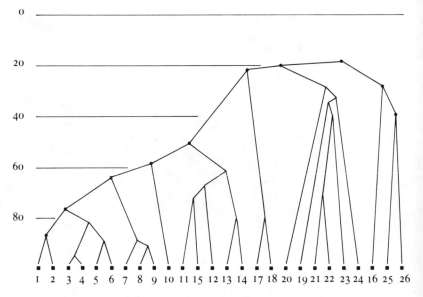

Figure 7-3. Result of clustering lexicostatistic percentage matrix.

A MULTIDIMENSIONAL SCALING APPROACH

A realistic diffusion model cannot proceed on the assumption that two-dimensioned geographical space is a homogeneous medium for the propagation of linguistic innovations. The eight-thousand-foot mountains between the Buang and Azera speakers or the five-thousand-foot range between the Buang and the coast, cannot be compared with the expanse of ocean between the various coastal villages nor with the canoe-navigable Markham River linking the Azera groups. Migration, trade, and cultural patterns complicate the picture. Which two-dimensional representation, then, should we use as the space in which "lexical waves" are propagated? The space that would be most compatible with a diffusion model would, of course, be that where the distances are most consistent with the lexical similarities. This leads us to use a multidimensional scaling procedure (INDSCAL) developed by Carroll and Chang (1970) on the lexical similarity matrix, which produces the configuration of Figure 7-4. The only major difference between this and Figure 7-2 is that the Azera are no longer in their outlying position but have assumed a position close to the Hotec group. This closeness is an artifact of the two-dimensionality. In a three-dimensional scaling, Hotec and Azera are widely separated in the third dimension, and the Mumeng and Buang groups are further differentiated from each other.

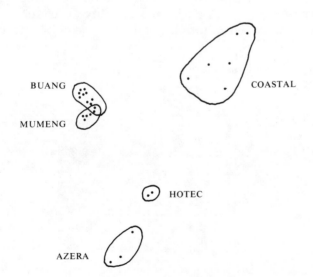

Figure 7-4. Result of multidimensional scaling of lexicostatistic percentage matrix.

THE WAVE MODEL

The assumptions behind our diffusion experiments are as follows:

1. Innovations in a test-list item occur at random among the twenty-six points in our two-dimensional space, and different test-list items innovate independently.

2. The wave "front" moves very rapidly with respect to the rate of innovation, so that the fate of any particular innovation in a test-list item is settled before the next one occurs.

3. The probability that an innovation is adopted (i.e., the "intensity" of the wave) at a given point depends only on the distance d between that point and the origin of the innovation; specifically the adoption probability is k/d where k is a parameter to be discussed later. Where $d \leq k$, the probability is 1.

In testing the diffusion model, we wish to have it produce simulated data as similar as possible to the real data. To do this we examine each test-list item in the original data and count how many different cognate classes have been elicited. The cognate classes are enumerated as follows. If for a given test-list item, all words are judged to be cognate, there is but one cognate class; if the words can be divided into two groups such that all the words within each group are considered to be cognate with each other, but not with any of those in the other group, then there are two cognate classes, and so on. Thus the number of cognate classes could conceivably range from one to twenty-six; in fact it ranges from one to sixteen, and the distribution of the number of classes is depicted in Figure 7-5. We would like to control the parameters of the wave model to mimic this distribution. To do this, the

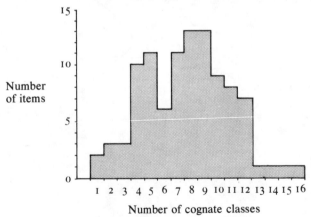

Figure 7-5. Distribution of the number of cognate classes per test-list item, in twenty-six lists.

diffusion experiment is conducted as follows. Each test-list item is treated separately. For a given item, one of the twenty-six points is chosen at random, and it is assigned cognate class 1. For each of the other twenty-five points a random number between 0 and 1 is generated. The distance d between this point and the innovation point is calculated and if the random number is less than k/d, the innovation is "adopted" at this other point. After the fate of this innovation at all twenty-six points is thus decided, a second innovation (i.e., cognate class 2) is randomly introduced and adopted according to the same procedure. This is continued for thirty innovations. At first sight it may seem that there are two parameters relevant to the final number of cognate classes for an item: the intensity constant k, and the total number of innovations during the time interval being simulated. In fact the number of innovations has no effect on the number of classes except at the very beginning of a simulation run. After a short while, the effect of each new innovation is to completely obscure, on the average, one of the previous innovations, so that an equilibrium number of cognate classes is more or less maintained. Thus our fixing a total of thirty innovations per test-list item has little effect on the final number of cognate classes. The only relevant parameter remaining is k. This may be set low, making for innovations of low intensity which interfere relatively little with each other, yielding a large number of cognate classes. High intensity innovations cover wide areas and lead to a low equilibrium number of classes. (In our program, k is not a constant but the mean of an exponential random variable. This merely increases the variability of the model.)

By suitably fixing k, then, we were able to control rather closely the number of cognate classes for a test-list item. So by varying k appropriately for different items, we were able to produce simulated data with the same distribution of cognate class numbers as in the real data.

A TREE COMPATIBILITY CRITERION FOR DATA SETS

In an ideal *Stammbaum* model, a cognate class for a given test-list item has a unique origin, i.e., each set of cognate words for the item can be traced to a single innovation in an ancestor language. This means that no identical coincidental innovations can occur, or that for no item will the situation of Figure 7-6 arise.

In reality, of course, no one disputes that independent innovation, borrowing, and mistaken cognation occur, and lead to situations such as Figure 7-6. To the extent that the tree model is valid, however,

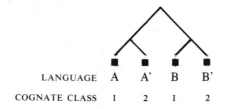

LANGUAGE	A	A'	B	B'
COGNATE CLASS	1	2	1	2

Figure 7-6. Forbidden configuration in ideal tree model. Either class 1 was innovated twice or class 2 was innovated twice.

we can expect significantly few such situations. Significantly few compared to what? Compared to some alternative to the tree model, namely the data generated by the wave model.

For each test-list item, then, we would like to calculate the number of coincidental innovations necessary to account for the cognacy data for that item, with respect to the family tree we have constructed (Figure 7-3). To compute this number, we used an algorithm which has been described several times in the literature, e.g., by Fitch (1971) or Hartigan (1973).

RESULTS AND DISCUSSION

In Figure 7-7 it is clear that the distribution of the number of coincidental innovations is concentrated on much smaller values than the diffusion-generated predictions, and hence the pure wave model is rejected by the test based on the number of coincidental innovations. It is equally clear that a pure tree model does not accord too well with the data either, because a pure tree model can generate only data with zero such innovations and the real data contain only 31 items with zero coincidences, out of 100 items total. We conclude that to account for the data we require a tree model, but one in which a certain amount of diffusion or borrowing occurs between geographically proximate languages.

To what extent do our results depend on the details of our wave model? Is it possible to construct a diffusion process which generates a distribution of coincidences more in line with the real data? We have already biased the test in favor of the diffusion model by using not the true geographical configuration of the languages, but the one obtained by multidimensional scaling of similarities. We might be able to improve the behavior of this model still further by using a three-

Wave Versus *Stammbaum* Explanations

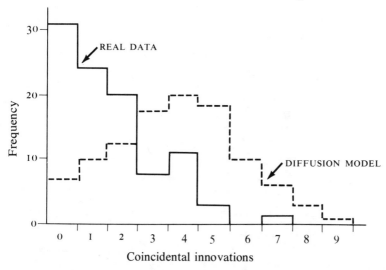

Figure 7-7. Distribution of numbers of coincidental innovations showing the relative lack of coincidence in real data, compared to diffusion-generated data.

dimensional configuration of languages, since this could be even more compatible with the configuration of similarities between the test-lists. On the other hand, many of the coincidences noted in the real data could be the result of our liberal cognation judgment procedure. Strict use of criteria of cognation would result in fewer coincidences in the real data and a better fit to the pure tree model.

One shortcoming of our version of the wave model is that it assumes a fixed position for each speech variety. More realistic versions would have to allow for migration or movement of speech communities in the course of simulation. These effects are captured to some extent in other models based on the evolution of planar graphs, which were explored by Sankoff and Dobson (1971), D. Sankoff (1972b) but which have not yet been integrated with empirical data.

8.

Cognitive Variability and New Guinea Social Organization: The Buang *Dgwa*

The following three extracts (translated from Buang) are taken from a single interview with a Mambump villager, on the subject of the location and ownership of his gardening land. The speaker mentions the names of three gardens, each of which, he says, belongs to a different kin group, each time confidently, almost casually, including himself in the kin group in question.

R: "*Sagomalo* [garden] belongs to *Mapas* [group]; it's *our* land."

Q: "In what other gardens do you have yams planted this year?"
R: "One at *Npeb*."
Q: "To whom does that land belong?"
R: "It belongs to *us Igiskone* people."

Q: "Do you have any other yam gardens this year?"
R: "Yes, one at *Pabup*."
Q: "To whom does that land belong?"
R: "To *Aying*, to *us Aying* people."

(Mambump village, July 1967)

This chapter originally appeared in *American Anthropologist* 74 (1972): 555–66. It is reprinted here with only minor editorial revisions. Field work among the Buang of Morobe Province, New Guinea, was carried out from September 1966 to August 1967 with the aid of a Canada Council Pre-doctoral Fellowship, and in July and August 1968 with the aid of a Canada Council travel grant. Generalizations in this paper apply mainly to the eight "headwaters" Buang villages, located near the source of the Snake River. I wish to thank the Canada Council for its support, and the people of Mambump and Rari villages for their patience and generosity. In addition, I would like to thank John Gumperz, Dell Hymes, Teresa Labov, and Richard Salisbury for helpful discussion of an earlier draft, read at the NEAA meetings, Ottawa, May 1970.
Orthography for Buang terms (except for village names) follows my outline of the headwaters Buang dialect (1968, chapt. 5). Briefly, voiced stops are prenasalized (as in Hooley 1962, 1964a on the central Buang dialect); consonant clusters are separated by unaccented schwa; γ is a uvular trill. Back velar consonants have not been distinguished from the velar series in this chapter.

The apparent paradox here is that the three italicized pronouns are all first person plural exclusive (Buang *ey*); the speaker, however, in identifying himself in the space of about ten minutes with three of the five major kin groups, does not appear to feel that there is anything contradictory or peculiar about having concurrent claims on all three.

Even to an ethnographer expecting irregularity in New Guinea social organization (see, e.g., Burridge 1957; du Toit 1962; Langness 1964; Epstein 1964; Watson 1965, 1970; de Lepervanche 1967–68; Strathern 1969), the statements made by the Buang about their kinship affiliation come as somewhat of a shock. In asking questions about kin group membership, it is disconcerting not only to find a very considerable lack of consensus among villagers as to the group to which any given individual belongs,[1] but also to find the same individual giving different answers on different occasions. The ethnographer's problem would appear to be that enunciated by Frake (1964: 132): to find "the questions that go with the responses."

One might start by trying to explain the situational and contextual constraints on verbal behavior. What factors influence an individual's decision about what group he/she will say he/she (or someone else) belongs to on any particular occasion? This line of attack does give us some insights. A complete understanding, however, requires more than a statement of the cultural rules that dictate particular choices (or, in other words, that explain why and under what circumstances seemingly contradictory statements are found perfectly acceptable by the hearers). It is obvious that claims to kin group membership occur within the context of a whole set of understandings about kin groups, the relationships between them, and the criteria for membership in them. Only by an investigation of these and related questions will we be able to satisfy our curiosity about whether or not people *really* belong to one group or another, or to several at once, or even to what extent they really *think* they do.

In this chapter I shall attempt to answer these questions in such a way as to relate individual choices to the cultural system of which they are a part, and to relate this cultural system in turn to the social and physical conditions of Buang society.

I. INVESTIGATION OF BUANG SOCIAL ORGANIZATION

"Which kin group do you belong to?" represents a rather unlikely question in a village of two hundred people in any kind of normal con-

1. Forty-two Mambump men, asked separately to identify the 47 men living in Mambump at the time, agreed completely on only 5 of them, as described in chapter 9 below.

versation (though the question is plausible coming from an anthropologist or other unenlightened foreigner). Such an enquiry, moreover, presumes a great deal, e.g., the existence of kin groups, that people belong to one or other of them, etc. The question of kin group membership in Buang society is, however, not one of purely academic or theoretical interest, and my introduction to Buang kin group categories came not from my asking specific questions about them, but from people's unelicited explanations of the relevance of kin groups to particular events.

The first occasion on which I heard kin groups mentioned was a communal garden planting in September 1966. In response to my questions about whose garden it was, I was told either the names of specific people who were planting sections of it, or given the name *Mapas.* What was *Mapas?* This was *Mapas* land, and *Mapas* was the name of a group of people, related by descent, representing part of the population of the village. All the people to whom this garden belonged were identified as "being" *Mapas.*

I subsequently learned that within the village in which I lived there were five or six entities analogous to *Mapas,* and that each of these was a specific instance of a general category called *dgwa.* (See Table 8-1.)

It will be useful at this point to demonstrate how people talk about *dgwa* by citing some direct quotations, all of which have been translated rather closely into English from tapes recorded in Buang.

Village names	Kin group (*dgwa*) names
Mambump	*Mapas* *Reγes* *Igiskone* *Iŋiay* *Aying*
Rari	*Rari-sodk*
Wins	
Bugwev	
Buweyew	
Sinagei	

TABLE 8-1. Village and kin group names mentioned in text.

In the first group of quotations, speakers are stressing the exclusiveness and uniqueness of *dgwa* groups, emphasizing that people who belong to a particular *dgwa* are separate and different from other people.

(1) *"Rari-sodk* is one itself alone." (Informant 1, Rari village, September 1966)

(2) *"Reyes* built its own men's house, and *Igiskone* built its own men's house. . . . The *Igiskone* people eat, and *Mapas* and *Reyes* people won't eat together with them." (Informant 2, Mambump village, July 1968)

(3) "Those people's *dgwa* doesn't go back to that of my father." (Informant 3, Rari village, September 1966)

People frequently report themselves as being members of the same *dgwa* as other people in their immediate vicinity during a conversation. This emphasis on inclusion and solidarity is evident in the next group of quotations. Note how Informant 1, who in example 1 had been emphasizing the uniqueness of his own group, *Rari-sodk,* shifts in 4 to stressing his solidarity with members of a visiting delegation of *Reyes* people from Mambump village, going so far as to claim he *is* a *Reyes* person, and covering any possible objections by providing an acceptable (see section 2) justification.

(4) "I am *Reyes;* I am not from another men's house. *Rari, Reyes,* they two have only one men's house." (Informant 1, Rari village, September 1966)

(5) "Our ancestor was *Mon Rubŋ,* we *Reyes* and *Igiskone* people's ancestor was *Mon Rubŋ.*" (Informant 4, Mambump village, July 1968)

(6) "We people of Rari, Mambump, Wins, and Bugwev, our *dgwa* was first at *Guzuviz* [toponym]. Our big men lived there." (Informant 2, Mambump village, September 1966)

Three more quotations from Informant 1 appear to contradict further his belief (if we take his statement in 1 seriously) in the exclusiveness of *dgwa* groups. All of these were recorded during a two-day period in September 1966.

(7) "My mother was a *Mapas* woman. . . . My *dgwa* is at *Mapas.*"

(8) "We here originated from a woman called *Kez Γamon* from Buweyew. . . . Our *dgwa* is at Buweyew

(9) "A woman from far far away came and bore our ancestors, our grandfathers, our fathers. . . . We originated from *Byek Bpek* from Sinagei."

Taken as a group, these nine quotations show not only how people on different occasions stress different aspects of the *dgwa* concept, but also how they cite different kinds of evidence to justify their claims.

What I found puzzling in discussions of *dgwa* membership was that an informant chosen at random from almost any small group of men who happened to be together for some reason would take great pains to explain to me how they were all members of some one particular *dgwa*, say *Mapas*. The explanation would take the form of a genealogical discussion, often mentioning how some ancestor of each had "come from" *Mapas*, which he could offer as a justification of the statement *ke Mapas* 'I [am a] *Mapas* [person]'. Further, he would often insist that those present were in fact the nucleus of the *dgwa* in question, that they formed an exclusive group in the *dgwa* by virtue of the special character of their ancestry. The interesting thing was that the same informant, on another occasion with another group of people present, would be quite likely to identify himself as being a member of a different *dgwa*, again giving a plausible explanation in terms of his genealogy. This might be easier to understand if it were considered normal for people to belong to numerous *dgwa*; however, the emphasis on exclusiveness shows that multiple *dgwa* membership runs counter to Buang ideology.

When confronted with these apparently contradictory statements, an informant tended to adopt one of two main lines of argument. Sometimes he would go to great lengths to show why his identification with one of the two or more *dgwa* mentioned was the most "real" or "true" (though it most often appeared to me that the one chosen was the one the informant was currently concerned with justifying). Alternately, he would begin, "Well, you see, everyone has two parents . . ." and finish with a statement that he was "half" (Buang *valu;* Tok Pisin *hap kas*) a member of one *dgwa* and "half" a member of the other. No one ever explained or justified to me his/her membership in more. than two *dgwa* on any one occasion, though many people claimed membership at one time or another in more than two.

A tentative rule for predicting which group an individual will say she/he belongs to might be: in the presence of a relatively small group of people (say two to five), a speaker will, wherever possible, name that *dgwa* most reasonable for all or most of those present to have in common. Like many rules, however, this one perhaps suggests more questions than answers. In addition to the most general and obvious question of why inclusion and solidarity appear to receive so much emphasis, we might ask what makes some claims more plausible than others. What does it mean to be a "real" or "true" member of a particular *dgwa?* To what extent does immediate social context predict people's answers?

In answering these questions, I will attempt to show that although, in general, individual Buang cannot be assigned absolutely to one kin group or another, *dgwa* organization is nevertheless systematic, and people's affiliation with *dgwa* is a crucial element in Buang social organization. Several different kinds of data will be brought to bear in making this argument. First, I will discuss the multiplicity of referents of the term *dgwa* and the way in which *dgwa* membership is related to other aspects of Buang social organization, notably land tenure (section 2). Second, the accepted conventions for discourse about *dgwa* help to indicate how people avoid bringing to light obvious discrepancies (section 3). In the last section, I attempt to treat the variation systematically.

2. THE CONCEPT OF DGWA AND ITS IMPORTANCE AS A UNIT OF SOCIAL ORGANIZATION

In its broadest sense, the term *dgwa* refers to the base or point of origin of a wide variety of objects (e.g., the base of a tree or a house) and abstractions (e.g., the origin of a dispute or custom). In many of the examples cited above, we see that *dgwa* is also used in the domain of kinship to refer to the source or origin of a particular "line" of kinship. In addition, it is the generic term for a series of named units such as *Aying, Igiskone, Mapas, Iŋiay,* etc., in the examples cited. Each of these specific *dgwa* names is a category label for a group of people presently alive and some subset of their ancestors. In this regard it is interesting to note that although there was considerable lack of accord regarding the specific *dgwa* to which to assign living people, the question appeared to have been resolved for ascending generations, and though people would occasionally state that their parents belonged half to one group and half to another, grandparents and up were assigned unequivocally to one or other *dgwa.*

Dgwa that, when referring to kin groups, may optionally be made more specific in the compound *alamdgwa* (literally 'people's origin') are conceived of as descent groups, although people claiming to belong to a given *dgwa* cannot trace their descent directly to a common ancestor. And although each *dgwa* has some sort of charter myth, this is not necessarily an origin myth. For at least some *dgwa* there does not appear to exist any one particular named ancestor.

Specific *dgwa* names also refer to men's houses, as each *dgwa* has only one, which carries the *dgwa* name. In fact, as can be seen in examples 2 and 4 above, the existence of a men's house is often used as justification for a statement regarding the status of particular *dgwa*. According to informants, the men's house constituted a nucleus for *dgwa*-based residential groupings or hamlets in former times when, they say, people were not congregated in villages as they are at present. Currently, headwaters Buang villages range in size from about 150 to 300 residents, and generally contain from four to six *dgwa,* membership in which constitutes at least to some extent a basis for residential groupings within the village. Though some villages contain several men's houses, others have dropped the custom of building them.

Each specific *dgwa* name is also a toponym, referring to a relatively large territory that comprises a number of smaller named places. Thus *dgwa* are also the names of places that specific ancestors can be said to have come from, and that mark the points of origin of particular lines of descent from these ancestors. In theory, Buang land is completely subdivided into a series of named plots or pieces of land, each of which can be said to form part of the territory of one or other *dgwa*. In practice, complete agreement among informants about which *dgwa* a given plot belonged to was almost as rare as it was in the specification of *dgwa* membership of particular people.[2] This is all the more difficult to explain in the light of the fact that *dgwa* territories are relatively compact; i.e., plots belonging to any one *dgwa* are contiguous and do not tend to be interspersed with other *dgwa*'s plots. In addition, informants agree on the general location (focus) of the territory of any given *dgwa*.

Like the Choiseulese *sinangge* (Scheffler 1965: 59), Buang *dgwa* are agamous. People deny the existence of any type of marriage rule or preference, and insist that marriage is a matter of individual freedom of choice. Men may even marry women whom they call "sister" (i.e., parallel cousins, even first cousins). Speaking of marriages within a *dgwa*, informants explain that it is good to consolidate land holdings

2. In interviewing 18 Mambump men, separately, about the *dgwa* ownership of 146 named plots, I found that for less than 60 percent of the plots (83) could I obtain a consensus of 15 or more of the respondents. There was a serious lack of consensus (less than 12 out of 18 agreeing) on 36, or 25 percent of the plots (cf. chapter 9 below).

within a *dgwa,* or at least within the village, and occasionally object to proposed marriages with other villages[3] on grounds of the subsequent loss of *dgwa* resources to that village.

As subsistence horticulturalists (Girard 1957, 1967), land is of primary practical importance to the Buang, and it is instructive to consider briefly the way in which land is owned and inherited. A garden plot theoretically belongs to the person who first cleared it and who, during his own lifetime, designates the person to whom it will next belong, usually a son but possibly a daughter or daughter's husband, or even a distant relative or unrelated person (this latter case usually involves the apprenticeship of an adolescent boy, who for some reason has few claims on any land of his own, to an older man who has a lot of land). Individuals have the right to clear new gardens in the bush land of their own *dgwa.* It is also common for plot owners to invite others to garden with them and to use a section of the plot, or to lend an entire plot for one planting, even to non-*dgwa* members.

Though it is true that individual owners of plots are recognized, the *dgwa* still maintains a certain interest in all its land, and the most senior man or men in each *dgwa* are considered to be stewards who oversee all *dgwa* land, and make decisions regarding length of fallow for communal gardens and other matters pertaining to the *dgwa* and its resources. (Such men are not necessarily "big men" or "managers" in the political sense.) Thus for any garden plot, it is theoretically possible to specify who is currently using it, who owns it, and who oversees it, i.e., which *dgwa* it is part of.

3. DGWA AFFILIATION IN DISCOURSE

We have seen in section 2 that a person's *dgwa* identification is of considerable social importance, particularly with respect to land rights. The quotations have shown that people refer to their *dgwa* in different ways: sometimes stressing the uniqueness of the one particular *dgwa* with which they are currently identifying themselves; at other times claiming to belong to other *dgwa* or emphasizing the commonality of two or more *dgwa,* in a show of solidarity with others present. People cite *dgwa* groupings to strengthen or prove an argument, or as evidence for statements they make about social relationships. The salient point here is that *whatever* argument is being made can be, and usually is, phrased in *dgwa* terms. In a social context where it is important to

---

3. In all cases I heard about where objections were voiced, men objected to daughters of the *dgwa* or village leaving it for some other group. Objections were never made to bringing women in.

stress unity (as, for example, in a discussion of cooperative gardening or other work), *dgwa* boundaries will be stretched, and it can justifiably be claimed that almost everyone present is, say, a *Mapas* person. Conflict, on the other hand, is frequently phrased as one *dgwa* group pitted against another.

It is important to note that *dgwa* membership in itself does not constitute a subject of argument. This would appear to be functionally related to the almost complete lack of argument about another important subject, land tenure. Land is not perceived as being in short supply among the headwaters Buang, and it is the object of very little conflict. Further, in the two cases I heard about in over a year, the question at issue did not bear on whether the principals were or were not members of a particular *dgwa*.

In other words, *dgwa* affiliation can be used as a piece of evidence in argumentation; it does not itself constitute the reason for or subject of an argument. A pertinent example concerns the case of a young boy who fell while climbing a tree and broke his arm during a communal garden planting organized by *Reγes* people. The boy's dead father had been a pillar of *Reγes dgwa*. The next day, a leader of *Mapas dgwa* was heard storming up and down the village square, berating *Reγes* people for having let "our" (*Mapas!*) child come to grief in "your" (*Reγes*) garden. As the boy's maternal uncle was an important man in *Mapas,* no one disputed the *Mapas* claim on the child in that context, but rather made arguments that it was not their fault, etc.

In most cases where people mentioned their *dgwa* affiliation either in conversation or in argument, they did not also give a justification for their claim. My own discussions with informants, however, provide considerable data on the kinds of evidence which are accepted in constituting valid claims. People justify their claims to membership in a particular *dgwa* on the basis of (1) father's affiliation; (2) mother's affiliation; (3) the affiliation of some grandparent or even great-grandparent; (4) being *vet* or apprenticed to a *dgwa* member; (5) spouse's affiliation (which applies mainly to those marrying in from a distant place, usually though not always women). Most of those whose primary claim is on the basis of (4) or (5) can, however, supply some evidence, usually tenuous, for one of the first three. The five justifications that I have listed are ranked in order of what I perceive to be decreasing strength. That is, a man who can cite his father and grandfather as having been members of *x* is much more likely to be regarded as a "true" member of *x*. Those with the strongest claims are considered to be the core or true members of a *dgwa,* and these are the men who become stewards of *dgwa* land. These "central" men, who rarely cite themselves or are cited by others as members of other *dgwa* are clearly in the minority. For most individuals, there is variability in the way they are assigned to *dgwa* (by themselves and others), as documented in chapter 9 below.

4. Discussion

Data underlying the present description of Buang *dgwa* organization have been of two major types: (1) myths and genealogies from which most of the quotations from Buang were excerpted, which displayed conflicting emphases of inclusion on the one hand versus exclusion on the other, and demonstrated how it was possible for a given speaker to identify himself/herself with a number of different *dgwa*; (2) evidence taken from casual discussions about *dgwa* membership, justification of claims to particular pieces of land, etc., which showed that many individuals do in their everyday behavior find it efficacious to claim membership in a number of *dgwa*, though almost everyone will insist, on any one occasion, that he is really a member of some one particular *dgwa* (this with the limited exception of a small minority of people who claim half-and-half status in two *dgwa* groups). A third body of data, consisting of the assignments of land and people made by a number of informants during interviews, and analyzed in chapter 9 below, confirms the pattern of variability described here.

In attempting to describe the cultural system, which allows certain seemingly contradictory statements on the part of Buang informants about social organization and their own place in it, I have presented data showing variability at more than one level. Specifically, (1) isolated informants present conflicting reports about the kin groups (*dgwa*) to which both people and plots of land should be assigned, and (2) individuals change their assignments according to immediate circumstances, and are not challenged by others when they do so. I propose that these two types of variation are related in a systematic way.

It would appear that Buang social organization represents an extreme case of a pattern already well described for New Guinea—that of a highly flexible social system that permits manipulation by individuals to suit their own ends, and in which individual choice does not upset the system; rather, it is an important *part* of the system. In recent years, much attention has been paid to this problem in the highlands of New Guinea (see, e.g., Barnes 1962; du Toit 1962; Langness 1964; Watson 1965; de Lepervanche 1967–68), where many of the societies appear to consist "ideologically" of segmentary, agnatic, exogamous lineages, but where "sociological" variation (up to 50 percent nonagnates in some local groups) is high. Cases with other ideologies, from other parts of New Guinea and Melanesia as well as the highlands, appear, however, to be equally problematic. (See Hogbin and Wedgwood 1953; Lawrence 1955; Burridge 1957; Epstein 1964; Scheffler 1965; Wagner 1967; Glasse 1968.) Authors describing both highlands New Guinea and other Melanesian societies have tended to propose that although variation exists at the "sociological" level, there is commonality at the ideological level. Langness, for example, discussing the Bena Bena, says that "the fundamental problem is the discrepancy between ideology and statistical norms" (1964: 182), and Epstein, dealing with the Tolai of Matupit where "the ideology is unequivocally matrilineal" (1964: 3) feels that variation ("sociological") is explicable in terms of "the expression of the working out of a uniform set of structural principles in the varied circumstances of social life" (1964: 2).

Most of these authors appear to feel that "ideology" is the locus of commonality or sharedness in culture.[4] In my view, the Buang data I have presented argue against a simple dichotomy between behavior (variable) and ideology (shared). Following Goodenough (1964: 11), I would agree that

> The ideational order is a property *not of the community but of its members* . . . [it] is nonmaterial, being composed of ideal forms as they exist in people's minds, propositions about their interrelationships, preference ratings regarding them, and recipes for their mutual ordering as means to desired ends [emphasis mine].

In the Buang case, the problem is to discover what the categories and their interrelationships are as they exist in people's minds, and to relate these in turn to the way people talk about them, which, as we have seen, is highly variable. There are several possible lines of explanation.

First, it is possible that variability in the assignment of items to categories (people and plots of land to *dgwa*) reflects a hierarchical taxonomy of *dgwa* groups, such that some informants used a more inclusive *dgwa* name, and others a more specific name, but were in effect referring to the "same" groups. This does not in fact appear to be the case. *Dgwa* are conceived not as units in a segmentary system, but rather as being independent, with independent territories. Although according to myth or history particular *dgwa* stand in special relationships with each other, none will admit to being a segment of some other

4. Watson (1970) presents an interesting analysis of Tairora social organization that differs from the static, social structural type of analysis in its emphasis on the dynamic elements of population flow between local groups.

group and each stands as an independent unit, in contrast with the others, controlling its own resources. It is clear that when people used different *dgwa* names, they were talking about different *dgwa*.[5]

Two other possible lines of explanation hinge on people's knowledge (or lack of it) of the "correct" assignments. On the one hand it is possible that, in response to my questioning, some people were ignorant of the correct assignments of some items, but preferred to give a "wrong" answer based on some faulty or misleading piece of evidence (e.g., a *Mapas* person is known to be working garden plot *x*, therefore *x* must be in *Mapas* territory) instead of admitting their ignorance. This was clearly not the case; first, because people who did not know an answer were usually reluctant to guess, preferring to say that they did not know; second, because it does not explain how individuals can and do assign *themselves* publicly to different categories.

At the other extreme, it is possible that there does exist an absolute assignment of individuals and plots of land to *dgwa*, of which everyone is aware, but the conventions of discourse about *dgwa* permit a great deal of leeway in making claims on *dgwa* other than one's "true" *dgwa*. Scheffler, for example, described such a situation for the Choiseulese, stating that:

> When one wishes to say that he is in some sense a "member" of a particular *sinangge* [the cognatic kin group], he says, "I am *sinangge* x" . . . but he says this about many *sinangge*. . . . "belonging" to *sinangge* is an idiom of broader kinship relations. (1965: 46)

He continues:

> When it is said that one belongs to many *sinangge* it is meant that one has interests in the personnel and estates of many descent groups and, furthermore, the rights of access to and residence upon the estates of those groups. (p. 48)

Scheffler goes on to discuss how people, through their actions, bolster their claims on one or other descent group, and the emphasis

---

5. Some confusion can, however, be caused in the identification of people by the fact that, strictly for government purposes (the record keeping of the Australian Administration in New Guinea), villagers have registered themselves according to a much simplified system. Thus in Mambump village, the whole population has been registered in the village book as belonging to one or other of two *dgwa*. This problem can usually be circumvented by explaining to informants that it is *not* the "village book" identifications that are required.

appears to be on eventual affiliation with some one group.[6] Although we know that individual Buang are also eventually assigned to one group (usually by their descendants, after they are dead), the problem we are dealing with is whether, at any one point in time, it can be said that all or most individual Buang "really" belong to only one group, as most of them affirm. If this were the case, it might be possible to explain an individual's assignment of himself to different groups on different occasions (by specifying the characteristics of the interaction situation that influence people to claim different groups). It would not, however, explain the lack of consensus on assignments of both people and land in response to individual questioning. (During these interviews, conducted ten months after my arrival, when I was well known in the community, each respondent understood that I wanted the best or truest categorization for each item, and people were very cooperative in giving me the answers they considered to be the best.) Discrepancies in such a situation should have been at a minimum, as an informant stating that "*x* is a member of *Mapas*" was not trying to give the wildest possible acceptable assignment, but the one he considered best. If there did exist only one "right" assignment for each item, there should have been much less discrepancy in the questionnaire data, as reported in chapter 9 below.

I feel that an analysis of the Buang *dgwa* system that insists on an absolute categorization would do violence to the data, and would fail to relate the two kinds of variability I have discussed. Rather, I propose that each individual item (person or plot) occupies a position defined in terms of *degree of centrality* with respect to each *dgwa*. As suggested in section 3, certain individuals and plots form a core or center for any particular *dgwa;* others are more peripheral and can thus be assigned, reasonably, to one of two or three possible *dgwa*. Because it is possible, in the abstract, for all but the most central members of some one *dgwa* to be assigned to several *dgwa,* this enables people to adjust to their immediate social context in making claims on various *dgwa,* in some contexts stressing inclusion and in others stressing separation.

In giving an abstract description of the *dgwa* structure, then, we could show that for each *dgwa* there exists a continuum, defined in

6. Although Buang and Choiseulese social organization appear to have much in common, they differ on several points: in conflicts over land (almost none for the Buang; numerous for the Choiseulese), in the depth of genealogies (five or six generations for the Buang; up to twelve for the Choiseulese), in the major disagreement among Buang on abstract assignments (at least, this kind of variation is not described for the Choiseulese in Scheffler's analysis), and in the fact that most Buang do not admit multiple membership.

terms of the centrality of the position of individuals (and plots) within the *dgwa*. For any given *dgwa*, the most central people are those with the strongest claims, as outlined in section 3 (e.g., someone with four *Mapas* grandparents would normally have a more central position in *Mapas* than someone with only three). The centrality of plots can be viewed in terms of their use by more or less central members of the various *dgwa*, or possibly in terms of absolute geographical distance from some point agreed upon as the focus of each *dgwa*'s territory.

How does this abstract structure correspond to the cognitive models of individual Buang? It is safe to say that every normal adult has a knowledge of the categories (*dgwa*) into which items can be classed, and of the criteria which permit an item to be classed in a particular category. In addition, I would argue that each person has a more or less clear (personal) idea of a continuum for each *dgwa*—not only who is most central to it (the stewards of each *dgwa*'s resources), but also who is a "member in good standing," who is a half or part member, and who has no claims at all. Similarly, every individual "knows" that certain plots are central to a particular *dgwa* (those plots on which communal *dgwa* gardens are periodically made), that others definitely do not belong to that *dgwa*, and that still others have an intermediate status. Stated conversely, every Buang has a mental image of which *dgwa* every member of his community can claim (and which each plot can be said to belong to), and of the relative strength of these claims.

It is probable that no two individuals have completely overlapping models, just as no two individuals share precisely the same knowledge of data by which items can be classed (exact kinship connections, land use, etc.). The greatest degree of overlap among people's models can be presumed to occur at both ends of the continuum for any one *dgwa* (which items are central; which definitely do not belong).

This formulation of what an individual's model should look like helps us to understand the high degree of variability in assignments made during individual interviews. The set of assignments of some forty people made by an informant during an interview does not, in my view, adequately represent his cognitive model of the place of these forty people in the *dgwa* system, as informants mentioned only the one or two *dgwa* they considered most important to each individual. The set of assignments given any one individual or plot by all informants, however, might be regarded as a closer approximation to the "average" position of that item over all informants' models. This is not to assign any absolute priority to the questionnaire as giving the "right" answers, and I would still maintain that there are no absolute "right" assignments. Quantitative analysis (chapter 9 below) shows, for example, that in assigning other people to the various *dgwa*, an individual draws not only on the concrete facts relating to their kinship connections, land use, etc., but also tends to be influenced by his own place in the social structure. That is, a person who considers himself as belonging to *Mapas* will tend to assign any dubious or peripheral cases to *Mapas*, and so on for the other groups. The same principle holds true for land assignments. *Mapas* people will tend to claim borderline land as belonging to *Mapas*.

It is more difficult to specify adequate rules for the way *dgwa* identifications are made in conversation. We can, however, state that such rules would have to take into account both the speaker's own position in each *dgwa* and the relevant situational factors, primarily the intention of the speaker to include or exclude others present. In both cases, we would also have to take account of the positions of the hearers, as well as the seriousness of the occasion, with respect to its relevance to the possible actualization of a claim; e.g., making a claim to be a *Mapas* person in the context of the distribution of *Mapas* resources would be more serious than making such a claim in a story-telling context. The former might require a central position in *Mapas* whereas the latter might require only a peripheral one. It is reasonable to suppose that further study of the contexts in which *dgwa* identifications are made, concentrating on the factors mentioned above, would provide fairly specific usage rules. The continuum for each *dgwa* would tell us which groups an individual may claim; the usage rules would specify the circumstances under which he may make these claims, and we could then better understand the way people manipulate their claims to their own personal and social advantage.

From this vantage point, we can return to two questions posed earlier in the chapter. The first has to do with the functioning of a system that permits such a high degree of individual manipulation. As far as any one individual is concerned, having a strong claim on a particular *dgwa* is valuable because it assures him a central place in the distribution of the resources of that *dgwa*, and perhaps the possibility of becoming a steward of its land; on the other hand, his claims on the other *dgwa* are reduced proportionally. It is also advantageous to have the maximum number of claims on other *dgwa*, providing a wider network of relationships to draw on should this become necessary. Given the numerous criteria for making claims on *dgwa*, most people have a large number of possibilities from which to choose, and can manipulate the way they stress particular ties from among these.

From the perspective of the overall socioeconomic system, *dgwa* flexibility provides a mechanism for regulating short-term demographic imbalances in the man-land ratio and making possible a more equitable distribution over all individuals in the society. Thus, for example, the sons of an in-marrying man (there are usually at least two or three at any given time in a village) are often apprenticed to a land-rich man, or else use land to which their mothers and/or wives have rights. Such men may come to be considered to belong to the adoptive or land-granting *dgwa,* especially as time goes on. One old man, from a distant village, who married an *Igiskone* woman and has lived with her at Mambump for the past forty-odd years, still identifies himself as a *Reγes* person, claimed through a great-grandmother who was from *Reγes.* Fifteen out of the twenty older men asked to identify him said he was *Reγes,* but his two sons are generally identified as being *Igiskone,* and fourteen of the twenty younger men identified him as being an *Igiskone* person. In families where several sons (three or four) grow to adulthood, one or more may marry a woman who has no brothers, use his wife's land rather than his father's, and become identified with his wife's *dgwa.*

The second question is in my view more fundamental, as it concerns the kinds of knowledge and assumptions about their social organization that can be presumed to be shared by the Buang, and bears upon the way in which we define the concept of culture. If we accept a definition of culture that stresses the sharing of particular pieces of knowledge, this might imply in the Buang case some kind of malfunctioning, breakdown of communications, or serious (mis)information problem in Buang society. If on the other hand we accept that the Buang share the knowledge of the system, meaning its categories, the variable criteria for how elements are fitted into those categories, the situations when it is acceptable to stress different criteria, or to stretch or narrow the categories, and sufficient facts about individual elements to allow for their manipulation, then our definition of culture can be that of a system in which people participate (Aberle 1960) but where it is not at all necessary for them to share the *same* cognitive map (in fact it is functional that they do not). It is important to note, however, that the "cultural idiolects" (Aberle 1960: 14) do not define the culture in some sort of additive way; rather, they fit together as variant strategies within a single system that is defined in terms of common understandings not at the level of pieces of specific information, but at the level of rules of acceptability of what the system permits.

9.

Quantitative Analysis of Sharing and Variability in a Cognitive Model

In their comprehensive review of various formulations of the concept of culture, Kroeber and Kluckhohn (1952: 109ff.) deal at some length with the problem of "the relationship of the abstraction, culture, to concrete individuals." The issue of homogeneity, commonality, or sharedness is of considerable importance in culture theory, since analyses of a culture necessarily proceed by abstraction from observations of the behavior of individuals, including their verbal behavior, and seek to arrive at generalizations.

Early formulations of culture tend to make the tacit, or even explicit, assumption of cultural homogeneity. To take only a few examples from the Kroeber-Kluckhohn compendium, Linton (cited on p. 50), talks of "the collection of ideas and habits which [members of a society] learn, share, and transmit"; Young (cited on p. 56) of "common and more or less standardized ideas, attitudes, and habits"; and Gorer (cited on p. 56) of "shared patterns of learned behaviour." In recent years, however, a number of anthropologists, including Aberle (1960: 15) and Wallace (1961a) have argued that culture is not homogeneous, but should be conceptualized rather as a complex structure or system that does not require cognitive sharing on the part of all individual members of a particular society. Wallace (1961b: 37) takes perhaps the most extreme position on cultural heterogeneity, stating that:

. . . the advocate of togetherness may argue, whether or not it is necessary that *all* members of society share *all* cognitive maps, they must share at least *one*. Such an argument, however, is not convincing. No criteria known to the writer would specify

This chapter originally appeared in *Ethnology* 10 (1971): 389–408. It appears here with only minor editorial revisions. I wish to thank the Canada Council for sponsoring the two trips to New Guinea during which the data on which this chapter is based were collected (September 1966 to August 1967, and July to August 1968). I would like to thank Richard F. Salisbury for comments on an earlier draft, read at the American Anthropological Association meetings, November 1970; and especially the people of Mambump village for their most generous cooperation. I am grateful also to Lilyan Brudner for many useful editorial suggestions.

what one map it is functionally necessary that all members of a given society should share.

In this chapter I discuss a general problem in the investigation of cognitive models in ethnography, that of analyzing the diversity of the cognitive models or maps of individual informants, referred to by Aberle (1960) as "cultural idiolects" and by Wallace (1961b, 1961c) as "mazeways," in relation to a unified sociocultural system. The issues that I am concerned with are to what extent are cognitive maps shared, which aspects of them are not shared, and how do these latter aspects vary from individual to individual? In effect, how is intracultural diversity organized?

The specific data discussed here are part of a larger study of the kin group organization and land tenure of the Buang, a mountain people of northeastern Papua New Guinea. As reported in chapter 8 above, this system is characterized by a high degree of variability both in informants' verbal reports of the affiliation of individuals and in their assignment of agricultural plots to kin groups (Buang *dgwa*).[1] Verbal statements assigning individuals and plots to kin groups vary across informants as well as among reports made by the same informant on different occasions.

The variable way the Buang talk about their kin groups may be investigated as the result either of variation in the immediate interaction situation or of actual differences among individual cognitive maps. These lines of investigation and explanation emphasize the shared versus the idiolectal aspects of culture. The first kind of explanation accounts for variation in verbal behavior—in this case, the assignment of a particular individual to different kin groups—in terms of a number of situational or contextual factors, such as the nature of the speaker's audience, his/her aims in making a particular claim, or the formality of the occasion. The implicit assumption behind the analysis of verbal behavior in this type of sociolinguistic explanation is that the members of the speech community in question share in some important sense the same sociolinguistic system. This system permits speakers to both encode and decode the social meaning of variable messages. These messages are generally examined at the expression level in terms, for example, of phonology, morphology, or syntax, rather than at the content level, for example, in terms of the objects, ideas, or concepts being referred to,

---

1. Orthography for Buang terms follows my outline (Sankoff 1968: chap. 5) of the headwaters Buang dialect. Briefly, voiced stops are prenasalized (as in Hooley 1970); consonant clusters are separated by unaccented schwa; γ is a uvular trill. Back velar consonants have not been distinguished from the velar series in this chapter.

or, in sum, comprising the referential meaning of terms. We might say that sociolinguistic analysis considers variation as a surface-level phenomenon of expression,[2] for it focuses on the sociological aspects of speech events and assumes that everyone shares the same cognitive model and simply expresses ideas differently as a result of various situational and social constraints. In this perspective, factors having to do with the interaction situation are presumed to account for variation in verbal reporting.

Studies of intracommunity variation in language use on the content, rather than on the expression, level are relatively rare.[3] Since a speaker is likely to be attentive to content as well as to the social situation, it is possible that variation in verbal expression represents real differences in individual cognitive maps of the content of the discourse, rather than simply the influence of the social situation. This second line of explanation, which I shall refer to as cognitive, treats variation as resulting from a lack of congruence among speakers' individual cognitive models. Here explanation focuses on deep-seated, underlying cognitive differences among individuals.

The present analysis of Buang social and cultural organization has several related goals. First, I demonstrate the applicability of the techniques and general theoretical stance of cognitive anthropology (see Tyler 1969a) to the analysis of social organization, a domain of culture which has received relatively little attention on the part of scholars working within this framework.[4] In adopting a cognitive approach to cultural analysis, I take as a point of departure the understanding that individual members of Buang society have of the way their society is organized. Second, I propose that if culture is to be understood as having a structure or system (see Kroeber and Kluckhohn 1952: 118–24, 385–89, passim; Wallace 1961a, b, c; Aberle 1960: 5–15; Conklin 1964: 25–26; Hymes 1970b: 28off.), the general practice of cognitive anthropology to date must be broadened so as to provide for the systematic incorporation of data obtained from a wider sample of informants than is presently the case. I argue that current socio-

2. My use of the surface-underlying distinction is prompted by, but does not strictly correspond to, the use of these terms in linguistics. The distinction I intend is between actual instances of verbal behavior, on the one hand, and the underlying cognitive structure of which it is an expression, on the other.

3. Two studies which constitute notable exceptions to this generalization, dealing with variable usage of referential terms, are Tyler (1969b) and Swartz (1960). Studies such as those of Friedrich (1966) and Brown and Gilman (1960), on variation in pronominal usage, are also of interest here.

4. Though much work has been done on kinship terminology, most other aspects of social organization have been neglected, here with the exception of the important body of work by Goodenough.

linguistic methodology[5] has much to offer in this respect, and describe the research strategy I developed in dealing with the Buang *dgwa* system. Third, I contend that an adequate description of the structure of culture, or of any domain of culture, can only be hampered by the adoption of an extreme position on the issue of cognitive sharing. If, however, we accept the fact that we cannot determine a priori the areas and levels at which differences among individual cognitive models will occur, we are able to deal with sharing and variability as matters of degree (see also Gladwin and Gladwin 1970) as well as of kind. Thus, instead of automatically attributing differences among statements made by informants to situational factors (in the case of the "shared" view of culture) or to differences in their cognitive models (in the case of the "heterogeneous" view of culture), variation and sharing are treated as problematic, and the explanation of differences among informants' statements is a result, rather than a determinant, of the analysis.

In this chapter I shall not attempt to provide sociolinguistic usage rules for kin group terms, since I have elsewhere (chapter 8 above) given numerous examples of variation at this level and have suggested probable contextual constraints on usage. Rather, I will show how informants' diverse verbal statements about kin groups can be interpreted in terms of a cultural system incorporating the cognitive maps of individuals and underlying the surface-level behavioral phenomena.

THE *DGWA*: A BRIEF OUTLINE

As I have elsewhere (Sankoff 1968; chapter 8) described the nature of the Buang *dgwa* in detail, I shall only briefly summarize its main characteristics here. The *dgwa* is the most important unit of Buang social organization, serving as the primary focus of identification for individuals. The Buang conceive of *dgwa* as being basically descent groups, and possess no other named kin groups, though *dgwa* are roughly organized into (named) villages and (unnamed) alliances. According to Buang theory, all Buang are members of some one or other *dgwa*, with the exception of a few individuals who are acknowledged to have half-membership in each of two *dgwa*. In fact, most Buang have claims on a number of *dgwa*, claims which may be substantiated in a number of ways.

In addition, each *dgwa* is associated with a certain territory, including both named garden plots and larger bush areas, access to which is in part contingent on membership in the *dgwa*. *Dgwa* territories are in theory unitary; that is, plots are not dispersed, and people

5. See chapter 2 above.

agree on the location of the general area belonging to each *dgwa*. All Buang land is conceived of as belonging to some *dgwa* or other.

As has been mentioned, *dgwa* are not organized into any hierarchy of kin groupings. Moreover, each *dgwa* is autonomous, and people do not admit to any relative differences in prestige or importance among the various *dgwa*. Here again theory differs from the actual state of affairs, as some *dgwa* are larger than others and, by virtue of this fact, command a proportionately higher allegiance (see discussion below) on the part of a large number of individuals. Claims to *dgwa* affiliation are made by individual Buang in a number of different kinds of social circumstances, and although on any given occasion an individual will generally insist that he is a member of some one *dgwa,* he may change his claim on another occasion, substantiating it, if requested to do so, through a different ancestor (for further details, see chapter 8 above).

In the village of Mambump, where the present study was carried out, there are five *dgwa* which are represented in terms either of large membership, of land holdings, or both. These are: Aying (A), Igiskone (I), Mapas (M), Reγes (R), and Iŋiay (X). Of these, M and R have the most members, followed by I (which, however, has a large amount of land), followed by A and X with only a few members (A having a lot of land, X a rather small territory).

INVESTIGATION OF THE *DGWA* SYSTEM

In working out a methodology which would clarify the Buang *dgwa* system, I had to consider how to collect and interpret verbal data in order to make meaningful inferences about the underlying cognitive structures of the speakers. During my first eight months of residence in Mambump, I had noted a large number of conflicting statements about the *dgwa* affiliation of both individuals and agricultural plots, and had concluded that a systematic collection of *dgwa* assignments was essential to an understanding of the unified sociocultural system of the Buang.

My analysis was initially complicated by the helpfulness of Mambump villagers who initiated me in the mysteries of *dgwa* organization by way of the simplifications they had already devised for the benefit of the hapless foreigner. A number of years before, the Buang had decided that to simplify matters for the purposes of the record keeping of the Administration of New Guinea, they would all register themselves as belonging to either M or R, the two largest *dgwa*. People other than M or R decided which of the two they had the strongest claim on, and registered themselves accordingly in the village book. (This does not imply, however, that the other *dgwa* are in any sense segments of M and R, and I will return to this point later.) Only when informants regarded me as being sufficiently well informed to understand, did they supply me with the other *dgwa* names: I, A, and X. At this point it became clear that variability in assignments did not result from relationships of inclusion among the various *dgwa*. Not only did people emphatically deny the existence of any such relationships, but the various *dgwa* claimed for any particular individual did not order in this way.

To obtain comparable data on the *dgwa* assignments on the part of a maximum number of informants, the construction of a controlled eliciting technique was essential in order to rule out the kind of variation I have called "sociolinguistic" (for a detailed discussion of this point see Black 1969: 172–74). My first step was to compile a list of all men currently (May–June 1967) resident in Mambump village. In a separate interview with each man on the list I asked the informant to tell me the *dgwa* of each person on the list, including himself, explaining that I did not necessarily want the "village book" identifications, but rather the "true" identification of each person. I was able to conduct interviews with forty-two of the forty-seven men on the list, and a comparison of their assignments of the forty-seven individuals to the various *dgwa* provided the basic data for my analysis of the place of individuals in the *dgwa* system.

Similar steps were taken in the collection of a set of assignments of garden plots to the *dgwa*. Again, the first step involved compiling a list of the plots to be assigned. The criterion I decided to use for inclusion of a plot on the list was its remembered use by at least one villager. Accordingly, during May and June 1967, I conducted detailed interviews with all available Mambump men on their gardening activities, concentrating on the highly valued cultivation of yams. I started by asking each informant the names of plots where he had yams under cultivation at that time, as well as how he came to be using each plot, what its particular cultivation history was, who had first cleared it and what relation to this person he was, and with whom he was cooperating in its use.

One aspect of yam gardening as practiced by the Buang[6] was especially useful in tracing cultivation history, and that is that each yam is trained on a tall pole, known in Buang as a *rirŋ*. These poles, which are cut in the forest, are used over and over when possible, and each year a man need only replenish a fraction of his supply. This means that instead of going to the bush to cut an entirely new set of yam poles each

6. For further details on yam cultivation among the Buang, see Girard (1967).

year, a man is principally involved in transporting last year's poles to this year's garden. This is such an important and time-consuming activity that men tend to have a clear memory, extending a number of years into the past, of which old garden the poles came from for any particular new garden. I pushed this line of questioning as far back as I could with each informant, and was thus able to obtain a fair number of names of plots each one claimed to have used.

Taking all the plots which had been mentioned by any informant, I ended up with 140 plot names. I then went back to eighteen of the men (chosen to represent all of the Mambump *dgwa*) and asked each one, in private, to tell me which *dgwa* each plot belonged to. As with the assignments of people, this investigation permitted me to construct a grid which served as a basis for the analysis of the place of land in the *dgwa* system. In dealing with plots, however, I also took into consideration their geographical location. In order to locate plots geographically, I asked a group of Mambump villagers to point them out to me on an aerial photograph, very much enlarged. Of the 140 locations assigned by informants, error resulted in having only 138 located on the aerial photograph.

INDIVIDUALS IN THE *DGWA* SYSTEM

The assignments of Mambump men, elicited during individual interviews, are presented in Table 9-1. It shows a fairly high degree of variability in the assignments received by all but a few individuals, even in a situation where informants tried to name that *dgwa* with which they felt each person was most truly affiliated. Claims made in everyday contexts, then, could be expected to vary a great deal more than this. If we decide to base our model of where individuals "really" belong in the *dgwa* organization of Mambump village on these data, we might decide to class each person as a member of the *dgwa* with which most people identified him. This, however, would destroy the subtlety of our model and ignore much of the data. A more natural model, I believe, would view each *dgwa* as being structured in terms of a core-periphery continuum, with members identified by all 42 "voters" as belonging to that *dgwa* at its core, and those members identified as such by only one or two "voters" at its periphery. Table 9-2 presents the membership of each *dgwa*, ordered in this way.

From the point of view of any individual, his rank order within a given *dgwa*, determined by the number of "votes" he got on that *dgwa* (the number of people who thought he was a member of that *dgwa*) can be directly related to the strength of his claim on that *dgwa*. Thus, for example, individual 5 has a very strong claim on M, and a rather weak

Assignees (identified by number)	\	Assigners (identified by number and in order of decreasing age, left–right)																																							
	5	6	7	8	10	11	14	17	19	20	21	26	32	34	37	38	40	41	42	43	44	50	58	62	64	66	69	87	88	89	92	93	95	97	99	100	101	102	111	125	126	134
5	M	M	M	M	M	M	M	M	M	M	M	MO	X	M	M	M	X	M	M	M	X	M	M	M	M	MO	M	M	M	M	M	M	M	M	M	M	M	M	M	M	M	M
6	R	R	R	R	R	R	R	R	R	R	R	R	R	R	R	R	R	R	R	R	R	R	R	R	R	R	R	R	R	R	R	R	R	R	R	R	R	R	R	R	R	R
7	M	M	M	M	M	M	M	M	M	M	M	M	M	M	M	M	M	M	M	M	A	M	M	M	M	M	M	M	M	M	M	M	M	M	M	M	M	M	M	M	M	I
8	R	R	R	R	R	R	R	R	R	R	R	R	R	R	R	R	R	R	R	R	R	RO	R	R	R	R	R	R	R	R	O	R	R	R	R	R	R	R	R	R	R	—
10	M	R	M	M	M	M	M	X	M	X	X	M	R	M	M	MX	M	M	M	M	M	X	RX	M	M	M	X	M	M	X	M	M	X	M	M	M	M	M	M	M	M	I
11	R	R	I	I	R	R	R	I	I	R	R	R	R	R	R	R	R	R	I	R	IR	I	I	I	R	R	I	I	I	I	R	I	I	R	I	I	R	I	I	R	I	M
14	R	R	R	R	R	R	R	R	R	R	R	R	R	R	R	R	R	R	R	R	R	MR	R	R	R	R	R	R	R	R	R	R	R	R	R	R	R	R	R	R	R	R
17	M	M	M	M	M	M	M	M	M	M	M	M	M	M	M	X	M	M	M	MO	M	M	M	M	M	M	M	M	M	M	M	M	M	M	M	M	M	M	M	M	M	M
19	M	M	I	I	M	M	M	M	M	M	M	M	M	M	M	MO	M	M	M	M	MO	M	M	M	M	M	M	MO	M	M	M	M	M	M	M	M	M	M	X	M	M	M
20	R	R	R	R	R	R	R	R	R	R	R	R	R	R	R	R	R	R	R	R	R	R	R	R	R	R	R	R	R	R	R	R	R	O	M	R	R	R	R	R	R	R
21	R	IR	I	I	I	R	R	I	I	R	IR	R	I	IR	R	I	R	R	I	R	I	R	IR	I	I	I	R	R	I	I	I	I	R	I	I	R	I	I	R	I	I	I
26	M	M	M	M	M	M	M	M	M	M	M	M	M	M	M	M	M	M	M	M	M	M	I	M	M	M	M	M	M	M	M	M	M	M	M	M	M	M	M	M	M	M
32	R	R	R	R	R	R	R	R	R	R	R	R	R	R	R	R	R	R	R	X	R	R	R	R	X	R	R	R	R	R	R	R	R	R	R	R	R	R	R	R	R	R
33	R	R	R	R	R	R	R	R	R	R	M	R	R	R	R	R	R	M	R	R	R	M	R	R	RM	R	R	R	R	R	R	R	R	R	R	R	R	R	R	R	R	—
34	M	R	M	M	M	M	M	M	R	X	M	X	X	RM	M	M	M	M	M	MX	M	X	M	M	X	M	M	M	M	M	M	M	X	M	M	M	X	X	M	M	M	I
37	I	R	I	I	X	I	R	I	I	R	I	I	A	A	R	I	A	AI	I	A	AI	I	A	A	I	I	A	R	R	I	A	I	I	I	I	I	I	IR	AR	I	I	M
38	M	M	M	M	M	M	M	M	M	M	M	M	M	M	M	M	M	M	M	X	M	AX	M	M	M	RM	M	X	M	M	M	RM	M	M	X	M	M	M	M	M	M	R
40	M	M	M	M	M	M	M	M	M	M	X	MX	M	M	X	M	M	M	M	M	M	M	M	M	M	M	M	M	M	M	M	M	M	M	M	M	M	M	M	M	M	I
41	M	M	M	X	M	M	M	M	M	M	M	X	M	X	MX	M	M	M	X	M	X	MX	O	X	M	M	M	X	M	M	M	O	M	M	—	M	O	MR	X	I	M	—
42	M	M	X	M	M	M	M	M	M	X	M	X	MX	M	M	M	X	MX	O	MX	O	MX	M	M	M	M	M	O	M	M	M	M	O	M	M	M	M	O	M	M	M	M
43	R	M	R	R	R	R	R	R	M	R	M	R	R	R	M	RM	M	R	M	M	M	R	RM	M	R	M	R	R	R	R	R	R	R	R	R	R	R	R	R	R	M	I
44	I	R	I	I	I	R	I	I	I	I	I	I	I	M	I	R	I	R	I	I	I	I	I	I	I	I	I	I	I	I	I	I	I	I	I	I	I	I	I	I	M	I
49	I	I	I	I	I	R	I	I	I	I	I	I	M	I	R	I	I	I	I	I	I	I	I	I	I	M	I	I	I	I	I	I	I	I	I	I	I	I	I	I	M	I
50	M	M	X	M	M	I	M	M	M	I	M	X	RM	M	M	M	M	AM	MX	M	M	M	M	M	M	M	X	M	M	M	M	IM	M	MX	MX	M	M	M	M	M	M	M
53	M	M	M	M	M	M	R	I	M	M	M	R	M	M	M	M	M	I	M	M	M	M	M	M	M	MR	M	M	I	M	M	I	M	R	M	M	M	R	M	I	M	M
58	M	M	M	M	M	M	M	M	M	M	M	M	M	M	M	M	M	M	M	M	M	M	M	M	M	M	M	M	M	M	M	M	M	M	M	M	M	M	M	M	M	I
62	R	R	R	R	R	R	R	R	R	R	R	R	R	R	R	R	R	R	R	R	R	R	R	R	R	R	R	R	R	R	R	R	R	R	R	O	R	R	R	R	R	R
64	R	R	R	R	R	R	R	R	R	R	R	R	R	R	R	R	R	R	R	R	R	R	R	R	R	R	I	R	R	R	R	R	R	R	R	R	R	R	R	R	R	I
66	R	R	R	R	R	R	R	R	R	R	R	R	R	R	R	R	R	R	R	R	R	R	R	R	R	R	R	R	R	R	R	R	R	R	R	R	R	R	R	R	M	R
69	M	M	M	M	M	M	M	M	M	M	X	R	M	M	M	M	M	M	M	M	M	M	M	M	M	M	M	M	M	R	M	M	M	M	M	M	M	M	M	M	R	M
77	M	M	M	M	M	M	M	M	M	M	M	M	M	M	M	M	M	M	M	M	M	M	M	M	M	M	M	M	MO	M	M	M	M	M	M	M	M	M	M	M	R	M
87	M	M	M	M	M	M	M	M	M	M	M	M	M	M	M	M	IM	M	M	M	M	IM	M	M	M	M	M	M	M	M	M	M	M	M	M	M	M	M	M	M	M	M
88	I	M	M	M	I	R	I	I	M	M	M	I	M	M	M	M	I	IMI	I	IM	M	I	I	MR	M	M	I	I	I	M	I	I	I	I	M	I	I	I	I	M	I	M
89	M	M	M	M	M	M	R	M	R	M	R	X	R	M	M	M	M	M	M	M	M	M	M	M	R	M	M	M	R	M	M	M	M	M	M	M	M	M	M	R	R	R
92	R	M	R	R	R	R	R	R	R	R	R	R	R	R	R	M	R	M	R	M	R	R	RM	M	R	M	R	R	R	M	R	M	M	M	M	M	M	M	M	M	M	I
93	M	M	M	M	M	M	M	M	M	M	M	M	M	M	M	M	M	M	M	M	M	M	M	M	M	M	M	M	R	M	M	M	M	M	M	M	M	M	M	M	M	M
95	R	R	R	R	R	R	R	R	R	R	R	R	R	R	R	R	R	R	R	R	R	IR	R	R	R	R	A	A	R	R	R	R	R	R	R	R	R	R	R	R	I	O
97	I	M	I	M	I	I	R	I	I	I	I	M	M	M	R	I	I	I	I	M	M	M	I	I	I	I	I	I	M	I	M	M	M	M	I	M	I	M	I	I	M	I
99	M	M	M	M	M	M	M	R	M	M	M	M	M	M	R	M	M	M	M	M	M	M	M	M	M	M	M	M	M	M	M	M	M	M	RM	M	M	M	M	M	M	I
100	I	IM	I	I	I	R	I	I	I	I	I	I	R	I	R	I	I	I	I	I	R	IR	I	I	I	I	I	I	I	I	I	IRI	I	I	I	I	T	I	I	I	I	M
101	M	M	M	M	R	M	M	R	M	M	R	M	M	M	M	M	M	M	M	M	RM	M	M	M	M	M	M	MR	M	M	R	M	MR	M	M	M	X	M	M	R	M	M
102	M	M	I	M	M	M	M	M	M	M	M	I	M	M	M	M	M	M	M	I	M	I	M	I	M	I	MO	M	M	M	M	M	M	M	M	I	M	I	M	I	M	O
111	M	M	M	M	M	M	M	M	M	M	M	M	M	M	M	M	M	IRI	I	I	I	I	I	I	I	I	I	I	I	I	I	I	I	I	I	I	I	T	I	M	O
125	I	IM	I	I	I	M	I	I	I	I	I	I	I	I	R	I	I	I	I	I	I	I	I	I	I	M	I	M	M	I	M	I	I	I	I	I	I	M	I	M	I	O
126	R	R	R	R	R	R	R	R	R	R	R	R	R	R	R	R	R	R	R	R	R	R	R	R	R	R	R	R	R	R	R	R	R	R	R	R	R	R	R	R	R	R
130	M	M	M	M	M	M	M	M	M	M	M	M	M	M	M	M	M	M	M	M	M	M	M	M	M	OR	M	M	M	M	M	M	M	M	M	M	M	R	M	M	M	M
134	M	M	M	M	M	M	M	M	M	M	M	M	M	M	M	M	M	M	M	M	M	M	M	M	M	M	M	M	M	M	M	M	M	M	M	M	M	M	M	M	M	M

TABLE 9-1. Assignment of 47 individuals to *dgwa* by 42 informants. Underlined assignments indicate the assigner's evaluation of himself. O = any *dgwa* other than A, I, M, R, X, and — = "don't know" response.

claim on X. This argument clearly depends on the assumption that even peripheral claims have a good chance of being recognized in these data, appearing in the response of one informant or another. On the basis of there being so many cases in which only one, two, or three people assigned an individual to a particular *dgwa,* I feel that this is the case. That is, if I had asked informants to rank people in terms of their centrality to each *dgwa* in turn, I would have come out with essentially the same results as those in Table 9-2, which we might call the "average" (not "shared") model.

The question here is: How well, or to what extent, do individual models correspond to the average, and what tendencies can be seen in the way individuals make their assignments? In studying the assignments made by any one individual, we must first note that we cannot infer an individual's cognitive model directly from the answers he gave, in the same way we did in the "average" model. This is because of the crudity implicit in giving only one, or at most two, assignments for each individual. Here it is interesting to note that overt responses did correspond to the sociolinguistic constraint that in any given situation people

No. of votes received	% of votes received (approx. strength of claim)	A	I	M	R	X
42	100			26, 134	6, 66, 126	
38–41.5	90–99			5, 7, 17, 40, 58, 77, 87, 93, 99, 130	8, 14, 20, 32, 62, 64	
34–37.5	80–89		44, 49, 100, 125	19, 38, 50, 101, 102	33, 92, 95	
21–33.5	50–79		21, 23, 37, 88, 97	10, 34, 41, 42, 53, 69, 89, 111	43	
8.5–20.5	20–49		11, 111	43, 88, 97	11, 21, 69, 89	34
4–8	10–19	37	53, 102	92	37, 44, 53, 101	10, 41, 42, 50
0.5–3.5	1–10	7, 38, 50, 95	7, 10, 19, 34, 38, 40, 41, 43, 50, 58, 64, 87, 93, 95, 99	11, 14, 20, 33, 37, 44, 49, 100, 125	10, 34, 38, 41, 42, 49, 50, 58, 77, 88, 97, 99, 100, 125, 130	5, 17, 19, 32, 37, 38, 40, 69, 89
0	0–0	42 others	19 others	9 others	11 others	33 others

TABLE 9-2. Assignment of individuals with respect to each *dgwa*. (Numbers identify individuals of Table 9-1.)

are referred to as belonging to some one, or at most two, *dgwa*. Though nothing in my question referred to the number of *dgwa* an individual could be assigned to, the great majority of assignments (more than 97 percent of a total of 1,974 assignments) were made in terms of one *dgwa,* and no one assigned anyone to more than two. Thus an individual's responses cannot be translated directly into the core-periphery continuum we assume to be his "competence model" for each *dgwa* (except very crudely in terms of "half-assignments").

There are several interesting things, however, that we can look at in the pattern of individual responses. Comparing individuals' assignments of themselves (underlined assignments in Table 9-1) with others' assignments of them (other assignments in the same row) shows that in a majority of cases (approximately 85 percent) people see themselves as others see them, and assign themselves realistically, that is, to the same *dgwa* that they are assigned by a majority of members of the community. There are two notable types of exceptions. The first consists of people who assign themselves to a larger *dgwa* when most of their fellows would assign them to a smaller *dgwa*. Though I have only two clear cases of this—number 37, whom a majority of people assigned to I but who sees himself as an R, and number 43, assigned by the majority to R but who sees himself as an M—there are several other cases of people on whom community opinion is more or less split, but who in assigning themselves mention only one of the two *dgwa* in question—that one having the most members. Second, there are those who assign themselves to one of the smaller *dgwa* (A or X), despite the fact that they receive more assignments to one of the larger *dgwa*. This is the case, for example, for number 34 and number 41.

This leads us to the next point, i.e., that some respondents, despite my urging, still answered only in terms of M and R, others assigned people only to M, R, and I, and still others made assignments to all five. (Assignments to *dgwa* other than these five accounted for only 1.2 percent of the 1,974 assignments made.) Table 9-3 gives the total number of assignments made to each *dgwa*, related to the number of people who are judged to have any claim on that *dgwa*, i.e., receiving at least one-half vote. It would appear that, in addition to the "village book" effect, there is a tendency for people to overassign persons to those *dgwa* which already have more members. Thus Mapas, for example, not only has the highest number of people with some claim on it—thirty-eight—but each of these people received an average of 24.9 votes. At the opposite pole is Aying, where only five people were mentioned as having a claim, and where each of these five received an average of only 2.2 votes. This tendency to overassign to the already larger *dgwa* reflects the stress on solidarity argued in chapter 8 above. In descending order both of size and of votes per person, the *dgwa* of Mambump village are M, R, I, X, and A. Though it could be argued that

	Mapas (M)	Reyes (R)	Igiskone (I)	Iniay (X)	Aying (A)
Total number of votes received	947.0	630.5	298.5	52.5	11.0
Total number of people having any claim	38	36	27	14	5
Average of votes/person having any claim	24.9	17.8	11.1	3.8	2.2

TABLE 9-3. Number of assignments of 47 people to each *dgwa* per person having a claim on that *dgwa*.

A received so few votes as to warrant its being discarded from our calculations, it has been retained there because of its importance as a land-holding unit, which will be described in the next section.

Further, we note that an individual's assignments of others tend to reflect his own affiliation. That is, M people (defined in terms of receiving a high number of M assignments) tend to assign more other people to M, and similarly for R and I. A positive correlation of the number of assignments made to a given *dgwa* with the assigner's own rank order in the *dgwa* (as shown in Table 9-2) is statistically significant at the .05 level for each of R, M, and I. There is a rather substantial range of difference among informants' individual models in terms of the size of the various *dgwa* (see Table 9-6). For example, the lowest number of assignments made to the largest *dgwa,* M, was thirteen (by an entirely R person), whereas the highest was twenty-nine (by someone with a personal score of 39.5/42 on M).

To summarize briefly the relationship between individual models of *dgwa* affiliation and the average model constructed from individual responses: individual models of *dgwa* groupings are of the same form as the average model, though the data I collected do not permit their refinement in terms of very subtle distinctions. This form is that of a nuclear or core group of men for each *dgwa,* surrounded by other men whose claims to membership in or affiliation with it are of ever-decreasing strength. Individual models, though the same as the average model in form, tend to differ from it in content in several systematic ways. These differences principally involve an individual's placement of himself within the network as a whole, as well as a tendency to enhance his own group by disproportionately assigning others to it.

I shall deal with the nature of individual cognitive models and their relation to the average model in more detail after discussing the *dgwa* system in terms of the ownership of land.

LAND IN THE *DGWA* SYSTEM

The results of my questioning eighteen Mambump villagers about the *dgwa* affiliation of 140 garden plots, presented in Table 9-4, differ in several ways from the results of questioning on the affiliation of people. First, I no longer had to stress that people should assign the plots to *dgwa* other than R and M, as the smaller *dgwa* were mentioned with much higher relative frequency than they were in the assignment of people. Table 9-5, which indicates the absolute number of assignments to each *dgwa*, as well as the number on which there was near-unanimous agreement, shows that people were unanimously willing to attribute at least some plots to A and X, whereas no one individual was

Plots (numbers as in Figures)	Assigners (numbers as in Table 9-1)																	
	20	69	58	62	41	333	44	34	6	43	17	14	21	7	37	11	32	50
1	X	-	Q	X	X	Q	X	X	A	Q	Q	A	A	A	X	A	A	R
3	A	Q	Q	A	A	A	-	-	-	-	A	A	A	Q	A	A	A	M
4	R	R	R	R	R	R	R	R	R	R	R	R	R	R	R	R	R	R
5	X	X	X	X	X	X	X	X	X	X	X	X	X	X	X	IX	X	X
6	R	M	I	O	Q	I	I	Q	IR	R	I	O	I	Q	I	I	R	IR
7	X	A	O	Q	A	A	A	Q	O	A	O	O	A	Q	O	A	A	O
8	M	X	X	X	X	X	X	X	X	X	X	-	X	X	X	X	X	X
9	M	A	M	A	A	A	-	-	-	-	-	A	O	A	A	A	A	AO
10	R	Q	M	Q	X	Q	Q	X	RX	M	MR	O	O	I	OX	OR	X	M
11	I	M	I	M	I	I	I	I	O	I	I	O	I	I	O	I	I	M
12	M	M	M	M	M	M	M	M	M	M	M	M	M	M	M	IM	M	M
13	R	R	R	R	R	R	R	R	R	R	R	OR	R	R	R	R	R	R
14	MO	M	M	M	Q	R	R	M	O	M	R	M	O	O	R	O	R	R
15	R	R	R	R	R	R	R	R	R	R	R	R	R	R	R	I	R	R
16	A	A	R	A	A	A	A	A	A	A	A	A	A	A	A	A	A	A
17	R	M	R	Q	O	M	R	Q	X	M	R	M	R	IR	O	IR	A	R
18	MO	M	M	M	O	M	M	M	M	M	M	O	O	M	M	MO	M	O
19	I	I	I	I	I	I	I	I	IX	X	O	IO	I	O	I	IO	I	I
20	M	M	M	Q	M	M	Q	Q	Q	M	M	MO	O	M	M	MO	O	O
21	I	I	I	I	I	I	I	I	I	I	I	I	I	I	I	I	I	I
22	MO	M	M	M	M	M	M	M	M	M	M	MO	MO	MO	M	O	M	M
23	M	M	M	M	M	M	M	M	M	M	M	M	M	M	M	M	M	M
24	M	M	M	M	M	M	I	M	R	M	M	M	M	M	M	IM	M	M
25	A	A	I	A	A	A	Q	A	A	A	M	A	A	A	A	A	A	A
26	R	A	I	A	A	A	A	A	A	A	A	A	A	A	I	A	A	A
27	M	X	X	X	X	X	X	X	X	X	X	X	X	OX	X	I	X	X
28	R	X	I	X	X	X	I	X	RX	R	X	O	X	I	X	I	X	X
29	I	I	I	I	I	I	I	I	I	O	O	IO	I	IO	I	I	I	I
30	A	I	R	I	I	MA	I	X	-	R	M	R	I	R	I	X	X	X
31	R	R	R	R	R	R	R	R	R	R	IR	R	R	R	R	IR	R	I
32	R	M	X	R	X	Q	X	X	M	X	X	X	X	X	X	IX	I	I
33	A	A	I	A	A	A	A	A	A	A	A	A	A	A	A	A	A	O
34	R	R	R	R	R	R	R	IR	R	R	R	R	R	R	MR	IR	R	R
36	R	M	M	M	M	M	I	IX	M	MR	R	I	O	R	O	O	R	M
37	R	R	R	R	R	R	IR	R	R	R	R	R	R	R	R	IR	R	R
38	M	A	I	A	A	M	A	A	A	M	M	A	A	A	A	A	A	A
39	R	R	R	R	R	R	I	R	R	R	R	R	R	R	R	IR	R	R
40	I	I	I	I	I	I	I	I	I	I	I	I	I	I	I	I	I	I
41	O	Q	I	O	I	I	I	I	IO	I	I	IO	I	I	I	I	I	I
42	I	I	I	I	I	I	I	I	I	I	O	X	I	O	I	I	I	I
43	M	M	M	M	M	M	M	O	M	M	M	M	M	M	M	M	M	M
44	X	X	X	R	X	R	X	X	X	X	X	R	X	X	X	IR	X	X
45	M	M	M	M	M	M	M	M	M	M	M	M	M	M	M	M	M	M
46	M	M	M	M	M	M	M	M	M	M	M	M	M	M	M	MO	M	M
47	M	M	M	M	M	I	M	R	R	R	I	M	M	IR	MR	MR	O	M
48	R	R	M	Q	R	O	R	R	R	R	O	OR	R	R	O	O	R	O
49	R	R	R	R	R	R	R	R	R	R	R	R	R	R	R	IR	R	R
50	OR	Q	I	I	O	I	I	O	O	I	O	O	I	I	I	IO	I	R
52	I	I	I	I	I	I	I	I	I	I	I	I	I	I	I	I	I	I
53	I	X	I	I	I	I	I	M	I	I	I	I	M	M	I	I	I	I
54	I	I	I	I	I	I	I	I	I	I	I	I	I	I	I	I	I	I
55	M	M	M	M	M	Q	M	M	M	M	M	M	R	MO	M	IO	M	M
56	M	M	R	M	M	M	M	M	M	R	M	O	M	M	M	IM	M	M
57	M	X	X	X	X	M	X	A	I	M	X	X	X	O	X	IX	X	X
58	X	A	I	A	A	A	A	A	A	A	AO	A	A	A	A	A	A	A
59	M	M	M	M	M	M	M	M	R	M	R	R	M	R	O	IR	R	M
60	R	X	R	R	M	Q	I	X	R	R	I	R	R	R	R	R	IX	R	R
62	R	IX	X	X	R	R	I	X	R	R	O	R	X	R	X	IO	X	X
63	R	I	I	I	I	I	I	I	I	I	I	IA	I	I	I	I	I	I
64	I	I	I	I	I	I	I	I	I	I	I	I	I	I	I	I	I	I
65	R	A	I	A	A	A	A	A	A	A	A	A	A	A	A	AI	A	A
66	R	A	I	I	AR	I	I	IR	R	R	R	R	A	R	AI	O	R	A
68	O	M	M	M	O	O	I	O	O	R	O	O	R	R	O	I	R	I
71	R	R	R	R	R	R	R	R	R	R	R	R	R	I	R	IR	R	R
72	O	A	O	O	A	A	A	A	A	A	A	AO	A	A	A	A	A	O
73	I	I	I	I	I	I	I	I	I	I	O	I	IO	I	I	I	I	I
75	R	X	R	R	R	R	R	X	R	R	R	R	R	R	R	IR	R	R
76	M	X	X	X	X	X	X	X	X	X	X	X	X	X	X	I	X	O
77	A	A	M	A	A	A	A	A	A	A	A	A	A	A	A	A	A	A
78	I	I	I	I	I	I	I	I	I	I	I	I	I	I	I	I	I	I
79	M	M	M	M	M	M	M	M	R	M	M	M	M	M	I	O	O	R	M
80	A	A	I	A	A	A	A	A	A	A	A	A	A	A	A	A	A	A
81	M	X	I	X	X	Q	I	X	M	I	X	X	X	X	X	I	X	X
82	M	M	M	M	M	M	M	M	M	M	M	M	M	M	M	M	M	M
83	M	M	M	M	M	M	M	M	O	M	O	M	O	M	M	MO	O	I

TABLE 9-4. Assignment of 140 plots by 18 individuals, numbered as in Table 9-1. O = any response other than A, I, M, R, X; Q = "don't know" response; indicates that the informant was not asked to identify that item.

180

Plots (numbers as in Figures) — Assigners (numbers as in Table 9-1)

Plots	20	69	58	62	41	333	44	34	6	43	17	14	21	7	37	11	32	50
84	R	R	R	R	R	R	R	R	R	R	R	R	R	R	R	IR	R	R
85	M	M	M	M	M	M	M	MO	MO	M	M	MO	O	MO	O	O	O	O
86	O	I	I	Q	I	I	IO	O	I	I	I	O	O	I	O	IO	I	O
87	R	R	R	R	R	R	R	R	R	R	R	R	R	R	R	R	R	R
88	R	A	R	A	A	I	A	A	A	R	AR	A	A	I	A	A	R	A
89	R	I	I	Q	A	I	I	I	I	R	IM	AI	I	I	I	I	A	I
90	Q	M	M	M	M	M	X	M	M	M	M	O	M	OX	O	OX	O	R
91	I	I	I	Q	I	I	I	F	I	I	I	I	I	I	I	I	X	I
92	I	A	I	A	A	A	AI	A	X	I	A	A	A	A	A	AI	A	O
93	R	M	R	M	M	I	I	M	M	R	R	Z	R	M	O	IM	R	I
94	M	X	X	X	M	X	X	X	X	X	X	X	X	I	X	IR	X	X
95	M	M	M	M	M	M	IM	X	MO	O	R	O	M	MO	O	O	M	M
96	M	M	I	I	A	A	AI	A	I	A	A	A	I	AI	A	I		X
97	O	O	R	Q	Q	O	O	O	O	O	O	O	O	O	O	O	O	O
98	M	A	I	A	A	I	A	A	A	M	AO	A	M	A	AO	A		M
99	M	M	M	M	M	M	I	M	R	I	M	M	I	I	M	I	M	M
100	M	M	M	M	M	M	-	-	-	M	M	M	M	M	M	M	M	M
101	M	M	M	M	M	M	M	M	MR	M	M	M	M	M	O	IM	M	M
102	R	M	M	M	M	R	I	M	R	X	R	R	R	R	R	IR	R	R
103	R	IA	I	I	I	I	I	A	I	I	I	I	I	I	I	I	I	R
104	R	X	X	X	X	I	IX	I	X	I	I	X	X	R	X	IX	I	I
105	L	I	I	I	I	I	I	I	I	I	I	I	I	I	I	I	I	I
106	A	I	I	A	I	A	A	A	A	A	AO	A	A	A	A	A		A
107	M	M	M	M	M	M	A	M	M	R	M	O	R	M	O	IM	R	M
108	M	M	M	M	M	M	M	M	M	M	M	M	M	M	M	M	M	M
109	R	R	R	R	R	R	R	R	R	R	R	R	R	R	R	IR	R	R
110	M	M	M	M	O	MO	IO	O	O	R	I	O	R	R	O	I	R	M
111	M	M	M	M	M	I	I	M	M	I	IM	O	R	I	O	IM	I	I
112	M	M	M	M	M	M	M	M	I	I	M	R	M	O	O	R		M
113	R	R	M	R	R	R	R	R	R	O	R	R	R	IO	R	R		
114	R	I	I	I	I	I	I	I	I	I	I	I	I	I	I	IO	I	I
115	R	M	M	O	O	M	I	O	O	R	R	O	O	R	O	IO	R	O
116	R	A	M	A	A	I	A	O	O	O	M	I	A	O	I	I	O	O
117	O	M	M	M	M	I	I	Q	O	M	I	O	I	I	O	I	M	M
118	I	I	I	I	I	I	I	I	I	I	I	I	I	I	I	I	I	R
119	M	M	M	M	M	M	M	M	M	M	M	M	M	M	M	M	M	M
120	R	R	R	R	R	R	I	R	R	R	R	R	R	R	R	R	R	R
121	I	I	I	I	I	I	I	I	I	I	I	I	I	I	I	I	I	I
122	M	M	X	X	X	X	I	X	X	R	I	X	X	O	X	I	X	I
123	R	I	I	X	X	I	I	I	I	O	O	O	X	I	I	I	X	X
124	M	X	X	X	M	X	X	X	X	X	M	X	X	O	X	XI	X	X
125	I	I	I	I	I	I	I	I	I	I	X	I	I	I	I	I	I	I
126	R	R	R	R	R	R	R	R	R	R	R	R	R	R	IR	R	R	R
127	M	A	I	A	A	A	A	A	A	A	AO	A	I	A	AI	A		M
128	M	M	X	X	X	M	M	X	X	M	M	M	X	O	X	I	X	M
129	I	I	I	I	I	I	I	I	I	I	IO	I	I	I	I	I	I	I
130	M	M	M	M	M	M	M	O	O	M	O	O	O	MO	M	O	O	MO
131	X	X	X	X	X	X	X	X	X	X	X	X	X	O	X	IX	X	X
132	M	M	M	M	M	M	M	M	M	M	M	O	M	X	M	MX	R	M
133	R	R	R	R	R	R	R	R	R	R	R	R	R	R	R	I	R	R
134	I	I	I	I	I	I	I	I	I	I	I	I	I	I	I	I	I	I
136	M	M	M	M	I	A	A	I	O	A	R	A	O	A	I	I	A	M
137	R	R	X	X	X	X	X	X	X	X	X	X	X	O	X	IX	X	X
138	M	M	M	M	M	M	M	M	M	M	M	M	M	M	M	M	M	M
139	X	I	I	I	I	I	I	I	I	X	O	IO	I	I	I	I	I	I
140	X	X	X	X	X	X	X	X	X	X	X	X	X	O	I	I	X	X
141	R	X	X	X	R	X	IR	X	O	R	R	I	I	R	IR	R		R
142	A	A	I	A	A	A	-	-	-	-	A	AO	A	AO	A	AI	A	O
143	A	A	I	A	A	A	-	-	-	-	M	AO	A	M	A	I	A	A
144	A	A	A	A	A	A	-	-	-	-	A	AO	A	A	A	A	A	A
145	R	A	I	A	A	A	-	-	-	-	-	AO	A	I	A	A	A	A
146	A	A	A	A	A	A	-	-	-	-	A	AO	A	A	A	A	A	A
147	A	A	IA	A	A	A	-	-	-	-	A	O	A	A	A	A	A	A
148	A	A	I	A	A	A	-	-	-	-	A	AO	A	A	A	A	A	A
149	R	M	M	M	M	M	-	-	-	-	-	-	M	M	M	M	M	M

	Mapas (M)	Reyes (R)	Igiskone (I)	Iŋiay (X)	Aying (A)
Total number of votes received	543.0	455.0	594.0	275.0	363.0
Total number of plots (of 140) ever mentioned as belonging	70	70	108	41	38
Number of plots on which there was near-unanimous agreement (17–18 of 18 votes)	10	11	12	1	5
Number of plots on which majority or more (9.5 or more of 18 votes) agreed	29	20	27	15	24

TABLE 9-5. Number of assignments of 140 plots of land made by 18 people to five Mambump *dgwa*.

considered to belong to A or X by even half of the assigners. The extent of variation in individual responses appears, however, to be about the same, whether it is people or plots being assigned, as can be seen in Table 9-6.

In considering plots, we have the added advantage of a geographical or two-dimensional representation which clearly indicates the pattern of overlapping concentric circles postulated as a model of the *dgwa* organization of people. Figure 9-1 shows both the nucleus of each *dgwa*'s territory (plots which received at least 17 of 18 possible assignments to one *dgwa*) and the surrounding area we can surely identify as belonging to each *dgwa* (plots receiving at least 9.5 assignments to one *dgwa*). Figure 9-2, which indicates those plots which were identified at least 2.5 times of a possible 18 as belonging to a particular *dgwa*, shows a great deal of overlapping.

With respect to the *dgwa* affiliation of plots, then, it is even pictorially clear that there are certain core areas that are more or less unanimously attributed to particular *dgwa*, and that as one gets farther and farther from the core area there is increasing variation in the *dgwa* attribution of particular plots.

Further analysis indicates that variation among individuals in the way they assign plots to *dgwa* is not random, and that certain trends and tendencies are evident in this variation. For example, informants do tend to overassign plots to those *dgwa* on which they themselves have strongest claims, i.e., to which they are most frequently assigned

	Assignments of 47 people to:					Assignments of 140 plots to:				
	Mapas (M)	Reγes (R)	Igiskone (I)	Iŋiay (X)	Aying (A)	Mapas (M)	Reγes (R)	Igiskone (I)	Iŋiay (X)	Aying (A)
Mean number of assignments by all informants (42 for people; 18 for plots)	22.6	15.0	7.1	1.3	0.3	30.2	25.3	33.0	15.3	20.7
Lowest number of assignments made by any informant	13.0	11.0	0.0	0.0	0.0	15.5	14.0	20.0	7.0	2.5
Highest number of assignments made by any informant	29.0	23.0	15.0	7.5	2.0	47.0	44.5	63.5	23.0	29.0

TABLE 9-6. Variation in assignment of people and plots.

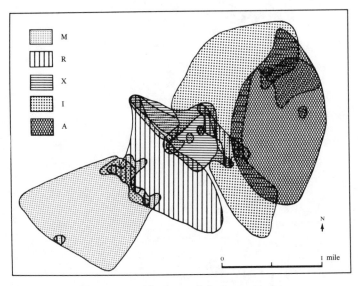

Figure 9–1. Nucleus of *dgwa* territories.

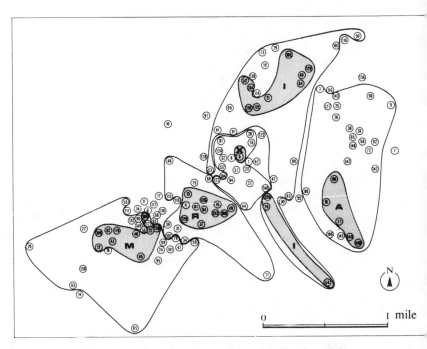

Figure 9–2. Overlapping peripheral territories of *dgwa*.

by others. The data on this relationship show a strong correlation for I, M, and X. An example of this tendency is evident in the case of informant number 44, who is rated by his fellows as being the "most I" in the village, and who gave 51 of his 140 assignments to I, as opposed to an average of 33 assignments I received. A further tendency observed for I, M, and X, though not as strong, was that people's biases in assigning land corresponded to their biases in assigning other people.

One other result came from looking at land people actually use. I had usage data on particular plots for 28 of the men in the sample. Correlating the assignments given to the men with the assignments given to the plots they claimed to have used proved significant in the cases of A, M, and R. That is, there is a relationship between the land people use and the way they are situated by their fellows in respect to the various *dgwa*. This relationship holds despite the fact that by no means all of the land the 28 people had used actually belonged to them, or even to the *dgwa* of which they considered themselves a part. Usufruct arrangements were, like many described in the ethnographic literature for New Guinea (see, for example, Brookfield and Brown 1963), extremely varied.

LAND AND PEOPLE: STABILITY AND CHANGE

The relationship between people's rights to land, both inherited and acquired, and the actual use they make of land, provides a dynamic element in the system. There are, clearly, stable elements involved. Claims an individual can make are clearly conditioned by the *dgwa* affiliation of his ancestors. For example, a person with four R grandparents would have a harder time making himself out to be, say, an M than would someone with one M grandparent. Nevertheless, it is probably the case that the affiliation of people with particular *dgwa* is less stable than the affiliation of plots. People have many important relationships other than descent (e.g., marriage, cooperation) which can, as it were, change their public image. Land, on the other hand, is definitely fixed in its physical relationship to the core area of each *dgwa*, though here, too, a situation in which a particular plot was used for some time by important men from a *dgwa* that had not previously had a claim on that plot might come to be thought of as at least peripheral territory of that *dgwa*.

We have seen that both land and people can be thought of as units that fit into the *dgwa* system of the Buang in very similar ways. I have proposed that the Buang model of *dgwa* organization consists of a core-periphery continuum in terms of the degree of centrality of each item (person or plot) to each *dgwa*. The degree of centrality of any item can only add up to 100 percent over all *dgwa*.

Land and people are associated by the fact that people inherit, and use, land belonging to one or more *dgwa* in which they have interests or with which they claim affiliation. Claims can be substantiated logically through a number of possible kin ties (see chapter 8 above), and practically through actual use of land. People appear to base their view of the place of particular items within the system both on what we might call their "fixed" or "ascribed" characteristics (i.e., ancestry for people; geographical location for land) and on current relationships between people and land. People's conceptions are also influenced by their own position with respect to the various *dgwa*.

Given these formulations, we do not need to view the fact that people are unanimous in their assignments of only a very small percentage of items as an indication of instability in the system. It is clear that items do change their position in the average model slowly, as individuals, reanalyzing their own knowledge of (and interest in) particular items, gradually come to shift their view of how the item in question should be placed.

INDIVIDUAL VERSUS "SHARED" CULTURE

The preceding paragraph has again raised the issue of the relationship of individual cognitive maps to the culture considered more broadly, as a system. So far I have referred to the model constructed by summing individual informants' responses as an "average," rather than a "shared" model. It is now time to examine the psychological reality of such a model, and to relate it to some of the broader issues in cultural theory.

In a discussion of the general orientation of cognitive anthropology, Tyler (1969a: 3) says:

> It is assumed that each people has a unique system for perceiving and organizing material phenomena—things, events, behavior, and emotions (Goodenough 1957). The object of study is not these material phenomena themselves, but the way they are organized in the minds of men. Cultures then are . . . cognitive organizations of material phenomena.

But "cognitive organizations" are, as Goodenough (1964: 11) rightly insists, the property "not of the community but of its members." If, then, the ethnographer must start by investigating the "cognitive organizations" of single informants, he runs into the same kind of problems that exist for the linguist who makes the mistake of thinking that a single informant's speech can be taken to represent an entire speech community because "language is shared." Tyler recognizes this problem, stating that systematic intracultural variation, explicable in terms of social and contextual factors, may be of great interest to the anthropologist. He (Tyler 1969a: 5) goes on to cite Wallace and Hymes in support of his contention that "variations are not mere deviations from some assumed basic organization; with their rules of occurrence *they are the organization*." Tyler's concept of systematic variation as enunciated here represents an important and, moreover, realistic qualification of his earlier statement regarding the "unique system" of "each people."

Analyses of culture from a cognitive perspective should deal with the issue of intracultural variation in cognitive maps, though it is often sidestepped in one way or another. To take one well-known example, Goodenough (1965: 111) discusses why only one informant was used in the construction of what he labels a "duty scale of 'setting oneself above another' in Truk." I will quote him at some length to make the point clear:

> Because status scales are worked out separately for each informant, they tend to be "perfect" scales, in which no item is distributed in a way that is inconsistent at any point with the distributions of other items in the scale. . . . In attitude and opinion surveys, where many informants are asked the same set of questions relating to a single object and their different responses are plotted so as to rank the informants and the specific answers to the questions against each other simultaneously . . . different informants do not share the same cognitive organization of the subject under study in all respects [and] perfect scales cannot be obtained. Here, however, we are looking at how identity relationships and duties are simultaneously ranked against one another in the mind of one informant as revealed by the distribution of his answers. Under such circumstances almost perfect scales may reasonably be expected.

Despite this caveat, the discussion continues as if the duty scale in question were in fact shared by all Trukese, and Goodenough (1965: 19–20) uses it to explain public reaction to various breaches of conduct (again defined in terms of the scale). We have no reason to doubt that most Trukese do in fact share many of the same rules relating to rights and duties, but the point is that the analysis was specifically stated by the author to have been based on work with one informant for reasons of elegance and rigor, and its relevance with respect to other members of the community appears simply to have been taken for granted.

My analysis of the Buang *dgwa* supports Goodenough's position that cognitive models must, theoretically, be construed as a property of the individual. I have posited that the basic model held by each individual Buang is constituted by his ideas of the degree to which each person or plot belongs to each *dgwa*. An individual's model is based on his knowledge of the kinship connections and land use activities relevant to each item. His verbal statements about *dgwa* affiliation reflect, however, not only this information, which can be expected to differ for each individual, but his interest, which also clearly differs for each individual. They also reflect conventions for speaking about *dgwa* (e.g., a maximum of two can be claimed at once; *dgwa* do not constitute a subject of argument; solidarity with others present is emphasized whenever possible).

An understanding of the precise nature of any individual's model thus involves the crucial methodological issues of how to interpret verbal statements in order to deduce from them the underlying cognitive model or map which permits those statements to be made. There is no way of identifying a particular statement by an informant (a surface-level phenomenon) as being a variant, or of identifying its rules of occurrence, in isolation from an analysis of the organizational or systematic aspects of the set of statements of which it is a member. An individual informant, in obeying the conventions of discourse and displaying sensitivity to the social context of his utterances, may display as much variation in the content of his responses as is observed between informants.

This intraindividual variability is the basis of my earlier statement that an individual informant's categorization of people and plots of land as reported during systematic interviews based on uniform eliciting procedures, should not be taken to represent his cognitive model. This set of answers constitutes, rather, only one surface representation of that model. By looking at tendencies that appear in the grouping of these representations, however, we can make certain inferences about the ways in which the individual models underlying these representations tend to differ, and, perhaps even more importantly, the ways in which they are the same.

In constructing a model based on tendencies observed over all informants, we rejected a "lowest common denominator" approach, which would lead to the inclusion in the various *dgwa* of only those items on which there was unanimity. This line of reasoning would in fact lead us not to accept the average model as represented in Table 9-2 and Figures 9-1 and 9-2, because it is not, strictly speaking, shared (e.g., we assume in the average model, Table 9-2, that number 53 has a claim of 10–20 percent strength on I, but in this representation at least, 80–90 percent of respondents did not admit any recognition of number

53 as having a claim on I, and thus might be said not to "share" this view of number 53's position).

The average model as we have constructed it represents, then, not the lowest common denominator, but rather that position for each item from which its position in all individual models will differ the least. The abstract model is probabilistic rather than deterministic in nature, since nothing in the system is considered to be fixed absolutely, even at the underlying cognitive level, and even for one informant. Individual models can thus incorporate change, and sharing is a matter of degree.

We are now in a position to clarify the relationship between the set of responses given by each informant in the formal interview, which provided the bulk of the data for this analysis, and the underlying model of which this is but one representation. I assume that what these data represent is a minimum first approximation to each informant's model. If, as we see in Table 9-1, informant number 5 says that subject number 6 is an R, we can safely assume that number 5 feels that number 6's most important claim is on R, but we reserve for further investigation the possibility that number 5 recognizes that number 6 has weaker claims on some other *dgwa*. The "average" model, though of course more abstract, permits a closer approximation to psychological reality at the community level, in that it provides us with a judgment of the degree of consensus and thus with a measure of the relative strength of claims. Checking what everyone said about number 6 in Table 9-2, and finding that he was rated 100 percent R, does not permit us to eliminate completely the possibility that number 6 has some recognized claims on *dgwa* other than R, but it would certainly lead us to suspect that number 6's claim on R is very strong and his claims on other *dgwa* very weak. Because the average model gives us a much more accurate view of the relative positioning of items, I would argue that it is the best starting point in any attempt to construct individuals' models.

CONCLUSIONS

The structure of the Buang *dgwa* system has been analyzed as an important part of Buang culture, at a level of abstraction higher than that of the cognitive models of individuals. This structure involves a basic set of assumptions, shared in very large degree by individual Buang, about the nature of *dgwa*, the rules of how items can be attributed to *dgwa*, and the appropriate ways to talk about *dgwa*. It also provides for systematic internal variation, in that the cognitive models of individuals are interrelated in specific ways, depending on their knowledge and interest (shared to varying degrees). The analysis of each item as occupying a variable range on a set of interrelated dimensions ("A-ness," "M-ness," "I-ness," etc.) resulted from the examination of a large number of responses by a large number of individuals.

In addition to the advantages of such a model in terms of descriptive adequacy (including the basis it provides for understanding the way people talk about and act towards *dgwa*), its incorporation of variability allows for the interpretation of differences in cognitive maps as being both "of degree" and "of kind," thereby escaping the sterility of an extreme stand on the issue of sharedness of culture. In addition, it can treat changes in both individual and shared models in a way which seems more closely related to the way in which such changes actually take place.

II. Studies of Particular Linguistic Variables

The papers in this section explore the distribution of particular linguistic variables within two speech communities. Chapters 10, 11, and 12 deal with aspects of the grammar of Tok Pisin, and chapters 13, 14, and 15 with French spoken in Montréal. Both studies were joint projects, begun as synchronic surveys of contemporary speech and speech variation, though both were concerned with problems of language change. In understanding our French data, we found it instructive to explore the history of the phenomena in question in the French language: this was relevant in particular to the deletion of ne (chapter 14) and to the alternation between the auxiliaries avoir and être (chapter 15). We were not able to find as much relevant material for the history of indefinite tu (chapter 13), since the type of discursive practices we describe for contemporary speakers are difficult to parallel in historical materials.

The history of Tok Pisin is much shorter, but here again we ran into similar problems as for the French. The more "discursive" the topic, the more difficult it was to find historical parallels. This was especially the case with respect to the development of the relativizer ia (chapter 11). The development of the future marker, bai (chapter 10) and the cliticization of subject pronouns (chapter 12) were somewhat easier to document in terms of their historical origins.

The main general interest we had in both cases was the process of grammaticalization. Initially, this was the focus of the Tok Pisin study, as Laberge and I set out to examine what features of Tok Pisin linguistic practice were becoming grammaticalized with creolization. We expected to find major differences between the speech of second-language (adult) speakers of Tok Pisin, and the new creolizing generation of first-language speakers. We found that such differences were fewer than we had thought, and were led to take a more broadly social and functional view of the relation between language use and grammatical elaboration (see also Sankoff 1977b). In the process, we developed a broader view of grammaticalization, one that also applied to our work on French. We became interested in how, through discursive practice, elements can change grammatical categories, become part of new paradigms. This process is *particularly relevant in chapters 11, 12, 13, and 15. All of the chapters deal with problems deriving from the overlapping of categories, and from the fusion of synchrony with diachrony. All of the chapters struggle with the notion of discursive equivalence of originally disparate grammatical elements during periods of change, before grammatical equivalence has been worked out (cf. also D. Sankoff and Thibault, in press). As such, we hope that they will be of some relevance to scholars working in other speech communities.*

10.

On the Acquisition of Native Speakers by a Language

GILLIAN SANKOFF AND SUZANNE LABERGE

This chapter deals with some changes currently taking place in the structure and use of the language known to linguists as Neo-Melanesian, Melanesian Pidgin, and New Guinea Pidgin,[1] and called Tok Pisin by its speakers. We describe in particular a number of changes in the grammatical structures used to indicate future time, and we link this change to the passage of Tok Pisin from a second-language *lingua franca* to the first language of a generation of urban New Guineans.

1. BACKGROUND OF TOK PISIN

New Guinea Tok Pisin is considered to be a descendant of the wide-spread South Pacific pidgin known in the nineteenth century as Beach-la-Mar (Churchill 1911)[2] and to have gained a foothold in New Britain,

This paper was first published in *Kivung* 6 (1973): 32–47. It appears here with minor editorial revisions. A preliminary version appeared in DeCamp and Hancock, eds., 1974: 73–85. We wish to thank all of those who helped in the preparation of this paper, particularly the residents of Lae who allowed us to record them and their families. Special thanks are due to Col. Harrington of the Pacific Island Regiment, who granted us access to Igam Barracks and extended many courtesies which were much appreciated; to Rev. Taylor and Rev. McCormack, for many kindnesses; and above all to the numerous residents of Igam Barracks who welcomed us in their homes. We also thank Eleanor Herasimchuk Wynn of the Language Behavior Research Laboratory, University of California, Berkeley, for assistance in compiling the data.

1. The standard source on the language has for many years been the work of Hall (1943, 1952, 1955a, 1955b), who used the term Neo-Melanesian, as did Mihalic (1957). Wurm (1971b) and Laycock (1970a) speak of New Guinea Pidgin; Mihalic (1971) and Brash (1971) of Melanesian Pidgin.

2. Churchill's book is based on a number of late nineteenth-century and early twentieth-century publications citing examples of the Beach-la-Mar "jargon." Despite the unevenness of his sources, examination of the many sentences compiled by Churchill reveals an unexpectedly close relationship with

the location of the German capital of New Guinea at one period, by the 1880s (Salisbury 1967; Laycock 1970b). The extreme linguistic diversity of New Guinea, with approximately seven hundred languages for its population of two and one half million, gave Tok Pisin a selective advantage in the colonial situation. It was, in fact, very rapidly adopted as a *lingua franca* among New Guineans having no other language in common and suddenly finding themselves in a number of new situations where communication was necessary: as laborers on plantations, crews on coastal vessels, domestic servants and other employees of government officers, and a host of other situations created by the colonial system. Most students of Tok Pisin maintain that from its beginning, it has been used primarily for communication among New Guineans rather than for communication between New Guineans and Europeans.

This very useful *lingua franca* function of Tok Pisin has been the principal reason for the way it has spread and flourished, presently numbering more than a half million speakers, more than double the number of New Guineans having any other language in common (Laycock 1970a: x; Table 5-2, p. 123). An important reason why Tok Pisin has had a selective advantage over the other languages with which one might say it has been in competition (the approximately seven hundred Papuan and Austronesian languages, German, Japanese, English) may be that it is easier to learn as a second language. Like other pidgin languages, it has been, up to the present, nobody's native language, but rather a second language for all its speakers. A language relatively easy to learn because, also like other pidgin languages, it had in comparison with natural languages a relatively limited vocabulary, relatively few grammatical categories, and a relative lack of grammatical complexity. This "relative ease of learning" contention is based not on the experience of native speakers of English in learning Tok Pisin, but on reports by many Papuans and New Guineans who have learned it as adolescents or adults.

2. PIDGINIZATION VERSUS CREOLIZATION

Hymes (1971) has recently proposed that pidginization as a process involves reduction and simplification of language structure that can be directly related to the reduction of linguistic (communicative) function. Thus the kinds of simplifications mentioned above generally appear to

---

Tok Pisin, a large number of the words and usages being still current in the language. It should be noted that there was also some input to Tok Pisin from the speech of returned laborers from the Queensland sugar fields, and for further historical details cf. Laycock (1970b) and Salisbury (1967).

be introduced in the interests of facilitating communication in a limited range of communication situations. That is, the pidgin is not used by anyone for the whole range of communication situations in which he/she participates: everyone has his/her native language to fall back on. This relationship between functional (communicative) and structural (grammatical) aspects can be characterized as follows:

> *Invariance in form,* rather than allomorphic variation; *invariant relation between form and grammatical function,* rather than derivational and inflectional declensional and conjugational variation; *largely monomorphemic words,* rather than inflected and derived words; *reliance on overt word order;* all have in common that they minimize the knowledge a speaker must have, and the speed with which he must decode, to know what in fact has grammatically happened. (Hymes 1971: 73)

Hymes goes on to say that, conversely, creolization as a process involves expansion and complication of language structure, again directly related to the expansion of functions of the language. Using the traditional definition of a creole as a pidgin which has acquired native speakers, Labov (ms., 1971) has also recently argued that creolization involves concomitant complication of structure, because pidgins do not seem to be grammatically adequate to function as natural languages, i.e., languages with native speakers. He says:

> Full competence in a pidgin grammar is still less than competence in one's native grammar. . . . we have objective evidence that pidgins do not provide all of the features which native speakers seem to demand in a language. When pidgins acquire native speakers, they change.

The goal of our research on Tok Pisin was not only to study the structure of the language as it is presently spoken in New Guinea but also to systematically investigate its contexts of use, including the range of competence displayed by different speakers. As such, it was important for us to make a series of recordings of Tok Pisin as it is actually used, over a wide range of communication situations. We hoped to discover systematic patterning of variation with respect to grammar and use, which would indicate the directions of linguistic change in the light of changes in usage.

3. PRESENT DAY USE OF TOK PISIN

During the last twenty years or so, Tok Pisin has undergone an impressive widening of its social and communicative functions. It has acquired the status of one of New Guinea's three official languages, and has been since 1964, the date of the inception of the first House of Assembly, the predominant language used in parliamentary debates. It has acquired two new channels other than the verbal. First, it has become a language of literacy, and is used in a host of newspapers, information bulletins, and the like. Second, it is the dominant radio language, though there are broadcasts in other languages as well. More important still, it has acquired a generation of native speakers. These people are the ever more numerous urbanites, more specifically, the children who have grown up in one of New Guinea's urban communities. Their parents may be from different areas, having no language in common except Tok Pisin, which is used as the household language. Even if the parents do have a native language in common, children growing up in towns frequently have little more than a partial and passive command of it. Parents commonly say: "The children only understand simple commands like when we tell them to go and get something, and they never answer us in our own language, but only in Tok Pisin." On the basis of observations we made during June–August 1971 (principally in Lae, but also in Wewak and Port Moresby), it appears that the native speakers of Tok Pisin are, by and large, under twenty years of age, and that their numbers are growing very rapidly.

4. NATIVE SPEAKERS (CREOLIZATION) AND LINGUISTIC CHANGE

The fact that Tok Pisin is presently undergoing creolization (or depidginization)[3] enables us to examine the ways in which the social and communicative functions of a language may be related to its structure. We thus attempted to discover in what respects the Tok Pisin spoken by this new generation of native speakers is different from that spoken by their (nonnative speaker) parents, in order to understand the kinds of changes that are taking place in the grammar of the language as it becomes a creole (i.e., a natural language). We hypothesized that native speakers in general tend to have little patience with or respect for a language with few grammatical categories, limited lexicon, virtually no morphophonemic reduction rules, insufficient redundancy, and little opportunity for stylistic maneuver. (These are of course *relative* characteristics; cf. also Kay and Sankoff 1973. The fact that Tok Pisin has been widely and extensively used in a great variety of communicative situations for several generations is sufficient explanation for its considerable stylistic resources, as clearly evidenced by Brash (1971), by the numerous literary works produced in the past five or six years,

3. The terms "creolization" and "depidginization" are used here synonymously.

and by listening to any fluent Tok Pisin-speaking politician. Our goal was to investigate what particular aspects of grammar appear to be changing in the language as spoken by native speakers.)

There is a great range of competence in Tok Pisin among speakers who have acquired it at different ages and different historical periods, and who use it for different communicative purposes: the newly arrived migrant in town (who at first may speak little and halting Pisin); the ex-*luluai* or *tultul*[4] in villages long used to government patrols, who may have learned their Pisin as plantation laborers in German times; the young generation of town-born children, for whom it may be a first language. Though we made recordings of all these and many more, we concentrated on families in which Tok Pisin is used as the normal language in the home. The parents were all fluent speakers of Tok Pisin, people who had lived in town for many years and who had for a long time spoken Tok Pisin rather than their native language. In looking for differences between their speech and that of their children, for whom Tok Pisin is a native language, it may be too much to expect, after only one incomplete generation, discrete, qualitative differences. Though more obvious differences might easily be found by comparing, say, new immigrants with the urban children, we wanted to specifically examine differences between *fluent* second-language speakers (the parents) and first-generation native speakers (the children). In making some preliminary comparisons, we have observed a number of tendencies which may represent ongoing changes in the language.

The children speak with much greater speed and fluency, involving a number of morphophonemic reductions as well as a reduction in the number of syllables characteristically receiving primary stress. Whereas an adult will say, for the sentence "I am going home,"

(1) Mì gó lòng háus;

a child will often say

(2) Mì gò l:áus;

three syllables rather than four, with one primary stress rather than two.

The particular phenomenon we examine in this chapter is related to a further generalization of Labov's. He says (m.s., 1971: 29):

It is not at all obvious that a pidgin will develop obligatory tense markers when it becomes a native language. Yet this has hap-

4. Government-appointed "headman" and "interpreter" respectively, under the earlier system of administration. These officials have been replaced by a system of elected Local Government Councils.

pened in case after case. . . . When pidgins become creoles, the system of optional adverbs gives way to an obligatory tense marker next to the verb.

After examining a corpus of tapes and transcriptions of second-language speakers of Tok Pisin collected by Gillian Sankoff during the 1960s, Labov suggested that the adverb *bai* is presently shifting to the status of a future marker. This, he said, is evidenced by:

1. its reduction from *baimbai* to *bai* (a change which has almost gone to completion, *baimbai* being rare in current usage);

2. its loss of obligatory stress;

3. its occurence with adverbs having a future meaning, e.g.,

(3) klostu bai i dai 'soon he will die';

(4) bihain bai i kambek gen 'later it will come back again'

4. its apparent tendency to be placed next to the main verb, after the subject, rather than at the beginning of the sentence or in presubject position.

We will deal with these four points in the light of our corpus of native and nonnative speakers, in order to see whether the usage of *bai* by the two generations of speakers indicates change in its grammatical function. The corpus on which the present discussion is based consists of 395 examples of *bai* in the speech of eighteen people: nine children and adolescents, between the ages of five and seventeen, and nine adults, parents of seven of the children, and between the ages of approximately twenty-five and forty-five. The children include four boys and five girls; the adults, four men and five women. Recordings were made of mealtime conversations among families, children's play, gossip, and storytelling (including the recounting of events), and our examples are drawn from all these sources.

4.1. *Baimbai* > *bai* in Historical Perspective

Among 395 cases, involving several hours of taped speech of various kinds, we found only five instances of *baimbai,* pronounced [bə′mbai] or [bə′bai]. These five cases occurred in the speech of three of the nine adults in our sample; there were no instances in the speech of any of the nine children.

Though *baimbai* is very infrequent in the ordinary conversational speech of the adults we observed, and nonexistent in the usage of the children, it is still used regularly within the speech community in some contexts, notably in radio broadcasts. Though it appears to be disappearing today, *baimbai* (< English 'by and by') was most probably the original form. Exactly when the reduction process from *baimbai*

		Approx. age	No. of cases
children	J.M.	5	20
	C.W.	6	15
	S.D.	8	47
	W.D.	11	12
	P.T.	11	21
	L.X.	11	12
	J.B.	12	25
	J.P.	15	20
	L.Z.	17	20
Total			192
adults	Mrs. M.	25–30	22
	Mr. W.	40	21
	Mrs. W.	25–30	20
	Mr. D.	35	20
	Mrs. D.	35	24
	Mr. T.	45	20
	Mrs. T.	30	24
	Mr. X.	40	20
	Mrs. Z.	35	32
Total			203
Grand Total			395

TABLE 10-1. Children and adults in the sample. Adults are parents of children with corresponding second initials.

to *bai* was initiated is very unclear from the existing documentation. Churchill (1911) contains no mention of *bai*, nor does Mihalic (1957), for over a decade the most reliable and respected source. Both of these do, however, list *baimbai*, as does Murphy (1966: 59), noted as "*adv.*, afterwards, later, in time, then (future)." Murphy, however, also lists *bai*, noted as "*conj.*, then, after, that, in order that, in consequence, so that." By 1971 (p. 63), Mihalic had added *bai*, listed with *baimbai* as being derived from English 'by and by', and having the same range of meanings (though for the 'in order to' meaning, the only example cited is that of *bai*).

Though it would seem logical that *bai* is the result of a reduction of *baimbai* (involving deletion of the first, rather than the second syllable), the two forms appear to have existed side by side for a long time. Ann Chowning (personal communication) reports that in areas of New Britain in the 1950s, *bai* was the exclusively used form, with *baimbai* appearing later as a novel introduction. We hope that further research into historical sources will help to shed light on this problem.

It is clear that for our subjects the change has already taken place, *baimbai* having virtually disappeared from ordinary conversation. Whether it can be said that *bai* has in fact become the regular "future" marker will depend, however, on a more detailed study of time relations in the verb system as a whole. *Laik,* for example, is frequently mentioned in the literature (Murphy 1966; Mihalic 1971; Laycock 1970a) as an auxiliary indicating immediate future. Though we have not examined *laik* in any detail, we find its occurrence to be very frequent in our sample, in many cases carrying the "immediate future" meaning, as in the following example from our corpus:

> (5) . . . nait, em i no inap kaikai, em *bai* pilei long graun igo igo igo nait tru nau, bai em i *laik* slip *bai* em *bai* kaikai.
> '. . . at night he didn't eat, he would play in the dirt right up until the middle of the night, until he would be about to go to sleep, then he would eat.' (S.D.)

The speaker employs a complicated tense structure in this story, using unmarked forms (not shown in this extract) for single completed actions in the past, *bai* to indicate habitual actions in the past, and *bai* with *laik* to indicate habitual being about to do something in the past. *Ken* has also been mentioned (Wurm 1971b; Laycock 1970a) as an indicator of future time; however, its use as a future marker by Lae area residents we recorded (including people from many parts of Papua New Guinea) was not sufficiently frequent for the type of quantitative analysis which follows.

4.2. Stress

Our data on *bai* indicate that it never receives primary stress. Transcribing the stress pattern for all sentences containing *bai,* we found that we could, however, distinguish three stress levels: secondary stress, where *bai* receives full syllabic weight, analogous to stressed syllables in nouns or pronouns; tertiary stress, where *bai* still retains syllabic weight, with stress equivalent to "unstressed" syllables in nouns or adjectives, or to most prepositions. The fourth stress level involves a reduction of the vowel nucleus to [ə], or even its disappearance, so that *bai* is barely if at all distinguishable as a syllable. Examples of each of these levels appear as examples 6, 7, and 8 below:

> (6) Em *bai* yu kam, *bai* yu dai. (Mrs. T.) 'You come; you'll die.'

> (7) Ating *bai* klostu belo. (Mrs. D.) 'It must be nearly noon.'

(8) Suga bilong mi klostu *bai* [bə] finis nau. (C.W.) 'My sugar cane is nearly finished now.'

A tabulation of the number of cases in which *bai* receives each of the three stress levels indicates that the children show a definite tendency to place less stress on *bai* than do the adults. Figures presented in Table 10-2 show that whereas adult usage is almost evenly split between levels 3 and 2, level 2 predominating slightly, children are twice as likely to use level 3 for *bai* as level 2. Children also show a significant tendency to reduce *bai* to [bə] (level 4), a phenomenon virtually absent among the adults.

Considering the data individually we can see from the plot in Figure 10-1 that the results of Table 10-2 are not simply an artifact of aggregating the data. There is a definite slope from left to right, and from lower to higher percentages, indicating that nonnative speakers (the adults) show a much greater tendency to stress *bai* than do native speakers (the children). The use of minimal stress (level 4) was used only twice by adults (two speakers), whereas five of the nine children used it a total of twenty times.

The data on stress support the hypothesis that the grammatical function of *bai* is changing from that of an adverb to that of a tense marker, as we would expect the latter to carry less stress. As a marker, however, we might also expect *bai* to show another characteristic of markers, i.e., to exhibit high redundancy.

4.3. Redundancy

We found numerous examples of *bai* being used in sentences containing either adverbs of time such as *klostu* 'soon' (cf. examples 7 and 8 above), *bihain* 'later', and *nau* 'right now' (including immediate future), or other indications of future time. In these cases, *bai* is not semantically necessary, future meaning already being present in the adverb or adverbial phrase.

Stress level	Children	Adults
2	29.1%	51.7%
3	60.4%	47.3%
4	10.4%	1.0%
Total cases	192	203

TABLE 10-2. Differential stress on *bai* for adults and children.

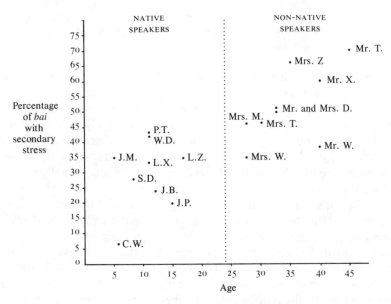

Figure 10-1. Percentage of cases of *bai* showing secondary stress for nine children and nine adults.

The redundant character of *bai* is also evident where it is used many times within a single sentence (as an alternative to the earlier system of marking a sentence, or even a longer segment, only once, usually at the beginning, for time, and using any following verbs in their invariant stem forms). The redundant, obligatory character of *bai* can be seen in the following quotation:

> (9) Pes pikinini ia *bai* yu go wok long,—*bai* yu stap ia na *bai* yu stap long banis kau bilong mi na *bai* taim mi dai *bai* yu lukautim na yu save wokim susu na *bai* yu givim long, wonem ia, stua, na *bai* ol i baim. 'You, first son, will go and work in,—you'll remain here and you'll stay on my cattle farm and when I die you'll look after it, and you'll be doing the milking and you'll send it to the, uh, store, and they will buy it.' (S.D.)

In this extract, every verb except *wokim* (qualified by the auxiliary *save*, meaning 'keep on doing') carries the marker *bai*. Application of the *bai* marker to every verb in compound sentences was extremely regular for all subjects studied, both adults and children, there being very few exceptions to this rule.

Dependent clauses in conditional constructions also appear to take *bai* obligatorily,[5] whether the independent clause contains *sapos* 'if' or not, as in examples 10 and 11.

(10) Sapos yu no lusim mi, *bai* mi kikim yu nau. 'If you don't let me go, I'll kick you.' (J.P.)

(11) Givim man i kaikai, em *bai* i dai. 'If you give it to somebody to eat, he'll die.' (Mr. T.)

Bai seems to be redundant and obligatory for both adults and children in the present sample, and we detected no significant differences in usage with respect to these characteristics. It is probable that the older generation of speakers, people in their sixties, do use *bai* less frequently, and we plan to examine our corpus of older speakers for this phenomenon.

4.4. Position of *bai* in the Sentence

(*Baim*)*bai* functioning as an adverb of time was free to occupy many positions in the sentence. It appears, however, that the clause-initial position has traditionally been favored. Mihalic (1957: 43) puts *baimbai* (glossed as 'in the future' or 'after a while') in a list of adverbs "to be found only at the beginning of a sentence." His 1971 edition modifies the position, putting it in a list of adverbs "found usually at the beginning of a sentence." If we interpret Mihalic's statement to include clause-initial as well as sentence-initial position, we find that all of the eleven examples of *baimbai* cited by Churchill (1911: 37) are of this type.

What is crucial in the switch to a marker function, however, is the position of (*baim*)*bai* with respect not to the sentence but to the verb. Here there appear to be three principal alternatives:

i. *bai* + NP + VP (NP = any noun phrase other than a pronoun);
ii. *bai* + pronoun + VP;
iii. *bai* + VP,

verbs normally being preceded by the predicate marker *i*. Of the eleven examples given by Churchill, four are of the first type. In our corpus, however, the frequency of this type is very low, as shown in Table 10-3. Cases where *bai* is separated from the verb phrase by more than a pronoun form only 5.9 percent of the total number of classifiable cases, twenty-two in all.

---

5. *Bai* indeed has broader functions than simply marking the future, as evidenced in example 6 above. An analysis of the whole tense-aspect system might show that it could be analyzed as an irrealis marker (cf. Bickerton 1975b).

	No. of cases
bai + NP + VP	22
bai + pronoun + VP	199
$\left\{\begin{array}{c}\text{NP}\\\text{pronoun}\\\emptyset\end{array}\right\}$ + bai + VP	151
Total	372^a

TABLE 10-3. Occurrences of *bai* in different positions.

[a] The twenty-three remaining cases were unclassifiable due to hesitations occurring after *bai*.

Looking at the data in detail, we can observe strong and consistent patterns of ordering with respect to the various pronouns and to the type of noun phrase involved. Table 10-4 indicates that virtually all the pronouns display a marked tendency to occur immediately adjacent to the verb phrase, with *bai* preceding the pronoun. This is the case for *mi, yu, ol, yumi, yu(tu)pela,* and *mi(tu)pela.* Of the fifteen cases where

	Order of *bai*	
subject NP	$bai + \left\{\begin{array}{c}\text{NP}\\\text{Pro}\end{array}\right\} + VP$	$\left\{\begin{array}{c}\text{NP}\\\text{Pro}\\\emptyset\end{array}\right\} + bai + VP$
mi	78	7
yu	52	1
ol	31	1
$\left\{\begin{array}{c}yumi\\\left\{\begin{array}{c}mi\\yu\end{array}\right\}\langle tu\rangle pela\end{array}\right\}$	22	6
subtotal	183	15
em	11	47
NP	22	36^a
$\emptyset$ subj.	—	53
subtotal	33	136
Total	216	151

TABLE 10-4. Order of *bai* with respect to various types of subject NP.

[a] Five of these cases also contain a *bai* preceding the noun phrase, of the pattern *bai* + NP + *bai* + VP.

NP =	Order of *bai*			Total
	bai + NP	NP + *bai*	*bai* + NP + *bai*	
I word	8	9	—	17
2 words	7	7	—	14
3 words	I	7	2	10
4 words	I	6	—	7
5+ words	—	2	3	5
Total	17	31	5	53

TABLE 10-5. Ordering of *bai* by number of phonological words in the subject NP.

bai was interposed between one of these pronouns and the verb phrase, eleven were found in the speech of children. *Em* is the only pronoun which tends to precede *bai*,[6] as do noun phrases.

Table 10-5 indicates that the number of phonological words in the subject noun phrase has an influence on the position of *bai*. In effect, *bai* rarely precedes a noun phrase longer than two phonological words, and when it does, the speaker frequently inserts another *bai* immediately before the verb phrase. Noun phrases composed of one or two phonological words are almost equally likely to precede or follow *bai*; longer noun phrases almost always precede *bai*.

Table 10-6 adds further clarification, showing that the relationships of Table 10-5 can perhaps be better understood in terms of grammatical conditioning. Noun phrases consisting of a single noun, a noun plus modifier, or a pronoun plus modifier can be either preceded or followed by *bai,* but more complex noun phrases are always followed by *bai.* It is interesting to note that subject noun phrases consisting of possessives (structures containing *bilong*) behave in the same way as subject noun phrases consisting of embeddings (i.e., containing surface verbs). Neither of these constructions occurs with a single preceding *bai.*

No significant differences with respect to the ordering of *bai* can be observed between the children and the adults. All speakers appear to share a rule that categorically inserts *bai* in immediate pre-VP position in the case of complex subject noun phrases, and which operates

6. The status of *em* as a pronoun that behaves similarly to the others is already dubious on other grounds. Its optional character permits its frequent omission, which accounts for the majority of 0-subject sentences in Table 10-4. See also chapter 12 below.

Structure of NP	Order of *bai*			Total
	bai + NP	NP + *bai*	*bai* + NP + *bai*	
{ mod. + Pro } { ⟨mod.⟩ + N }	15	16	1	32
{ mod. + Pro } { ⟨mod.⟩ + N } + adv.	2	1	1	4
{ N } { Pro } + *bilong* + { N } { Pro }	—	8	2	10
{ N } { Pro } + embedding	—	6	1	7
Total	17	31	5	53

TABLE 10-6. Ordering of *bai* by grammatical structure of subject NP.

with a probability of approximately 0.5 in the case of other nonpronominal subject noun phrases.

DISCUSSION

That *bai* has been undergoing a transition to the status of a future marker is supported by historical data indicating the anteriority of *baimbai,* with subsequent reduction through [bə'mbai] and [bə'bai] to *bai* ([bai] and [ba]), a process now almost gone to completion. A continuation of this process has led to further reduction (as is clear from the children in our sample) to [bə]. *Bai* has become a highly redundant, obligatory marker for fluent present-day speakers. The marker status of *bai* for the children in our sample is also indicated by the reduced stress it receives in their speech, compared with adult speech. A shift in the position of *bai* with respect to the verb also appears to have taken place in the past, though fluent second language speakers now show no difference from native speakers in this regard. Further work on the behavior of various kinds of embeddings[7] that clearly affect the *bai*-movement rule for all fluent present-day speakers, may also help to clarify the history of this change.

It is obvious that change in the status of *bai* was well under way prior to the existence of a large number of native speakers; native speakers appear to be carrying further tendencies which were already

7. E.g., relatives, as in chapter 11 below.

present in the language. We are not arguing that the presence of native speakers creates sudden and dramatic changes in a language, but rather that their presence may be one factor in influencing directions in language change.

Further, we feel that evidence presented here supports the argument that Tok Pisin is proving and will continue to prove adequate to handle whatever communicative demands are put on it, and that as these demands increase, the available linguistic resources will also increase, as they have clearly done in the past and continue to do in the present. *Olsem mitupela i bin suim yupela long dispela liklik toktok.*

11.

The Origins of Syntax in Discourse:
A Case Study of Tok Pisin Relatives

GILLIAN SANKOFF AND PENELOPE BROWN

The structure of relative clauses has attracted considerable attention in recent years, and a number of authors have carried out analyses of the syntax of relativization. In our investigation of syntactic structure and change in New Guinea Tok Pisin, we find that the basic processes involved in relativization have much broader discourse functions, and that relativization is only a special instance of the application of general "bracketing" devices used in the organization of information. Syntactic structure, in this case, can be understood as a component of, and derivative from, discourse structure.

We begin in sections 1–3 with a discussion of strictly syntactic issues: the processes used in the formation of Tok Pisin relative clauses and cleft sentences. In section 4, we broaden the analysis to show how the "relativizing" particle is used in deixis. In section 5, we examine a number of discourse considerations, including problems of sequencing. We then attempt to show, in sections 6–8, how a discourse-based analysis provides a means of understanding exceptions to the purely syntactic formulation. Finally, we indicate how our approach enables us to reconstruct a plausible sequence for the origin and spread of the relativization transformation, and address ourselves to the issues of syntactic complexity in a creolizing language.

This chapter first appeared in *Language* 52 (1976): 631–66. It is reprinted here with only minor editorial revisions. We first began working on the problem of relativization in New Guinea Tok Pisin (Melanesian Pidgin English, Neo-Melanesian) in 1972. Earlier versions of the present paper were presented in March 1973 at the University of Texas Conference on the Expanding Domain of Linguistics, in March 1974 at the Annual Colloquium on Directions in Linguistics at the University of Calgary, and in January 1975 at the International Conference on Pidgins and Creoles, University of Hawaii. We thank all those who made helpful comments on the earlier versions, particularly Susan Ervin-Tripp, Erving Goffman, William Labov, Stephen Levinson, Peter Mühlhäusler, John Rickford, Harvey Sacks, and Emanuel Schegloff.

1. Relative Clauses

The prototypical relative clause construction, as found in the cases we have studied, is illustrated in sentences 1–8,[1] all of which share the fact that the embedded relative is bracketed off from the matrix sentence by the particle *ia*. The left-hand (or initial) *ia* occurs immediately after the head noun, and the right-hand (or terminal) *ia* occurs at the end of the embedded clause.[2] In addition, these sentences demonstrate the flexibility of the *ia*-bracketing of relative clauses. First, the head noun modified by the *ia*-bracketed relative can occupy the three basic syntactic positions in the matrix sentence: subject (as in 1–4), complement (as in 5–7), and circumstantial or oblique (as in 8):[3]

1. This study is based largely on a series of recordings of Tok Pisin made in the town of Lae, Papua New Guinea, in July and August 1971 by Suzanne Laberge and Gillian Sankoff, though a few of the sentences analyzed date from Sankoff's earlier work in the Buang area. We thank the many kind people who agreed to recording of conversations among themselves and their children. We also thank Colonel John Harrington of the Pacific Islands Regiment, who facilitated contacts with residents of Igam Barracks, where a number of the recordings were made, and Suzanne Laberge, whose help throughout the study was invaluable.

Though the recordings were made in Lae and surrounding areas of the Morobe Province, it would be inaccurate to suppose that the Tok Pisin of the people recorded represents only a "Morobe Province dialect" of the language. The adults we recorded were from all parts of Papua New Guinea, were for the most part married to people with whom they did not share a *tok ples* (native language), and had lived in other urban centers besides Lae. Of the eighteen adults whose utterances we analyze here, nine were from various parts of the Morobe Province, five were from the Highlands, two were from Bougainville, one was from Madang, and one from West New Britain. Most of the children (eight of whom figure in this analysis) had also lived in towns other than Lae. All the people quoted in this paper are referred to by pseudonyms.

2. We are well aware that nonrestrictive relative clauses at least, and possibly also restrictive relative clauses, may be analysed otherwise than as sentences embedded into NPs; thus Thompson (1971: 94) proposes that "both restrictive and non-restrictive relative clauses must be derived from underlying conjunctions." In attempting to situate our understanding of relative clauses in a discourse framework, we take no particular stand on the transformational issues involved (cf. also n. 24 below); we use the term "embedded" temporarily (it will later be replaced by the term "parenthetical expression") and in the most general sense, corresponding to Benveniste's discussion of the relative in Ewe as a "phrase . . . encadrée" (1957: 40; the translator has rendered this in English as the "framed" clause, 1971: 182). For another discourse-based analysis of relatives, cf. Loetscher 1973.

3. Unless otherwise indicated, the head noun, and any other representation of it in the sentence, will be in large capitals both in Tok Pisin and in the English gloss; *ia,* used as a bracketing or embedding marker, is printed in boldface.

212

(1) *MERI ia*, [*EM i yangpela meri, draipela meri ia*], *EM harim istap* (Donald D.) 'This GIRL, [WHO was a young girl, big girl], was listening.'

(2) *Disfela liklik BOI ia*, [*tupela kisim EM ikam ia*], *EM, EM ilaik igo huk* (Elena F.) 'This little BOY, [THAT the two of them had brought], was going to go fishing.'

(3) *Na PIK ia* [*ol ikilim bipo ia*] *bai ikamap olsem draipela ston* (Elena Z.) 'And this PIG [they had killed before] would turn into a huge stone.'

(4) *Dispela MAN ia*, [*lek bilong EN idai ia*], *EM istap insait nau* (Diane G.) 'This MAN, [WHOSE leg was injured], stayed inside.'

(5) *E, yupela lukim MERI ia* [*bipo EM istap ia*]? (Noemi S.) 'Hey, did you see the WOMAN [WHO used to live there]?'[4]

(6) *Em yupela lukim MERI ia* [*bipo igo istap ia*]? (Noemi S.) 'Did you see the WOMAN [WHO used to live there]?'

(7) *Mama iputim DISFELA ia*, [*igat kon na muruk samting istap ia*], *em iputim igo* (Emma M.) 'Mother put THIS ONE, [WHICH has corn and cassowaries on IT], she put IT down.'

(8) *Olosem mipela tu ia save kros nabaut long GIRAUN ia* [*gavman isave kisim ia*] (Tony T.) 'Us too, we're pretty angry about the LAND [the government has taken].'

Note also that, in contrast to Malagasy and other Western Austronesian languages discussed by Keenan 1972, the coreferential NP can also occupy these three positions within the embedded sentence:[5] subject, as in 1, 5, 6, and 7; complement, as in 2, 3, and 8; and oblique, as in 4 and 7.

---

4. 'There' in the English glosses of 5–6 conveys part of the meaning of the verb *istap* 'to live, stay (somewhere)', which can be used without mentioning a place; it is not a gloss for *ia*.

5. This can be explained by categorizing Tok Pisin in Keenan's terms as "noun coding" (as opposed to verb coding). This is consistent with the fact that the means used "to indicate the role (subject, object, etc.) of the head NP in the subordinate clause" (p. 171) include both pronominalization (though as we shall see, this is highly variable) and word order. Though case-marking is typical of noun coding languages, Tok Pisin (like most pidgins and, of course, many other languages) demonstrates almost no case-marking. Interestingly, however, one place where it does show up is precisely in the marking of oblique cases, where *em* (3rd person pronoun, unmarked for gender, and used everywhere except in oblique cases) becomes *en* after *long* and *bilong*.

213

Another aspect of flexibility in *ia*-bracketed relatives is the way that the coreferential NP is represented within the embedded relative clause. It appears never to be simply copied as a noun, though sometimes it is represented by a pronoun. In 1, e.g., *meri* 'girl' is represented by the pronoun *em* 'she' in the embedded sentence. Similarly, *boi* 'boy' in 2 is pronominalized to *em* 'he', and in 5 *meri* again becomes *em*. In 4, *man* 'man' is pronominalized to *en* 'he'. In the other four sentences, however, the head NP has no surface representation in the relative clause. Thus there is an alternation between pronominalization and deletion of the coreferential NP within the embedded sentence. This alternation occurs in virtually identical syntactic environments. Comparing sentences 2 and 3, e.g., we see that each begins with a subject noun (*boi* and *pik* 'pig' respectively); then follows an embedding in which something was done to the boy (or the pig)—i.e., each is the complement in the embedded sentence; finally comes the predicate of the matrix sentence. In 2, however, *boi* is pronominalized to *em* in the embedded sentence, whereas in 3, *pik* has no surface representation at all in the embedded sentence. Sentences 5–6 present an even closer parallel. Said by the same speaker, only several minutes apart, and recounting two successive episodes in which two different groups of people were asked the same question, the sentences are virtually identical (in both cases *meri* is the complement of the matrix sentence and the subject of the embedded sentence)—except that in 5, *meri* is pronominalized to *em* in the embedded sentence, whereas in 6, it has been deleted altogether.

Exactly what constrains the alternation between pronominalization and deletion of the coreferential NP in the embedded sentence is not entirely clear. There are, however, several constraints about which we can be sure. First, when the head NP consists of a personal pronoun, deletion always seems to apply within the relative clause. There are, however, very few such sentences;[6] in most, as in 1–8, the head NP consists of a noun, or a noun plus an adjective or a demonstrative like *dispela* 'this'. Hence this generalization is not very helpful in accounting for the variation we observe. A second constraint deals with the syntactic position of the coreferential NP within the embedded sentence. This has three parts, as follows:

(a) In OBLIQUE cases (after the "prepositions" *long* and *bilong*),[7] the relativized NP always appears as a pronoun, and is never deleted.

6. One such sentence is cited as 67 below.
7. Though both *long* and *bilong* can be loosely said to function as prepositions, both have wider syntactic functions, including that of subordinators: *bilong* as an introducer of purpose clauses; *long* as a complementizer. For more details cf. Mühlhäusler 1975b; Laycock 1970a; Wurm 1971b.

An example of this with *bilong* (possessive) is provided in 4 above, where a more literal gloss of the embedded sentence would be 'the leg of his was injured.' An example with *long* (generalized locative, 'at, on, to') is:

(9) *Yu lukim DISPELA ia* [*kon ia wantaim muruk isanap long EN ia*]? (Emma M.) 'Did you see THIS ONE [THAT has corn and cassowaries on IT]?'

Since prepositions cannot be stranded, there is no analog to the English "Did you see the one that they put the design on?"

(b) In cases of COMPLEMENTS, the relativized NP very rarely appears as a pronoun, but is almost always deleted (in a ratio of about 4 : 1), as in 3 above. But there are a few cases where, as in 2, complements remain as pronouns in embedded relative clauses. In any case, there is a general rule which deletes complements of transitive verbs in a great many contexts (cf. Lattey 1975). Thus the fact that very few accusative pronouns show up in relatives is not chiefly the result of any rule specific to relativization.[8]

(c) It is where the coreferential NP occurs as the SUBJECT of the embedded sentence that we find the greatest variation. Here, too, the tendency is to delete rather than pronominalize, but in a ratio of only about 2 : 1.

The Tok Pisin sentences thus represent two of the syntactic variants sketched by Schwartz 1971, namely his types (ii) and (iii), schematized (p. 142) as follows:

(ii) N *that*$_s$[. . . $\emptyset$ . . .]
(iii) N *that*$_s$[. . . PRO . . .]

Noting that the element represented as *that* "is not case-inflected and cannot be the object of a preposition," Schwartz adds: "Type (iii) is only a variant of (ii), in that (iii) allows the accusative pronoun to surface, although it may be optionally suppressed. Both types allow the more oblique cases to be relativizable as surface pronouns, e.g., *the house that we live in-it.*" As we have shown above, Tok Pisin also allows the subject pronoun to surface, a possibility not discussed by Schwartz. Indeed, surface subject pronouns are more common in relative clauses than accusative pronouns.[9] Surface pronouns are obligatory in oblique cases.

8. Nor do any semantic features such as [+animate] or [+human] appear to have a role in constraining the deletion of accusative pronouns.

9. The fact that it is predominantly subject pronouns which "surface" has prompted Susan Steele (personal communication) to raise the question of whether there is normally a pronoun copy or clitic in simplex sentences of the

Where there is a surface pronoun in the embedded sentence, there appear to be no movement rules which would reorder constituents differently from their normal order in nonsubordinate sentences. Thus there is no evidence of a rule that would demonstrate a principle of pronoun attraction (cf. Givón 1972); and we have only one sentence (13 below) that might serve as a possible candidate for pied-piping (Ross 1967: 114)—an attempt that failed, as the speaker hesitated and reverted to normal order.

Another area of variation in the structuring of embedded relative clauses involves those cases in which the matrix sentence continues after the embedding. Since Tok Pisin is an SVO language, these sentences are, for the most part, those in which the head noun is the subject of the matrix sentence—as in 1–4 above, where the embedded relative is followed at least by the verb of the matrix sentence. Of the 49 such sentences in our corpus, 33 (67 percent) are like 1, 2, and 4, in that the coreferential NP is again represented after the embedding, as a pronoun. "Literal" glosses for these sentences would be as follows:

(1') 'This girl [who . . . . . .] SHE was listening.'

(2') 'This little boy [that . . . . . .] HE was going to go fishing.'

(4') 'This man [whose . . . . . .] HE stayed inside.'

In 3, however, the speaker does not repeat the pronoun after the embedding, and the initial English gloss given above respects its absence.

Thus there are four possibilities with respect to the surface representation of the coreferential NP, in sentences where the matrix and embedded sentences do not finish coterminously. First, the head noun, occurring prior to the embedding, can be pronominalized both within the embedding and again after it. Thus in example 1 we have:

meri ia [*em . . . ia*] *em . . .*
girl [she . . .] she . . .

There are fourteen such sentences in our corpus. Sentence 3 is the complete opposite of this, the head noun being unrepresented on the surface both within the embedding and after it. We have fourteen ex-

---

form *Tispela SKIN EM i bilong kapul* (Laycock 1970a: 24) 'This skin is a possum skin.' Indeed, there are many such sentences; but there are also many sentences of the form *Tispela BANIS i bilong gaten bilong mi* (Laycock 1970a: 25) 'This fence belongs to my garden.' We find such pairs in equational sentences as well as in sentences with various verb types (cf. also the contrast between 52 and 53 below). See chapter 12 below on pronoun copying.

amples of this type. A third possibility is Equi-NP Deletion within the embedding, coupled with pronominalization after it, as in the following (one of nineteen such sentences):

> (10) *BOI ia* [*igat fiftin yias ia*] *EM itokim ologeta liklik boi ol ikam* (Elena F.) 'This BOY [WHO was fifteen years old] HE told all the little boys to come.'

The last possible combination consists of a pronoun in the embedding, with no pronoun after it. This seems to be very rare; we have found only two such cases:

> (11) *Disfela MERI* [*EM pas tru, EM isave tru ia*], *o.k. bai kisim setifiket na igo nes* (Elena F.) 'Any GIRL [WHO really succeeds, WHO really knows], will get a certificate and become a nurse.'

> (12) *Na, ol long Moresby tok, 'Em, MASTA* [*EM igo long ples ia*] *ikam long wok ia.'* (Amanda Z.) 'And, the people in Moresby said, "The WHITE MAN [WHO went to the village] has come to work here."'

Both sentences lack the initial *ia*-bracket, and 11 is also interpretable as a conditional, glossed something like: 'If a girl really succeeds, really knows, she'll get a certificate and become a nurse'. Both of these matters will be discussed in section 8 below, where we shall see that the alternation between deletion and pronominalization of coreferential NPs is also related to aspects of the information structure of the discourse.

In summary, we have seen that the basic process used in relativization is the placement of *ia* at the beginning and end of the embedded clause, and that this device is used independently of whether head nouns and coreferential NPs are in subject, complement, or oblique positions. Within the embedded clause, the relativized NP may either be represented as a pronoun or deleted, and there are some syntactic constraints involved in this variation. Where the matrix sentence continues after the embedding, the head noun tends once more to be represented as a pronoun; but again it is often deleted, and there is a great deal of variation here too. Where Equi-NP Deletion has occurred within the embedding, a coreferential pronoun is slightly more likely to occur again after it than not (nineteen occurrences and fourteen nonoccurrences). The presence of such a pronoun within the embedding, however, makes it very likely that another will also occur after the embedding (fourteen occurrences versus two nonoccurrences).

2. OTHER POSSIBLE DEVICES FOR RELATIVIZATION

We shall now consider whether all relative clauses in Tok Pisin are constructed in this way, and whether any other mechanisms are used in relativization. Indeed, not all relative clauses are bracketed on both sides by *ia*—as we have already seen in 11–12, where *ia* marks only the end of the embedded relative. In other cases, *ia* marks only the beginning of the embedding; and in still others, *ia*-brackets are missing entirely. An attempt to describe and explain these phenomena will, however, have to await a discussion of the broader functions of *ia*-bracketing in discourse.

As far as other markers of relativization are concerned, it is important to note the role of intonation. Many embedded relatives end on a rising intonation contour, as will be examined in greater detail in section 5.

Another possible type of marker is WH-forms—a set of obvious candidates for relativizers in any language, given the relation between relatives and indirect questions as discussed, e.g., in an important paper by Keenan and Hull 1973. In Tok Pisin, these are *we* 'where', *husat* 'who', and *wonem* 'what'. In all the complex sentences we have examined, only five use WH. In 13, there is hesitation as the speaker first tries *long*,[10] then *we*, and then finishes off the relative with a right-hand *ia*-bracket:

> (13) *Nau bihain nau, em igo soim PLES [long, we pik isave slip long en ia]* (Elena Z.) 'And so then, she went and pointed out the PLACE, [at (to), where the pig slept].'

Sentence 14 is an indirect question:

> (14) *Nating tumara samting mi mas go bek long ples bilong mitupela ia na lukim [husat kilim dispela pik na tromoe]* (Elena Z.) 'Maybe tomorrow or so I should go back home and see [who killed this pig and threw it away].'

---

10. Had *long* not been replaced by *we* in this sentence, it would probably have been followed by the pronoun *en* (given the impossibility of preposition stranding), yielding something like 'at it the pig slept'. But this possible attempt at pied piping seems to have failed, in that the speaker replaced *long* by *we*, and then inserted *long en* ('at it') in its normal, postverbal position. However, since *long* also serves as a complementizer, its use here (and in 17, below) may have been as an intended subordinator rather than a preposition. Both sentences involve considerable hesitation on the speaker's part. A third possibility is that *long* represents an aborted attempt to introduce an indirect object: *soim ples long X* 'pointed out the place to X'.

In 15, *wonem* in fact modifies the head noun in the matrix sentence, rather than serving as a relativizer:

(15) *Na **wonem** MASTA [em ilaik kam long ples bilong en] tasol em pas long Pidgin tasol* (Emma M.) 'And ***whatever*** (any) WHITE MAN [(who) comes from his own country] must simply learn Pidgin.'

Sentence 16 is the only one of its kind in our corpus, in that the relative is preposed with respect to the entire matrix sentence—its head, *ol*, being the last word in the matrix sentence:

(16) *[**Husat** igat mani paul na istap long buk bilong mi yet], orait mi gat plantesin kopi, mi ken bekim dinau bilong OL* (Samuel K.) '[***Whoever*** has money gone astray and it's registered in my book], well, I have a coffee plantation, I can repay the debt to THEM.'

Had the relative not been preposed, the speaker would not have used a construction like **dinau bilong OL [husat igat . . .]* 'the debt of THOSE [*who have . . .*].' At any rate, our material yields no such sentences, and we have no hesitation in marking such a sentence as at least questionably grammatical. Lastly, 17 uses a WH-form (*husat*) as well as double *ia*-brackets, and it is doubtful that *husat* is really functioning as an embedding marker. Rather, it is probably a hesitation form used while the speaker searches for the lexical item *ol man* 'the people' (as described in section 4):

(17) *Em tokim tupela stori long PIK ia [husat ia, EM ol man, long ol man ronewe igo ia]* (Elena Z.) 'She told the two of them the story of the PIG [who, uh, the people, that the people ran away from].'

The paucity of sentences in our corpus using various forms of WH in the syntax of complex sentences does not, however, indicate the absence of such constructions in Tok Pisin. Indeed, on Manus Island, Peter Mühlhäusler (1977b: 572) has heard *we* used as a relativizer in sentences other than relatives of place.[11] Nevertheless, in the Tok Pisin

11. In our data, *we* is not used even in the formation of place relatives, the only case we have being 13. Mühlhäusler (personal communication) reports that his data for "those speakers who use *we* as a relative pronoun suggest that left-hand *ya* never appears but that right-hand *ya* is occasionally present." Nevertheless, "*ya* is strongly present in the speech of young people on the New Guinea mainland, particularly strong in the case of those who speak Tok Pisin as their first language." Mühlhäusler also cites data gathered by Malcolm Ross

familiar to us, the only common use of WH in complex syntax is in indirect questions such as 14. Though we do not treat indirect questions in this paper, our general impression is that *ia*-bracketing is not used in these constructions, and that WH is widely used. Cleft sentences, however, group with the relatives in using *ia*-bracketing, and we will turn briefly to a consideration of them.

3. CLEFT SENTENCES

Keenan and Hull's study of relative clauses, cleft sentences, and WH-questions in approximately a dozen languages sets forth a number of reasons why the syntax of the three constructions should present so many similarities. In addition, they find "a general tendency, on points where all three constructions are not similar, for WhQ and Cleft to pattern similarly, both differing from RelCl" (1973: 350). In the Tok Pisin we studied, however, it is relatives and cleft sentences which use a parallel construction, both differing from WH-questions (direct and indirect). Several examples of cleft sentences are:

(18) *Em liklik barata ia* [*mi tok ia*] (Noemi S.) 'It's the YOUNGER brother [I'm talking about].'

(19) *Nogat, em wantok ia* [*putim long maunten ia*] *na nau tasol senesim givim mi* (Tim D.) 'No, it was my FRIEND [who was wearing (it) on the mountain] and only now did he trade it with me.'

(20) *Em nambawan meri ia* [*igat nain bilong en* [*bai igo long Lae*]] (Sarah D.) 'It's the FIRST wife [who has the right [who will go to Lae]].'

(21) *Em wanpela America ia* [*iputim nain long en*] (Emma M.) 'It was an American [who gave her name to her].'

In 18–20, the emphasized word in the English gloss indicates that this is the focused element, being distinguished from some other possible referent. In 18–19, the speaker wants to correct an erroneous identifica-

---

in a high-school class of students from various parts of Papua New Guinea, for whom *ia* was consistently used in forming relative clauses: "The left-hand *ia* was consistently present, the right-hand one sometimes missing when it fell at the end of a sentence." Camden (1975) states that in contemporary Bislama (Beach-La-Mar), a sister language of Tok Pisin spoken in the New Hebrides, *we* is used as a "dependent clause marker." The examples he cites use *ya* postponed to the head noun, followed by *we*.

tion of the person being talked about by the previous speaker. In 20, which contains two embeddings, *nambawan meri* 'the first wife' is focused on in contrast to another woman who erroneously thinks SHE will be able to go to Lae. Sentence 21 looks parallel to the other three; i.e., it seems to focus on a particular referent which satisfies (in Keenan and Hull's terms) "the condition given by [the sentence] separated off from it. Further [such sentences] all presuppose that some member of the world satisfies this condition." We shall see later, however, that 21 does not quite correspond to this view, and an examination of it in its discourse context will help us sharpen our analysis of concepts like "focusing" and "presupposition."

Note that there is no surface copula in any of these sentences, not even the "predicate marker" *i-* (which would indeed be the only possible surface marking). Nevertheless, *i-* can be deleted in a large number of environments (cf. Smeall 1975; Woolford 1975); and we would argue that initial *em* in 18–21 is serving as the dummy "it" in what are, semantically, clearly cleft sentences. A semantic criterion is, incidentally, also used by Keenan and Hull, where cleft is identified as a construction which "can be negated to mean that there is something or someone satisfying the sentence, but not the one referred to by the construction" (p. 370). This is the case for all the sentences identified as cleft in this study.

One last point to note about 18–21 is that not all of them show complete *ia*-bracketing. Specifically, 20–21 do not terminate the embedded sentence with *ia*. For these cases (as for 11–12, in which initial *ia* was missing), we shall examine the constraints on the placement of *ia* in sections 6 and 8.

4. *ia* IN DEIXIS

In grammatical descriptions of Tok Pisin that we have consulted, *ia* has been treated as a place adverbial (Laycock 1970a: xxviii)—and, when co-occurring with *tispela* (*dispela*) or *em*, as a demonstrative (Mihalic 1971: 16, 22; Wurm 1971b: 12). Etymologically, it is derived from English *here* (Mihalic 1971: 98),[12] and the sources spell it *hia*. An example

12. Pawley points out that **ia* is the reconstructed form of the 3sg. focal pronoun for Eastern Oceanic (the Austronesian languages of island Melanesia other than New Guinea), and that it occurs in many currently spoken Eastern Oceanic languages. It does not, however, appear to function "emphatically" or demonstratively except in combination with personal pronouns, in which case it PRECEDES the pronoun. Pawley states (1972: 36): "The focal pronouns . . . are used when the speaker wishes to focus on or emphasize the pronoun. . . .

of its use as an adverb of place is 22, and two examples of its use as a demonstrative are 23–24:

(22) *Yu stap hia* (Mihalic 1957: 46) 'Stay here.'

(23) *Em hia* (Mihalic 1957: 46) 'This one here.'

(24) *Tispela haus hia* (Wurm 1971b: 12) 'This house.'

Though our data show very little use of *ia* as an adverb of place, they do confirm that this function (probably the original one, given a transfer of the English meaning of "here") still exists to some limited extent. (The final *ia* in 12 above is interpretable in this way). *Long ia* (literally 'at here') is sometimes heard; but *ia* is more frequently used to modify other expressions in place deixis, so that a more likely gloss for 'here' would be *ples ia* or *hap ia*.

But it is as a demonstrative or deictic marker that *ia* abounds in our data. It seems only a short step to extend the function of a lexical item that has served as an adverb of place to a demonstrative or generalized deictic function. At least, this is a phenomenon common to many languages; cf. Eng. *this here man,* which retains a nonstandard connotation, or Fr. *celui-ci* and *celui-là* ('this one' and 'that one' in standard French, from the adverbs *ici* and *là* respectively). We should point out that, although the argument in this paragraph assumes a "place adverbial" origin, with an extension to broader demonstrative or deictic functions (an argument which appears to have historical support in this case, as we shall demonstrate in section 9), the fact that the two functions are expressed by the same form on the synchronic level, in Tok Pisin as in many other languages, is understandable in terms of the close semantic analogy between the two uses, without assuming any directionality.

We have many sentences in our data like 23–24, in which *ia* is postposed to a noun or pronoun and has the function of focusing on that element. Sometimes it marks contrast with some other referent—'this

---

They act as emphatic or redundant subject, preceding the unemphatic subjective pronouns."

Despite this—and despite the fact that Tolai, the major Austronesian language contributing to Tok Pisin, also uses *ia* as one form of the 3sg. pronoun (Franklin 1962: 11)—Tok Pisin *ia* clearly does not have its origin in a personal pronoun, even a "focusing" pronoun. Rather, as will be explained in section 9, the more important parallel with Austronesian languages concerns the POST-POSED deictic marker found in a number of the Austronesian languages of Melanesia.

(here) N,[13] rather than some other'; but sometimes it simply fore-grounds the N. In 25, e.g., the speaker is asking a friend of hers about the price of a certain type of cloth the friend has bought. She says to her, pointing to the cloth in question,

(25) *Disfela ia, ol ikosim em haumas?* (Lita T.) 'This one, how much do they charge for it?'

Ia in deixis is sometimes best glossed as 'this' or 'that' (cf. Rickford 1973: 17),[14] sometimes as the weaker 'the'. But note that the distribution of *ia* (alternating with Ø) probably does not correspond in any neat way with the distribution of *this, the,* and *a* in English, certainly not with respect to the complexities of colloquial usage exemplified in sentences such as *So we ran into this friend of hers.* (Indeed, it will soon become apparent that the sentence is a very inappropriate unit for the analysis and understanding of these issues, and can therefore exemplify very little.) Like English *this,* however, *ia* can be attached either to a FIRST reference to a particular item in some discourse, or to a LATER reference to an item which has previously been mentioned. What is common to both cases is that, in saying *N ia* 'THIS ONE', the speaker uses a form that invites the addressee to recognize or uniquely identify the referent. Such recognition or identification may be accomplished in several ways.[15] First, there may be a gestural or nonlinguistic accompaniment to the speech act itself, occurring at the same time or in close

13. *Ia* almost always attaches to some nominal element, symbolized here by N. There is one class of uses of *ia,* however, with which we do not deal here: cases where *ia* attaches to verbal expressions or to whole sentences. Here the function could again be described as one of focusing or emphasis, as in the ubiquitous, emphatic *Nogat ia!* 'No sir!', alternating with *Nogat tru* as a stronger form than simply *nogat* 'no'. Two other examples of this verbal-qualifying, or "sentence-bracketing" use of *ia* are:
Ya, Susanna, yu no kaikai ia! (Lalia T.) 'Hey, Susanna, you didn't eat any-thing at all!'
Tasol narapela narapela olsem, ino inap ia! (Emma M.) 'But all sorts of other people, they're simply incapable of it!' (of speaking Tok Pisin well, in contrast to the speaker and her friends).
14. Rickford also points out that *ia* can mean "both 'this one here' and 'that one there' or both 'the former' and 'the latter'." We thank him also for helpful discussion of many of the problems of deictic *ia.*
15. Our use of the term "identification" corresponds rather closely to Sacks and Schegloff's (1979) use of "recognition"; i.e., the issues involve rec-ognition of a specific, known referent. It is also very similar to the use of "attribution" in Goffman (ms., 1975), which involves recognizing which speci-fic one of a known set is being referred to, where the referent refers hearers back to some schema of identification they are known (or believed) to have.

proximity to it, which makes very clear the referent of the word to which *ia* has been attached—e.g., Lita's pointing to the cloth in 25. Another case would be someone's asking, immediately after a very loud noise has visibly startled everyone present, *Em wonem ia?* 'What was that?', where 'that' clearly refers to the noise—or an even more laconic *Balus ia,* literally, 'This/That airplane', but understood by everyone under the circumstances to mean 'This/That noise was caused by an airplane.'

Second, the attaching of *ia* to some N (in the absence of concurrent nonlinguistic indication of the referent of N) may in itself be sufficient for the identification of its specific referent. This may be either because the referent has been specified earlier in the discourse (in the case of later references), or because of information shared by speakers and hearers prior to this interchange (in the case of first references). In both cases, talking about speakers and hearers "accomplishing" identification may seem to be putting the case somewhat strongly. Nevertheless, the issues here clearly deal with identification, whether or not there is any problem about the actual task of identification which a particular speaker or hearer has in a given case. For example, 26 is drawn from a long narrative about a whole community of people from a seaside village fleeing to the hills in fear of a tidal wave, expected to follow an earthquake foretold by a prophet:

> (26) *Na ol igo istap long MAUNTEN ia na wet long bikpela GURIA ia igo* (Noemi S.) 'And they went and stayed on this MOUNTAIN and waited for this big EARTHQUAKE.'

The mountain (*maunten*) in question and the impending earthquake (*guria*) have already been discussed in some detail by the narrator; references to them here are subsequent references. There is no problem in distinguishing this particular mountain and earthquake from some other possible candidates. In specifying *maunten ia* and *guria ia,* the narrator is alerting the listener to the fact that she has already been told "which mountain" and "which earthquake." Another example is taken from a narrative where the protagonists are two women, the *meri tru* 'real woman' and the *tevel meri* 'spirit woman'. The sentence starts by twice referring to them jointly with the dual pronoun *tupela*; the next reference is to only one of them, the *meri tru,* which is qualified by *ia* and refers back to a prior characterization:

> (27) *TUPELA igo, igo kisim kanu na TUPELA igo, igo igo nau, na MERI TRU ia em iwo—huk. EM iwok long pulim pis na tevel meri iwok long kaikai pis* (John P.) 'The two of them went and got a canoe and the two of them went off, and the REAL

WOMAN was—fishing. SHE was busy fishing and the spirit woman was busy eating the fish.'

The problem of identification appears fairly simple in narratives, where an item tagged with *ia* has generally been introduced and characterized earlier, as with *maunten, guria,* and *meri tru* in 26–27. In hundreds of cases like these, neither speakers nor hearers appear to encounter any problem in achieving mutual understanding of the correct referents of Ns to which *ia*s are attached. Indeed, speakers and hearers seem able to communicate correct identifications in many potentially more difficult situations than those of 26–27, e.g., where the N in question has not previously been mentioned, as in 28. Here the speaker has been engaged in an abstract discussion of the nature of a type of spirit creature known as *masalai* 'incubus'. "A *masalai* can turn itself into human form," he has been explaining, "in order to seduce you. You may just sit down and have a chat with it, thinking it's a real person. But it's invisible to everyone else; only you can see it. So if I were to come along and find you talking to one, I wouldn't be able to see it, and I'd exclaim:

> (28) '*E! MAN ia toktok wantaim husat?!*' (Tony T.) 'Hey! Who's this GUY talking to?!' "

Man ia is clearly the person who has up to now been referred to as 'you', the hypothetical character the *masalai* has been trying to seduce; and Tony's exclamation is addressed to some hypothetical third party. Though *man* in 28 was technically being used for the first time in the discourse in question, the identification of its referent was not problematic for any of the hearers.

Despite the fact that no problems of identification in fact occurred in 25–28, it is nevertheless the case that saying *N ia* 'THIS N' opens the door to the potential "identificational" query, "Which N?"[16]

16. Various observers have differed in their interpretations of just how problematic the identification of the N qualified by *ia* is. Thus Wurm states (1971b: 12): "*Hia* and *lohap* . . . are also used alone after nouns. . . . This is done when the object referred to has been mentioned before, or the person spoken to is familiar with it, or no doubt is expected to arise over what it is. The use of these postposed demonstratives carries the connotation of stressing the obvious, and the purely demonstrative function is sometimes quite weak, e.g., *mi hanggiri long mit hia*: 'I am hungry for tinned meat' (i.e. it should be obvious that I do not hunger for sweet potatoes)."
Rickford, on the other hand, says (1973: 3): "*Ia* seems to be used in just those cases where doubt or confusion might arise to who or what is being talked about, rather than the other way around." Our view is that *ia* is used in both of these apparently disparate ways—and that they are not in fact so very disparate, as we shall attempt to show.

Though on many occasions speakers in no way acknowledge such potential problems, we have several kinds of evidence that achieving identification CAN be problematic; all these involve cases in which speakers say *N ia,* but do not simply continue on with the sentence or discourse. The first kind of evidence comes from sentences where the speaker uses the slot opened up by *ia* after N to insert further information relevant to the identification of the referent of N. In 29, e.g., the speaker is telling a story about three brothers, the last of whom was called Dusty. Since he was mentioned, however, an episode has occurred in which an old man came walking along the road and broke his leg, an episode which takes several sentences to recount and ends with the beginning of the cited material. The next reference to Dusty first uses the term *dispela boi ia* 'this boy', but then the slot immediately after *ia* is used to insert his name, Dusty. Renaming appears to be one excellent way of assuring appropriate identification:

(29) . . . *na kar ikam na, brukim lek bilong en. Brukim lek bilong en na, dispela BOI ia, DASTI ia, lukim* . . . (Celia D.) '. . . and the car came and, broke his (the old man's) leg. Broke his leg and, this BOY, this DUSTY, saw . . .'

Another one-word reidentification is illustrated in 30. Here it consists not of a proper name, but of the term which has previously been used throughout the particular discourse to identify this referent, i.e., *masalai*:

(30) *O, mi toktok wantaim TAMBERAN MAN ia, MASALAI* (Lalia T.) 'Oh, I was talking with this SPIRIT, this INCUBUS.'

Whereas 29–30 illustrate one-word renamings of the referents of the first N (*boi* and *tamberan man,* respectively) for purposes of identification, 31 uses a longer expression to do the same sort of "identificational" work. Here, the speaker is recounting the plot of a cowboy movie in which the two main characters have already been identified as 'John' and his friend, an older man. Needing to identify this second man at a later point in the story, she says:

(31) . . . *na em, MAN ia, [lapun man ia], stap autsait ia* (Diane G.) '. . . and this MAN, [this old man], stayed outside.'

Later in the same story, the old man in the interim having been shot in the leg, Diane uses a sentence given above as 4, in which she identifies the old man: *Dispela man ia, [lek bilong en idai ia], em istap insait nau* 'This man, [whose leg was injured], stayed inside.'

A comparison of the *ia*-bracketed materials in 31 and 4 indicates that though their syntactic structures are different (an NP in apposition in 31 versus a relative clause in 4, above), their identificational function within the discourse is identical (they even refer to the same man, in the same story!), as is the structure of their insertion into their respective matrix sentences. In these two respects, both sentences are also identical to 29 and very similar to 30 (which differs only in that the sentence ends immediately after the reidentification, and is lacking the second *ia*—a feature which will be discussed later). All have the characteristic, rising, "comma" intonation marking the expression inserted after the first *N ia*.

In 25–28, the referents of items qualified by *ia* are fairly obvious, whether because of the immediate non-linguistic circumstances of the discourse, or because *ia* tags something whose referent had previously been made clear, or was correctly identifiable by hearers because of knowledge or understanding they had. In such sentences, *ia* can be seen as somehow backward-looking; it alerts listeners to the fact that they are supposed to know "which N." But 29–31 and 4 mark a subtle shift. Though *ia* is still "backward-looking" in the same sense, we see that the first N chosen and tagged with *ia* may not be felicitous (it may be inadequate for correct identification of the referent by hearers, or it may not be an identification appropriate for use in the immediate context).[17] Once there is any doubt about the referent of an item tagged by *ia,* a speaker may make another try at providing an identification. The most likely place to correct a potential trouble (e.g., misidentification of the correct referent) is immediately after the possibility of trouble has occurred, i.e., after the first N tagged by *ia*; hence *ia* becomes, in effect, the potential marker of a place where another try at identification may be made. Thus in 29, *boi,* a generic term whose referent (even in the context) might have been any of the three brothers, is replaced by *Dasti,* the name of the specific referent; in 30, a new term used to refer to the spirit-person, *tamberan,* is replaced by the only term which has previously been used for this referent in this discourse, *masalai.*

However, as we saw by comparing the function of the bracketed material in 31 and 4 with that in 29–30, such one-word reidentifications are but the simplest type of a class of expressions that can be inserted parenthetically after *ia,* and whose function is identificational. As the marker of the beginning of a parenthetical expression of some sort,[18] *ia*

---

17. Cf. the discussion of these issues in Schegloff 1972.

18. Our use of the term "parenthetical expression" will be restricted to relative clauses (both restrictive and nonrestrictive) and to other appositive expressions which relate informationally to some N in the matrix sentence. We do not mean it in Emonds' sense (1973: 335) of "parenthetical clauses" which

can be conceived as a left-hand or initial bracket. Indeed, this was the function of *ia* occurring after the head NP in the relative clauses of section 1, and after the focused noun in the cleft sentences of section 3.

An extension of this "identificational" use of the slot after *ia* occurs in more clearcut cases of "correction" than in the simple replacement of a term by a more precise one, or by a descriptive phrase;[19] and this provides a second type of evidence for our argument that problems of identification can occur, and that they are often repaired immediately after the first instance of *N ia*. Speakers, e.g., in replacing one term with another, may admit the first was an "error" by saying something like "whoops," "sorry," or "I mean," any of which could serve as a gloss for *wonem* (literally, 'what') in the following:

(32) *Tupela ikam long dispela KAR ia,—wonem, HOS ia!* (Diane G.) 'The two of them came in this CAR,—uh, on a HORSE!'

In other cases, speakers reassert that a first identification was correct. This is the function of *yes, kanu* below:

(33) *Nau ol igo long solwara tu na lukim stik bilong SAMAN ia, yes, KANU ia* (Donald D.) 'So they went down to the sea and saw the pole of the OUTRIGGER, yes, the CANOE.'

A third type of evidence for the use of *ia* in problems of identification comes from cases where the first N tagged by *ia* is not a noun at all, but one of the very general pro-forms typified by the interrogatives *wonem* and *husat*, which are glossed in English by words like *whatchamacallit, whosis, thingamabob, whatsisname*, etc. These are used in "word-searches"—e.g., in 17 above, where the proform was *husat*. Three examples using *wonem* are cited as 34–36. This usage is very frequent, particularly among children (all the cited examples come from the speech of children and adolescents):

(34) *Na em isingautim olgeta, WONEM ia, MAN long ples bilong kam luk sanap na lukluk* (Elena Z.) 'And she called out to all the UH, PEOPLE from the village to come and see, stand up and look.'

(35) *Na disfela seken pikinini ia bai em igo long wanpela bikpela WONEM ia, TAUN stret na bai em iwok* (Celia D.) 'And this

---

specifically do NOT "dominate a phrase node (such as NP)," but rather refer to, or comment on, a whole independent clause.

19. We do not mean to imply that ALL "correction" in Tok Pisin requires the use of *ia*, but simply that its existence provides one important mechanism for certain types of correction.

second child will go to a big WHAT, a real TOWN and he'll work (there).'

(36) *Ol ikilim disfela WONEM ia, MERI ia* (Paul T.) 'They killed this WHAT, this WOMAN.'

A fourth kind of evidence of the potentially problematic nature of identifications comes from sequences where speakers other than the one who has said *N ia* are involved in confirming, questioning, and adding to identifications. This evidence will be presented in section 5.

First, however, we must return to the notion of *ia* as a left-hand or initial bracket, introduced in the discussion of examples 29 ff. As we noted, these examples all involved "backward-looking" use of the slot after *ia*, inserting information designed to identify "which N." But a deictic marker which has become a potential initial bracket for a parenthetical expression provides another important structural possibility, viz., the "forward-looking" use of the slot for the insertion of "new" information. Thus, in using the expression *N ia* about an item mentioned for the first time, about which hearers may have no prior knowledge, a speaker can use the slot provided after *ia* to supply a description or CHARACTERIZATION, rather than an IDENTIFICATION. He is thus saying, in effect, "this N" (about which I am going to tell you something relevant) instead of "this N" (which you are supposed to know about). That is, IDENTIFICATIONS instruct hearers, "Search in your file to see which one this is"; CHARACTERIZATIONS instruct them, "Open a file on this N, and put this information in it."

The conversational use to which the information in characterizations is put is quite varied, and does not immediately concern us here. Suffice it to say that one important use is for later identifications. Thus sentence 7 above, re-cited here for convenience, characterizes a newly introduced item, a piece of cloth, as having corn and cassowaries on it: *Mama iputim DISFELA ia, [igat kon na muruk samting istap ia] em iputim igo* 'Mother put THIS ONE, [which has corn and cassowaries on IT], she put IT down.' The bracketed material here is not identificational; i.e., 'having corn and cassowaries on it' is not serving to distinguish this cloth from some other piece of cloth. It is obvious from the context and from the "comma" intonation that the cloth's referent is not in question, and that the description of the pattern on it is simply a characterization. Much later in the same conversation, the speaker uses this characterization identificationally, asking:

(37) *Yu lukim DISPELA ia, [kon wantaim muruk isanap long EN ia]?* (Emma M.) 'Did you see THE ONE [that had corn and cassowaries on IT]?'

Another previously cited example is sentence 1: *MERI ia [EM i yang-pela meri, draipela meri ia] EM harim istap* 'This GIRL, [WHO was a young girl, big girl], was listening.' Here, the question "which girl" is irrelevant, and (as with "which cloth" in 7) the bracketed material does not address itself to this question. This time, however, the bracketed material is used not for later identification of the girl, but is a necessary fact in understanding the next event in the story.

A last example of the use of *ia* in characterizations is taken from a conversation about the dangers involved in going alone to work in a garden. After expounding on the dreadful things that might happen to a person, Emma M. says, "So I carry this enormous bush knife," which statement is greeted by a round of laughter. During the laughter, she starts to go on with an episode of her story, "So I—"; but she interrupts herself, as soon as the laughter is over, with an additional characterization of the knife as belonging to her husband:

> (38) Emma: *Na mi karim draipela bus naip ia* 'So I carry this enormous bush knife.'
>
> 2 women: (laughter)
>
> Emma: *Na mi—[papa—bilong papa bilong John ia] mi karim* 'So I—[father—John's father's], I carry.'

There has been no previous mention of a knife in the conversation (nor is it mentioned again); and the characterization of it as belonging to "John's father" (Mr. M.) is not provided in order to help listeners identify it, the specific referent of *bus naip* being irrelevant. Comparing the syntactic structure of the bracketed material in the examples of characterizations (7, 1, and 38), as we did earlier with identifications, we see once more that there is variation from "full relatives," like 7 and 1, to genitives, like 38, though we have found no one-word parenthetical expressions analogous to those used in identifications.

We have seen how a demonstrative or deictic *ia*, postposed to the noun it qualifies, can come to act as a POTENTIAL left-hand bracket in providing a slot for the insertion of a parenthetical expression: potential, because in many cases the referent is clear, there is no identificational work to be done or new information to be inserted, and the possible slot provided after *ia* is not exploited, as in 25–28. We have not, however, exhausted the structural possibilities of the use of *ia* in discourse. In particular, we shall see in section 5 that *ia* provides a slot which is available to all participants in a conversation; thus its analysis bears on problems of discourse sequencing, as well as on those of the organization of information. Lastly, the reader may have noted that we continue to talk about "*ia*-bracketing," and even to insert left and right brackets in our transcriptions of examples, though as yet we have provided an analysis only of how *ia* can come to act as a left-hand or initial bracket. *Ia* as a right-hand or terminal bracket is a further problem dealt with in section 5.

5. *ia* IN DISCOURSE (USE BY MORE THAN ONE PARTY)

In section 4, above, we argued that *ia*, postposed to a particular N, has the basic function of focusing on that N—its deictic force being used to specify THIS N as opposed to some other, or simply to foreground a particular NP among others in the discourse. Its focusing function and its position make it an ideal place, we have argued, for re-identifications, in the case that the first N may somehow be inappropriate, or that its referent may be in some doubt. We showed two examples of this, 29–30, in which speakers replaced an infelicitous first N with another. Such renamings were, however, seen not to be the only way to remedy an unsatisfactory identification, since speakers may use the parenthetical slot after an initial *ia* to refer to properties of the N, as seen in 31 and 4. In both cases, however, the parenthetical expression served to IDENTIFY the N.

In the examples considered so far, potential problems of identification have been dealt with or corrected by the speaker's using the slot after N *ia* either to rename more appropriately or specifically, as in *boi* → *Dasti* in 29, or in *tamberan man* → *masalai* in 30, or to provide a description which refers back to a previous characterization, as in 31 and 4. But in none of these cases did speakers manifest much doubt about whether hearers were in fact having problems of identification: there was no hesitation, no rising intonation on the *ia* after the bracketed material, and speakers continued on without interruption (Sacks and Schegloff report parallel findings in such cases). *Boi, tamberan man,* and *man* may have been insufficient initial identifications; but the parenthetical material included to clarify or correct was apparently entirely adequate to do the job. In 29, hearers had been told that the boy's name was Dusty because he played in the dust; in 30, the *masalai* had been discussed at great length; in 31 and 4, the facts that the man was old and had broken his leg had very recently been mentioned, clearly did not apply to any of the other characters in the story, and were almost sure to identify the *man* uniquely.

In other cases, however, a potential doubt about the adequate identification of an item is evidenced by an ACKNOWLEDGMENT of identification by the hearer immediately after N *ia*, sometimes only a nod but often a very soft 'Mm' or 'Mm hmm', 'Yes', or 'Yeah'. Such acknowledgment sometimes occurs after a first *N ia,* as in 39, where the speaker uses rising intonation (marked by accent):

> (39) Diane G.: *Na biain disfela MISIS ĭa* 'And later this (white) LADY?'
>
> Lalia T.: *Ye* 'Yeah.'
>
> Diane G.: *em igo* 'she left.'

In such cases, the speaker may not insert any parenthetical material after the identification has been acknowledged; but we also often find MULTIPLE renamings, as in 40, or descriptions, as in 41–42. In such cases, speakers wait until they have clearly satisfied themselves and/or hearers before ceasing to re-identify. In 40, Mrs. M. begins by resolving the previous topic (the mission store where she buys sewing supplies) by coming up with the name of the storekeeper, Pastor Brown, to which Mrs. T. responds with an affective comment (which already indicates that she recognizes the referent). Then Mrs. M., in the course of changing the topic to discuss the linguistic abilities of Mrs. Brown, a topic which then continues for some time, renames Brown three times, beginning with *Fata* (the term usually used for a Catholic priest), replacing it with *bingsu* (the term for a Lutheran missionary, which Brown is), and replacing this in turn, emphatically, with his name. Each successive try is followed by *ia* (without question intonation), and by an acknowledgment by Mrs. T.:

> (40) Mrs. M.: *Em bingsu, bingsu, . . . Brown* 'It's pastor, pastor, . . . Brown.'
>
> Mrs. T.: *Em taranggu, i gutpela man* 'Yes, poor dear, he's a good man.'
>
> Mrs. M.: *Bingsu Brown, misis bilong, misis bilong, FATA ia,* 'Pastor Brown, the wife, the wife, of this FATHER,'
>
> Mrs. T.: *Mmm.*
>
> Mrs. M.: [*Em, BINGSU ia*], 'Uh, this PASTOR,'
>
> Mrs. T.: *Mm-hmm.*
>
> Mrs. M.: [*BROWN ia*], *man! Tok Yabem bilong en,* [claps hands once] *olosem tok ples bilong en!* 'This BROWN, wow! Her Yabem [handclap] is just like her native language!'[20]

20. Yabem, or Jabêm, is an Austronesian language from the north coastal area of the Huon Gulf; it has been spread as a *lingua franca* by the Lutheran Mission throughout much of the Morobe Province (Renck 1977a).

Example 41 goes even farther in resolving problems of identification:

> (41) N.S. *Ologeta karim kago nai igo pinis*—'They all carried their belongings and went off—'
>
> G.S. *Long maunten?* 'To the mountain?'
>
> N.S. *long HAP ia* [*yu lukim bikpela VILIS ĩa*] 'to this PLACE [where you see a big VILLAGE]'
>
> G.S. *Mm.*
>
> N.S. [*Em yumi go, na igo long Mumeng ĩa*] '[that you go to, to go to Mumeng]'
>
> G.S. *Yes*
>
> N.S. *EM ia,* [*ol igo istap*] 'THAT'S [where they went and stayed].'

Here the speaker's rising intonation on *ia* after *vilis* 'village' and *Mumeng* indicates some doubt on her part as to whether it will be adequate to do the job of identification. The hearer, G.S., has asked for specification of the place, and the speaker, N.S., uses two *ia*-bracketed relative clauses to explain exactly where the place is. As in 40, the hearer's first acknowledgment, "Mm," is very soft, and the second (here "*Yes*") is louder and more assertive. N.S. then finishes the interchange with an emphatic cleft sentence, "THAT'S where they went and stayed." Note that there is no rising intonation on either the initial *ia* after *hap* 'place' or the *ia* in the final cleft sentence, a fact which will inform our discussion of the different functions of initial *ia* and final *ia* in general.

A last example, showing some doubt on the speaker's part coupled with acknowledgement of identification, is intermediate between 39, with no parenthetical expression, and 40–41, with two each. Example 42 has just one such expression:[21]

> (42) E.M.: *Em nau, dispela nupela NU TESTAMENT ia* 'Now, this new NEW TESTAMENT.'
>
> S.L.: *Mm hmm.*
>
> E.M.: *BUK ia* 'this BOOK,'

---

21. The left bracket indicates two speakers beginning at the same time. Conventions used in the transcription of overlaps are those proposed by Sacks, Schegloff, and Jefferson (1974: 731).

S.L.: ⎡ *Mm hmm.*

R.T.: ⎣ *Mmm.*

E.M.: *Em nau,* . . . 'Well, now, ...'

We saw in 39–42 that the identification accomplished by *ia*-bracketed material is not necessarily assumed, or automatic; it involves interactional work, a checking-out of acknowledgment, negotiation of what is mutually understood. Acknowledgment may occur after the first N, as in 39, 40 and 42; or hearers may wait until after the first parenthetical expression, as in 41. They may then, of course, continue to acknowledge after subsequent parentheticals. But the interactional use of *ia* goes much deeper than this. As a point at which further information about the item set off or qualified by *ia* can be inserted, the potential bracket opened after a potential left-hand *ia* can be used not only by present speaker, but also by any other speaker who wishes to insert pertinent information. As soon as an item has been qualified as "THIS one," there is the possibility of a parenthetical expression consisting of (a) smoothly-inserted information by present speaker, as in 29–31 and 4; or (b) a self-interruption (often in the form of a correction) by present speaker, as in 32–36; or (c) an interruption by a new speaker, as we shall see below. Thus, like many other elements of the turn-taking system (cf. Sacks, Schegloff, and Jefferson), *ia* is open for use by all conversational participants, and provides an opening for any new speaker.

Word replacements, e.g., need not be done by present speaker, but may be done by a next speaker, as in 43, where Nat corrects Paul's description of a sorcerer's spell:

(43) Paul T.: . . . *wokim olosem na rausim wanpela ston na wanpela, a, NIL ia* '. . . they do it like that and take out a stone and a, uh, NAIL,'

Nat P.: *NIDOL ia* 'a NEEDLE,'

Paul T.: *bilong sowim samting* 'for sewing things.'

The next example of the use of the slot after *ia* by a next speaker also extends the analysis in another way. At the end of section 4, we sketched an argument that held that speakers use *ia*-bracketing not only to provide identifications ("backward-looking" in the sense that they ask hearers to draw on some information they already have, in order to identify the N), but also to provide initial characterizations of some "new" N ("forward-looking" in the sense that the slot is used to supply information hearers do not already have). Of course, the information supplied in an initial characterization may later be used parenthetically for identification (another important sense of "forward-looking"), and initial characterizations may be done in a variety of ways. What is of interest here, however, is that they are often done in exactly the same was as are identifications, i.e., with a parenthetical expression bounded on both sides by *ia*. We illustrated this in 1, 17, and 38. But whereas in identifications the question of adequacy is always relevant (is the N, and/or the parenthetical material provided, adequate or appropriate for identification?), giving hearers something to acknowledge (as in 39–42), the fact that characterizations provide "new" information means that very often there is nothing for hearers to acknowledge. How are they to know whether a characterization is "adequate" until later on, when they find out how it is to be used?

In some circumstances, however, participants may be able to acknowledge or challenge a characterization. This can happen, e.g., when there are several hearers present, and one or more of them shares the information which the speaker is imparting. Thus characterizations, as well as identifications, can be accomplished jointly (though this is a rarer event).

We mentioned, in discussing the issues of identification involved in 31, that the "man" in the cowboy movie had already been characterized as "old," and that the parenthetical material used in the identification was pulled out of the previous characterization. We shall now see how that initial characterization was made, collaboratively, by the three people who have seen the movie and who are jointly recounting it to a group of listeners. Diane G. is the chief narrator; but the two young boys who saw the movie with her, Paul T. and Nat P., pay close attention and interrupt her on a number of occasions (curly braces enclose the whole "characterizational" transaction):

(44) Diane: *Dispela John wantaim*   'This guy John with this
           narapela PREN bilong   other FRIEND of
           en ia,   his,
           {[*dispela MAN ia*],   {[this MAN],'
           ⌈*tupela—*   ⌈'the two of them—'
  Paul: ⌊*Wanpela lapun*   ⌊'An old ⌈father!'
                  ⌈*papa!*   ⌊'his father!'
  Nat: ⌊*Papa bilong*
                     en!
  Diane: *Yes, papa—ah, ino papa*   'Yes, his fa—uh, not
           bilong en, PREN   his father, his
           bilong en ia!} *Tupela*   FRIEND!} The two
           ikam . . .   of them went . . .'

235

The problem here concerns the proper characterization of John's sidekick, here being mentioned for the first time, and whose name no one seems to remember. Diane initially refers to him as John's "friend," but immediately inserts (using *ia*-brackets) a parenthetical expression characterizing him as *dispela man ia* 'this man'. (This may seem completely uninformative as a characterization to the reader unfamiliar with Tok Pisin; but note that the usual meaning of *pren* is 'friend of the opposite sex, lover'; saying he is a MAN clears up a possible confusion that a girlfriend is the referent.) Paul, who had waited for Diane to provide SOME characterization by not interrupting after the first *ia* (the initial bracket), now with split-second timing interrupts after Diane's second *ia* (the terminal bracket), apparently judging her characterization of the second man to be insufficient, and himself provides a characterization of the man as *wanpela lapun papa* 'an old father'. Meanwhile (back at the ranch) Diane has begun to continue her story with *tupela* 'the two of them', which is overlapped by Paul's *wanpela*, at which point she desists. Paul continues with *lapun* 'old' in the clear; but then Nat, anticipating what Paul is going to say, chimes in with *papa* at the precise time Paul is saying *papa*—continuing, after Paul has finished, with *bilong en* 'of his'. Diane recommences, starting to adopt this new characterization of the man as 'John's father', but then denies it, returning to her original statement that he is simply John's friend. She closes the material within braces, in which there has been an interaction among all three participants as to the proper characterization of the man, with a final *ia,* and continues with *tupela* as she had been doing when interrupted by Paul. Note that what was finally established was that John's friend was a man old enough to be his father, though not his father, but definitely an 'old man' (*lapun man*), the precise words Diane later uses to identify him in example 31.

Like Keenan and Hull (1973), we have rejected a strictly syntactic view of relative clauses, in order to show some of the properties which relative clauses share with other constructions. But whereas their analysis is based on a study of isolated sentences from a logical and semantic perspective, ours examines sequences of utterances within a discourse context, trying to understand how the relevant construction types are actually used in the exchange of information. Thus Keenan and Hull (p. 350) state that one of the logical similarities shared by WH-questions, relative clauses, and cleft sentences is that they all "have a condition given by a sentence S that they impose in some way on the noun phrase separated off from it. Further, they all presuppose that some member of the world satisfies this condition, and are concerned with the member or members that actually DO satisfy the condition." This is one way of understanding why a focusing particle is such a likely candidate for doing the syntactic work of separating the NP off from the embedded sentence in the three types of constructions, as is true in a number of the languages on which Keenan and Hull present data. But we would argue that this is, in fact, better understood as a property of any parenthetical expression which does identificational work. Use of *lapun man ia* 'this old man' in 31 presupposes that there is such a member of the world, just as does the embedded relative *lek bilong en idai ia* 'whose leg was injured' in 4 and the use of the name *Dasti* in 29. All these cases involve the identification of 'the member or members which actually DO satisfy the condition.'

But not all sentences which use the forms available for doing identificational work in fact use them in this way. Characterizations, e.g., often use *ia*-brackets, though the work they do is not identificational (cf. sentences 1, 7, and 38). To illustrate with a sentence which was cited earlier, let us reconsider the cleft sentence 21, "It was an American who gave her her name." Though, logically, we could say that it is "presupposed" that someone named the little girl in question, and that the sentence is focusing on "which member of the world" is the one to have done it, this is in fact not how the sentence functions in the context. Rather, the speaker is attempting to introduce a new topic, and is using this construction for arranging two NEW bits of information: that someone named the child, and that the person was an American. In this case, *ia* has a clear focusing function; but an analysis of the sentence as locating which member of the world satisfied the "presupposed" condition is not the most useful way of understanding it.[22] In other words, we feel that it can be misleading to use the formal properties of a construction in arguing about its possible function, the understanding of which is more readily observed from the uses to which it is put.

It should come as no surprise that a focusing particle like *ia* is not specific to the three syntactic types discussed by Keenan and Hull, but that its use is governed by discourse considerations dealing with the structuring of information exchange. In analyzing how *ia* is actually used, we have seen that, for speakers and hearers, "presupposition" is often problematic, and that the structures which seem to be built for dealing with presupposition (in our terms, determining whether or not the bracketed material is adequate or appropriate for identification or characterization) contain the mechanisms necessary for the interactional negotiation of these problems. Thus, in some cases, speakers

22. On related problems of out-of-context discussion of presupposition, see Sherzer 1973. For an illuminating discussion of the relationship between syntax and information structure, see Halliday 1967, especially pp. 203 ff. on "information focus."

manifest doubt about whether hearers will be able to identify a particular N, either by using a rising intonation on the *ia* which follows it (the first or left-hand bracketing *ia*), as in 39, and/or by adding one or more identificational expressions after it. A rising intonation on the *ia* following such an expression (the second, or later *ia*) is also not at all uncommon, as speakers use it to check whether the identification or characterization given has been sufficient (cf. also Sacks and Schegloff). But note that such a right-hand or "terminal" *ia* is only potentially terminal: if the identification or characterization still turns out to be insufficient, the speaker may well continue to provide further information, and each potentially terminal *ia* then also marks the slot at which a new parenthetical expression can begin. Further, the system provides an opening for a next speaker to use the slot, whether to question or correct the identification or characterization, to confirm that it has been understood, or to provide further information for a third party.

We saw earlier that left-hand or initial *ia* is also only potentially so, since an N may be tagged with *ia* (usually with emphatic or fading intonation) and nothing more. But this (potential initial) *ia* may also receive a rising intonation, when there is doubt about the identification of the referent. Any *ia* (with rising intonation or not; potentially initial or potentially terminal) can mark a slot where hearers can question or acknowledge, and where either present speaker or a next speaker can provide a parenthetical expression; but most identifications and initial characterizations are limited to one such expression. Thus *ia* occurring after any such expression is very likely to be serving as a terminal bracket, functioning to announce to hearers that the parenthetical expression is over, and that what follows belongs to the matrix or higher sentence.

6. An Initial View of the Placement of *ia* with Respect to Relative Clauses and Cleft Sentences

We indicated in sections 1–3 that some relative clauses and cleft sentences do not use *ia*-bracketing; i.e., they lack either initial *ia*, or final *ia*, or both. We shall now attempt to use what we have learned about the wider functions of *ia*, in deixis and in discourse, to understand those cases in which *ia* is not used. Our analysis treats as crucial the deictic or focusing function of *ia*, the different roles of *ia* as an initial and final bracket, and the question of word order in syntax.

Table 11-1 presents the 112 relative clauses and cleft sentences we have considered according to the syntactic position of the head noun in the matrix sentence, and the presence or absence of initial and

Type of *ia*-Bracketing	Place Relatives	Relative Clause Comp.	Relative Clause Subj.	Relative Clause Obl.	Cleft Sentences	Total (excl. place relatives)
ia . . . *ia*	5	6	11	6	6	29
ia . . . ø	1	6	4	7	9	26
ø . . . *ia*	1	6	9	1	1	17
ø . . . ø	12	16	14	4	6	40
Total	19	34	38	18	22	112

TABLE 11-1. *Ia* bracketing according to sentence types.

final *ia*. The 19 place relatives are not included in the totals for each type of bracketing, as they do not typically use *ia*-bracketing and are not dealt with in this discussion (figures on them are included for comparative purposes).[23] Of the 112 other sentences, 72 use some form of *ia*-bracketing, as opposed to 40 in which neither initial nor final *ia* is used.

Though the different syntactic types in Table 11-1 do show different patterns of use of *ia*-bracketing, an examination of these patterns yields only partial answers in understanding the constraints on the distribution of *ia*. First, we observe that the highest frequency of use of *ia* is in cleft sentences and in sentences where the head noun follows a preposition (oblique cases); here, approximately 75 percent of the cases we have examined use some form of *ia*-bracketing. In addition, both of these sentence types show particularly frequent use of initial *ia* (i.e., *ia*

23. Neither time nor place relatives use *ia*-bracketing to any degree. Our data on time relatives confirm the descriptions provided by Laycock (1970a: xxxii) and by Wurm (1971b). The latter states (p. 72): "If a conjunction is used, the concept expressed in English by *when* is rendered by *taim* or *long taim,* and the temporal clause usually precedes the main clause." An example from our data is: *Tasol disfela TAIM [mitupela igo long Mumeng], em istap long Lae yet* (Lalia T.) 'But WHEN [the two of us went to Mumeng], she was still in Lae.' Here, as in many such sentences, the speaker uses rising intonation to mark the end of the embedded temporal clause.

Place relatives are, however, more interesting: though they do not typically use *ia*-bracketing, some speakers appear to have extended this marking either as an adjunct to, or in replacement of, the usual construction, an example of which is: *Na igo stret long PLES [igat maunten long EN]* (Tim D.) 'And he went straight to the PLACE [THAT had a mountain on IT].' We see that there is no marking other than the pronominalization of *ples* as *en* after *long* in the embedded sentence; *long en* occurring in final position within the embedded sentence (as it regularly does) is sufficient to indicate the end of the embedding, if the matrix sentence continues. *Long* cannot occur without *en,* as noted in connection with sentence 9. But *long en* can be left out entirely, in which case *ia*-bracketing normally applies.

following the head or preposed noun), but rather infrequent use of *ia* after the embedded sentence.[24]

The frequent use of initial *ia* in cleft sentences can best be explained as concerning the focusing function of *ia*. The preposing of the noun to which *ia* attaches is one way of topicalizing; and many such sentences are said very emphatically, the specific referent being vigorously contrasted with another possible candidate. Indeed, as in 18–20 above, speakers often use cleft sentences in correcting misidentifications by a previous speaker. We will repeat only partial glosses:

(18) 'it's the YOUNGER brother' (previous speaker had thought the elder brother was being discussed).

(19) 'no, it was my FRIEND' (not me, as previous speaker had claimed).

(20) 'it's the FIRST wife . . . [who will go to Lae]' (not the new girlfriend or "second" wife, who has packed her bags in vain).

Of the seven cleft sentences not using *ia* after the preposed NP, two use alternate focusing words: *tasol* 'only, the very one' in 45, and *yet* (intensifier, often glosses as '-self') in 46:

(45) *Yu dispela BOI tasol [ikam na stilim kararuk bilong mi]?* (John L.) 'Are you the **very** BOY [who came and stole my chickens]?

(46) *Em MAMAPAPA bilong mi yet [ol ibaem em]* (Melissa K.) 'It was my PARENTS **themselves** [who paid for it].'

In neither case is the speaker correcting a misidentification; but there are, of course, many cleft sentences using *ia* which also do not correct misidentifications, e.g., 21, which we discussed in section 5, in connection with presupposition.

24. We do not propose to debate the transformational issues involved in the underlying structure of cleft sentences. Here we follow Keenan and Hull's reasoning: "in saying 'the constituent is MOVED OUT of the sentence', we only use this metaphor to make the nature of the surface syntactic form clear, and do not want to commit ourselves to this as the transformational origin of the constructions" (1973: 370, n. 2). Interestingly, as noted by Rickford, *ia* is frequently used in sentences of the predicate nominal type, such as: *Em WANTOK ia* (Tim D.) 'It's (that's) the friend' and *Em TUMBUNA STORI ia* (Tim D.) 'That's an ancestral story.' The addition after *ia* of a parenthetical clause that "modifies" the predicate nominal in such sentences yields a cleft sentence of exactly the type we are considering, thus: (19) *Nogat, em WANTOK ia [putim long maunten ia]*. . . . 'No, it was my friend [who was wearing it on the mountain]. . . .'

The five remaining cleft sentences that use neither *ia* nor any other focusing particle to separate the preposed noun from the following embedded sentence seem to rely on intonation and word order (the preposing itself) to accomplish this separation, and are not otherwise analytically distinct from the cleft sentences using *ia*. Examples are:

(47) *Em ino bus, em ROT, [mama bilong en wokim]* (Paul T.) 'It wasn't the forest, it was the PATH, [his mother had made].'

(48) *Em DISPELA [mi toktok long EN]* (Tony T.) 'That's THE ONE [I'm talking about].'

Despite such exceptions, it is clear that most cleft sentences are syntactically specific examples of a general "topic-comment" structure which involves left dislocation or preposing of the "topicalized" element, attaching *ia* to it, and making a comment about it.

Before returning to a consideration of why right-hand or final *ia* is rather infrequent in cleft sentences, as well as to a discussion of the other cases of Table 11-1, it is important to re-examine in greater depth the distinction made in section 5 between IDENTIFICATIONS and CHARACTERIZATIONS.

7. MORE ON IDENTIFICATIONS AND CHARACTERIZATIONS

In section 4 we stated that any N having a definite, specific referent can have *ia* postposed to it, which can in turn be followed by a parenthetical expression. We distinguished IDENTIFICATION, where the parenthetical expression (whether a re-identification or a description) asks hearers to search to identify a specific referent already known to them, from CHARACTERIZATION, where the N used has a definite, specific referent, but where hearers are not asked to identify it—the slot after *ia* being used to provide a characterization which is often "forward-looking" in that it will later be used for identification. Though the information states of hearers differ radically in the two cases (cf. Goffman 1974: 133–34, 506–8) we argued in section 4 that, in both identifications and characterizations, referents are definite and specific from the speaker's point of view, and therefore can have *ia* attached to them. (It is important to note that many relatives qualify neither as identifications nor as characterizations; but we shall postpone a discussion of this until section 8.)

The distinction between identification and characterization is based mainly on the work done by the parenthetical expression. We noted that IDENTIFICATIONAL expressions use information presumably known to hearers (whether a renaming or a description),[25] to identify specifically one of two things: (a) an item that has been mentioned and characterized earlier in the same conversation; or (b) an item that is being mentioned for the first time here, but that hearers can uniquely identify from prior knowledge.

A classic example of the first sub-type (which abounds in storytelling) was the man "whose leg was injured" in 4, the man having been so characterized earlier in the same conversation. The second type is much less common, and also poses a number of analytical difficulties—because, although the parenthetical expression does function principally to identify the item, it is also often serving simultaneously as a characterization of the item for purposes of the present conversation. One fairly clear case is the excerpt cited as 41 above, in which N.S. identifies a *hap* 'place' mentioned for the first time in this conversation, but which she assumes is already known to the hearer, and her two parenthetical expressions seek to enable G.S. to identify it specifically. Another example is:

(49) *Na em, wanpela MERI ia,* [*bos bilong mipela ia,* [*MERI bilong en*]], *EM igat bel nau* (Emma M.) 'And this WOMAN, [our boss, [his WIFE]], SHE was pregnant then.'

Wanpela meri ia 'this woman' is here being mentioned for the first time; but Mrs. M.'s parenthetical expression, 'our boss's wife', does indeed seek to identify her specifically. (The hearer in this case had seen the boss's wife, but did not know her personally—and so would not have recognized her name.) And though the parenthetical expression could in some sense be said to provide an initial characterization of the woman, the information which Mrs. M. uses to identify her later in the discourse is the fact that she was pregnant. In both examples, then, the identificational function is primary.

A similar distinction can be made with respect to parenthetical expressions which provide characterizations. Here the work done by the parenthetical expression is that of providing new information about the N it qualifies; but it may characterize a new N being introduced for the first time, or it may tell hearers something new about an N whose referent has already been clearly identified (in storytelling, these are often recharacterizations). In addition to the characterization of the

25. "Presumably" here is an inference about the function of the parenthetical material provided by speakers. In such expressions, speakers seem to supply material which will be adequate to the job of identification, and which we can therefore suppose that THEY PRESUME will work, i.e., be known to hearers. If it does not work, of course, speakers can "recycle," recursively, with a further, again "presumably known" parenthetical expression.

piece of cloth in 7, of the girl in 1, of the bush knife in 38, and of the old man (collaboratively) in 44, other examples of initial characterizations (of N's being introduced for the first time) are:

(50) *Mi save lukim wanpela DOK ia,* [*ya bilong EN blekpela*], *na mi save fret long EN* (Elena F.) 'I saw this DOG [that had black ears], and I was afraid of IT.'

(51) *Em igo na kisim wanpela MERI ia* [*em, disfela papa bilong mi ia,* [*susa bilong en, liklik bilong en*]] (Sarah D.) 'He went and got this WOMAN, [uh, this "uncle" of mine, [his sister, his little sister]].'

To understand that the parenthetical expression in 51, superficially so similar to 49, is not functioning to identify, it is necessary to know that none of the hearers knows either the uncle or his little sister, who figure here in a story of long ago and far away. No one is expected to identify them specifically, or recognize them.

In the second type of characterization, which we referred to above as "recharacterizations," the N about which a new comment is made is virtually always the immediately previous topic; there is no question at all that the "comment" expression following it might be doing identificational work, since its referent is absolutely clear. For reasons that will be explained below, it is rare for the form of recharacterizations to be truly "parenthetical," in the sense of having the "comment" expression followed by any other material in the same sentence. Two examples of recharacterizations typically lacking this parenthetical structure are 52, from a story in which there is only one dog, which has already been mentioned many times, and 53, from a story where the hero, a king, has similarly been often mentioned:

(52) *Dok ia, em naispela dok* (Paul T.) 'This dog, he was a nice dog.'

(53) *King ia, wok long wetim pikinini bilong en, pikinini bilong en ino kam* (Wilma D.) 'This king, kept on waiting for his child; his child didn't come back.'

Let us summarize the similarities and differences among the four types of expressions we have discussed. First, referents are always definite (the precise sense in which this is meant is explained in section 8), and also specific, certainly for speakers. But only in the case of recharacterizations can hearers uniquely identify the referent on hearing N *ia* without its immediately following parenthetical expression. Thus, in this case, the expression following *ia* serves only to insert new information about a known N. But in two other cases (those involving identification), the parenthetical expression itself enables hearers to uniquely identify the N. That is, speakers may use such an expression in this way to identify an N uniquely, whether or not it has previously been referred to in the current conversation. Note that both sub-types of "identificational" parentheticals correspond to restrictive relative clauses, insofar as they restrict the universe of possible referents of the N to which they are attached. (The correspondence is not complete, in that the form of the parenthetical may be anything from a single noun, to an NP, to an embedded sentence.) In the last type of expression—new characterizations—hearers are not expected to be able to identify the referent uniquely even after the parenthetical expression, since it applies to a new N which they are not expected to recognize; its function is to tell them something relevant about it (they may, of course, be expected to use this information in making a later identification). Thus in the two sub-types of "characterizations," hearers are simply told certain "new" facts, possibly additional facts, about a particular N. In both cases, these correspond to some extent to appositive or nonrestrictive relative clauses, in that the information they contain does not function to identify or restrict the universe of possible referents of the N to which they are attached.[26] However, in recharacterizations they do not do the work of identification, because the referent of the N is already totally obvious; and in characterizations of new Ns, they cannot identify the referent, because the N in question is completely new to hearers.

8. CONSTRAINTS ON *ia*-BRACKETING

We are now in a position to see why identifications (both sub-types) are more likely than characterizations to be truly "parenthetical," i.e., to have some material in the same sentence occurring AFTER the parenthetical expression. In "topic-comment" terms, both cleft sentences and characterizations use the slot after initial *ia* to make a comment about the preceding N; but this is not the case with identificational parentheticals, which occur in sentences which make their comments elsewhere (either before or after the parenthetical expression). Cleft sentences, on the other hand, usually consist only of the preposed-topic N and the embedded-sentence comment; thus there is no need to sepa-

26. Though only nonrestrictive relatives have traditionally been considered "appositive" (cf., e.g., Langendoen 1969: 148–49), many of the parenthetical expressions we have been discussing appear to be both "restrictive" in function and "appositive" in form. This is the case for renamings, as well as for some "descriptive" parentheticals (whether full relatives or not).

rate the embedded sentence from any following material. And characterizations have a parenthetical structure only when the sentence in
which they occur makes two comments, the first "parenthetical"—as
in 50, where we are told both that the dog had black ears and that Elena
was afraid of it. Most, however, are like 52 in containing a single
comment, and thus no relative clause.

The fact that the embeddings attached to head nouns in oblique
cases and those in cleft sentences are virtually always coterminous with
the end of the sentence (we found only one exception, in an oblique
case) is what makes them so unlikely to have a final *ia*. There is no
following material from which they need to mark a separation. (A pause
or other intonational mark will usually indicate separation from the
succeeding sentence.) Initial *ia,* however, has an important focusing
function in cleft sentences. In oblique cases, *ia* may carry extra weight
in view of the greater complexity which usually characterizes such
sentences (e.g., most have both a direct and an indirect object); and
surface marking of the embedding probably makes them easier to
parse.[27] This greater importance of initial *ia* as opposed to final *ia*
appears to constitute a specific illustration of Goffman's suggestion
(1974: 255–56) that:

> the bracket initiating a particular kind of activity may carry
> more significance than the bracket terminating it. For . . . the
> beginning bracket not only will establish an episode but also will
> establish a slot for signals which will inform and define what sort
> of transformation is to be made of the materials within the epi-
> sode. . . . Closing brackets seem to perform less work, perhaps
> reflecting the fact that it is probably much easier on the whole to
> terminate the influence of a frame than to establish it.

In this case, the use made of the bracketed materials can involve identification or characterization, and can apply to an N which may or may
not be meant to be initially recognized; the "informing signals" include
intonation on both the N and initial *ia.* Closing or terminal *ia,* on the
other hand, can function to confirm an identification emphatically, simply to separate the embedded material from the continuing sentence, or

---

27. Susan Ervin-Tripp and Dan Slobin have brought to our attention
evidence, from the psycholinguistic literature, that sentences with relative pronouns deleted are more difficult to parse than those retaining relative pronouns.
Cf. Fodor, Bever, and Garrett 1974; Shipley and Catlin ms.: 6; and
d'Anglejan-Chatillon 1975: 32–33, as well as Bever's discussion (1970: 313–16)
of "perceptual strategy" constraints on the deletion of relative pronouns in
English. On perceptual and processing constraints in relation to the surface
forms of relatives, cf. also Bever and Langendoen 1971; Kuno 1974.

(usually with rising intonation) to do double duty as a potential initial *ia* for a new parenthetical expression.

It is clear from Table 11-1 that terminal *ia* is less frequent in our data than initial *ia* (forty-six cases versus fifty-five cases). Table 11-2 indicates that the favored environment for missing final *ia* is at the end of embeddings which are coterminous with the end of the matrix sentence. Of the forty-nine sentences in which the matrix sentence continues after the embedding, half do not mark the end of the embedding with *ia*.

Where the matrix sentence does not continue after the embedding, two-thirds (forty-two out of sixty-three sentences) do not mark the end of the embedding with *ia*. Table 11-2 also shows that there are twenty-four sentences in which the matrix sentence does continue after the embedding, but which are not marked with final *ia*. Of these, eighteen are also missing initial *ia*, and the majority of them have special discourse characteristics which will be discussed below. The remaining six again seem to rely on word order and intonation to clarify the syntax. Two examples are:

(54) *EM ia* [*bai kapsaitim igo insait*] *EM orange juice* (Jack W.) 'This STUFF [she's going to pour in] IT's orange juice.'

(55) *Na, MERI ia* [*kam long Manam*] *tok, 'No, yu noken igo.'* (Alice D.) 'And this GIRL [who came from Manam] said, "No, you can't go."'

In both these cases, the parenthetical material is said very rapidly and in an undertone, and the following matrix sentence recommences in a louder, more emphatic style. Once more, we observe variation with respect to pronoun-copying after the parenthetical expression; 54 repeats the subject pronoun *em*, while 55 deletes it.

Lastly, we come to the problem of missing initial *ia*. The first constraint of importance here is related to discourse considerations: with only one exception, *ia* does not attach to Ns whose referents are

	Matrix sentence continues	Matrix sentence terminates	Total
Final *ia*	25	21	46
No final *ia*	24	42	66
TOTAL	49	63	112

TABLE 11-2. Presence and absence of terminal *ia* according to co-occurrence with the end of matrix sentence.

indefinite, as shown in Table 11-3. The "definite-indefinite" distinction drawn here is not syntactically defined (though it has syntactic consequences with respect to *ia*-placement). For example, the "indefinite" article *wanpela* can qualify a noun whose referent is definite in our terms, as in 'it was an (*wanpela*) American' in 21 above, or as in the following:

> (56) *Wanpela lapun MERI ia* [*isave stap long . . . , EM lapun meri ia*] *ikam nau tokim JEK, "Jek!"* (Sogana L.) 'This (an) old WOMAN [who lived at . . . , SHE was an old woman] came and said to Jack, "Jack!"'

Morgan (1972) adduces similar arguments to show that in Albanian "the coreferential NP in the relative clause is definite when the head NP is indefinite" (p. 67), and that for English, "the coreferential NP in a relative clause on a true indefinite NP is underlyingly definite" (p. 71). But rather than treating the problem in terms of either the surface syntactic categories of definiteness and indefiniteness—as marked, e.g., by the article—or even dealing with notions of what is (presumably semantically) "underlyingly" definite or indefinite, we prefer to consider the REFERENT of the NP in question in terms of the information structure of the discourse. Thus, even when the examples cited are individual sentences, as in sections 4 and 6, their explication involves recourse to facts such as whether the N is a "first" or "later" reference to an item in a particular discourse, and whether or not the parenthetical expression does identificational work—i.e., facts that are available only by examining the discourse or sequential context.

Recall that both types of parenthetical expressions (identifica-

		Definite Referent	Indefinite Referent
Initial *ia*	with final *ia*	29 }	0 }
		} 54	} 1
	without final *ia*	25 }	1 }
No initial *ia*	with final *ia*	15 }	2 }
		} 34	} 23
	without final *ia*	19 }	21 }
Total		88	24

TABLE 11-3. Presence and absence of *ia* according to definiteness of referents.

tions and characterizations) are considered to have definite, specific referents. In these terms, *wanpela N ia* is one way of introducing a new, but definite, specific N into a conversation. It says, in effect: "Consider a new N whose specific referent you don't know, but I do, and I'm going to tell you something further about it." In contrast, Ns whose referents we consider to be INDEFINITE are those referring to ANY MEMBER OF A CLASS defined by the parenthetical expression, but not some particular specified one or group. Indeed, not only do hearers not know "which specific one," but speakers also do not claim by their reference to identify or characterize "some specific one"; rather, the parenthetical expression qualifies "any such one." Thus, in 57 (instructions to a child about how to make orange juice from powdered crystals), ANY spoon having the qualities specified in the parenthetical expression (i.e., being wet) will have the undesired consequence of making the orange juice powder fizz up:

(57) *Nogut putim SPUN [igat wara] bai igo insait liklik ia taksim em bai ologeta iboil* (Jack W.) 'Don't use a SPOON [that's wet] lest it go in even a little bit and touch it and it'll all fizz up.'

It is therefore not coincidental that many Ns having indefinite referents are also qualified by quantifiers, such as *planti* 'many' in 58 and *ologeta* 'all, every' in 59; or occur within the scope of a negative, as in 61; or are found in existential sentences like 60–61, as well as 58; or in statements of general facts, truths, or conclusions about the nature of the world, as in 62–64:

(58) *Igat planti MAN [bai igo]* (Alice W.) 'There are a lot of PEOPLE [who'll go].'

(59) *Na OLOGETA SAMTING [istap long giraun, wonem kain gol], EM bilong gavman* (Bob B.) 'And EVERYTHING [that's in the ground, whatever kind of precious metal], IT belongs to the government.'

(60) *Yutupela noken wari, bai igat narapela KAR [bai igo]* (Jack W.) 'Don't you two worry, there'll be another CAR [that'll go].'

(61) *Inogat wanpela TOK [ikamap stret long mi]* (Peter E.) 'There is no NEWS [that has come directly to me].'

(62) *MAN [igat inap mani] ken baim* (Tony T.) 'PEOPLE [who have enough money] can pay.'

(63) *EM* [*ol ikolim sangguma*] *EM man tasol* (Tony T.) 'THAT [which they call *sangguma*] (i.e., anything called *sangguma*) IT is really human (i.e., not supernatural).'[28]

(64) *PIKININI* [*ino inap long save long tok ples bilong mama o papa*] *bai yusim Pidgin* (Emma M.) 'CHILDREN [who don't know their parents' languages] will use Pidgin.'

Now though the embedded sentences in 57–64 would qualify as "restrictive relatives," we see that the distinction of restrictive and nonrestrictive is analytically rather unhelpful; what is important to understand about these embedded sentences is that none of them is doing identificational work, since identification of the specific referent of N is not at issue in any of them. Nor indeed is it the function of the parenthetical expression to "characterize" the N in any way, i.e., to provide information about a particular N. Rather, in all except the existential sentences 58, 60, and 61, the parenthetical expression states the condition under which ANY SUCH N would satisfy the statement made in the matrix sentence. Thus they are all paraphrasable as conditionals, e.g.,

(57) If a spoon is wet, it'll make it fizz up.

(59) If there is any precious metal in the ground, it belongs to the government.

(62) If a person has enough money, he can pay.

(63) If a thing is called a *sangguma*, it is really human.

(64) If a child doesn't know . . . , he'll speak Pidgin.

Note, however, that these sentences can also be paraphrased in Tok Pisin with WH-forms, "whichever," "whoever" etc., as in 15–16 above. The sentences we are considering here might look something like:

(57) *Wonem SPUN* [*igat wara*], *bai* . . .

(59) *Wonem SAMTING* [*istap long giraun*], *em* . . .

(62) *HUSAT (MAN)* [*igat inap mani*], *ken baim*.

(63) *Wonem SAMTING* [*ol ikolim sangguma*], *em* . . .

(64) *Husat PIKININI* [*ino inap . . .*], *bai* . . .

28. Mihalic (1971: 169) defines *sangguma* as 'secret murder committed by orders from sorcerers'. Our texts also indicate that it can be used to refer to the sorcerer himself.

As in 57–64, most sentences in which the relative qualifies an N with an indefinite referent lack not only initial *ia,* but also final *ia.*

From Table 11-3, we see that there are still 34 sentences which have definite referents and lack initial *ia.* Of these sentences, however, 15 do employ final *ia,* generally serving to mark off N + parenthetical from the ongoing sentence. Further, in these sentences, the parenthetical expression itself is often minimal—consisting, e.g., of a verb alone (with or without pronoun copy):

> (65) *Em MAMA bilong tupela [EM idai ia] EM swim swim istap* (Paul T.) 'The MOTHER of the two [WHO had died], she kept on swimming.'

> (66) *Nogat, MAN [isindaun ia] MITUPELA stori* (Tony T.) 'No, the MAN [who is sitting] HE and I are telling stories.'

But what of the 19 sentences so far unaccounted for, in which no *ia*-bracketing is used, though referents of Ns are definite? Six of these are unmarked cleft sentences, discussed above. The remaining 13 include every syntactic type of relatives, with the coreferential NP acting as subject in both the matrix and the embedded sentence, as in 67; as subject of the matrix sentence and complement of the embedded sentence, as in 68; as complement in the matrix sentence and subject in the embedded sentence, as in 69; or as complement in both, as in 70:

> (67) *Na MIPELA [ikam long Lae], MIPELA igo* (Noemi S.) 'And THOSE OF US [WHO had come to Lae], WE left.'

> (68) *Na narapela LAPUN [EM yu lukim], EM iHolzknecht* (Alice W.) 'And the other OLD MAN [THAT you saw], HE was Holzknecht.'[29]

> (69) *Lucy, yu kirap igo lukim SISIS bilong mama [istap long dro bilong masin]* (Emma M.) 'Lucy, go get Mommy's SCISSORS [WHICH are in the machine drawer].'

> (70) *Ol itok, wetim dispela, wonem, RIPOT [ol ikisim igo nau ating bai ol iputim we long. . . .]* (Tom S.) 'They said they'd wait for this, uh, REPORT [THAT they took and that maybe they were going to put somewhere. . . .]'

This group of sentences provides evidence that the *ia*-bracketing rule has not been completely generalized as yet (see the historical discus-

---

29. Preposed *em* here would appear to constitute a counter-example to our claim, in section 1, about lack of evidence for a pronoun-attraction principle. Object preposing is, however, a stylistic variant not specific to relative clauses.

sion in section 9), and remains to some extent variable or optional in the population under study. The 13 sentences in question come from nine different speakers, all but one of whom used *ia*-bracketing in other sentences.

A last possible constraint on *ia*-bracketing which we investigated is social; i.e., we wondered whether particular speakers or groups of speakers tend to use *ia*-bracketing with greater frequency than others. The 112 sentences we examined are uttered by 26 speakers, the number of sentences from any single speaker varying between 1 and 15. The relatively low number of sentences per speaker (a problem endemic to studies of variability in syntax) makes it difficult to discern differences among speakers; however, most display variable usage, alternating among the various possibilities we have discussed (double *ia*, initial *ia* only, final *ia* only, no *ia*). Only one speaker (Tony T.) has an inordinately high ratio of sentences unmarked by *ia* (8 out of 11, with one each of the other three types), but 4 of the 8 unmarked sentences are indefinites. Grouping the speakers in various ways, we found a slight tendency for women to use *ia*-bracketing more frequently than men (72 percent versus 56 percent), and for children to use it more than adults (75 percent versus 60 percent). We would not claim that these differences are significant, given the sampling error inherent in having relatively few sentences per speaker, and we find it remarkable that speakers behaved so similarly.

To return briefly to an issue raised in section 1, regarding the interaction between *ia*-bracketing and Equi-NP Deletion, it would at first glance appear that *ia*-bracketing acts as a constraint on the alternation between deletion and pronominalization of the coreferential NP. Of the 40 sentences in Table 11-1 in which *ia*-bracketing is not used, 80 percent delete the pronoun, as opposed to only 60 percent of the 72 sentences in which some form of *ia*-bracketing is employed. This, however, is entirely due to the presence of the 21 indefinites in the "unmarked" category, since deletion is almost categorical in these sentences, only one of them retaining a coreferential pronoun in the embedded sentence. Of the 19 remaining unmarked sentences, 63 percent delete the pronoun, i.e., deletion occurs with the same frequency as in the *ia*-bracketed sentences.

9. THE PUTATIVE ORIGINS OF *ia* AS A RELATIVIZER: IMPLICATIONS FOR CREOLIZATION

It is fairly clear that *ia* has not been used as a relativizer throughout the history of Tok Pisin. It is definitely not so used in the earliest source in which we searched for examples of relatives, Churchill's account of

Beach-La-Mar (1911). Beach-La-Mar was a western Pacific trade pidgin of the 19th century, the ancestor of the language still called Bichelamar (Guy 1974) or Bislama (Camden 1975), currently spoken in the New Hebrides. Tok Pisin is also considered to have its roots in Beach-La-Mar (Salisbury 1967; Laycock 1970b); and indeed the bulk of Churchill's data comes from New Guinea, culled from a dozen or so publications published around the turn of the century.

The four clear examples of relative clauses that we have been able to extract from Churchill are not syntactically marked, except for an Equi-NP Deletion rule. They are presented below, preserving Churchill's highly anglicized spelling (bracketing and glosses represent our analysis):

(71) *He look out all men* [*stop this place*] (Churchill [1911: 50]; originally from Wawn 1893: 386) 'He looked for the people [who lived (t)here].'

(72) *Some place* [*me go*] *man he no good* (Churchill [p. 48]; originally from London 1909: 361) 'Some places [I went] the people were bad.'

(73) *You savez two white men* [*stop Matupi*] *he got house* (Churchill [p. 42], originally from Wawn [p. 290]) 'You know that the two white men [who live at Matupi] have a house.'

(74) *Chief he old man* [*he no savey walk good*] (Churchill [p. 49], originally from Wawn [p. 43]) 'The chief is an old man [who can't walk properly].'

Sentence 74 in particular might lead one to suspect the NON-application of Equi-NP Deletion to explain the presence of the second *he,* or indeed to interpret this sentence as two coordinate clauses without a conjunction—i.e., "The chief is an old man, he can't walk properly." However, we believe that the correct interpretation is that *he* (present-day *i-*) was already functioning as a "predicate marker,"[30] not a pronoun, as appears to be the case in 72, *man he no good.*

Thus relativization in this early period seems to have involved no markers in the matrix sentence, and an Equi-NP Deletion rule in the embedded sentence. Hearers probably deduced the embeddedness from word order and juxtaposition of elements alone, with perhaps some help from prosodic features like stress and intonation. Moreover, the relatives observable in citations and texts published in Hall 1943

---

30. Cf. Smeall (1975) and Woolford (1975) for more detailed analyses of current usage. Early sources (including Churchill and Queensland 1885) contain numerous examples of N + *he* + verb.

(recorded by various anthropologists during the 1930s), as well as those in Wurm 1971, Laycock 1970a, and Mihalic 1971 (recorded during the 1950s and 60s), show virtually nothing but this pattern (apart from time and place relatives, discussed in fn. 23). The only clear exceptions are five sentences drawn from Hall's copious texts, collected in the Sepik area during the 1930s. They constitute a small minority of all the relatives observable in Hall's texts; but they demonstrate the same structure exhibited by the sentences we have been analyzing, in that four of them (one of which is given as 75) use initial *ia,* and one uses final *ia* (none use both initial and final *ia*). We regularize Hall's transcription slightly, add brackets and underlining, and quote his English gloss:

(75) *Tufela i-fainim MUN* **hir,** [*i-stap long sospen*] (Hall 1943: 46) 'They found the MOON here, [WHICH was in the kettle].'

Interestingly, Hall glosses *hir* as 'here', but treats the following material as a relative.

Since examination of available texts leads us to believe that relatives were largely unmarked with *ia* until fairly recently, we have attempted to investigate how *ia* was used in these earlier texts. The earliest source (Queensland) contains no *ia* at all; but Churchill (1911: 43) has one sentence, corresponding to the "place adverb" usage mentioned by Laycock, Wurm, and Mihalic (cited in section 4):

(76) *Here no kaikai* (from Seligman 1910: 10) 'There is no food here.'

Texts cited by Hall dating from twenty or thirty years later, however, contain several examples of deictic *ia,* two of which are quoted (with his glosses) as follows:

(77) *Ol i-go nau, em TUFELA PIKININI* **hir,** *TUFELA i-go lukautim banana i-mau* (Hall 1943: 46) 'When they had gone, these two children both went to look for ripe bananas.'

(78) *Na disfela MERI,* [*doktor i-kisim*], *disfela namberwan MERI bilong em* **hir,** *i-pikinini bilong luluai* (Hall 1943: 56) 'Now this woman, [whom the doctor took], this number-one wife of his, was the luluai's daughter.'

Sentence 78 in particular is noteworthy because the relative 'whom the doctor took' is unmarked (as appears to be typical), whereas *hir* is deictic. In both 77 and 78, Hall glosses *hir* as 'this, these', though he does not recognize this function in his grammatical discussion, and lists *hir* simply as an "adverb" (p. 100). Deictic or demonstrative *ia* is also attested in the texts and examples cited by Wurm 1971b, Laycock 1970a, and Mihalic 1957, 1971.

Our reconstruction follows simply from this historical account. That is, we propose three stages: (1) the original "place adverb" *ia*; (2) extension for use as a postposed deictic or demonstrative; and (3) further extension for general "bracketing" use, including topic-comment structures, relativization, and cleft sentences. That these uses are semantically and functionally related has been shown in sections 4–8.

We can now relate this development to the creolization process. First, we know that the existence of creole speakers of Tok Pisin in any significant numbers can be dated no earlier than the mid-1950s; and we have five clear cases of *ia*-marked relatives attested from more than a decade earlier. Certainly there is no reason why fluent second-language speakers of Tok Pisin could not have made the transfer between stages 2 and 3 in the use of *ia*. That they indeed did so is confirmed by the adults in our sample, who have this usage well established in their speech and have not learned it from their children.[31] This is particularly likely not only because of the semantic and functional relationships among the three usages, but also because many Austronesian languages of the New Guinea and island Melanesian area show striking parallels.

Thus, in Buang,[32] the deictic particle *ken* is used as a place adverbial, e.g., *ke mdo ken* 'I'm staying here'; as a postposed demonstrative, e.g., *ke mdo byaŋ ken* 'I'm staying in this house'; and as a relativizer, e.g., *ke mdo byaŋ ken gu le vkev* 'I'm staying in the house that you saw yesterday'. Ray 1926 provides some evidence for similar structures in a number of island Melanesian languages, including Iai (p. 89), Nguna (p. 208), Tasiko (p. 237), Uripiv (p. 286), and Tangoa (p.

31. Some of the young adults in our sample had no children older than infants. We do not, of course, mean to imply that children's most important input to language learning comes from their parents (or vice versa, in a creolizing situation!). We believe that the creolization process can shed much light on various problems of language universals (cf. Traugott 1973; Slobin 1975), though we do not agree with Bickerton's assertion (1974: 127) that this view necessarily implies that "adults have readier access than children to linguistic universals." Taking a somewhat wider view of linguistic universals than simply how linguistic universals may relate to "specific neural properties of the human brain" (Bickerton, p. 135), we also feel it important to understand how linguistic means are shaped by their situation within, and relation to, the communicative patterns of human societies (cf. Hymes 1971). We therefore agree with Bickerton that close study of the particular social circumstances of both pidginization and creolization is necessary for the solution of these problems.

32. Buang is an Austronesian language spoken in the Morobe Province south of Lae, and studied by Sankoff. Bruce Hooley, who has done extensive research on another dialect of Buang (where the cognate for *ken* is *sen*) has confirmed these examples. Hooley (personal communication) has correctly pointed out that Buang relatives usually, but not invariably, have a closing particle other than *ken* (or *sen*), one of a set of deictic forms.

254

360). As for Tok Pisin's contemporary "sister" languages, Bislama appears to use *ia* as a postposed deictic marker, sometimes in conjunction with its relativizer *we* (cf. Camden [1975] and fn. 11 above); and in the Solomon Islands, *ia* has been described as a "particle which refers back to, e.g., *desfala man ia*" (S.I.C.A., n.d., p. 13).[33]

Whether fluent, adult, second-language Tok Pisin speakers initially extended deictic *ia* for "bracketing" use in complex sentences as a "logical" outgrowth of its focusing functions, or whether some of them at least were influenced by grammatical parallels in their first languages, it is fairly clear that we should attribute the source or ORIGIN of this construction to adults. But it is also clear that the rapid SPREAD of the *ia*-bracketing rule (i.e., its regular use in a majority of relatives) is a recent phenomenon, characteristic of that community which uses Tok Pisin as its primary language, including both "pidgin" and "creole" speakers.

33. We thank Aletta Biersack for bringing this to our attention.

12.

Variability and Explanation in Language and Culture: Cliticization in New Guinea Tok Pisin

1. FUNCTIONALISM AND LANGUAGE CHANGE

In the last ten or fifteen years, we have come a long way from the one language = one culture assumption that once characterized much of our thinking about the relationships between language and culture. No longer can it be maintained, in any strict or simple sense, that "language is the mirror of culture," for we now know that in many societies there is widespread bi- and multi-lingualism, and that even where there exists what people call "one language," it is never totally uniform, or totally stable.

In the innocent one language = one culture days, linguistic differentiation was explained in terms of a split-and-divergence model, i.e., as the result of the separation and isolation of populations. Dialect and even language leveling was thought to be the unavoidable consequence of language contact. Today, a great deal more is known about the relationship between social and linguistic facts. Largely through the work of John Gumperz, we know, for example, that linguistic differences can be maintained, even created, *within* speech communities where the segments of the population concerned are in "regular and frequent interaction" (Gumperz 1964: 137).

After all, we have only to note the numerous differences now described for many communities between men's and women's speech to come to the conclusion that speech differences can be maintained

This chapter first appeared in M. Saville-Troike, ed., *Linguistics and Anthropology*, Washington, D.C., Georgetown University Press, pp. 59–73. It is reprinted here with only minor editorial revisions. An earlier version was read at the Conference on Mechanisms of Syntactic Change, organized by Charles Li, Santa Barbara, May 1976. I am very grateful to Suzanne Laberge for the major part she played in the data collection in Papua New Guinea in 1971, and to David Sankoff and Pierrette Thibault for their generous contribution to the data analysis. I also thank the many kind residents of Lae and environs, Papua New Guinea, who permitted us to record them and their children.

among interacting groups. Similar observations can be made about generational differences in situations of very rapid language change, as is the case in creolization, for example, in the New Guinea situation I will discuss in this chapter. The sex and generational differences have one thing in common: the creation and maintenance, among subsegments of a population, of linguistic differences *not* caused by isolation or lack of contact between the subsegments in question.

This lack of linguistic homogeneity, which has been well documented in numerous studies of variability over the last decade, has raised a number of questions that are crucial in rethinking the problem of the relationship between language and culture. First, what are the sources and functions of linguistic heterogeneity (at whatever level) that one finds? Second, how much such heterogeneity can be tolerated (i.e., without seriously impeding communication), and in what areas of language?

My own work on language variation has led me to take issue with the position that language is autonomous, a Saussurian "système où tout se tient." Rather, I have come to see that much of the structured variation that exists in language can be ascribed to the social nature of its use, and to the plurality of functions that it serves. Thus the study of linguistic variability also leads to the rejection of a one-to-one relationship between form and function. What remains problematic, then, is just how, and to what extent, these functions influence the shape of language.

I am not, however, advocating "functionalism" as a panacea for understanding the relationships between language, society and culture, especially in the light of the fact that in several disciplines functionalism seems recently to have run its course. Indeed, it has been widely criticized in social anthropology as not constituting an *explanation* at all. Critics note that within this framework, aspects of culture and social institutions were construed as a kind of homeostatic system, (one analyzed the correlation of, say, bride wealth and divorce rates as mutually interdependent, necessary to each other), but that it was difficult to say what might cause any such cultural fact or social institution to be some other way.

In contrast to this, however, I think that approaches identified as "functionalist" within linguistics have always had an explanatory thrust.[1] This is because the problem has been conceived in essence as one of explaining linguistic facts in terms of nonlinguistic facts. More

---

1. Most of the work I have in mind is European, including the Prague school, Vološinov in the U.S.S.R., Frei and Bauche in Switzerland, Martinet in France, and Halliday in England.

subtly put, one looks at the influence of nonlinguistic considerations in the explanation of linguistic facts. So in linguistics, it seems, no contradiction is felt to exist between explanation and functionalism. Kuno, for example, has recently claimed that "wide varieties of linguistic phenomena are in fact primarily controlled by nonsyntactic factors," listing among these factors such things as "the speaker's belief about the universe that he lives in, presupposition, discourse influences, perceptual strategies" and so on (Kuno 1975: 276).

Until very recently, few twentieth-century American linguists have adopted a functionalist position. It is no accident, however, that the principal champion of such a view in the U.S. for many years has been a scholar whose work has been centrally concerned with relating anthropology and linguistics. I speak of course of Dell Hymes (e.g., 1964a, 1970a), who has written that:

> A sociolinguistic critique . . . is structural, in seeking to show the existence of structural relationships in language, and in the use of language, beyond those usually taken into account by linguists. It is also functional, in that discovery of new structural relationships depends upon the recognition of the functions they serve. (Hymes 1970a: 112)

He argues for "the priority, plurality, and problematic (empirical) status of the functions of speech" (p. 113).

But for many years, the majority of modern American grammarians did not embark on the functionalist project, perhaps, at least in part, for the following reasons: (1) the seductiveness of the orderliness of synchronic linguistic structure, viewed as an abstract formal system that (whether from a structuralist or generative perspective) in itself overpowered other problems and perspectives, giving linguists plenty to work on without getting their hands dirty; (2) the distastefulness, especially to those holding a relativist position, of functionalist arguments when pushed to the extreme (viz., critiques of Martinet's conception of "functional load"). One is easily led into considerations of how "well adapted" a particular form is to the function it is supposed to serve, or to analyzing a particular synchronic state as being "better adapted" than a previous one, etc. To our ears, the following quotation sounds old-fashioned, somewhat Durkheimian, and certainly overly mechanistic:

> The functional cycle is constituted by a stimulus (the deficits); a means (the processes); an end (linguistic needs). And as in biology, the stimulus creates the function and the function the organ. In linguistics the deficit awakens a need (in any case always latent) that in turn triggers the process which satisfies it. (Frei 1929: 22—my translation)

As an alternative to falling into teleological circularity, or having to make distasteful comments on "utility," then, how much more pleasant to consider linguistic change as simply the reanalysis or reorganization of formal rules!

I think that a way out of some of the traps of overly mechanistic functionalism involves a clear recognition of both the multifunctionality of language as stressed by Hymes, and some of what Hockett (1963) has called the "design features" of language, which seem to be structurally important and enduring. As an example, I will examine a case of dynamic tension between a discourse function—foregrounding or topicalization—and a language pattern feature—morpho-syntactic regularization. In describing this tension, I will be looking at innovation in speaker strategies as discourse-related. My view is that we can describe as grammaticalization processes the transition between what initially appear to be ad hoc speaker strategies and what later can be fairly confidently described as syntactic rules.

2. TOK PISIN SUBJECT PRONOUNS

The specific example to be discussed in this paper concerns the cliticization of subject pronouns in New Guinea Tok Pisin, during the period 1885–1970. The data on which this analysis is based are taken from four historical stages of the language:

I (1885): Queensland, Hearings of the Royal Commission on Recruiting Polynesian [*sic*] Labourers in New Guinea and Adjacent Islands. These data are copious, but must be used with caution.[2] They consist of thousands of question-answer pairs where the judge questioned several hundred laborers about the conditions of their employment on the Queensland sugar plantations. Transcription of the responses appears somewhat anglicized—the official view was, after all, that the laborers spoke English more or less well (or not at all, in which case an interpreter was used). Responses citing what was said at the time a laborer was hired appear closer to what we imagine the language to have been like (e.g., using "me" as a subject pronoun more frequently, as opposed to the "I" in most responses to the judge).

II (1911): Churchill's *Beach La Mar,* a compendium of sources (mostly accounts by travelers, including ships' captains and European resi-

---

2. One reason for caution concerns the fact that the language spoken in Queensland by 1885 may already have to be considered a sister language, rather than a direct ancestor, of contemporary Tok Pisin (Mühlhäusler 1976a). The differences were, however, probably slight at such an early stage.

260

dents of various islands) dating mainly from around 1900. Again, the quality of the data is variable, and care must be exercised.

III (1930s): Hall's (1943) account provides texts collected in New Guinea (mainly the Sepik region) in the 1930s by various anthropologists.

IV (1971): Recordings collected by Suzanne Laberge and myself of (1) adult ("pidgin") speakers of Tok Pisin and (2) children and adolescent ("creole") speakers of Tok Pisin.

Cliticization of the subject pronoun *i* 'he' seems to have taken place between 1885 and 1935, and our data on the first three periods indicate this quite clearly.

2.1. Stage I (1885)

Of a sample of approximately 750 sentences containing subjects, the subject noun phrase consisted in over 99 percent of cases of either (1) a *single noun* sometimes with but generally without modifiers as in 1, or more rarely several conjoined nouns as in 2, or (2) a *pronoun*, as in 3–6. Pronoun subjects represented about 73 percent of subjects; the rest were noun subjects:

(1) Boatswain gammon me. (399)[3] 'The boatswain lied to me.'

(2) Sister, father, and all people belong a me plenty cry. (484)

(3) We fellows no savez talk. Dixon talked. (517)

(4) Me no count him. (77)

(5) I no savez count him moons. (235)

(6) He say all same, "three yams go work." (330)

A few remarks are in order with respect to these sentences. Concerning the subject pronouns, the three which clearly dominate are *I* (244 cases), *he* (124 cases) and *you* (109 cases). There are enough instances of *me* (18) for us to be sure that it *was* being used as a subject pronoun at this time, but we have no way of telling to what extent the *I*s in the text represent "corrections" or changes made in transcribing the hearings. (*I* shows up to a limited extent in Stage II, and completely disappears in subsequent stages.)[4]

3. Numbers which follow sentences from the 1885 Royal Commission report designate lines as indicated in the Report. Orthography for the first three stages follows the orthography of the original sources.
4. The only vestige of *I* in current Tok Pisin is found in the form *ating*, glossed 'perhaps' or 'maybe'. Interestingly, 4 of Churchill's 10 cases of *I* occurred with the verb 'think'.

We can also be quite sure that *he* was functioning as a strong pronoun. First, there are no alternates (as with I/me); *him* (> *em*, the current form) shows up for the first time in subject position in Churchill's 1911 materials. Second, *he* remains in significant proportions in the 1911 texts, and its descendant *i* is still with us—thus it is not the figment of the transcriber's imagination that I suspect "I" of being.

But we do also see the beginnings of *i*'s cliticization. There are 5 sentences (of some 200 with noun subjects) in which the noun is followed by *he*. This was clearly a little-used option in the grammar, or perhaps a strategy which was just being invented, and at least one of our examples would appear to indicate that it had contrastive force:

(7) Q. Did you talk to captain at Townsville? (496)

R. No; Jack he talked.

Contrast this with the more usual "Dixon talked" in 3. A second example shows another case of "switch reference," this time the subject "you" is replaced by "ship" in the second speaker's response.

(8) Q. Then you went along ship?

R. Yes, and ship he go. (548)

In the other three sentences using *N* + *he* + *V*, the subject noun phrases are *two fellow moon* and *three fellow moon*, as in 9, all unusual in having relatively long (i.e., other than one-word) subjects.

(9) Two fellow moon he die, one fellow come up, then you go back. (554)

For comparison's sake, let us consider briefly the object pronoun 'him'. There are far fewer cases of 'him' than 'he' occurring as an independent pronoun—only 7, one example of which is given as 4 above. But there is again evidence of the beginning cliticization of 'him', in that there are seven further sentences with V + him ± NP complement, as in 5. This is fairly similar to the number of subject NPs occurring with the "candidate clitic" *he*. However recall that the proportion for *he* was 5 of 200 sentences with noun subjects; here there are 7 of only 80 sentences with noun complements. Of the verbs occurring with *him*, several in current Tok Pisin have an obligatory -*im* suffix: *count, call, hear,* and *feel*. Modern descendants of *like* and *finish* take the -*im* suffix when used transitively. The four others (*took, get, shut,* and *tell*) have not survived in modern Tok Pisin.

2.2. Stage II (1900–1910)

Churchill's data look remarkably modern compared to the situation of Stage I. The most dramatic change is the cliticization of *he* (*i*), evident in the frequency of the *NP* + *he* + *V* type. Whereas it represented only 2.5 percent of all sentences with noun (nonpronominal) subjects in 1885, this type accounts for 65 percent of 81 noun-subject sentences I have examined in Churchill's data, as shown in Figure 12-1. Sentences with *NP* + *he* + *V* are illustrated in 10 and 11; with *NP* + *V* in 12 and 13.

(10) One fella tree he tambo ('forbidden') along you altogether. (Churchill, p. 34)

(11) Pappa belong me he go finish yes'erday. (Churchill, p. 34)

(12) That fellow break plenty match. (Churchill, p. 36)

(13) Plenty boy die. (Churchill, p. 36)

It is unclear from Churchill's data whether *he* can be analyzed as an agreement phenomenon as discussed in Givón (1976), given that it

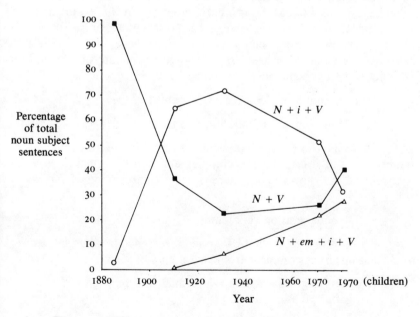

Figure 12-1. Time course of the successive cliticization of *i* and *em.*

263

marked neither number or gender. Churchill provides numerous examples of its use in four categories: "masculine," "feminine," "neuter," and "plural," including sentences 14 and 15.

(14) Queen Victoria he look out. (Churchill, p. 42)

(15) All a Malekula man he say. (Churchill, p. 42)

Note, however, that (1) Tok Pisin was already reorganizing its pronominal system to obliterate useless English distinctions such as gender in the third person singular (Churchill cites only four cases of *she*) and to set up more reasonable categories such as duals; and (2) the English pronominal forms that might have served in marking agreement had almost disappeared from Tok Pisin even at this time (if ever their presence was anything more than transcription error). In addition to *she*, these include *they* (only three cases in Churchill) and *it* (never cited). The "second wave" of cliticization to be discussed in section 3.3 most certainly did involve agreement.

Though I think we can safely say that cliticization of *he* (*i*) has taken place by this time, it seems that *he* (*i*) still retains some of its force as a strong pronoun. My main reason here (in the absence of any data on stress) is that *he* still occurs as a sole subject pronoun in a fairly significant number of cases, with only two cases of *him* occurring as a subject pronoun. *He* is the sole subject in 60 sentences, or 43 percent of the third person subject sentences—including those with *N* + *he* (53 cases) and *N* alone (28 cases). *He* as a subject pronoun is illustrated in 16; one of the two sentences with *him* as subject is cited as 17.

(16) He find him along reef. (Churchill, p. 33)

(17) Him go dead. (Churchill, p. 37)

Him has also made great strides as a clitic. Of 42 complement sentences, 15 have *him* alone as complement as in 16; 11 have *him* + *N* *complement*. As shown in 18, there is some transcription of *-him* as a suffix.

(18) He make'm one big fennis. (Churchill, p. 33)

There is one somewhat exceptional sentence in Churchill's material that deserves comment from two points of view:

(19) God big fella belong white man him fella he make'm altogether. (Churchill, p. 34)

First, there is the rather odd *him fella*, a form that has not survived to the present as part of the standard paradigm *mipela, yupela,* etc., but which seems to represent a productive possibility which keeps cropping up in the language. Hall (1955) mentions its use on one occasion in 1954 as a demonstrative adjective. The interesting thing is that *him fella* is followed by *he*, and seems to be a case of a "strong pronoun" followed by a weak or clitic pronoun. Churchill's data contain several other cases of such constructions: *all he* (one case); *me fellow me* (three cases); *these two fella they* (one case); *you me two fellow we* (one case); and the doubtful *altogether you boy . . . you* (one case).

	Churchill (1911)	*current usage*
3rd sing.	em fellow he	em (i)
1st dual (incl.)	you me two fellow we	(yu)mi tupela (i)
1st pl. (excl.)	me fellow me	mipela (i)
2nd pl.	you . . . you	yupela (i)
3rd dual	these two fellow they	tupela (i)
3rd pl.	all he	ol (i)

These cases seem to represent the initial extension of clitics with strong pronouns, a development subsequent to their use with nouns.

The second thing about sentence 19 is that it is the first case we have of a full noun phrase, followed by a strong pronoun, followed by the clitic *he*, a development that continues in later stages. It is of interest that the initial noun phrase is long and complex, one of the two factors we shall see later as favoring a pronoun copy.

2.3. Stage III (1930s)

All of the trends evident in Churchill's material are continued at this stage. Principally:

1. The proportion of NP subjects followed by the clitic *i-* (now represented as such in Hall's orthography) is even higher: of the 100 sentences with full noun phrase subjects, 71 are of the form *NP + i + V*.

2. There is an increasingly small proportion of sentences with *i-* as sole subject (24 cases), and these are almost as clearly restricted to a small set of constructions as they are today, i.e., mainly existential sentences beginning with *igat* or *inogat,* as in 20, and in narrative "over-laid" structures (cf. Grimes 1972) as in 21.

(20) Na em, bifor, i-no gat mun—no gat mun long klawd antap. (Hall, p. 46) 'Now previously there was no moon—there was no moon up in the clouds.' (Hall's gloss).

(21) Na em i-no laik askim tufela, em papa i-haid tasol, i-stap. Istap nau, i-tudark nau. (Hall, p. 46) 'Now he did not want to

265

ask the two of them, and the father just kept silent, and stayed there.' (Hall's gloss)

3. There is a greatly augmented use of *i-* in combination with other pronouns. Whereas there were 8 such cases in Churchill's material, we now see 75 percent of pronouns followed by *i-*, as *em i-* in 21.

4. The complement clitic -*im* now appears to be firmly attached to all the verbs it attaches to today, and no more will be said about it in this paper. A detailed discussion may be found in Wurm (1971b), section on "transitivity," pp. 22–38. See also Lattey (1975).

5. *Em* is firmly established as a subject pronoun (40 cases), as shown in Figure 12-2.

6. The most striking development at this stage concerns what appears to be the beginning of a second wave of subject-pronoun cliticization, i.e., *N* + *pronoun* + *i* + *V*. I have so far found 6 cases: 5 with *em* (sing.) and one with *ol* (pl.), as illustrated in 22–25:

(22) Putim umben long rot bilong pik, *Ngwambwa em i-*kisim pik. (Hall, p. 49) 'If we put a net on the road where the pig has been, a spirit of the dead takes the pig.' (Hall's gloss)

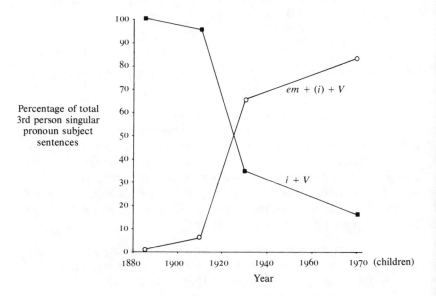

Figure 12-2. Weakening of pronoun *i* and introduction and spread of *em*.

(23) Mitufela sutim, givim long kandari, Bandarap. *Bandarap em i*-kukim. (Hall, p. 48) 'The two of us shot it, and gave it to my mother's brother, Bandarap. Bandarap cooked it.' (Hall's gloss)

(24) Man i-mekim singsing long Mbabmu, *meri em i*-go long em, em i-pekpek blut, . . . (Hall, p. 48) 'Men utter a spell over (Mbabmu); if a woman goes near them, she will have dysentery. . . .' (Hall's gloss)

(25) *Na papa bilong tufela pikinini, wantaim mama bilong tufela, ol i*-go wok saksak long bus. (Hall, p. 46) 'Now the father of the two children, and their mother, went to cultivate sago in the bush.' (Hall's gloss)

In these sentences even more than was the case with the initial cliticization of *he* (*i*), it is clear that the pronoun *em* performs a particular discourse function, being used in the case of long or complex subject NPs as in 25, where it serves as a reminder of the subject of the verb, and as an emphatic topic-changing marker as in 22–24. In 23, for example, the whole story is about the narrator and his hunting-companion, referred to throughout as *mitufela*. The very last sentence, following a string of sentences in which *mitufela* was the subject, changes the subject to *Bandarap*, and inserts pronoun *em*.

2.4. Stage IV (1971)

The data for this period have been separated into two groups, the adults, who are "pidgin" or second-language speakers (as indeed were all of the people whose speech we have looked at in the first three stages), and their children, or "creole" speakers. Though in many ways the grammars of these two groups are very similar with respect to subject clitics, they do differ in some degree. This raises the question of the extent to which these differences are to be accounted for in the kind of terms we have so far employed in accounting for changes over the first three stages (i.e., to what extent they are a continuation of previous trends and innovative possibilities), or in terms of some special properties of "creolization." Let us first try to see what is common to both groups (adults and children).

Most importantly, both adults and children show a marked increase in the proportion of noun-subject sentences employing the $N + pronoun + i + V$ construction type, as illustrated in 26 and 27 (adults) and 28 and 29 (children):

(26) Bifo *ol Gieman ol i*soim ol bikpela man bifo. (Jack W. 2:2:028) 'Before, the Germans taught our forefathers.'

(27) Na *narapela em i*putim blakfela. (Tim D. 13:1:070) 'And the other guy wore a black one.'

(28) *Wanpela meri em i*go nau, . . . (Paul T., age 11, 5:2:240) 'So this woman went. . . .'

(29) *Planti kain man olsem ol i*save stap long Lae (Joe S., age 11, 5:2:263) 'Lots of that kind of people live in Lae.'

Among both adults and children, *em* is used for singular subjects and *ol* for plurals, but there are several cases of children hesitating over the choice, as in 30, and there may be some tendency among children towards generalizing *em* to plurals as well. Duals, as in 31, pose even more of a problem:

(30) Yu save ol disfela, *ol man ol, em, ol, i*kilim disfela wonem ia, meri ia? (Colin K., age 11, 5:2:250) 'Do you know those men (who) killed this, uh, woman?'

(31) *Tupela liklik man em* blong, *ol* blong, wonem, Butibum. (Celia D., age 9, 7:2:098) 'The two little boys were from, were from, uh, Butibum.'

The more usual pronoun to use with duals is *tupela*:

(32) Wanpela taim, *Jack na mama bilong en tupela i*save slip. (Sogana L., age 11, 8:1:203) 'Once upon a time, Jack and his mother were sleeping.'

Among the adults of our 1971 sample, 23 percent of noun-subject sentences follow the subject noun phrase with a pronoun (*em, ol,* or *tupela*) agreeing in number with the subject, and among children, the figure is very similar, 27 percent. The frequency alone, however, should not necessarily lead us to make any particular statements about whether this represents a "second wave" of cliticization. It is clear that the former subject pronoun *i*- long ago lost its emphatic force as it became a clitic—but *em* and *ol* (*tupela* is of very low frequency) still retain it to some extent. Thus their inclusion still serves in topic-changes as in 27 and unemphatic contexts like 28.

Data I have assembled on the children show a continuing decrease in *i*- as sole subject, almost entirely specialized to the existential sentences and overlaps discussed in stage III. Indeed, the decrease in the proportion of such sentences over the whole time span considered is very regular. They represent half of the NP subject sentences at stage I, one third at stage II, one fourth at stage III and one sixth at stage IV.

This leads us to the main difference between adults and children at stage IV. Both groups have less *i*- in noun-subject sentences than do

Hall's stage III subjects in the 1930s, as indicated in Figure 12-1. But the children have even fewer than the adults. This looks like a reversal of the earlier trend—cliticization of *i-*, which as far as our present indications go, seemed to have reached a peak in the 1930s. Smeall (1975) and Woolford (1975) have shown the complex syntactic and phonological conditioning of *i-* deletion in our 1971 data, and Woolford's comparison of these data with materials collected by Wurm in the late 1950s indicates that *i-* was more frequent then than at the 1930 date indicated in Figure 12-1. I will not discuss this conditioning here, but it appears (1) that it is not totally related to current *em*-cliticization, i.e., *i-* is dropping out a little more rapidly than *em* is coming in, and (2) it represents a further complexity in the children's grammar, where *i*, having lost its semantic and then syntactic weight, could undergo morphophonologically conditioned deletion. And it is in phonology in general that children appear most significantly to differ from adult speakers of Tok Pisin at present (e.g., the differences in stress documented in chapter 10 above).

3. CONCLUSION

We have followed the vagaries of the progressive grammaticalization of a particular linguistic practice. This practice, the insertion of the pronoun *he* after a subject noun, appears to have originated as a device marking and emphasizing particular nouns in particular discourse contexts, e.g., topic changes. The progressive grammaticalization has involved loss of the original pragmatic or semantic force, along with greater interaction with other syntactic rules, until such time as the pronoun-clitic loses all force and is subject to the grim reaper, phonological deletion. Overlapping with this is another, later, but similar, wave involving the same kinds of strategic-cum-grammatical processes.

Further work will attempt to clarify the discourse constraints involved in this "second wave," expanding the analysis to all of Hall's texts (only a small sample was treated here), those of Wurm and Laycock (not treated at all here), and our conversational materials from 1971. It is suggested that these may aid retrospectively in the interpretation of the "first wave" in the early texts that are less rich in terms of sequential discourse.

It is clear that change in the pronominal and agreement systems has been very rapid in Tok Pisin. The changes documented in this paper cover a span of only eighty-five years, implying that at virtually any point within this span, there has been a great deal of variability. Such variability, however, does not appear to have obstructed communication, or to have led to difficulties in language learning. The number of Tok Pisin speakers continued to grow throughout the period, and only very recently (and then only partially) as a result of the birth rate. As innovations having particular discourse functions underwent rapid diffusion, generalization, and regularization, they lost such functions and were subsequently supplemented by other innovations. All of which has led, among other things, to greater redundancy in Tok Pisin. Variability has been not a symptom of disorder, but an indication of growth.

13.

Anything *You* Can Do

SUZANNE LABERGE AND GILLIAN SANKOFF

INTRODUCTION

Discourse equivalents—even grammatical equivalents—need have nothing in common but their contemporary struggle: not history, and especially not a common "underlying" form, unless it be one in which the tortuous path to the surface is unnecessarily ad hoc and messy.

In this chapter we will begin with the story of the French *on*. Before the current episode begins, plucky little *on* has shed the disyllabic baggage of its ancestor *homo*, and has made it out of the content-word status of the masses into the elite corps of grammatical elements— this, by adhering strictly to Benveniste's dictum: "'Nihil est in *lingua* quod non prius fuerit in *oratione*'" (1966: 131). From lowly beginnings as an indefinite referent, *on* has succeeded in infiltrating the personal pronouns. Not only does it take over at will from *je, tu, ils,* and the rest, but it has also virtually ousted *nous.*

In the present episode, we shall see how the personal pronouns hit back. *Tu* and *vous* have taken up the challenge, and are now locked in combat with *on* in a bout for indefinite champion, a title *on* thought it had locked up. Will this battle for the hearts and minds of the speakers of French be a fight to the finish, or can the adversaries live in peaceful coexistence? (In the meantime, interested parties are advised that they needn't be overly concerned about keeping their grammars tidy.)

This chapter first appeared in Talmy Givón, ed., *Discourse and Syntax,* New York: Academic Press, 419–440. It is reprinted here with minor editorial changes. The work reported here was made possible in large part by a Killam Grant from the Canada Council. Laberge (1978b) contains a full account of this research, and this paper is grounded in that analysis. We owe much to our coworkers on the Montréal French project, especially Pascale Rousseau, David Sankoff, and Pierrette Thibault. We also thank the many participants at the Discourse and Syntax symposium who made useful suggestions, particularly Talmy Givón.

Studies of Particular Linguistic Variables

1. *On,* INDEFINITE PAR EXCELLENCE

The versatility of the subject clitic *on* ('one') in French is legendary. Derived from Latin *homo* ('man'), its original, and perhaps still in some sense basic referent is an indefinite 'anybody'. It is found, for example, in proverbial expressions such as the following, cited from our corpus of Montréal French:

> (1) Mon père disait tout le temps, "Bien, quand *on* est valet *on* est pas roi." (65: 6)[1] 'My father always used to say, "Well, when one is a jack, one is not a king."'

Over time, *on* has acquired the ability to substitute for any and all of the personal pronouns, and contexts making clear its anaphoric capacity can readily be shown.

1.1. Use of *on* for *je*('I')
(Recalling an automobile accident):

> (2) *b.* J'ai cassé le steering avec mon genou parce que j'étais assis de côté.
>
> *a.* Et puis vous êtes correct?
>
> *b.* Ah, oui, *on* s'en vient petit vieux, mais *on* est correct. (114: 22)
>
> *b.* 'I broke the steering wheel with my knee because I was sitting on the side.
>
> *a.* And you're o.k.?
>
> *b.* Oh yes, the *old man*'s getting on, but *he*'s all right.'

In 2, as in other examples, we have glossed very liberally in trying to find an English expression with the same flavor. In this case we have used "the old man" rather than any English pronoun, to convey the distance the speaker expresses in calling himself a *petit vieux* (coreferential with *on*).

---

1. Examples are taken from our corpus of 120 interviews in Montréal French. The first figure in parentheses indicates the speaker's number, the second indicates the page in the transcription. This example comes from speaker 65, page 6. For further details on the methodology of the project, cf. D. Sankoff et al. (1976).

272

1.2. Use of *on* for *tu* ('you')
(Said to a habitual fellow crossword-puzzler)

> (3) Comme ça *on* fait des mots croisés sans nous attendre? 'So *she*'s doing crossword puzzles without waiting for us?'

In this case, the speaker is using *on* to address his partner. Another possible English gloss would be: 'So we're doing crossword puzzles without waiting for our partner?'

1.3. Use of *on* for *elle* ('she')
(Said about the female interviewer, to a third party who has arrived in mid-interview)

> (4) Je suis en train d'être interrogé. *On* me demande si j'étais un bon petit garçon. (115: 15) 'I'm in the middle of being interviewed. I'm being asked (one is asking me) if I was a good little boy.'

1.4. Use of *on* for *ils* ('they') and *nous* ('we')

The specific referents of *on* substituting for *ils* ('they') and *nous* ('we') may be more difficult to identify, since these pronouns themselves often refer to incompletely defined collectivities. This is particularly the case with *ils* in sentences like 5:

> (5) Moi je me comprends bien dans ma langue, de la manière que je te parle,—mais *ils* disent à la télévision qu'on parle cheval un peu. (24: 25) 'I get along fine in my own language, the way I'm speaking to you, but *they* say on television that we speak *joual* (= lousy French[2]) a bit.'

Here '*they*, the people on television' is about as specific as '*they*, the people in Luther's day' in the following example, in which *on* substitutes for *ils*:

> (6) C'est à l'époque de Luther . . . il y avait des sorciers qu'*on* brûlait. (73:17) 'It was in Luther's day . . . there were witches that *they* burned.'

2. "Lousy French" was the expression used to refer to Quebec French in general by Canadian Prime Minister P.-E. Trudeau in a much publicized interview several years ago.

What these last two examples have in common is that they clearly exclude the speaker and the hearer, even though the third parties they refer to are not well defined. Indeed, one also finds nouns meaning "people" that are semantically rather empty, such as *les gens* and *le monde*[3] used in very similar constructions. *Le monde* often gets plural agreement:

> (7) Il y a des places comme à Outremont, ces affaires-là, on dirait que *le monde* sont plus civilisés ou parce qu'ils sont plus riches. (109: 16) 'There's places like in Outremont, and like that, it seems like *the people* are more civilized, or maybe because they're richer.'

On for *nous* has become the most common substitution. Indeed, it has very nearly replaced *nous* (about 98 percent) in current spoken French in Montréal.

> (8) *On* se ramassait tous dans la salle à diner, puis la télévision, puis *on* écoutait le hockey. (6: 7) 'We all got together in the dining room, with the television, and *we* listened to (watched) hockey.'

As such, *on* co-occurs with *nous* (*autres*), in the paradigm *moi, je; toi, tu; lui, il;* etc.

> (9) Tu sais, ils veulent pas que *nous-autres on* reste dans la même marde qu'eux-autres. (88: 21) You know, they don't want us to stay (that *we* stay) in the same shit as them.

So great is the association of *on* with *nous* that 'we' has become the unmarked, unless-otherwise-indicated reading of *on*. What, then, of the classic, indefinite *on*? We find that this *on* is in fact being replaced by *tu* and *vous,* as will be described in the next section.

2. *Tu~vous* as Indefinite: Contexts of Alternation with *on*

The use of *vous* or *tu* as a substitute for *on* has been noted by numerous authors, including Brunot (1922) and Sandfeld (1928). Benveniste has this to say on the subject:

> La définition de la deuxième personne comme étant la personne à laquelle la première s'adresse convient sans doute à son emploi le plus ordinaire. Mais ordinaire ne veut pas dire unique et con-

---

3. *Le monde*'s semi-clitic status is supported by the fact that it rarely co-occurs with another clitic, e.g., *le monde, il(s)*. Most true nouns rarely occur in subject position *without* a following clitic.

stant. On peut utiliser la deuxième personne hors de l'allocution et la faire entrer dans une variété d' "impersonnel." Par exemple, "vous" fonctionne en français comme anaphorique de "on" (ex. "on ne peut se promener sans que quelqu'un *vous* aborde"). En mainte langue, *tu* (*vous*) sert de substitut à *on*. (Benveniste 1966: 232)

The definition of the second person as the person addressed by the first doubtless corresponds to its most ordinary use. But ordinary does not mean unique and unchanging. One can use the second person outside of the address system to serve as a kind of "impersonal." For example, *vous* 'you' functions in French as anaphoric for *on* 'one' (e.g., "one cannot go walking without someone addressing you"). In a great many languages, *tu* or *vous* serve as substitutes for *on*. (Translation by G.S.)

Our corpus confirms this, and a detailed study of the contexts of use of indefinite *on* shows that *tu* and *vous* can be used in virtually all of them. Perhaps the most central element unifying these various contexts is the theme of *generality*, or of *generalization*. The cases we have studied can be usefully grouped into three broad linguistic classes, each involving specific means of expressing generality. It is important to note that the indefinite referent here is always vague as to the possible inclusion of speaker and hearer: *anybody* "means" just that—possibly you, possibly me, or anyone else in like circumstances. The referent here is in this sense "more indefinite" than the *on* equivalent to *ils, les gens, le monde*, which is clearly [–speaker], [–hearer].

2.1. Lexical and Syntactic Indicators of Generalization

There are a great many lexical items, as well as morphological and syntactic structures that can convey generality. Often these markers co-occur. Many of them work to dissociate reference from specific places and times. Infinitives like *à travailler* and *à lire* in 10 are by definition atemporal, and adverbs like *toujours* 'always' can also contribute to the timelessness of an assertion. Other common adverbial indicators include *de nos jours, à c't heure,* and *aujourd'hui* (all glossed as 'nowadays').

> (10) J'en ai peut-être regagné un peu. . . . A part ça, à travailler puis à lire *on* s'améliore toujours un petit peu. (30: 40) 'I've perhaps made a little progress. . . . Besides, in working and in reading *one* always improves somewhat.'

> (11) Disons quand j'ai mis les pieds dans le vrai monde là, dans le monde où *tu* recontres toutes sortes de gens et puis tout ça

. . . (58: 5) 'Let's say that when I stepped into the real world, into the world where *you* meet all sorts of people and all that . . .'

The generality of the statement in 10 makes it virtually impossible to decode *on* as 'we, the members of some (even vaguely defined) group'. It is clear that the speaker intends *on* to refer to *anyone* who works and reads. In 11, the speaker's evocation of "the world where" sets up a general situation that "anyone" could participate in. His *tu*, suddenly appearing in the middle of a first person account can hardly be heard as 'you, the person I'm talking to'.

One syntactic indicator of generality is a tense change, always from a past tense (usually the *imparfait* or *passé composé*) to the present, as illustrated in 11. Such a tense change frequently accompanies a subject change, again as in 11, from *je* to the indefinite *on, tu,* or *vous,* where a speaker generalizes from his or her own experience, phrasing it as something that would apply to anybody.

There are four further morphological or syntactic structures that serve to identify generalized statements, all of which permit both *on* and *tu* or *vous,* though for brevity's sake only one case of each will be cited.

2.1.1. *Coreferential le, la, les*

(12) *On* choisit *les* amis. (12: 16) '*One* chooses *one*'s friends.'

This would contrast with "On choisit *nos* amis," which would generally be glossed, 'We choose *our* friends'.

2.1.2. *Coreferential Indefinite Noun Phrase*

(13) Quand *une personne* élevait une famille dans ce temps-là, *vous* étiez pas capable d'avoir de luxe. (37: 16) 'When *a person* was bringing up a family in those days, *you* couldn't have any luxuries.'

Though we did not study reflexives per se, the following example (one of many) confirms the identity of "second person" and indefinite forms:

(14) *Quelqu'un* qui veut travailler normalement, c'est plus facile *t*'exprimer dans ta langue que d'essayer de *t*'expliquer dans une autre. (6: 19) '*Anybody* who wants to work properly, it's easier for them (you) to express themself in their language than to try to explain yourself in another.'

2.1.3. *Definitional Structures with c'est*

> (15) L'inconvénient c'est qu'*on* fait des réparations dans un logement, et puis quand *on* part, *on* est obligé de laisser ça là. (16: 16) 'The trouble is that *you* make repairs in a rented place, but when *you* leave, *you* have to leave it all there.'

2.1.4. *Certain Existential Structures, Usually with the Verbs avoir ('have'), voir ('see'), and trouver ('find')*

> (16) Le joual, c'est une déformation, comme *tu* as des patois en France. (112: 34) '*Joual* is a deformation, like the *patois you* get in France.'

This structure is found in contexts where the existential *il y a* would also have been possible.

In addition to these very diverse indicators of generality, there are two specific types of utterances that deserve special mention. These are implicative constructions, and constructions headed by a presentative.

2.2. Implicative Constructions

Implicative constructions are statements of cause and effect. They consist of two sentences, the first of which (the protasis) sets up a supposition and the second (the apodosis) states the implications. Conditionals with *if* are common examples of implicative constructions. The syntactic relation between the two sentences need not be one of embedding, however. Sentences may be coordinate as in 18, or simply juxtaposed.

> (17) Bien si *on* laisse faire les hommes c'est tout' des grosses bêtes. (79: 17) 'Well if *one* lets men do what they want, they're all big brutes.'

> (18) *Vous* allez voir deux Français de France, puis ils parleront pas tous les deux pareil. (6: 22) '*You* take two Frenchmen from France, and they won't both speak the same.'

2.3. Propositions Headed by a Presentative Construction

Presentative clauses constitute a particularly striking way of announcing the generality of the proposition that they introduce. The forms of presentatives are numerous, but they all work to put interlocutors on notice that what is coming next is a generally admitted truth, or a personal opinion that speakers hope are shared, if not universally, at least by their interlocutors.

Indefinite referents in these cases occur not in the presentative clause itself, but rather in the following sentence. Some of the presentative forms found in our corpus are:

il me semble	'it seems to me'
$\left\{\begin{array}{l} \text{il} \\ \text{c'} \end{array}\right\}$ est vrai	'it is true'
faut dire	'it must be said'
disons	'let's say'
je dis	'I say'
je pense	'I think'
je trouve	'I find'
d'après moi	'according to me'
il est certain	'it's certain'

The force of such presentatives in affirming the generality of the succeeding proposition is evident from the examples:

(19) Puis ça, moi j'ai pour mon dire, *on* peut pas se mettre dans la peau d'un autre. (42: 12) 'There's this, I would say, *one* cannot put oneself into the skin of another [another person's shoes].'

(20) D'après moi, c'est pas avec des guerres que *tu* réussis à faire un pays, *tu* t'assis puis *tu* discutes. (6: 17) 'As far as I'm concerned, *you* don't build a country with wars, *you* sit down and *you* discuss.'

2.4. Lexical and Syntactic Constraints on Choice among Variants

We have shown that the three major classes of 2.1–2.3 all permit both *one* and *you* as indefinite referents. Though our theoretical framework led us to seek out distributional parallels and relations of partial equivalence, it did not force us to postulate total equivalence. Specifically, we were quite prepared to consider the possibility that some contexts might favor a particular form, or even to find some contexts where one or other form was obligatory. There are only a couple of the latter. For *on*, there are a few frozen forms: structures with

$$\text{QU} + \text{on} + \left\{\begin{array}{l} \text{dire} \\ \text{appeler} \end{array}\right\} \text{ such as } \textit{comme on dit, qu'on appelle,} \text{ with}$$

glosses like 'as it's called', i.e., by anybody who might have occasion to call it. Here is a typical example from a word-search:

(21) On allait manger chez Gerassimo, puis je voyais toujours euh . . . *comment est-ce qu'on appelle* donc, euh, Ti-Coq là. (57:

15) 'We used to eat at Gerassimo's, and I always used to see uh, *what's his name,* uh, Ti-Coq.'

Toward the end of our data analysis, we found that *on* is not quite categorical in these contexts. There were 8 cases (5 speakers) of *tu* or *vous* in such expressions, representing only 1.3 percent of the total. This may be a beginning of the invasion of *on*'s last stronghold. Here is an example, again from a word-search:

> (22) D'ailleurs les professeurs font une espèce de petite grève, comment est-ce que *tu* appelles ça, d'écoeurement, quelque chose du genre, enfin. (53: 8) 'In fact the teachers are on a kind of little strike, what'cha macallit, a slowdown, something like that, anyway.'

(She's looking for the term *grève du zèle,* which is a work-to-rule campaign.) In addition to these expressions involving *dire* and *appeler,* there are some sequential constraints that lead to the obligatory use of *on,* as indeed there are also for *tu* and *vous.* These, however, will be explained in section 6. The only case of categorical *tu–vous* not involving sequential matters involves co-occurrence with a past tense verb. In such utterances, *on* would always be interpreted as meaning 'we'; to express the indefinite referent, *tu* or *vous* must be used. Thus, speaking of the Depression to someone who wasn't born then,

> (23) *Vous* aviez pas une cenne pour vous acheter un habillement à toutes ces années-là. La femme non plus. (37: 24) '*You* didn't have a cent to buy clothing for all those years. The wife neither.'

The same constraint works spatially as well as temporally. In co-occurrence with *ici* ('here'), *on* would be decoded as 'we' in the following example. Instead, *vous* is used:

> (24) *a.* Est-ce que vous pensez que la cuisine qui était faite avec le poêle à bois, c'était bien meilleur?
>
> *b.* Oui c'est pas la même chose, ça restait chaud plus longtemps aussi. C'est pas pareil. Ici *vous* chauffez là, puis le manger est froid tout de suite. (116: 17)
>
> *a.* 'Do you think that food was much better, cooked on a wood stove?
>
> *b.* Yes it's not the same, it used to stay warm longer too. Here *you* heat, and the food gets cold right away.'

Leaving these categorical contexts, which were not tabulated in the quantitative study, let us return briefly to the three major contexts of section 2, keeping in mind decoding problems that might occur, given that all three forms (*on, tu,* and *vous*) have readings other than indefinite. Specifically, as we saw in the discussion of 23 and 24, *on* may run into trouble by being decoded as 'we', and *tu* and *vous* by being decoded as 'you, the hearer(s)'. The hypothetical nature of implicatives, however, seems to work to diminish the possibility of ambiguity with the second person referent when *tu* (or *vous*) is used. This would lead us to suspect that implicatives are fertile ground for the spread of *tu* and *vous*. With presentatives, on the other hand, the metalinguistic framing that these utterances accomplish often signals a distance the speaker is adopting with respect to his or her own views, thus dissociating the speaker from the referent of the subject of the sentence. The possibility of ambiguity between indefinite *on* and first person plural *on* is thereby diminished, leading us to expect the *on* variant to be numerous in this class.

Before looking at whether, and how, such considerations of speaker strategy in facilitating disambiguation may intervene to make particular syntactic categories more or less amenable to the use of particular forms, there are a few other considerations to introduce. First, what are people doing with these indefinite referents, and how might this influence the choice of form? Second, do all speakers make use of all the forms? If there are interindividual differences among speakers, what are the theoretical consequences of this for an understanding of language use and language structure? Third, once having taken into account everything we know about the properties of the indefinite *on, tu,* and *vous,* and their distribution among speakers, can we go any farther by looking at syntagmatic considerations and examining them in sequence?

3. DISCURSIVE EFFECTS: WHAT ARE INDEFINITE REFERENTS USED FOR?

In addition to examining the forms of utterances containing indefinite referents, we have also looked at their place and function within the discourse. We have arrived at two broad discursive or pragmatic categories, which we label "situational insertion" and "the formulation of morals or truisms."

3.1. Situational Insertion

The utterances we are concerned with are generalizations involving an indefinite person, and they all have the effect of locating this person in a potentially repeatable activity or context. Anyone's experience may constitute the basis for generalization, though most often it is the speaker's.

(25) J'aime mieux boire une bonne brosse, c'est mieux que fumer de la drogue, je trouve. Le lendemain matin *tu* as un gros mal de tête mais ça fait rien, *tu* es tout' là, tandis qu'avec la drogue *tu* sais pas si *tu* vas être là le lendemain. *Tu* peux te prendre pour Batman ou Superman puis *tu* te pitches dans les poubelles. (62: 11) 'I prefer to drink myself stoned, it's better than smoking dope, I feel. The next morning *you* have a bad headache but that's no big deal, *you* are all in one piece, whereas with drugs *you* don't know if *you* will be there the next day. *You* might decide you're Batman or Superman and take off into a garbage can.'

(26) Ben *on* a qu'à prendre l'autobus puis *on* se rend compte comment les jeunes parlent; disons ça c'est le mauvais langage. (3: 30) 'Well, *one* only has to take the bus and one realizes how young people talk. Let's say it's poor language.'

At issue in 25 is the speaker's own experience with alcohol and drugs. By using *tu,* he assimilates himself to a much wider class of people, downgrading his own experience to incidental status in the discourse, phrasing it as something that could or would be anybody's.

Example 26 is an example of a hypothetical activity open to anyone, that of "taking the bus." In this case as in many others, it is fairly clear that the "indefinite agent" serves as a rather transparent guise for the speaker's own experience and opinions. There is clearly more going on here than the simple avoidance of "I" due to the politeness or "refinement" that the classic French grammarians have attributed to the seventeenth-century nobility. Speaking of the *on* "of modesty," Brunot says:

"Le moi est haïssable." Pour éviter de se mettre en avant, au nominal personnel, les raffinés substituaient souvent l'indéterminé *on,* qui, étant plus vague, ne choque pas. (1922: 276)

"The *me* is hateful." To avoid putting themselves forward, in the personal nominal, refined persons often substituted the indeterminate *on* which, being vaguer, is less shocking. (Translated by G.S.)

In saying 'you have only to take the bus to hear the bad language of the young people' the speaker is not, however, being particularly "modest." Rather, she is claiming more weight for her assertion, phrasing it as verifiable by anybody. The discursive effect of inserting an un-specified agent into a hypothetical situation seems to function to elevate her statement to the plane of conventional wisdom—thereby, perhaps, rendering it more difficult to challenge. The special status of assertions containing indefinite referents is even more evident in the class of utterances to be discussed in the next section, where "conventional wisdom" is explicitly invoked.

3.2. The Formulation of Truisms and Morals

Cases we have analyzed as the formulation of a truism or moral seem to involve a speaker in evaluating a situation. The form of this evaluation is such as to break or at least greatly attenuate the tie with the speaker's own experience that we saw in the previous section.

> (27) Ça sert à rien de savoir compter de nos jours; ou *tu* es bien riche puis *tu* as un comptable qui compte pour toi, ou *tu* es très pauvre puis *tu* as pas d'argent à compter. (6: 24) 'It's no use knowing how to count these days. Either *you*'re really rich and *you* have an accountant do your counting, or else *you* are very poor and *you* have no money to count.'

> (28) J'ai horreur d'entendre crier, puis pourtant faut que je crie avec les petites. Ca me déplaît beaucoup. Mais je me dis, des enfants c'est des enfants, *on* peut pas les faire penser comme des adultes, *on* peut pas. (9: 13) 'I can't stand to hear yelling, but just the same, with the little ones, I have to yell. I really find it unpleasant. But I say to myself, children are children, *one* can't make them think like adults—*one* just can't.'

As was the case with the general class of "situational insertion," morals are not characterized by particular lexical or syntactic markers. They can be formulated using any of the three construction types of section 2. Illustrated here are an implicative in 27 and a presentative heading (*je me dis*—'I say to myself') in 28. A moral is understood as such essentially because of its particular relation to the discourse as a whole. One thing that distinguishes morals and truisms from the category we have called "situational insertion" is that morals constitute a kind of reflection based on conventional wisdom, whereas "situational insertion" seems to be an attempt to elevate particular experiences and ideas to that status. Morals of course inherently involve the evocation of a situation, but they also generally possess a strong judgmental or evaluative connotation. This is particularly clear when the utterance is a saying or proverb overtly borrowed from the oral tradition of the community, as in the first example cited in this paper. It is no accident that a moral often appears at the beginning or at the end of a narrative sequence or a description. Labov's *codas* (1972: 365), which he analyzes as functioning to avert the "so what" reaction, often take the form typical of morals and truisms, showing similar timelessness and indeterminacy.

3.3.

Morals, then, are like situational insertion, only more so. There is a great difference between the discursive effect of a sentence like "When I get drunk I wake up with a headache" and that of "When one gets drunk one wakes up with a headache." The first is a natural for the "so what" reaction, whereas the second seems to constitute its own *raison d'être*. Moreover, the first can call forth a reaction of disapproval from one's interlocutor, but he or she can do little more than disagree with the second. Morals or truisms are even further removed from challengeability insofar as they function to evalute or demonstrate the point of something else. "Children are children, one can't make them think like adults" is in itself serving to justify the speaker's statement that she "has to" yell at her children. Though it would be possible for an argumentative interlocutor to respond that indeed one ought to be able to reason with children, the evaluative role of the proverbial utterance combines with the nonsituated quality of its reference to give it a greater measure of protection from such a riposte.

As to the use of *on* versus *tu* and *vous* in the two pragmatic categories described here, it seems likely that morals might favor the retention of *on*, the older and more "formal" variant. Morals are at a greater remove from the running discourse, more metalinguistic in functioning as considered, "official" pronouncements.

4. SYNTACTIC AND PRAGMATIC TYPES AS CONSTRAINTS

Exempting the cases where one or other form is mandatory, we analyzed a total of 4,367 cases of use of indefinite subject clitics. In Table 13-1, we present a breakdown of these cases according to the three utterance types and two pragmatic effects discussed in sections 2 and 3.

As was to be expected, the bulk of our examples were found in the more general "situational insertion" category (3,593 cases as opposed to 774 "morals"). Looking first at which utterance types are used to convey each of the two discursive effects (percentages given at the right of each of the two major columns), we see that the two special syntactic constructions are used a higher proportion of the time in the more marked discursive category, that of the formulation of morals. The rate of use of implicatives rises from 38 percent in "situational

Linguistic factors	Pragmatic factors						Total	
	Situational insertion			Formulation of morals				
	on	*tu-vous*	total	*on*	*tu-vous*	total	*on*	*tu-vous*
Generalizations	899	951	1,850 (52%)	176	78	254 (33%)	1,075	1,029
Implicatives	505	878	1,383 (38%)	220	140	360 (46%)	725	1,018
Presentative heads	233	127	360 (10%)	109	51	160 (21%)	342	178
Total	1,637	1,956	3,593	505	269	774	2,142	2,225

TABLE 13-1. Occurrence of indefinite referents according to linguistic and pragmatic context.

insertion" to 46 percent in morals, and the rate of use of presentative headed constructions more than doubles, from 10 percent to 21 percent.

Scanning the marginal totals also gives us a good first impression of the effect of the linguistic and pragmatic categories on the use of *on* versus *tu* and *vous*.[4] Though the total number of each is almost identical (2,142 versus 2,225), they are not used equally frequently in all contexts. In particular, *on* is very much preferred in presentative-headed constructions (342 cases versus 178 of *tu* and *vous*), and dispreferred in implicatives. As for the pragmatic categories, the heavy use of *on* for formulating morals (505 cases versus 269 for *tu* and *vous*) is very striking.

In order to better gauge the interaction of the environments, however, we undertook a variable rule analysis according to the methods set forth in Rousseau and D. Sankoff (1978b). For the factors described so far, this analysis gave us probability weights that accord with the hypotheses formulated in the discussion of the constraints and confirmed the tendencies observed in the marginal totals. Probability weights are as follows (higher numbers indicate that *on* is favored; lower numbers favor *tu* and *vous*).

$p$syntax:	Implicative	0.32
	Presentative	0.65
	Others	0.54
$p$pragmatic:	Situational insertion	0.37
	Moral	0.63

Further details of the statistical analysis are given in Laberge 1977a and 1977b.

5. SPEAKERS' REPERTOIRES

Differences among speakers have been both a blessing and a curse in variation studies. On the one hand, the fact that in no known speech community are linguistic resources distributed equally has been a key observation in the understanding of the social underpinnings of linguistic change. On the other hand, there is always the "multiplicity of dialects" bugaboo, haunting sociolinguists with images of perfect synchronic "solutions" which will somehow do away with all the "remaining variation" after an analysis such as that reported in section 4 has been carried out.

Of course, not every speaker operates according to the probabilities obtained from the group data of 120 people. Indeed, we know

---

4. For purposes of the statistical analysis, we have grouped *tu* and *vous* together in opposition to *on*. Further discussion of this is provided in section 5.

that the use of *tu* or *vous* to express an indefinite referent is the more recent as well as the less "proper" form. We would therefore be surprised to find it as popular with older and more careful speakers as it is with younger and less careful ones. We also know who the more careful speakers are likely to be: those for whom speaking "well" pays off. A detailed discussion of this issue, as well as an analysis of the degree of integration of each of the 120 speakers into the *marché linguistique* (Bourdieu and Boltanski 1975) is available in Laberge 1977b. For present purposes, we note simply that speaking "well" is, in contemporary Québec society, likely to be characteristic of women and of those men whose socioeconomic life history has put a premium on proper, careful, normative speech.

Given all these considerations, we looked at each speaker separately, attempting to find out what it is about them that might help to account for their usage preferences. The variable rule assigned each speaker a probability weight from 0 to 1.0 according to his/her preference for *tu~vous* or *on* respectively.

Looking first at the 60 male speakers, we found that 7 used *tu~vous* categorically, 7 used *on* categorically, and the remaining 46 showed a range of probabilities between these two extremes. There was a fairly strong age correlation with *on* use, older speakers quite clearly preferring the conservative *on* to *tu* or *vous*. Sixty-six percent of male speakers over forty preferred *on* to *tu~vous*, whereas only 28 percent of those forty and younger preferred *on*. These results are displayed in Table 4-5, p. 92.

Dividing the women into the same age groups, the older women seemed to pattern with their male counterparts, 69 percent of them preferring *on* to *tu* and *vous*. The younger women, however, showed a surprising difference: even more of them (76 percent) favored *on*.

On then, is the markedly female variant. Not a single woman used *tu~vous* categorically, though 11 used *on* categorically (7 of whom were in the younger age group). Apart from the striking sex difference, and the major age difference among men, no other social attributes of speakers seemed to be relevant. (At least not social class, as measured by the *marché linguistique* index. Education, as measured by years in school, was barely significant.)

These results, coupled with those of section 4, give the following picture. Seven speakers use *tu~vous* categorically; 18 use *on* categorically; and 94 alternate. (One further speaker didn't use any indefinite pronouns). These 94 are more likely to use *on* if they are women, and particularly if they are less than forty years of age. They are also more likely to use *on* in formulating morals or truisms, as well as in constructions headed by presentatives. We might now ask whether these likeli-

286

hoods apply in more or less the same way to all 94 of the variable speakers or whether there are subgroups of these people who show very different patterns, that is, whether the weights obtained for the linguistic and pragmatic categories derive from improperly lumping speakers.

A statistical procedure developed by Rousseau (see Rousseau and D. Sankoff 1978) made it possible to test the hypothesis that speakers fell into two or more distinct groups. Rousseau found two groups whose members were significantly dissimilar. The main difference between them was that for the first group of 57 speakers, the probability weights of the linguistic factors were ordered in the same way as was reported in section 4, except that their effects were more distinct, whereas for the remaining 37 speakers, these factors seemed to level out. That is, there was one group whose members were supersensitive to the linguistic constraints, and a second whose members were insensitive to them. The two groups showed almost identical behavior with respect to the pragmatic constraints.

We have not yet investigated what might be the social basis underlying these differences among speakers, particularly as concerns the last binary grouping. What does seem clear from the sex differences is that a simple "contagion" theory of dialect differences is inadequate. Differences between men's and women's speech in this case can hardly be due to any kind of "communicative segregation." The *tu~vous* variant, though it is clearly the innovative form, has certainly been around enough for everybody to catch it, if that were all that was involved.

Though in the past, many studies of grammatical variation have suffered from small samples and insufficient data, we do not think this is a problem here. With 4,300 tokens, each of which has been carefully studied as to its syntactic and discursive role, we feel we have an accurate idea of how each speaker uses these resources. The usage preference so clearly demonstrated by men for *tu~vous* and by women for *on* represents one instance of linguistic resources being marshalled to symbolize a social distinction—the fact that the difference is largely a question of degree bears witness to the subtlety that such processes can resort to, without making much of a ripple in communicative efficacy.

One issue we have not yet dealt with may have some bearing on this point, and that is speaker preference between indefinite *tu* and *vous*. So far, we have considered the two as equivalent, and as distinct from *on*. It is, of course, the case that the distinction between *tu* and *vous* as terms of address is interactionally significant in French. And, interestingly enough, this is another area where our sample showed a great sex difference. Of the 60 women, 54 addressed the interviewer as *vous*; of the 60 men, only 25 did. (This includes 9 people who alternate between *tu* and *vous*.) Moreover, the unanswered question of the relationship between the form of address used to one's interlocutor and the form of the indefinite used is a complicated one. Certainly there is no one-to-one relationship. Fifteen people who restricted themselves to *vous* in addressing the interviewer *never* used *vous* as an indefinite; a further 19 such speakers used both *tu* and *vous* as indefinites. One interesting fact, however, was that none of the 28 speakers who used only *tu* in addressing the interviewer used only *vous* as an indefinite (a few of them used both).

Indulging in a little speculation, we might guess that since indefinite *tu* and *vous* have the corresponding pronouns of address as their source, there may still be a little contamination in the choice of form as between *tu* and *vous*. We would guess that for a number of reasons (including the distributions cited in the preceding paragraph) *tu* is currently the less marked of the two.

We still insist, however, that all three forms function quite equivalently in the most semantically empty contexts, where even *on* is so impersonal as to be serving more as a dummy element than anything else. Consider the following idiomatic expressions equivalent to "everything you might imagine" or "what you will," functioning as a kind of etcetera at the end of a list.

(29) Et puis c'était la grande fête, les cadeaux, l'excitation des cadeaux, puis les chants, puis les déclamations, puis *tout ce que vous voudrez*. (115: 435). 'And it was always a big party, with presents, the excitement of the presents, and signing, and recitations, and *everything you might want.*'

(30) Le gars il peut avoir un char, une maison puis le yacht puis *tout ce que tu voudras,* mais il a le droit, hostie. (95: 6) 'The guy might have a car, a house and a yacht and *everything you might want,* but he has the right (to have them), for chrissake.'

(31) Et bien il y avait . . . le chanoine X là qui était longtemps doyen de la Faculté des Lettres et qui était en plus vice-recteur et puis en plus professeur et puis en plus doyen et puis en plus, je ne sais pas, administrateur et *tout ce qu'on veut*. Bon, il était le seul. (81: 12) 'And so there was . . . Canon X there who for a long time was Dean of the Arts Faculty and who was also Vice Rector and who was also a professor and also dean and also, I don't know, administrator and *everything one might want.* Well, he was the only one.'

288

In a further such idiomatic expression, evidence of the emptiness of the forms is given by the fact that they are in alternation with a completely clitic-less version. Three of the several possibilities are illustrated here, with *on* appearing in 32, *tu* in 33, and no clitic at all in 34:

(32) *Qu'on le veuille ou non,* la fille qui sort avec son jeune homme, en tout cas, elle sort, elle, sur son côté. (1: 10) '*Like it or not,* the girl that goes out with a young man, in any case, she goes out on her own.'

(33) Tu as la chaîne d'état puis le canal 10, ben la plupart du monde c'est le canal 10, tsé, *que tu le veuilles ou pas,* tsé, le monde ils sont pas intéressés à voir un programme instructif. (88: 22) 'You have the state channel as well as Channel 10, well most people are going to watch Channel 10, y'know, *like it or not,* y'know, people are not interested in seeing an educational program.'

(34) Je suis pas bilingue, je me débrouille disons. Mais mes soeurs, eux-autres, deux langues; d'ailleurs j'ai mes deux frè-res qui ont marié des pures anglais, fait que, *veux veux pas,* hein, faut, faut-. (29: 19) 'I'm not bilingual, let's say I sort of get along. But my sisters, two languages!—in fact I have my two brothers who married pure English girls, so, *like it or not,* eh? you have to, have to—.'

That *tu* and *vous* have wormed their way into these very empty, parenthetical slots, even for many vigilant but unsuspecting speakers, is, we feel, strong evidence of their growing equivalence with impersonal *on,* and their interchangeability with other impersonal constructions.

6. SEQUENTIAL CONSIDERATIONS

Our approach to the study of *on, tu,* and *vous* has involved syntagmatic considerations to a greater degree than has been usual in variation studies. Indeed the very definition of categories like the formulation of a moral has involved the relation of the utterance to other pieces of discourse. Here we examine specifically how the occurrence of a particular clitic may be constrained by the sequence immediately to its left.

6.1. Sequential Constraints Leading to Categorical *on*
Indefinite *tu* or *vous* cannot be used in contexts where there is a definite 'you' immediately to the left, for fear of confusion with the latter.

(35) *Vous* [+def.] me demandez de vous raconter une partie de ma vie là, mais il y a des choses, qu'*on* [−def.] peut pas expliquer pourtant. (9: 13) '*You* (the interviewer) ask me to tell you a part of my life, but there are things that *one* just can't explain.'

* . . . que *vous* [−def.] pouvez pas expliquer.

* ? . . . que *tu* [−def.] peux pas expliquer.

The problem of confounding an indefinite with a definite *you* sometimes also comes up in cases where the ungrammaticality is one of social relations rather than referential confusion. Thus:

(36) a. Quel âge avez-vous?

b. Je dis pas d'âge moi. Je parle pas des âges; *on* parle pas de ça aux femmes, des âges. (5: 25)

a. 'How old are you?

b. I don't say any age. I don't talk about ages. *One* doesn't talk about that to women, about ages.'

This is clearly both a refusal to reply to the question and a counterattack; the asker is reproached for asking. But saying "you don't talk" would have been, again, too clearly "you, the asker."

6.2. Obligatory *tu* and *vous* in Sequence
Recall that the "ambiguity" problem for *on* is that of being confused with 'we'. Thus when there is a definite subject clitic, especially 'I' or 'we' in the immediate left hand context, *on* is useless as a representation of 'anyone', because it would be identified with 'we' (unless of course there are additional markers such as the tense change discussed in connection with 11). In the following example, the speaker, a secretary, is talking about her boss's family:

(37) La famille, *je* les reconnais presque tous parce qu'ils viennent au bureau. *Tu* les reconnais, tsé, *tu* les vois arriver puis *tu* dis ça, ça c'est de la famille. (4: 36) 'The family—I recognize almost all of them because they come in to the office. *You* recognize them, y'know, *you* see them coming and *you* say, that, that's gotta be family.'

If she had said *on*, this would have immediately been decoded as 'we the office employees' and the generalizing function would have been lost. What she wants to convey is that *anybody* would recognize these people as family, and the use of *on* wouldn't have permitted her to do this.

6.3. Sequential Constraints with Noncategorical Consequences

The statistical analysis described in section 4 proceeded first by excluding all cases of categoriality (categorical speakers and all categorical environments, including sequential ones), and then by treating each instance of an indefinite as an independent binomial trial. But the fact that for this particular study we had so much data, including a fairly large number of contiguous tokens, enabled us to explore the noncategorical effects of contiguity.

Specifically, we attempted to characterize the effect of syntagmatic proximity of three types between neighboring tokens. We focused in each case on the relation a second token bears to a first. The three types are embedding-constrained tokens, sequence-constrained tokens, and unconstrained successive tokens.[5] In the case of embedding-constrained tokens, a single referent is the subject of two sentences, one of which is embedded in the other, as in 38:

> (38) Ah! bien c'est entendu qu'*on* est mieux, mieux en campagne quand *on* est jeune. (116: 26) 'Well for sure you're (*one* is) better off in the country when you're young.'

Implicative structures obviously offer considerable scope for such analysis.

In sequence-constrained tokens, a single referent is the subject in two or more sentences which are conjoined or simply juxtaposed:

> (39) L'influence de la finance, c'est ça, *vous* payez tout en l'utilisant, *vous* en êtes pas privé. (41: 18) 'The point about borrowing money is that *you* pay for it while *you*'re using it, so *you* don't have to go without.'

The weakest of the three relationships is that between unconstrained successive tokens. Here, two successive occurrences of a same variable are too distant to qualify for either of the above categories.

Though we noted that a switch of variants *can* occur even in the most constrained environment, that of embedding-constrained tokens, our hypothesis was that the stronger the syntagmatic relationship between the two tokens, the less likelihood there would be for a switch of

---

5. There is a further type involving hesitation phenomena that had to be discarded due to the heterogeneity of hesitation types.

Speaker number	5	6	13	44	115
Proportion of *on*	.45	.24	.24	.30	.39
tu-vous → *on* switch rate for unconstrained pairs	.50	.33	.17	.33	.50
tu-vous → *on* switch rate for sequence-constrained pairs	.12	.12	.06	.19	.20
Proportion of *tu-vous*	.55	.76	.76	.70	.61
on → *tu-vous* switch rate for unconstrained pairs	.25	.60	.63	.67	.73
on → *tu-vous* switch rate for sequence-constrained pairs	.37	.33	.24	.57	.05

TABLE 13-2. Comparison of variant proportions with switch rates for two types of neighboring variable pairs. In almost all cases, variant proportion approximates switch rate for unconstrained pairs, while sequence-constrained switch rates are much lower. (Reproduced from D. Sankoff and Laberge 1978.)

variant to occur when the second token was uttered. This hypothesis was statistically validated in D. Sankoff and Laberge (1978). Table 13-2 presents data from five speakers who demonstrated at least a modicum of switching behavior in their sequence data, and shows that the sequencing context is much more restrictive than simple proximity between variables.[6] Indeed, as D. Sankoff and Laberge point out, "switching rates for unconstrained pairs are not clearly different from the overall proportion of the variants" (1978: 126). This would seem to indicate a form of text-cohesion operating between adjacent sentences that are syntactically related.

7. CONCLUSIONS

We began this chapter by considering a syntactically and semantically well-defined and fairly circumscribed problem: subject clitics used for an indefinite human referent. In trying to understand the distributional facts about the three forms currently employed, we studied a great range of construction types and where they occur. This led us to seek a broader understanding of the place of such constructions in discourse, and forced us to realize that there were a plethora of other construc-

6. Embedding-constrained tokens could not be tabulated because they were not sufficiently numerous in the data.

tions serving somewhat similar functions, including passives, as well as other, progressively more nouny indefinites (*quelqu'un, un gars,* etc.), and expressions with no clitic at all like *veux, veux pas.*

The fact that *tu* and *vous* can be used even in constructions where the indefinite is so "bleached" that it serves only as a dummy (analogous to 'what*cha* [*you*] macallit') is clear evidence of their migration across morphological categories, from the definite to the indefinite system. This supports our view that forms with disparate grammatical origins can come to be discourse equivalents. Further, we believe that such discourse equivalents sooner or later come to have an official place in the grammar as linguistic equivalents. In other words, it is through discursive practice (as Benveniste noted in our citation at the beginning) that grammar changes.

14.

The Productive Use of *ne* in Spoken Montréal French

GILLIAN SANKOFF AND DIANE VINCENT

The French language, as spoken in many parts of the world, seems to be losing the negative morpheme *ne*. This disappearance of *ne* has not gone unnoticed among scholars. According to Gaatone, "The frequent—and increasing—omission of *ne* is one of the characteristics of the spoken language" (1971: 67). Pohl, in a series of articles on *ne*-deletion in contemporary spoken French (1968, 1970, 1975) has confirmed this disappearance, citing *ne* deletion rates for several areas of France and Belgium. Ashby has provided detailed studies of *ne* deletion in Paris (1976) and Tours (ms., 1977).

Historical grammars testify to the remarkable time depth of the phenomenon. According to Gougenheim (1951), *ne* has been subject to deletion since the sixteenth century: "Some writers . . . delete *ne*, as does the modern spoken language when the verb is followed by a grammatical function word like *point* 'not at all' or *jamais* 'never'" (p. 217). Brunot and Bruneau (1949) cite Molière in support of their assertion that "as of the 17th century, *pas* 'not', *point* 'not at all', etc., suffice for negation" and that "one often finds the absence of the negative *ne* in interrogatives; it was considered elegant" (p. 517, accompanied by an example from Pascal).

Nyrop deals more extensively with this phenomenon, explaining the change as follows: "The negative complements are . . . originally positive terms; through being used in negative expressions, little by little they acquire a negative value, and this curious contagion results in

This study was partially supported by a Killam research grant from the Canada Council (S74-1483). I wish to thank Diane Vincent, my coauthor, for her painstaking work on the analysis, as well as for her permission to publish an English version here; to thank also the other members of our research group who helped us in the preparation of the article, and Jacques Pohl, whose comments were extremely useful. The actual writing was done at the Center for Advanced Studies in the Behavioral Sciences while I was a Fellow there in 1975. I have prepared the English version (including the translation of all citations from the French) specifically for this volume.

the negative *ne* becoming superfluous, and being omitted" (1930: 37). This "superfluity" of contemporary *ne* is stressed by Gaatone, who states that "*ne*, in modern French, is a redundant marker of negation" (1971: 99). According to Nyrop, the change involved has progressed very slowly:

> The deletion of *ne* has gained ground bit by bit. Originally, it was restricted to interrogatives; but, during the Renaissance period, it was also extended to conditionals. Over time, *ne* was omitted from other subordinates and also in the main clause: thus *il ne marche pas* made way for *il marche pas.*[1] (1930: 38)

Pohl (personal communication) suggests that "the evolution of *ne* deletion probably did not follow the same route" in the spoken and in the written language. The "elegant" *ne*-less turns of phrase of seventeenth- and eighteenth-century written French would, Pohl suggests, scarcely be possible in modern written French, and would have an "archaic or pretentious connotation." In contemporary written French, *ne* is the ninth most frequent word (Juilland et al. 1970: 387), whereas in spoken French, scholars are agreed that the omission of *ne* continues to "gain ground." Pohl proposes that "it was between 1820 and 1850 that the spoken language began to diverge from the written, by a quite rapid acceleration of omissions" (1975: 22). Pohl's student Roelandt (1975) has, however, documented a fairly high frequency of *ne* deletion in ordinary (*populaire*) spoken French as of 1730.

Pohl's comparison of different dialects of French had already suggested that in Québec French, *ne* deletion was very far advanced. Daoust-Blais (1975) confirmed this, observing that in Québec, *ne* has almost completely disappeared. Its redundancy (negation is always indicated by some other marker) and its extremely low frequency lead one to ask why it is ever used at all. The present quantitative analysis attempts, then, to account for why, in the final stages of a grammatical change, *ne* lingers on. We attempt to show that *ne* can still be used productively (i.e., other than in frozen forms) and to explain what it is about the contexts of its production that leads to its retention.

THE DATA

This analysis is based on 60 of the 120 interviews of the Sankoff-Cedergren corpus of spoken French in Montréal (Sankoff and Sankoff

---

1. The example *il ne marche pas* is chosen precisely because the original use of *pas* in negation was derived from its meaning of a 'step', thus 'he doesn't walk a step'. Over time, *pas* as a marker of negation completely lost its meaning of 'step' (though when preceded by an article, it can still mean 'step' or 'pace').

1973). The general theme of these interviews was "life and customs in Montréal," and most of them were between an hour and an hour and a half in length. All of the examples cited here are numbered according to our transcription: 57.798 means that the example was taken from interview number 57, line 798 of the transcription.

The very low frequency of *ne* made it rather pointless to listen to all of the negative sentences, in the hope of occasionally finding an instance of *ne*. Instead, we located the cases of *ne* (including, of course, *n'*) in the transcriptions, then checked them all by listening to the relevant sections of the tapes. The habits of written French died hard with our transcribers: more than 80 percent of the instances of *ne* we had listed turned out to be figments of the transcribers' imaginations. We controlled for the opposite problem (i.e., the occurrence of *ne* not being transcribed) by listening to a subsample of our tapes, and concluded that error in this direction is negligible. We are therefore fairly certain that the extremely low frequency of *ne* we documented is not the result of transcription error.

Frozen Forms

Ne is most frequently found as an invariant element in certain frozen forms that do not represent productive syntactic rules in the current spoken language. Expressions like *n'importe quoi* ('no matter what', 'whatever'), *n'empêche que* ('even though', 'nevertheless'), and *n'est-ce pas* (tag, 'it is not', 'isn't it the case') do not represent the productive use of *ne*. For the same reasons, we did not include in our study the two cases of "uniceptive" *ne* (Pohl 1968: 1343) that we observed: *si je ne m'abuse* ('if I am not mistaken') and *ne serait-ce que* ('were it not that'), which appear once each in our material. Again, they do not result from the productive use of *ne*.

Occurrences of [n] Due to Phonological Processes

In tabulating the instances of *ne* use, we discovered a phonologically ambiguous environment: occurrences of [n] preceded by the subject clitic *on* (literally 'one' but usually 'we')[2] and followed by a vowel. In such cases, it was impossible to discern whether the audible [n] indicates the presence of *ne* or whether it is due to the liaison of *on* with the following vowel:

$$
\left.\begin{array}{c}
\textit{on n'a pas} \\
\text{vs.} \\
\textit{on a pas}
\end{array}\right\} \quad \text{both 'we haven't', both } [\tilde{\mathfrak{z}}\text{napɑ}]
$$

2. Cf. Laberge (1977).

(Note that the positive *on a* [ɔ̃na] also features the same liaison.)

Further, we found that the object clitic *en* ('some', 'any') preceding the verb, is itself often preceded by a [n] which is in no way a negative marker. There were many positive sentences like 1 and 2 in which the *en* was preceded by [n].

> (1) Elles s'aperçoivent que ça n'en prend de l'argent pour vivre. (3.727) 'They learn that it takes money to live.'

> (2) C'est pour n'en revenir au procès de Rose. (2.560) 'So to get back to the Rose trial.'

In the sixty interviews we examined, we found five cases of *en* in negative sentences, associated with *pas* ('not') or *plus* ('no more'), where the *en* was preceded by [n].

> (3) Mon Dieu, je m'embarque dans une conversation moi là, à n'en plus finir. (10.713) 'My God, I get myself into a conversation that never ends.'

> (4) C'était à la mélasse là. Il y en a qui mettent du raisin, d'autres qui n'en mettent pas. (10.836) 'It was made with molasses. Some people put raisins in; other people didn't put any in.'

> (5) Le monde à cette heure, ils n'en font pas de cas de leurs enfants. (18.566) 'People these days, they don't care enough about their kids.'

> (6) Ah non, je trouve qu'ils n'en profitent pas assez. (20.390) 'Oh no, I think they don't get enough out of it.'

> (7) Ceux qui veulent en profiter, comme de raison. Ceux qui n'en profitent pas, bien tant pis. (44.910) 'Those who want to get something out of it, that's o.k. Those who don't get anything out of it, well that's just too bad.'

In these cases, it was impossible to say whether the [n] resulted from the phonological processes observed in 1 and 2 or from the negative morpheme *ne*. We asked a number of native Montrealers about the acceptability of *positive* versions of 3–7, listed here as 8–11, and discovered that they were unanimously acceptable:

> (8) Il faut n'en finir avec ces histoires-là. 'We have to finish with that stuff.'

> (9) Il y a du monde qui n'en mettent trop. 'There are some people who put in too much of it.'

(10) Le monde ils n'en font toujours trop. 'People always make too much of it.'

(11) Louise n'en profite toujours. 'Louise always gets something out of it.'

We concluded that we could not with certainty analyze 3–7 as containing *ne,* and these sentences were left out of our quantitative study.

THE USE OF *ne*

The approximately seventy-five hours of recorded speech in the sixty interviews we studied gave us over 12,000 negative sentences. All of these contained the morpheme *pas* 'not' and/or *rien* 'nothing', *jamais* 'never', *plus* 'no more', and *personne* 'nobody'. In all of these sentences, we found only 46 cases[3] of the productive use of *ne,* as shown in Table 14-1. We omitted the doubtful cases of *ne* possibly due to phonological processes as described in the last section, as well as the frozen forms. We estimated that of the more than 12,000 cases of *pas,* less than 15 percent would be elliptical forms, or frozen forms like *pas mal.*[4] Subtracting these cases, we were still left with approximately 10,000 sentences containing *pas,* where the speaker could have used *ne.* We did not add to this total the cases of *rien, jamais,* etc., because of the frequency of their co-occurrence with *pas.* However, calculating the deletion rate for the 10,000 cases with *ne* (the rate would be still higher if the instances of *rien,* etc., were included) it is clear that speakers use *ne* in only the tiniest minority of cases. The overall rate of "omission" of *ne* would be something like 9,954/10,000, i.e., 99.5 percent. Indeed, it is more reasonable to talk of these as the unmarked cases, with the presence of *ne* treated as an insertion.

These results are in marked contrast to those reported in

3. We listened to one case that we eventually decided to leave out of our analysis because the speaker reformulated it in the middle, omitting in the reformulation the *ne* he had originally used:
   (12) Ah le samedi soir, le hockey, ah bien, oui. . . . ça. . . . on ne . . . on le voyait pas mais on l'écoutait. (30.378) 'Oh yeah, Saturday night hockey, well, yes, . . . that . . . we didn- . . . we didn't watch it but we listened to it.'
4. *Pas mal* literally glosses as 'not bad', but is usually used in the sense of 'pretty much' (cf. examples 36 and 37 below). Elliptical forms and short answers also had to be omitted because *ne* cannot occur in them:
   (13) Q. Est-ce que les filles jouent avec les garçons? 'Do the girls play with the boys?'
   A. Pas beaucoup. 'Not much.'

	pas	*rien*	*jamais*	*plus*	*personne*
With *ne*	42	—	1	3	—
Total for 15 interviews[a]	3,528	144	232	123	27
Approx. total for 60 interviews	12,140	680	780	500	120

TABLE 14-1. Sentences containing *ne* as compared with the total number of negative sentences.

[a] The 15 interviews are those containing at least one *ne*. For these interviews, all negative sentences—including those with *jamais,* etc.—were carefully examined. The number of negative *jamais, plus,* and *personne* in the other 45 interviews was estimated from these 15.

Gougenheim et al. (1967), from a study of spoken French carried out in the early fifties. Gougenheim et al. report 3,283 cases of *ne* for 5,308 cases of *pas,* giving a deletion rate of about 38 percent. Though it is possible that this rate is slightly too low because of the difficulty typists had in not "correcting irregularities and lapses" (p. 67), this work as well as Pohl's indicates a real difference between Québec and France as concerns the use of *ne.* Pohl (1968: 1351–52) states that there is considerable difference among the various regions of France, and his figures show:

> the more advanced character of this change in a vast zone which includes Paris as opposed to the rest of France; in France as opposed to Belgium, in the city as opposed to the country. . . . ; of young people, especially children, as opposed the middle aged and elderly. [These figures] also permit us to presume that certain professions—for example teaching or bookish professions—have a conservative effect.

Even in Paris, the region of France in which *ne*-omission is most advanced, the deletion rates given by Pohl vary from 25 percent to 86 percent (Pohl 1975: 19). Ashby's study of upper middle class Parisian speech, based on Malécot's corpus, reported 569 sentences with *ne* from a total of 1,020 negative sentences, or a deletion rate of 55.8 percent (1976: 120). These figures are much lower than those of the 60 Montréal speakers we studied. The woman with the highest use of *ne* still had a "deletion" rate of 92 percent.

The 46 cases of the productive use of *ne* are listed in the Appendix, as examples 14 through 59. In none of these cases was its use obligatory. *Ne* could have been omitted from all of these sentences without altering their negative meaning.

The Productive Use of *ne* in Spoken Montréal French

THE SPEAKERS WHO USE *ne*

Fifteen of the 60 speakers we studied used *ne* at least once during the course of the tape-recorded session. It is important, however, to note that none of these people regularly used *ne* to form negative sentences. Eleven of the 15 used *ne* only once or twice during the whole interview, and even the heaviest user of *ne* (speaker 31,[5] who accounts for 13 of our 46 cases) has a "deletion" rate of 92 percent. These frequencies alone would seem to indicate that it is more reasonable to talk of insertion of *ne* than of deletion, especially since, as we shall see in the next section, *ne* is used when speakers are maximally attentive to speech.

Are the speakers who used *ne* at least once during the interview different in any significant regard from those who refrained from using it at all? Table 14-2 indicates that *ne*-users tended to be slightly older, to have had somewhat more education (i.e., to have completed high school), and most importantly to have a much higher level of integration into the "linguistic marketplace" (D. Sankoff and Laberge 1978b). This relationship is further documented in Table 14-3, which shows that speakers having a linguistic market index greater than .5 are much more likely to make occasional use of *ne* than are speakers whose linguistic market index is less than .5. Eleven of the 19 speakers whose index is greater than .5 were observed to use *ne*, in comparison with only 4 of the 41 speakers whose index is less than .5.

Given the very low frequency of use for all speakers (setting aside speaker 31, the other 14 speakers use *ne* in only about 1.5 percent of their negative sentences), we are loath to interpret our results as indicating that the other 45 speakers lack a *ne*-insertion rule. We feel

Speakers	Number of speakers	Mean age	Mean years in school	Mean linguistic market index	Mean number of *ne*	Mean number of *pas*
using *ne* at least once	15	44.2	11.5	.55	3.1	235
not using *ne*	45	38.9	9.0	.25	—	191

TABLE 14-2. Comparison of speakers who used *ne* with those who did not.

5. Speaker 31 is a sixty-one-year-old woman, daughter of a wealthy business and professional family, who spent several years studying in France before marrying a man in the same social bracket as her parents.

301

	Mean linguistic market index	
Speakers	>.5	<.5
using *ne* at least once	11	4
not using *ne*	8	37

TABLE 14-3. Use of *ne* according to linguistic market index.

rather that had we had a large enough sample of speech from these people, we would have been able to catch them using *ne* productively at some point. Though most of the people who used *ne* were members of the bourgeoisie and of the professions, or white collar employees, they also included two housewives with only primary school education, a young electrician, and an unemployed handyman. We are thus led to believe that *ne*-insertion is a syntactic resource available to most, if not all, speakers of Montréal French. It is, as we shall argue in the next section, a characteristic of careful speech. Indeed, perhaps such social differences as we have found here among "users" and "nonusers" of *ne* are due to the fact that bourgeois speakers are in general more likely to use "careful" speech, marked with rare and bookish features.

Most studies of linguistic variation have concentrated on variables whose variants are in much more serious competition. Indeed, there is a tendency to feel that once the frequency of application of a rule has passed beyond a certain level—say 90 percent or 95 percent—it might as well be treated as categorical, since in any case the inertia of linguistic change will soon push it to 100 percent. We disagree. We suggest that a linguistic change in progress may be halted, even very close to categorical status. This is particularly likely when the alternation serves to mark some social or stylistic difference. We have seen that in the case of *ne,* socially based differences among speakers provide only a partial explanation. However, as we shall see in the next section, *ne* is also involved in stylistic differences.

RHETORICAL CONTEXTS THAT FAVOR THE USE OF *ne*

The range of topics that appear in the 46 sentences of the Appendix is surprisingly limited, considering the rather broad range of topics covered in the interviews. First, there are 12 sentences dealing with language itself (those examples whose English gloss is preceded by "L" in the Appendix). Many, though not all of these have to do with "proper" speech. One might argue that in talking about language, people may be more aware of their own speech, and thus make greater use of forms thought to be more correct.

Six further sentences also focus on speech itself, whether by quoting the words of another (examples 55 and 58) or by phrasing thoughts in a formulaic way. Sentences 18, 19, 31, and 33 are proverbial in character, since their content (general, moralizing statements about "human nature") as well as their form are reminiscent of the proverbs of the oral tradition.

Two other topics seem to favor the use of *ne*. There are a further 16 examples in which the topic is either religion, or the education of children (both moral education at home and formal instruction at school). The theme of discipline runs strongly throughout these excerpts.

It is of course possible to use *ne* outside of these contexts, but such cases form a small minority of our examples. The 12 remaining sentences involve talk of travel to Europe, putting on shows, being allergic to dye, not having money for family feasts, and so on. There are several cases of negation of verbs of thought, opinion, or speech—cases of not believing, not knowing, not remembering.

In general, *ne* appears in contexts where speakers are most likely to be aware of speech itself, and to be monitoring their own speech. The topics of language, instruction, discipline, and religion tend to spirit people back to a normative world in which "proper language" becomes very salient. The speech that seems appropriate to these topics thus comprises a number of features of formal style.[6] It is not surprising that in the same sentences as those containing *ne*, we find other forms that are very rare in Montréal French. These include *nous* instead of *on* as a subject clitic in 16 and 17; *alors* rather than *donc* or *ça fait que* as a conjunction in 46; nonreduced forms of *elle* and *elles* in 43 and 44, a continuative relative in 24.[7] In addition to co-occurrence with these formal variants, we find other "literary" touches: present participles, passives, subjunctives, and learnéd vocabulary.

It is important to note that even those themes that heighten people's awareness of speech and encourage self-monitoring do not

6. Ashby (1976: 131) shows that in a corpus of Parisian French, *ne* appears more often in discourse where speakers address each other as *vous* than in that where *tutoiement* prevails—a nice indicator of formal style and exactly in line with what we would predict.

7. These are all variables that have been studied by members of our research group. On continuative relatives, see Kemp (1978) and Sankoff et al., in press. On the alternation between *donc*, *alors*, and *ça fait que*, see Dessureault-Dober 1975. On *on-nous*, see Laberge 1977 and chapter 13 above. *Elle* and *elles* are treated in both Sankoff and Cedergren 1971, and Laberge 1977.

categorically produce *ne* in negative sentences. The application of *ne* insertion remains variable even in the environments most favorable to it. Thus speaker 31, who says 'it is clear that we do not have (N'*avons pas*) the accent' in 46, and 'I do not believe (*je* NE *crois pas*) that in Montréal we speak *joual*' in 47 continues slightly farther on the same theme, using no *ne* in explaining that *notre parler est pas tellement différent* (31.613) ('our speech is not so different'). Of course, as noted above, *ne* can also occur in less favorable environments, though even more rarely.

CONCLUSION

We have seen that in spoken Montréal French, *ne* is used in a very small percentage of negative syntactic environments, environments in which its use would be possible. A high proportion of the cases of *ne* are attributable to conversational themes that favor a careful, even precious, style. However, it is clear that on the one hand, the use of *ne* is not restricted to these favorable contexts, and that on the other, these contexts themselves do not make the use of *ne* obligatory. Most literate speakers would use *ne* much more frequently in writing, but we do not know to what degree its obligatory presence in standard written French (which people encounter in reading) contributes to its maintenance in those verbal styles that approach the written. In any event the morpheme *ne*, despite its redundancy and rarity of use, seems not to be disappearing completely. It is maintained as a syntactic and stylistic resource, available to the speakers of Montréal French to use as they see fit.

APPENDIX: THE 46 SENTENCES CONTAINING *ne*.

(14) Puis ma mère n'aimait pas qu'on aille déranger alors elle nous tenait plutôt à la maison. (3.46) 'And my mother didn't like us to go out and make nuisances of ourselves, so she pretty much kept us at home.'

(15) Pas loin. . . . La maison n'existe plus, elle a été démolie. (3.137) 'Not far . . . the house doesn't exist any more, it was demolished.'

(16) Bien, nous n'avions pas beaucoup d'argent pour faire des gros repas. (3.197) 'Well, we didn't have much money to make big meals.'

(17) Le règlement y était et puis nous observions les règlements plus faciles. Tandis qu'aujourd'hui les règlements on ne peut pas leur imposer. (3.417) 'The rules were there and we obeyed the rules more. Whereas today you can't impose the rules on them.'

(18) Puis, pour bien vivre, il faut avoir la paix, puis les gens ne semblent pas s'y prêter. (3.547) 'And to live well, you have to have peace and quiet, and people just don't seem to want to be that considerate.'

(19) Ah bien, je lui parlais de la même façon que je vous parle là . . . à mon enfant la même chose. Je pense qu'on ne change pas. On est comme on est. (3.585) (L) 'Well, I spoke to him the same way I'm speaking to you now . . . and I speak the same way to my child. I think that we don't really change. We are what we are.'

(20) Q. Mais est-ce que vous pensez qu'il fera une carrière?

R. Non. Je n'y tiens pas du tout, moi. (3.632)

Q. 'Do you think he'll make a career of it?'

A. 'No. Personally, I'm not particularly enthusiastic about it.'

(21) Disons que . . . nous autres, on a connaissance dans le groupe que je me tiens là, je ne crois pas. (6.586) 'Let's say that . . . for us, the group I hang around with, we know about it, so I don't think so.'

(22) Quand on employait des mots canadiens, il nous répétait: "Je ne comprends pas." (6.770) (L) 'When we used Canadian words he would always say, "I don't understand."'

(23) J'ai commencé à travailler sur une machine IBM: sur plusieurs sortes de machines IBM, que je ne connaissais pas. (9.566) 'I began working on an IBM machine, on various types of IBM machines with which I wasn't familiar at all.'

(24) Et puis je suis allergique à la teinture, ce que je ne savais pas. (9.573) 'And I'm allergic to dye, something of which I was unaware.'

(25) Ma mère est très croyante . . . e . . . ma mère e . . . aujourd'hui ne pratique pas mais est toujours croyante. (9.702) 'My mother is very religious . . . uh . . . my mother . . . uh . . . now she doesn't practice any more but she still has her faith.'

(26) Il est parfait bilingue . . . e . . . ma mère ne parle pas un mot anglais. (9.967) (L) 'He's completely bilingual . . . uh . . . my mother can't speak a word of English.'

(27) Mais on a tous appris à parler l'anglais, c'est-à-dire qu'à la maison, on parlait anglais-français. Fait que pour moi, je trouve que ce n'est absolument pas un problème. (9.971) (L) 'But we all learned English, that is, at home we spoke English and French. So for me, I find that it's really not a problem.'

(28) Q. Est-ce qu'il y avait des balançoires, des carrés de sable? R. Je m'en rappelle pas. Je ne crois pas. (12.53)

Q. 'Were there swings, sand boxes?'
A. 'I don't remember. I don't think so.'

(29) On pourra pas discuter sur un problème familial, mais qui n'existe pas dans la famille. (13.412) 'We wouldn't be able to discuss a family problem, but that doesn't exist within the family.'

(30) Elle va avoir des mots . . . e . . . des mots spécifiques . . . des termes exacts, d'accord. Mais e . . . s . . . son langage quotidien n'en sera pas influencé plus que ça. (13.685) (L) 'She'll have words . . . uh . . . specific words, exact terms, all right. But uh . . . her everyday speech won't be affected as much as all that.'

(31) Quand ils seront instruits, ils prendront les commandes de tout ce qu'il y a à prendre. Le travail, bien, puis l'épargne. Les jeunes n'épargnent pas. (20.349) 'When they're educated, they'll have to take on all the responsibilities. Work, and saving. The young people don't save.'

(32) Ils ont pas . . . les jeunes n'ont pas . . . On avait une formation autrement nous autres . . . religieuse. (20.406) 'They don't . . . the young people don't . . . we had another kind of training, a religious training.'

(33) Les gens n'y croient plus mais quand arrive un mauvais coup, vous savez, c'est bon d'avoir quelque chose pour . . . e . . . s'appuyer. (20.408) 'People don't believe in it anymore but when something bad happens, you know, it's good to have something to . . . uh . . . lean on.'

(34) Ils ont peut-être des raisons qui sont valables mais je pense que c'est une idée qui ne doit pas être rejetée complètement,

qui doit être sûrement analysée. (25.356) 'They may have valid reasons but I think that it's an idea that should not be completely rejected, which surely ought to be analysed.'

(35) Pour le gars qui a . . . disons qui a une formation un peu plus poussée, plus que lui, c'est . . . ces explications-là ne satisfont pas, bien là, on peut pousser un peu plus, jusqu'où le gars peut aller. (25.511) 'For the guy that has . . . lets say who has a little more education, more than *he* does, it's . . . those explanations are not satisfying, so then, you can go a little farther, just as far as the guy can go.'

(36) Puis l'autre est e . . . arrivée pas mal longtemps après moi. Elle n'a pas été pensionnaire, c'était le petit bébé celle-là. (31.101) 'And the next one uh . . . arrived quite a bit after me. She didn't go to boarding school—she was the baby of the family.'

(37) Oui. J'ai pas mal voyagé . . . e . . . ça fait seulement quelques années que je ne voyage plus, mais je suis allée en Europe plusieurs fois. (31.238) 'Yes. I've traveled quite a bit . . . uh . . . it's only the last few years that I no longer travel, but I've been to Europe several times.'

(38) Ca je trouve que ça a beaucoup changé, ah peut-être, il y a des raisons, vous savez, que . . . je ne connais pas. (31.320) 'This I find has changed a great deal. Oh, perhaps there are reasons, you know, that . . . I don't know.'

(39) La religion elle-même n'a pas changé. La manière de la pratiquer peut-être. (31.335) 'Religion itself hasn't changed. Perhaps the way it's practiced.'

(40) C'est évident mais sûrement que la religion n'a pas changé. (31.337) That's true, but surely religion hasn't changed.'

(41) Q. Est-ce que votre père était trés autoritaire?
R. Le grand . . . oui, l'autorité, le grand respect, la personne à ne pas déranger e. . . . (31.382)

Q. 'Was your father very authoritarian?'
A. 'Great. . . . yes. Authority, great respect, a person not to be bothered uh. . . .'

(42) . . . à ne pas demander rien, vous savez? (31.382) '. . . not to ask anything, you know?' (continuation of 41)

(43) Elle est comme un cheveu sur la soupe. Elle est entrée dans ce grand monde qu'elle ne comprend pas. (31.411) 'She's like a lost soul. She came into this big world that she doesn't understand.'

(44) Puis avant, elles ne pensaient même pas à ces choses-là. Elles étaient pas malheureuses. (31.434) 'And before, they didn't even think about those things. They weren't unhappy.'

(45) Mais pas nécessaire de mettre des fichus, puis des permanentes, puis e . . . des bijoux e . . . ça je ne comprends pas. (31.438) 'But they don't have to wear fancy scarves, and permanents, and uh . . . jewelry uh . . . that I don't understand.'

(46) Une fois j'avais dit à quelqu'un: "Bien je viens du Canada." "Ca se voit." Il voulait dire ça s'entend. Alors, c'est évident que nous n'avons pas l'accent de. . . . (31.540) (L) 'Once I said to somebody, "I come from Canada." "I can see that." He meant he could hear it. So it's clear that we don't have the accent of uh. . . .'

(47) Mais je ne crois pas qu'à Montrèal, on parle joual. Non. (31.562) (L) 'But I don't think that in Montréal we speak *joual*. No.'

(48) Q. Trouvez-vous qu'on se fait juger par notre façon de parler?
R. Je ne crois pas. Vous voulez dire d'une façon habituelle? (31.589)
(L) Q. 'Do you think we're judged by our manner of speaking?'
A. 'I don't think so. You mean, in general?'

(49) C'était des gens qui montaient des shows intéressants puis qui n'étaient pas payés. . . . (34.625) 'They were people who put on interesting shows and who were not paid. . . .'

(50) Bien non, maman n'est pas venue. . . . (35.8) 'No, mother didn't come. . . . (from Montréal).'

(51) C'est une de mes tantes, la soeur de maman qui est venue rester avec nous autres pour avoir soin de nous autres, et puis je vous dis qu'il fallait écouter.

Q. Trouvez-vous que c'était. . . ?

R. Je n'ai pas trouvé ça dur. (35.108)

'It was one of my aunts, mother's sister, who came to live with us to look after us, and I tell you we had to listen.'

Q. 'Did you find it. . . ?'

A. 'I didn't find it hard.'

(52) Il y en a qui parlent un drôle de langage. Question d'instruction e . . . c'est surtout une question d'instruction. N'ayant pas été à l'école et puis écoutant certaines émissions . . . (39.552) (L) 'Some of them speak a strange kind of language. A question of education and . . . it's mainly a question of education. Not having been to school and listening to certain programs. . . .''

(53) Mais eux autres, n'ayant ja . . . n'ayant jamais eu l'entraînement que nous autres qu'on a eu à l'école, ils s'arrêtent complètement là. (39.561) 'But as for them, never havi . . . never having had the training we had at school, they just give up completely.'

(54) Je n'ai pas tellement l'occasion d'être e . . . beacoup avec les jeunes, mais il me semble qu'en les entendant parler. . . . (44.912) (L) 'I don't get much opportunity to be uh . . . with young people, but it seems to me when you listen to them talk. . . .'

(55) Mais faire la liaison des verbes, là comme on dit "il sera pas," en réalité il faudrait dire "il ne sera pas" (47.527) (L) 'But making the liaison with the verbs, like when you say *il sera pas* really one ought to say *il ne sera pas*.'

(56) . . . puis que les Français n'emploient pas. Nous autres, en réalité c'est le vieux français qui se parle. (47.575) (L) '. . . . and which the French don't use. Us, really we speak Old French.'

(57) Prends la majorité des gens de mon âge, je . . . je pense que . . . la très forte majorité ne pratique plus. (53.819) 'Take the majority of people my age. I . . . I think that . . . the very great majority no longer practice (their religion).'

(58) Puis quand que mon grand-père est mort, il a dit: "N'oub-

liez pas le quatre juillet.'' (57.657) 'And when my grandfather died, he said, "Don't forget the fourth of July." '

(59) On parlait d'après la religieuse ou nos livres. Notre cerveau ne travaillait pas. Là, eux autres, tout travaille. (57.798) 'We went according to what the sister said or what the book said. Our own brains weren't working. For *them,* everything's working.'

15.

The Alternation Between the Auxiliaries *avoir* and *être* in Montréal French

GILLIAN SANKOFF AND PIERRETTE THIBAULT

1. INTRODUCTION

Anyone who has ever tried to learn French—at least in a second-language classroom—has encountered the *"être"* verbs. These verbs form a small group for which French grammar prescribes conjugation with the auxiliary *être* 'to be'. This distinguishes them from the majority of French verbs, conjugated with the auxiliary *avoir* 'to have'. Though the second language student of French is usually presented with a fixed list of sixteen *être* verbs, in fact the membership of the list, as well as the exact number of verbs to be included, has varied over time, as we shall see below. Nevertheless, the verbs of this small class have certain properties in common. They are all intransitive. Most are verbs of motion, like *aller* 'to go', *monter* 'to get up', *sortir* 'to go out', and so on, or stative verbs, like *rester* 'to stay' and *demeurer* 'to live'. These semantic properties, however, do not uniquely define the set of *être* verbs. The fact that other verbs with the same semantic properties are prescribed as being conjugated with *avoir,* and the fact that the list of *être* verbs varies according to the prescriptive grammarian one consults, combine to indicate that the list of *être* verbs is at least to some extent arbitrary.

This chapter was originally published in French in *Langue Française* 34 (1977): 81–108. I thank my coauthor, Pierrette Thibault, for her permission to include in this collection an article to which her contribution was at least as great as my own, and for her detailed comments on the English version that I prepared for this volume. The research on which this article was based took two years to complete, and we gratefully acknowledge the cooperation of many who contributed in one way or another, especially Pascale Rousseau for the quantitative data analysis, Suzanne Laberge for the choice and checking of examples, and David Sankoff, whose material and intellectual aid throughout our work on this paper was inestimable. Discussion with Claire Blanche, Jean-Claude Chevalier, Simone Delesalle, John Fought, Françoise Kerleroux, William Labov, and Beatriz Lavandera helped clarify several aspects of our analysis.

Despite the rules of normative grammar, Montrealers often use *avoir* in conjugating the *être* verbs. This chapter is a detailed report on this phenomenon. Our methods are essentially quantitative and distributional. Our analysis is based on the 120 interviews of the Sankoff-Cedergren corpus of Montréal French (Sankoff and Sankoff 1973). In these materials we examined not only the syntactic context of the occurrences of *avoir* and *être*, but also semantic and discursive features of each case, as well as various social facts about the speaker.

We originally listed all the verbs for which we had found an alternation between *avoir* and *être* as auxiliaries. The frequency of several of these was, however, too low to give us any indication of the effects of the various constraints on the choice between the two auxiliaries. This was the case, for example, for *diminuer* 'to diminish', conjugated 11 times with *avoir* and only once with *être*. Here is a list of the verbs we studied, in order of frequency:

arriver	'to arrive'	467 occurrences
aller	'to go'	404
venir	'to come'	353
rester	'to stay'	339
partir	'to leave'	240
sortir	'to go out'	133
passer	'to pass (by)'	128
déménager	'to move'	113
rentrer	'to enter'	109 (literally 're-enter', but used by most speakers instead of *entrer*)
revenir	'to come back'	104
demeurer	'to live, stay'	77
tomber	'to fall'	74
retourner	'to return'	39
monter	'to go up'	33
entrer	'to enter'	19
descendre	'to come down'	18

Note that in presenting the list of verbs we studied, we defined the problem as involving the alternation between *avoir* and *être* **as auxiliaries,** that is, in doing the **same** grammatical work. Given that elsewhere in French grammar, *avoir* and *être* have **different** functions, a major part of our task was to define the variable. This meant locating that area of *avoir/être* variation which does **not** convey any subtle temporal or aspectual differences. In particular, this involves separating the use of *être* as a copula from its use as an auxiliary. Accordingly, we devote section 2 to a detailed investigation of the question of defining the variable. This is followed by a discussion of the distribution of *avoir* and *être* for the various verbs we studied in section 3. Section 4 deals with the variation among speakers. In the remainder of the present section, we will review what previous authors have had to say about *avoir/être* alternation.

For at least the past three centuries, grammarians have remarked on this alternation, tending to propose two major types of interpretation. Some grammarians have said that *avoir* marks the imperfective (*révolu*) aspect whereas *être* marks the perfective aspect of the verb. Thus, speaking of the sixteenth century, Gougenheim[1] writes (1951: 122): "The possibility of choosing between the auxiliaries *être* and *avoir* was greater than it is today for the verbs of movement. *Avoir* marked the movement considered in and of itself, *être* the movement considered in its completion." He cites as evidence a sentence from Marot where the author conjugates the verb *entrer* with *avoir,* focusing on the movement as such. This distinction is very similar to the distinction Benveniste makes between the aorist and the perfect (1966: 243–44).

Other grammarians have taken the view that the aspectual distinction is of a somewhat different sort. They feel that *avoir* or *être* is chosen according to whether one wishes to stress the action itself or **the state that results** from the action. This group of grammarians analyzes the contrast as being between the past action 'he went' and the state 'he is gone', as opposed to the first group, which contrasts the past action, imperfective 'he went' with perfective 'he has gone'. The seventeenth-century grammarian Ménage clarifies the "resulting state" interpretation with the following remarks on the verbs *entrer, sortir, monter,* and *descendre.*

> *Il est entré, il est sorti, il est monté, il est descendu.* This is how M. de Vaugelas claims that we must conjugate the preterits of these four verbs. And indeed this is the way one usually speaks. But one can also say *il a sorti, il a monté.* As in these examples: *monsieur a sorti ce matin* 'monsieur went out this morning', that is to say that he went out and came back. For if he had not come back, one would say, *M. est sorti, M. est sorti dès le matin.* 'M. is out, M. has been out since this morning.' *Aussitôt que Madame est venue de la messe, elle a monté en sa chambre.* 'As soon as Madame had returned from mass, she went up to her room.' *Un tel écolier n'a pas monté en troisième, il est demeuré en quatrième.* 'Such and such a schoolboy has not gone up to third, he has

1. The translation of this and all other citations from the French was done by Gillian Sankoff.

remained in fourth.' *J'ay monté à cheval sous Arnolfini.* 'I rode horseback under Arnolfini.' (Ménage 1676: 274)

The "rules of usage" given in some prescriptive grammars of modern French are based on a similar aspectual distinction, though they usually state that this is disappearing from current usage. Brunot and Bruneau, for example, explicitly state (1969: 311) that the differential use of the auxiliaries, according to whether reference is being made to an action or its result, was maintained until the middle of the nineteenth century, since the 1848 edition of the *Grammaire des Grammaires* still gives this "rule of usage." For Grevisse, the distinction has been maintained only in certain verbs. *Entrer, partir, repartir, rester, sortir,* and *tomber* were, according to him, formerly conjugated with the two auxiliaries, though the use of *avoir* is currently proscribed in the "composé" tenses. However, for a second list of verbs that comprises, among others, *changer, déménager, descendre, monter,* and *passer,* he claims that one uses *avoir* "when one wishes to express an action which happened at the time of which one is speaking, and *être* when one wishes to express the state resulting from an action previously accomplished" (Grevisse 1969: 605).

Not all authors make a clear distinction between the two types of interpretation. We sometimes find an amalgam of the two interpretations, as in the following citation from Frei:

> We note that "advanced French," drawing on the coexistence of the two auxiliaries, *être* and *avoir,* in the past tense of intransitive verbs, tends to give them distinct values according to whether it is a case of the perfect ("state which follows a process": *être*) or of the preterit ("process in the past": *avoir*). (Frei 1929: 86)

More recently, linguists have conceived the problem in other terms. For Benveniste as for Guillaume, the auxiliary, like the participle, has a double function: grammatical and lexical. In Benveniste's terms (1974: 182), conjugation with *avoir* conveys *l'acquis d'opération* "process attainment," and conjugation with *être* conveys *l'acquis de situation* "situational attainment." The verbs are grouped into two classes, semantically compatible with one or the other trait.[2] Guillaume (1970: 26) accounts for this double function as follows: "The auxiliary *avoir* leaves open the continuity of the continuation of the verb. The auxiliary *être* comes from this continuity of continuation being broken, from the very meaning of the verb."

2. Along these lines, Claire Blanche has suggested (1977: 101–2) that the verb *partir* may have different meanings according to whether it is conjugated exclusively with *être* or alternatively with *avoir* and *être.*

In the spoken language, forms of the type *j'ai parti* still exist, and their use has become socially marked. Thus we find in Brunot and Bruneau (p. 311), "Today, *je suis rentré* is the only current form; *j'ai rentré* is 'common' (*populaire*)." Frei is a proponent of "popular" French. His view is that it is an "advanced" language that maximally puts to use all of its resources. Nevertheless, he recognizes the opprobrium that attaches to the use of *avoir*.

Does the current variation in the auxiliaries still convey a trace of the aspectual distinction? Can it be explained in terms of the semantics of the verbs to which it applies? Can it stem rather from a process of social differentiation, the residue of a former aspectual distinction whose nature is not entirely clear?

In approaching the actual linguistic practice of speakers of Montréal French, we try to answer these questions and to add new elements to the debate. We attempt to show what can be contributed to grammatical analysis through the study of a gamut of individuals displaying markedly different linguistic behavior. In particular, we try to demonstrate how a sociolinguistic study that is necessarily restricted to synchronic data can nevertheless best be understood within a diachronic framework.

2. THE QUESTION OF ASPECT: ANALYTICAL CRITERIA

Though we are aware of the ambiguity in a sentence like *je suis rentré* ('I came back', 'I'm back') when taken out of context, we claim that the vast majority of the sentences that we studied were not ambiguous. That is, there were indices *other than* the presence of *avoir* or *être* that made possible the distinction between an act and its completion, or the state ensuing from its completion. We obviously could not rely on *avoir/être* to give us this information, as one object of our study was to examine exactly whether and to what extent the choice between *avoir* and *être* does mark the distinction.

It is important before proceeding further to recall the consequences of the loss of the *passé simple* from spoken French. The preterit/perfect distinction that had been marked by *passé simple/passé composé* was neutralized, with the *passé composé* taking over preterit functions. Thus *j'ai marché au bureau ce matin* is properly glossed 'I walked to the office this morning'; whereas *j'ai marché énormément dans ma vie* is 'I have walked a tremendous amount in my life'.

With the *"être"* verbs of movement considered here, we claim that the action/resulting state distinction is more appropriate than the completed action/incompleted action distinction. For these verbs, completion of the action results automatically in a state. "Having gone

315

out'' results in "being out." For this reason we prefer not to use traits like [±completed] or [±perfective], which call to mind the preterit/ perfect distinction.

The stative sense of the completed action makes the use of *être* in these contexts a natural parallel to its use as a copula. Thus *il est sorti* 'he is gone' (better in English, 'he is out') is synonymous with *il est absent* 'he is absent'. Indeed, the construction is the same one used with descriptive adjectives like *beau* 'handsome', thus *il est beau* 'he is handsome'. All of these cases, we argue, are cases of COPULA + AD-JECTIVE. The problem is that *il est sorti* is also used to convey the preterit 'he went out', which we would analyze, as in the case of *j'ai marché* above, as AUXILIARY + PAST PARTICIPLE. In order to understand how *avoir* and *être* are variably used as auxiliaries in the preterit, we must rely on other indices to convey information about which cases of *ÊTRE* + PAST PARTICIPLE are to be read as COPULA + ADJECTIVE, i.e., "resulting state."

The strength of such other markers can readily be seen by examining sentences 1 and 2. The distinction here is conveyed by temporal expressions of some sort:

(1) Hier, mon petit frère il était ici, puis il *est parti* à dix heures et demie. (2.381)[3] 'Yesterday my little brother was here and he left at 10:30.'

(2) Il *est parti* en France maintenant. (117.9) 'He's away in France now.'

Clearly both sentences make mention of an act of leaving that has been completed in the past, but whereas the first sentence deals with the moment of the act itself, the second talks of the ensuing state. In sentence 1, the temporal expression "at 10:30" punctualizes the departure. It suffices to indicate that *est parti* refers to the moment at which the act took place. In contrast, in sentence 2, the adverb "now" indicates that the verbal expression doesn't refer to the accomplishing of the act (that is, to the time of its execution), but indeed to the state following the act, a state that prevails at the time in question (the "reference point,"[4] "now," which corresponds here to the time of the

---

3. Each sentence taken from our corpus is numbered according to the speaker (from 1 to 120) and the line of the transcription in which it occurs. Here, speaker number 2, line 381.

4. Following Reichenbach (1966: 288), we understand that the "past" conveyed in sentences such as 1 and 2 is not absolute, but relative, since it must always be located with respect to a point of reference. This reference point may be situated at the time of the event to which the verb refers, or at the time of the speech act in which it is found, or at a time other than these two. This concept

utterance). In sentence 1, the verbal expression *ÊTRE* (IN THE PRESENT) + PAST PARTICIPLE is interpreted as a *passé composé* representing the preterit; here, *être* is acting as an auxiliary. In sentence 2, the same verbal expression is interpreted as a present; *être* is therefore acting as a copula and the participle, as an adjective.

Two facts are associated with the use of the verb *être* as a copula: (1) the time is always the same as the tense of the copula itself (here it is the present); and (2) the participle acts as an adjective. This is why, in such sentences, it is always possible to substitute a nonparticipial adjective without changing the temporal point of reference. This is never possible in the "preterit" cases. We could say "he is happy in France now" but not "he is happy at 10:30" (that is, not without changing the temporal point of reference).

In the present analysis, we are interested in those sentences that refer to the carrying out of acts in the past, and which can thus be interpreted unequivocally as *composé* tenses (rather than as COPULA + ADJECTIVE). We believe we can show that the variation observed between the two auxiliaries in such contexts is not subject to any aspectual constraints. This aspectual distinction does not enter into the paradigm of the *composé* tenses because in sentences like 2, the verb *être* is acting not as an auxiliary but as a copula. Note that except in very unusual circumstances, only the verb *être* can occur in "resulting state" sentences (cf. 2.5). There is thus no variation in these contexts.

When we first began working on *avoir/être* variation, we had no clear understanding of what exactly led to the interpretation of one instance as focusing on an action, and another as focusing on an ensuing state. Initially, we worked from our intuitions about what was being conveyed. Perhaps our most challenging analytical task was to make explicit how we came to have these intuitions. The result of this work, then, was the development of a set of indices that we present in the following sections.

The indices enabling us to determine that reference is being made to the accomplishing of an action in the past apply somewhat differently according to the verbs considered and according to the tenses involved. We shall return to these questions in grouping the verbs according to their semantic traits. In the presentation of the indices that follows, we attempt to show that they all have the function either of focusing on the carrying out of an action or process in the past, relative to a time of reference (*COMPOSÉ* TENSES), or of indicating a state

---

is useful in accounting for *composé* tenses other than the *passé composé,* and we develop it in 2.1.3 below.

that prevailed at the time of the point of reference (COPULA + ADJEC-TIVE).

Most of the time, we find co-occurrence of several indices. Nevertheless, we have attempted to locate examples in which each one is found alone in order to show to greater effect its value as a marker.

2.1. Temporal Indices

The *passé composé* of the verbs of motion we studied corresponds to the aorist or preterit. Indeed we hold that there is no perfective sense associated with the use of this tense for motion verbs, because the action is transformed into a state as soon as it is completed. (This is not the case for the stative verbs; cf. 3.4.) In a large number of cases, we find markers that focus on the time of the action itself. These are temporal indices that, in Reichenbach's terms, situate the point of reference at the time of the event. The expression 'at 10:30' in sentence 1 is one illustration. Our analysis also applies to the other *composé* tenses since we could imagine sentences in other tenses where such indicators play the same role. *Ce matin-là, il était parti à 10 h. 30 puisqu'il avait un rendez-vous à 11 h.* 'That morning, he had left at 10:30 because he had an appointment at 11:00'. Or, *Quand il a appris que sa soeur était arrivée à 10:35, il regrettait d'être parti à 10:30.* 'When he learned that his sister had arrived at 10:35, he was sorry to have left at 10:30'. In the presentation of the various indices, we restrict outselves to the *passé composé*. The other tenses will be treated in section 2.4.1.

2.1.1. Indices that Situate the Point of Reference at the Time of the Event Itself: Locating COMPOSÉ Tenses

Some temporal indices appear in the immediate environment of the verb, whereas others emerge from the sequence of the discourse. Among indices of the first type, we find not only adverbs like *hier* 'yesterday', but also a variety of other expressions that serve to punctualize or indicate a specific time. *Une fois* 'once', *un jour* 'one day', *la semaine suivante* 'the following week', *á l'âge de douze ans* 'at the age of twelve', *en 1922* 'in 1922', etc. Here are several examples (in these, as in all further examples, we italicize the indicators under consideration):

(3) Oui, j'ai descendu *à matin.* (114.688) 'Yes, I went down this morning.'

(4) *Le 7 juillet,* je suis descendu à Reykjavik (75.305) 'On the 7th of July, I set down in Reykjavik.'

(5) Parce qu'on a parti nous-autres, *le 29 avril*. (44.192) 'Because we left, we did, on the 29th of April.'

(6) On est parti *à 11 h. du matin,* on a arrivé *à 7 h. du soir*. (98.94) 'We left at 11 a.m.; we arrived at 7 p.m.'

In the immediate environment of the verb, we also find adverbial expressions like *souvent* 'often', *bien des fois* 'many times', etc., which do not refer to one specific time but which mark iterativity or the repetition of the same action. We illustrate with the verb *déménager* ('to move'), something about which we asked everyone, and which most had done more than once in their lives:

(7) On a déménagé peut-être *cinq six fois*. (110.59) 'We moved maybe five, six times.'

(8) On est déménagé *trois quatre fois*. (61.13) 'We moved three or four times.'

In terms of the sequence of discourse, the setting of an action within a sequence of actions is generally sufficient to indicate that the point of reference is the time of the action. Mostly, but not always, these series are accompanied by adverbial markers or conjunctions like *là* ('there, at that point'), *après ça* ('after that'), *puis*[5] 'and, then', *alors* 'thus', etc. In 9 and 10, the act of "leaving a job" is situated between two others:

(9) C'etait rien que pour trois mois. J'ai sorti de là. *Là,* j'ai essayé de me placer ailleurs. (96.945) 'It was only for three months. I left there. Then, I tried to get another job.'

(10) Puis *après ça* comme j'étais diplomé, j'ai enseigné au Collège St-Romuald pendant un an, puis *après ça* je suis sorti, je me suis en revenu en ville. (47.646) 'And after that since I had my diploma, I taught at the Collège St-Romuald for a year, and after that I left, I came back to town.'

Even when the action following the verb in question is not mentioned, membership in a series is generally sufficient to clearly indicate the focus on the action itself even without the further temporal specifications that are so often present. In 11, 'during the war' provides a further temporal specification.

(11) *Après ça,* j'ai parti de là en temps de guerre. (28.34) 'After that, I left there during wartime.'

5. Cf. Giacomi, Cedergren, and Yaeger (1977).

(12) Au début on jouait avec eux-autres *puis après ça* eux-autres sont partis puis nous-autres, on a continué avec d'autres, plus jeunes. (112.164-65). 'At the beginning we played with them but after that they left, so we continued with other, younger kids.'

Here are two further examples with the verb *retourner*.

(13) Mais j'y ai retourné *par après*. Mon père il dit: "Tu vas retourner en bicycle." (86.168) 'But I went back after that. My father said, "You're going back on your bicycle."'

(14) *Puis après ça,* il y est retourné. Il avait encore deux mois et demi à faire. (10.528) 'And after that, he went back. He still had two-and-a-half months to do.'

The indices of focus on the accomplishing of an act are often found in combination with each other. The next example contains several. In addition to the iterative marker *souvent* 'often', there is *après ça* 'after that', which indicates a series and an embedded sentence with *parce que* 'because' (cf. 2.2.2).

(15) *Après ça,* on est déménagé *souvent parce qu'*il faisait des spéculations. (110.45) 'After that, we moved often because he was involved in speculating.'

2.1.2. Indices that Situate the Point of Reference after the Time of the Event: Locating COPULA + ADJECTIVE

When the focus is on the state resulting from the act, the point of reference shifts away from the time of the act itself. Thus, when the state in question prevails at the time of the speech event, the copula that expresses it is in the present. This is why we used temporal expressions that refer to the present as indicators of "resulting state," or COPULA + ADJECTIVE constructions. These include *maintenant* 'now', *à cette heure* 'now', etc.

(16) Là, ils sont déménagés ici mes parents *maintenant.* (120.251) 'Now, they're settled here now, my parents.'

In sentences like 16, the only possible reading of the verbal expression is the following: *être* (or copula) in the present + adjective. *Ils sont déménagés* describes the state consequent to a previous act whose temporal referent is immaterial.

In terms of discourse sequencing, it sometimes happens that the reference to the present is simply indicated by the presence of another proposition for which the one under consideration constitutes a paraphrase. Here is an illustration:

(17) Leur problème *est soulagé,* leur mal est parti là. Ils peuvent se replacer. (51.648) 'Their problem is relieved, their sadness is gone now. They can get back to normal.'

The proposition *leur mal est parti* is glossed 'their sadness is gone' (not 'their sadness went away'), and the verbal expression is interpreted as COPULA + ADJECTIVE because its time reference is the same as that of the paraphrase *leur problème est soulagé.*

In narratives where the speaker is recounting past events, the copula in the *imparfait* accompanied with an adjective represents a state that prevailed at the time of the past events, as in the following sentence:

(18) A ce moment-là, mes parents étaient partis en Europe puis eu . . . je sortais pas. (117.381) 'At the time my parents were away in Europe and, uh . . . I didn't go out.'

The expression *à ce moment-là* refers to a specific time in the past. It is associated with a verbal expression in the imperfect (*je sortais pas*). Moreover in the proposition *mes parents étaient partis en Europe,* the time of departure of the parents was before the state described and has no importance at the time evoked in the narrative. We interpret the verbal expression of this proposition as follows: COPULA (in the imperfect) + ADJECTIVE. If the sentence had been *à ce moment-là, mes parents sont partis en Europe* 'at that point, my parents left for Europe', the temporal expression would have constituted a marker of reference to the point at which the act was accomplished, as with the examples presented in 2.1.1. Making the distinction thus requires taking into account the discursive sequence in which the sentence under consideration is situated. The importance of this becomes even more apparent in the following section.

2.1.3. *Temporal Relations Involved in the Sentence*
In order to distinguish between reference to an action or to an ensuing state when the reference point is not indicated by any adverbial markers, prepositional phrases or sentence paraphrases, we must examine the temporal relations within complex sentences. For example, there are two possible readings of verbal expressions following *quand,* depending on the tense of the verb in the higher sentence.

When the verb of the higher sentence is in a simple (non-*composé*) tense that is the same as the tense of the verb *être*[6] in the sentence embedded under *quand,* this verb is interpreted as a copula

6. As we mentioned in section 2 above, we find only *être,* not *avoir,* in "resulting state" contexts.

and not as an auxiliary. In this case, the tense of the verb of the higher sentence fixes the reference point after the event and thus serves to indicate that the verbal expression in the embedded sentence conveys a state. This is the case in the following examples. Note that the tense of the copula is always the same as the tense of the verb in the higher sentence: the *présent* in 19, the *imparfait* in 20, the *futur* in 21.

(19) Quand on *est parti* dans une discussion, des fois tu *cherches* des termes. (39, p. 25) 'When you're really into a discussion, sometimes you have to grope for words.'

(20) Quand les gardiens *étaient partis,* là, on *jouait* une bonne partie de la nuit au ballon-balai. (88.769) 'When the caretakers were gone, we played broomball a good part of the night.'

(21) Et puis, elle disait, "Quand je *serai partie,* ma petite, tu *pourras* rien savoir." (57.844) 'And she used to say, "When I'm gone (=dead), my little one, you won't be able to find out anything."'

In contrast, when the verb of the higher sentence is in any *composé* tense, or in a simple tense other than that of the *être* in the sentence embedded under *quand,* this embedded *être* is interpreted not as a copula but as an auxiliary. The tense of the verb in the higher sentence fixes the reference point at the time at which the *quand* sentence happened, as is demonstrated in the following examples:

(22) Quand elle *est partie* d'ici, sa mère *est venue* la chercher. (78.169) 'When she left here, her mother came to get her.'

(23) J'*avais* ça même quand on *est arrivé* ici à Pointe St-Charles. (51.263) 'I had it even when we arrived here in Point St-Charles.'

(24) Oui, ils *pensaient*—bien, quand ils *ont arrivé* à l'hôpital, fallait, paraît qu'ils le *pensaient* mort. (51.345) 'Yeah, they thought—well, when they got to the hospital—they had to—it seems that they thought he was dead.'

(25) Je pense que ça fait dix, onze ans. Ça *faisait* pas longtemps quand je *suis arrivée* ici, ça *était* ouvert quand j'*ai arrivé* ici moi. (101.306) 'I think it's about ten or eleven years. It hadn't been open long when I arrived here, it was open when I arrived here.'

Not all the combinations of tenses that this interpretive rule implies were found in our data. We found mostly the types of sentences in

22–25, though there were also one or two with both verbs in the *plus que parfait,* referring to the distant past, as in *quand tu étais parti, je t'avais conduit à l'aéroport* ('When you left, I drove you to the airport').

We can summarize the possible combinations for each reading as follows: Reference point at the time of the past act: *composé* tense.

$$1. \left[\underset{s_1}{x + \text{verb}} \left[\begin{smallmatrix} \text{passé composé} \\ \text{imparfait} \end{smallmatrix} \right] + y \left[\underset{s_2}{quand + A + \left\{ \begin{smallmatrix} \hat{e}tre \\ avoir \end{smallmatrix} \right\}}_{[\text{présent}]} \right. \right.$$

$$\left. \left. + \text{ past participle} + \underset{s_2}{B} \right] + \underset{s_1}{Z} \right]$$

$$2. \left[\underset{s_1}{x + \text{verb}_{[\text{plus-que-parf.}]}} + y \left[\underset{s_2}{quand + A + \left\{ \begin{smallmatrix} \hat{e}tre \\ avoir \end{smallmatrix} \right\}}_{[\text{imparfait}]} \right. \right.$$

$$\left. \left. + \text{ past participle} + \underset{s_2}{B} \right] + \underset{s_1}{Z} \right]$$

Reference point after the time of the act: copula + adjective.

$$3. \left[\underset{s_1}{x + \text{verb}_{[\text{tense}]}} + y \left[\underset{s_2}{quand + A + \hat{e}tre}_{[\alpha \text{ tense}]} \right. \right.$$

$$\left. \left. + \text{ past participle} + \underset{s_2}{B} \right] + \underset{s_1}{Z} \right]$$

The feature [tense] in 3 can be either the present, the imparfait, or the future.

2.2. Nontemporal Indices

The nontemporal indices presented in this section are all used to focus on the action itself. In describing the circumstances of an act, they fix the reference point at the time of the act. In making explicit the manner in which an act was accomplished, or in stating the goals of an act, or in providing other circumstantial details, a speaker is pointing to the act itself rather than the resulting state. Indeed, on examining the wider context of discourse, we find that speakers simply do not typically refer to the circumstances of states, whereas they do talk about the circumstances of acts. These nontemporal, circumstantial indices are often supplemented by temporal indices, but as the examples illustrate, they are sufficient, even on their own, to situate the reference point at the time of the act.

All of the nontemporal indices take the form of prepositional phrases, in contrast with the temporal indices, most of which are adverbs. However, not all prepositional phrases indicate a focus on the action itself. Locational specifications, for example, often take the form of prepositional phrases, but supply little information about the modality of an act. Indeed, they are often found in sentences containing indicators that the focus is on "resultant state" (e.g., in examples 2 and 16 above). Thus we have chosen to group the nontemporal indices according to semantic criteria, i.e., according to the question to which they respond.

2.2.1. *Response to the Question "how"*
Here we are concerned with prepositional phrases that indicate manner or instrument. First, a sentence in which the instrumental specification is reinforced by temporal indices:

(26) Quand qu'on a été à Québec, on a parti *à pied*. (23.463) 'When we went to Québec, we left on foot.'

Nevertheless, as we see in 27 and 28, any provision of details about the manner of accomplishing an act is generally sufficient to block a "resulting state" reading:

(27) Ca c'est comme vous, vous rentrez ici, je sais pas, *la manière vous* avez arrivé. (2.1153) 'It's like when you, you come in here—I dunno, the way you arrived.'

(28) Je suis arrivé *comme un cheveu sur la soupe*. (81.33) 'I arrived out of the clear blue sky.'

2.2.2. *Response to the Question "why"*
Another way to accentuate or focus on an act is to state its reasons, its goal, or its cause. This is usually done with a prepositional phrase beginning with *pour* 'for':

(29) J'ai parti de là *pour me marier*. (45.33) 'I left there to get married.'

(30) On est parti de là *pour aller à Pointe-aux-Trembles*. (88.106) 'We left there to go to Pointe-aux-Trembles.'

2.2.3. *Response to the Question "under what circumstances"*
The indices discussed up to this point, though based on semantic criteria, still had well defined surface forms (PP with *pour* or *avec* or *comme,* and so on). In contrast, the markers in this last category are extremely varied. We can only say that they all serve to make precise the circumstances of an act, to furnish the sort of information that prevents us from interpreting the verbal expression as denoting a state resulting from the act. In making an interpretation, it is important to

situate the sentence in its wider context. In sentences 31 and 32, for example, one could not reasonably hold that the person who had fallen was still in the state of being under the bed or the tree, given that 31 is part of a narrative sequence, and in 32 the speaker is sitting on a chair talking to the interviewer:

> (31) Elle a tombé *de son lit en bas,* hein? (72.305) 'She fell out of her bed to the floor, eh?'

> (32) Je suis tombé *en bas d'un arbre.* (117.749) 'I fell out of a tree.'

These last two examples are taken from recountings of accidents:

> (33) Ca ici là, c'est les broches qui ont arrivé *bord en bord de ma jambe.* (51.338) 'This here, that's the staples that went *right through my leg.*'

> (34) Il rentrait au garage mais c'est l'autre qui est arrivé *sur eux-autres.* (44.593) 'He went into the garage but it was the other guy that landed *on top of them.*'

2.3. Indicators of Duration

It is true that states generally perdure longer than acts, and that in general, there is some durative feature associated with states. It is not, however, this durativity that qualifies a verbal expression as a "resulting state." Some acts, by their very nature, are of longer duration than others. The fact that the act of returning on a bicycle in 13 took longer than the act of falling out of bed[7] in 31 is immaterial to the distinction we are interested in.

Recall the discussion of sentences with *quand.* The various combinations of tenses enable us to distinguish between *quand* referring to "the point when" in the case of acts, and *quand* referring to "the period during which" in the case of ensuing states. Duration was thus an important criteria. Nevertheless, durative expressions like *toujours* 'always', *tout le temps* 'all the time', *la plupart du temps* 'most of the time', etc., do not in themselves constitute indices of resulting states. Their value as indicators depends on their relationship with the reference point. Most of these indicators can be employed either as markers of duration or of iterativity. In this latter case, the focus is on the repeated act.

---

7. We can of course imagine contexts where the act of falling is prolonged, e.g., by a parachute. There is also the celebrated case of Alice in Wonderland's fall down the rabbit hole.

Consider the following sentence:

(35) Toutes les fins de semaine en été, on était *toujours* partis. (14.105)

We gloss this as:

'Every weekend during the summer, we were always away.'

rather than

'We always left on weekends during the summer.'

Our reasons are as follows. Suppose we were to substitute *on partait toujours* for *on était toujours partis*. In this case, *toujours* would definitely be read iteratively ('we always left'), but it would in fact be the use of the imperfect that marked iterativity—the adverb *toujours* could be eliminated and the sentence would still have the punctual, iterative reading. In 35, however, we interpret the verbal expression in terms of a state mainly because of the specification 'on weekends', which, in combination with the verb *être* in the imperfect, situates the act of departure before the reference point. The sentence points to absence during the weekends, absence created by the regular act of departure at the beginning of each weekend period.

2.4. Application of the Criteria to Other Sentence Types

The reader will have noticed that the example sentences presented up to this point have all been in the affirmative. In addition, almost all the examples of sentences focusing on "acts," have been in the *passé composé*. This was a deliberate choice on our part in illustrating the application of the various criteria, first, because the majority of sentences we considered were in fact in the affirmative, *passé composé*, and second, in order to facilitate comparison between the sentences. In this section, we devote our attention to some of these other sentence types.

2.4.1. *Tenses Other than the* PASSÉ COMPOSÉ

Sentences conjugated in tenses other than the *passé composé* deserve some attention despite their rarity (they constitute only 5 percent of all the sentences analyzed). When the motion verbs that we studied are conjugated in the pluperfect or the future perfect (*plus-que-parfait* and *futur antérieur*), they do not refer to acts unless they are situated within a narrative sequence that consists of a series of verbs in the tense in question. Otherwise, as we saw in 2.1.3 and 2.3, they get a "resulting state" reading.

There is one tense in which the accent is systematically placed on the act itself. This is the *conditionnel passé* (past conditional). In 36, this interpretation is reinforced by the use of *tout de suite* 'right away', which punctualizes:

(36) En avoir vu une, j'aurais déménagé *tout de suite*. (96.81) 'If I'd seen one, I would have moved right away.'

Here the fact that the act is hypothetical in no way detracts from the "act" reading—indeed, it enhances it. Thus *tout de suite* is not the only indicator. *En avoir vu une* 'had I seen one' also directs attention to the act itself. Had the speaker seen a suitable house, the act of moving would have ensued. The reference point is thus the time of the hypothetical act. A "resulting state" interpretation is completely blocked. In all cases of the *conditionnel passé* that we looked at, there is a specification of the hypothetical circumstances in which an act would have occurred. These cases are similar to those described in 2.2.3, where it is the description of the circumstances of an act that indicates the reference point.

2.4.2. *Sentences Other than Affirmative*

Interrogative sentences were relatively easy to deal with, keeping in mind the problem of establishing the reference point in relation to the time of the act. In 37, the specific time of the act is being questioned, and there is no doubt that the focus is on the act itself:

(37) Marie, *à quel âge* que tu es arrivée à Montréal? (89.3) 'Marie, how old were you when you came to Montréal?'

Direct questions like 37 are fairly rare in our corpus, and we will not discuss them further here. Note in passing that the criteria apply in the same way to indirect questions:

(38) Je sais pas *à quel âge* qu'il est arrivé à Montréal. (5.176) 'I don't know how old he was when he came to Montréal.'

The case of negative sentences is somewhat similar to those in the past conditional (cf. 2.4.1). Before treating the effect of the negation on the potential aspectual distinction, we must consider the scope of the quantifier. In some sentences, it is not the verb but a complement that is negated. In 39, for example, it is clear that the person did arrive and that the *pas* 'not' applies to the prepositional phrase *dans un bien bon temps* 'at a very good time'. *Dans un (pas) bien bon temps* thus constitutes a response to the question "when," since it puts the accent on the precise time at which an act took place, and thus resembles the cases described in 2.1.1.

(39) Vous avez pas arrivé *dans un bien bon temps,* je suis pas habillée. (51.188) 'You didn't come at a very good time, I'm not dressed.'

In the more frequent cases where the quantifier applies to the verb, the problem is not to establish a distinction between the negation of an action and the negation of the state that results from it, but rather to distinguish between a nonaction and the state results from this nonaction. The markers that indicate focus on an act that took place are similarly applicable to an act that might have, but did not, take place. In 40, we have an indicator of cause (response to the question "why"), which focuses on the precise moment of the nonact, rather than the state that ensues from this act's not having taken place:

(40) Ils m'ont donné une place pour que je rentre dans l'hôpital puis j'ai pas rentré . . . *parce que j'ai pas voulu me faire opérer.* (72.531) 'They gave me a place in the hospital but I didn't go in . . . because I didn't want to have the operation.'

Compare with a case in which the focus is on a state that resulted from a nonact. In 41, the result of not having accomplished an act would have grave consequences for the individual in question:

(41) Puis si elle était pas rentrée *à minuit une,* elle sortait pas pour une semaine. (67.252) 'And if she wasn't in at one minute after midnight, she wasn't allowed out for a week.'

This sentence was analyzed according to the same criteria of temporal concordance that were used to identify the "resulting state" sentences in 2.1.2.

To complete our discussion of negatives, consider the following sentences that contain an indicator specific to negatives, the adverb *jamais* 'never'.

(42) Puis après ça, je suis plus *jamais* rentré dans les pavillons. (113.290) 'And after that, I never went back to the pavillions.'

(43) Puis j'ai dit—on a tellement détesté les Vêpres, puis l'église—à cause de ça qu'on est *jamais* retourné aux Vêpres. (47.322) 'And I said—we so detested going to vespers, and the church—that's why we never went back to vespers.'

Jamais in both cases is interpreted as 'not a single time', and thus can be identified with the indices of iterativity in affirmative sentences.

2.4.3. Special Cases

We found only a dozen cases at most for which we could agree intuitively that the focus was on either the act or the ensuing state, but for which we couldn't specify any particular indices such as those presented in the preceding sections. One such sentence is:

(44) Après qu'on a passé ça là, notre rage est passée il me semble. (16.319) 'After you've been through that, your anger is all gone, it seems to me.'

It seemed to us that the proposition *notre rage est passée* describes an ensuing state, though we could specify no formal criteria as to why this reading should be the preferred one. In the few cases like this, we based our classificatory decision on the fact that our intuitions were in agreement, and were thankful that there were not too many of them.

2.5. "Resulting State" and Auxiliary Variation

At the beginning of section 2.0, we pointed out the parallel between "resulting state" constructions consisting of AUXILIARY + PAST PARTICIPLE, and COPULA + ADJECTIVE constructions. This equivalence was thought to hold only for cases where the auxiliary was *être*. We have, however, found two cases where *avoir* is used in constructions analyzed as "resulting state," as follows:

(45) Mettons que j'aurais parti *cinq ans*. (52.318) 'Let's say I'd have been away for five years.'

(46) Mais *maintenant, eu,* . . . bah! ça a passé. (113.281) 'But now, uh, . . . well, it's gone.'

On the basis of only two cases, we think it would be somewhat hasty to conclude that *avoir* can fill the copula role, though we note that there are copula-like constructions with *avoir* in French, e.g., *avoir faim* 'to have hunger' = 'be hungry'; *il y a,* existential 'there exists', etc.)

2.6. Composé Tenses and Variation

In the cases we have identified as focusing on the act itself, i.e., the cases of *composé* tenses rather than COPULA + ADJECTIVE, we find considerable variation between the two auxiliaries in parallel contexts. The following sentence constitutes a striking illustration; with a switch in auxiliary from *a parti* to *est parti:*

(47) Dans un sens quand elle *a parti,* ça m'a fait plus de peine que quand mon père *est parti.* (107.32) 'In a sense when she died, I felt worse than when my father died.'

Still, the parallelism of the contexts is not in itself proof of our contention, and we rely on the indicators of action versus resulting state that we have developed throughout section 2. We hope to have demonstrated in

329

this section that the distinction between an action and an ensuing state corresponds to a difference in the temporal point of reference. The result of this analysis is that in sentences where the focus is on the act itself, there can be no question of any aspectual nuance being marked. In this context, then, we can consider variation between *avoir* and *être* as two variants of the variable "auxiliary,"[8] and proceed to a systematic examination of their distribution. This will be the topic of section 3.

2.7. Potentially Ambiguous Sentences
There exist in our corpus some sentences that contain no aspectual indices and for which the point of reference is difficult to establish. When these sentences are constructed with the auxiliary *être*, they are potentially ambiguous. In these cases, it is possible to interpret them either as sentences in a *composé* tense, where the focus is on the action itself (that is, when the reference point coincides with the time of the event), or as sentences constructed of a COPULA + ADJECTIVE that focus on the state resulting from the action or process (that is, when the time of the event is situated earlier than the point of reference). In this type of sentence, where the reference point is difficult to establish, the same speaker may alternate between the two auxiliaries. With no other temporal or aspectual indicators, the choice of *avoir* still gives an unambiguous reading, since it always expresses a past tense. With *être*, however, the reading of the sentence can remain ambiguous. Compare the following sentences:

(48) On les voit plus—soit qu'ils travaillent ou ils ont déménagé. (6.100) 'We don't see them any more—whether it's because they're working or because they $\left\{ \begin{array}{l} \text{moved} \\ \text{have moved} \end{array} \right\}$,

(49) Tous ceux qui restaient sur la rue ici sont tous déménagés. (6.533) 'All those who used to live on the street here $\left\{ \begin{array}{l} \text{moved} \\ \text{have moved} \\ \text{are gone} \end{array} \right\}$.'

In sections 2.5 and 2.6 we established that only *être*, never *avoir*, is found in the "resulting state" environment. Thus in 48, *ont déménagé* is definitely to be construed as a passé composé, though like all other *passé composé*, the preterit/perfective tense distinction is neutralized—thus an English gloss of 'moved' or 'have moved' may be

8. On the concepts of variable and variants, see Labov 1969: 738, and chapter 3 above.

equally valid. But the copula or "resulting state" reading is blocked. With *être*, however, as in *sont déménagés* of 49, the copula reading is perfectly possible: 'are moved', like 'are gone', or 'are elsewhere'. We feel that for some verbs not discussed here, e.g., *changer* 'to change', the presence of *être* categorically gives a copula reading, but that for those we deal with in this paper, *être* can be either copula or auxiliary.

3. THE VERBS

This section will be devoted to the study of the distribution of *être* and *avoir* as **auxiliaries** for the various verbs we studied. This implies, of course, the prior elimination of all the "copula" contexts as described in section 2. Note that for the stative verbs *rester* and *demeurer*, the distinction between "act" and "ensuing state" is not appropriate. These verbs will be discussed separately in 3.4.

Before proceeding to examine the two main subgroups of verbs, we present an overview of all the verbs studied (with the exception of *rester* and *demeurer*). Table 15-1 shows all of the uses of these verbs in all the various tenses for the 119 individuals who used them (one person did not use any of these verbs in a *composé* tense throughout the

Verbs	I. copula	II. "ambiguous"	III. *composé* tenses			
			avoir	être	% avoir	prob. of avoir
1. aller	—	—	3	401	0.7	.002
revenir	3[a]	25[a]	4	72	6.5	.004
venir	—	12[a]	24	317	7.0	.01
arriver	11	30	45	381	9.0	.04
entrer	1	2	1	15	6.0	.07
2. partir	56	36	54	94	36.0	.37
retourner	—	2	17	20	46.0	.57
descendre	—	2	8	8	50.0	.66
monter	2	3	19	9	68.0	.71
sortir	10	21	70	32	67.0	.76
rentrer	7	10	68	24	74.0	.81
tomber	—	7	48	19	72.0	.85
déménager	1	10	70	32	70.0	.85
passer	17	9	92	10	90.0	.96

TABLE 15-1. Distribution of *avoir* and *être* for all verbs except *rester* and *demeurer*.

[a] Estimates based on 40 interviews.

recorded interview).[9] Not only is it clear that the frequency of the use of *avoir* varies considerably from verb to verb (from 0.7 percent to 90 percent), but that the number of "copula" and "potentially ambiguous" cases also varies, as we can see from comparing, say, *aller* with *partir* or *sortir*.

The first stage in the statistical analysis of the alternation between *avoir* and *être* in contexts we had analyzed as *composé* tenses consisted of simultaneously estimating (1) the tendencies of each of the speakers to use the two auxiliaries and (2) the tendencies of the different verbs to be conjugated with each of the two auxiliaries. This calculation, using the variable rule model (cf. Cedergren and Sankoff 1974; Rousseau and Sankoff 1978), gave us the "probability" figures in the last column of Table 15-1. They indicate the probability of using *avoir* for each of the verbs. This method of estimating the probabilities levels the effects of inequalities among the figures for the various speakers, in calculating the effect for each verb.

Given the very great differences in the use of *avoir* for the various verbs, it seemed likely that the meanings or syntactic features of the verbs themselves might influence the variation. We shall treat this question according to the two subgroups of Table 15-1, subgroupings that correspond to differences in the syntactic distributions of the verbs, as well as to a rather marked difference in the probability of *avoir* use. The stative verbs *rester* and *demeurer* will be treated separately.

3.1. *Aller, revenir, venir, arriver,* and *entrer*
All the verbs of this group are very much less frequently conjugated with *avoir* than are the other verbs we studied, as is clear from Table 15-1.[10] Indeed, examining these data in detail, we find that for *aller, revenir, venir* and *entrer,* only 11 of the 119 individuals in our sample used *avoir* at all. These 11 speakers are found among the 13 individuals of the first subgroup of Table 15-2. All of the other speakers who had occasion to use these verbs in *composé* tenses restricted themselves to *être*. And even among those speakers who did sometimes use *avoir* in

9. We listened to approximately a third of these recordings in order to locate all the examples of the verbs in which we were interested. For the remainder of the interviews, we relied on the transcriptions carefully corrected by Suzanne Laberge. We listened to any examples that seemed at all unusual. Thus, for example, we listened to all the cases of *avoir* for the verbs *aller, revenir, venir,* and *entrer*. A total of approximately twenty cases were excluded because of phonetic problems, e.g., the difficulty of distinguishing *a* from *est*.

10. The ordering of these verbs among themselves is of little importance, given the very slight differences among the probabilities.

TABLE 15-2. Use of the two auxiliaries in all *composé* tenses, for six subgroups of the 119 speakers. For each verb, *avoir* is the left-hand column; *être* in the right-hand column. The stepwise diagonal indicates scaling.

Number of speakers	aller		revenir		venir		entrer		arriver		partir		retourner		descendre		monter		sortir		rentrer		tomber		rester		déménager		passer		demeurer	
13	3	22	4	5	24	17	1	—	14	12	8	3	1	—	1	—	1	1	11	1	6	—	6	—	30	1	8	1	6	—	8	—
13	—	29	—	13	—	62	—	2	28	32	12	2	2	1	—	3	3	1	8	3	24	—	12	3	30	5	17	—	16	1	12	1
21	—	77	—	12	—	87	—	1	—	111	30	14	14	—	4	—	12	1	21	6	20	2	12	3	64	5	13	3	23	2	12	1
23	—	97	—	30	—	67	—	2	—	86	—	26	—	4	1	2	2	3	28	9	15	1	5	3	35	12	17	7	25	2	17	—
20	—	63	—	7	—	44	—	3	3	57	3	26	—	8	—	2	1	2	—	6	2	13	13	6	38	15	13	4	10	2	12	—
29	—	113	—	5	—	40	—	7	—	83	1	23	—	5	—	4	—	2	2	7	1	8	—	4	—	17	2	17	12	3	3	—

conjugating these verbs, the majority used *être* most of the time. The variation for one such speaker is illustrated in the following example:

(50) J'ai manqué souvent cet hiver, *j'ai pas allé* à cause on a eu tellement de mauvais temps, hein? Là, non, *je suis pas allé* cet hiver, moi. (101.292–93). 'I was absent often this winter, I didn't go because we had such bad weather, eh? No, I didn't go this winter.'

Insofar as *arriver* is concerned, twice this number of speakers occasionally use *avoir* in its conjugation (20 of the 25 individuals in the first two subgroups of Table 15-2). Here again, very few of them use *avoir* categorically. Sentences 23 and 24, as well as 25, illustrate the variation in auxiliary use with *arriver* on the part of a single speaker.

It remains the case, however, that the use of *avoir* seems to be blocked for most speakers in conjugating these five verbs. Interestingly, none of them appears in the lists of verbs that, according to prescriptive grammars, may take, or may in the past have taken, *avoir*. What, then, do they have in common?

We notice first that it is almost impossible to use the participles of *aller* or *venir* in expressing a state. We have no COPULA + ADJECTIVE uses for either of them, and only a few AMBIGUOUS cases for *venir*. *Aller* is the only verb that has no AMBIGUOUS cases at all. This is in accord with the nongrammaticality of using the past participle of *aller* adjectivally. In Montréal French, a sentence like 51 would be much more acceptable than 52, which was found to be totally ungrammatical by all of the people with whom we discussed the matter:[11]

(51)? Un voyageur *arrivé* (d'un long voyage) est souvent content de retrouver son pays. 'An arrived traveler is often happy to return to his own country.' or 'A traveler, arrived from a long journey . . .'

(52) *Un enfant *allé* (à l'école après une longue maladie) est souvent content de retrouver ses copains. 'A child gone (to school after a long illness) is often happy to rediscover her friends.'

Though neither of these sentences sounds very acceptable in English, Montréal French speakers found that 51, especially when accompanied by the adverbial support 'from a long journey', was fairly acceptable.

11. Blanche has applied this type of test to all of our verbs and seems to find differences between her dialect and the Montréal dialect discussed here as to the acceptability of the sentences.

They had no trouble at all, however, in accepting the past participle of a verb like *sortir* as an adjective, even without adverbial support:

(53) Après minuit, les pensionnaires *sortis* ne peuvent plus rentrer. 'Boarders out after midnight cannot get back in.'

It seems, therefore, that the motion verbs of Table 15-1 can be hierarchized according to the possibility of using their past participles as adjectives in order to express a state, and that this hierarchy is related to the acceptability of using *avoir* in their conjugation. The greater the possibility of using the past participle as an adjective in expressing a state, the greater the likelihood of the verb being conjugated with *avoir* in *composé* tenses. The verbs that offer the strongest resistance to the use of *avoir* in the *composé* tense conjugations are precisely those whose participles can only with difficulty be used to express states.

We have found it impossible to make clean cuts in this hierarchy. The scale of Table 15-2 shows certain thresholds at which the relationship between *avoir* and *être* is reversed. *Aller* is clearly situated at one extremity, and *revenir* (probability the closest to *aller*: .004 and .002 respectively) acts like *venir* (probability .01). We shall not discuss *entrer* because of its systematic replacement with *rentrer* by most Montrealers (cf. section 3.2). The fact that *entrer* is employed mainly by members of the bourgeoisie explains both its very low frequency in our data and its infinitesimal probability of being conjugated with *avoir*. As for *arriver*, we have already mentioned that of the verbs in its group, it is the most likely to be useable in expressing a state, as in the following example:

(54) Bien là, vu que l'été *est arrivé*, bien on va se baigner chez une de mes amies. (69.65) 'Well, now that summer's here, we'll go swimming at my girlfriend's place.'

3.2. *Partir, retourner, descendre, monter, sortir, rentrer, tomber, déménager, passer*
These verbs are very different from those discussed in 3.1. Compared with them, the participles of this class of verbs can much more easily be used as adjectives to express a state. Thus, there are many more cases in the "copula" and "ambiguous" columns of Table 15-1. Moreover, all of these verbs have transitive uses. The *Petit Robert* cites them as transitives as well as intransitives, with examples like *rentrer les foins*

'take in the hay' and *retourner une lettre* 'return a letter'.[12] Here are three examples from our corpus:

(54) En Corée, j'ai—, on a jamais descendu un Chinois. (95.683)
'In Korea, I—, we never killed a Chinese.'

(55) . . . qui est-ce qui aurait pas monté la chaudière en haut.
(7.541) '. . . who wouldn't have taken the boiler up.'

(56) Il a sorti Chartrand du trou combien de fois? (2.689) 'How many times has he gotten Chartrand out of the hole?'

Because *avoir* is categorically used with transitive verbs, we omitted cases like 54–56 from our compilations, and counted only intransitives.[13]

To claim that the transitive uses with *avoir* have an influence on the intransitives would be to postulate some kind of analogy operating on the intransitives.[14] This explanation would not, however, cover the cases of *avoir* being extended to verbs that cannot be used transitively, like *arriver* or *venir*.

We are at a loss to explain the special case of *partir*, which, in terms of its probability of taking *avoir*, is quite distinct from the other members of the second group. It is equally used transitively, and its participle seems to adjectivize as readily as the other participles in the group (*parti* is currently used adjectivally to mean 'high' or 'stoned').

Whether the adjectival hierarchy or the transitivity explanation seems to carry the more weight in explaining why different verbs are more or less susceptible to conjugation with *avoir*, there remains much that is arbitrary about the short list of verbs for which *être* is prescribed. Other verbs in French that have the same semantic characteristics are nevertheless conjugated with *avoir*, as is the case, for example, with the verb *grimper* 'to climb'.

3.3. Rester, demeurer

Rester and *demeurer* are stative verbs. Semantically, they express the absence of movement. The opposition between *arriver* and *partir*, be-

12. Of these, only *tomber* is not used transitively in Québec, where one speaks of dropping something as *échapper*, or sometimes *laisser tomber*. Also, the semantic extension of *partir* is much greater in Québec, being used for things like starting a car or a business.

13. Note that in the passive voice, a transitive verb takes the same form as the adjectival use of a past participle with intransitives. The result of the act described in 55 would be *la chaudière est montée en haut* 'the boiler is (has been) taken up'. We took care not to include any such cases in our data, and most of the sentences we analyzed had animate subjects.

14. Canale et al. (1978) propose this explanation in studying the extension of *avoir* to the classical *être* verbs by speakers of French in Ontario (1978).

tween *entrer* and *sortir, aller,* and *venir* has to do with directionality, but at another level, all these verbs are opposed to *rester* and *demeurer,* since they all have to do with movement rather than its absence.

The aspectual distinction used in separating *composé* tenses from COPULA + PAST PARTICIPLE cases for the motion verbs had to do with a movement/nonmovement distinction (the resulting state of the "copula" cases involving lack of movement). The relevant distinction in the case of the stative verbs has little to do with this opposition. In fact the preponderant use of both of these verbs is as synonyms for the verb *habiter* ('to live'), a verb always conjugated with *avoir*.[15] If all of the instances of *rester* and *demeurer* in the sense of *habiter* were conjugated with *avoir,* we could assume that the variation is limited to other contexts. This is, however, not the case, for one finds examples like:

(54) Mais un mois après, on est parti puis on *est resté* juste en haut sur Mentana là-bas, juste en face du Parc Laurier. *J'ai resté* là jusqu'à six ans. (39.11–12) 'But a month later, we left and then we lived just above there, over on Mentana, right across from Laurier Park. I lived there till I was six years old.'

How do we account for the high rate of use of *avoir* for these verbs of state? (cf. Table 15-2). For *rester* and *demeurer,* the aspectual distinction of section 2 does not apply. It could hardly be relevant to distinguish here between an action and the resulting state. We find, however, that it is possible to distinguish between a state that is terminated and a state that persists up to the reference point. The cases which correspond to the *composé* tenses for movement verbs are those in which the state is terminated prior to the reference point. Most of these sentences contain a specification of duration:

(55) Il est resté ah! *34 jours* à l'Institut de Cardiologie. (8.373) 'He stayed, oh, 34 days at the Inst. of Cardiology.'

(56) Il a resté *une semaine* aux soins intensifs là, . . . (8.374) 'He stayed a week in intensive care, there, . . .'

The parallel established here between the aspectual distinction relevant for the motion verbs and the more properly temporal distinction relevant for the stative verbs is by no means artificial. The recognition of a particular case as being a state terminated before the reference point makes use of similar criteria as are required in indicating, for the movement verbs, a focus on the action itself. The analogy between the "continuing state" and the "copula" contexts is also clear. There are,

15. On the distribution of verbs of "habitation," cf. Sankoff, Thibault, and Bérubé 1978.

however, two major differences between stative verbs and the motion verbs discussed in section 2.

First, we do not consider there to be any "ambiguous" contexts for stative verbs. When there is no clear indication that a state has been terminated, we assume that it persists.[16] Consider the following examples:

(57) Depuis la naissance, j'ai toujours demeuré à Montréal. (103.4) 'Since I was born, I've always lived in Montréal.'

(58) Eu . . . on est demeuré . . . à Ahuntsic, on a dé . . . bien, là-bas, bien j'ai, . . . je suis toujours dans Ahuntsic. (11.25) 'Uh . . . we stayed . . . in Ahuntsic, we mo . . . well, there, well, I, . . . I'm still in Ahuntsic.'

In the second sentence, it seems that the final explanation 'I'm still in Ahuntsic' reinforces the current-state reference of the first verb, *est demeuré*. But this state is indissociable from its beginning. It is not, like the past participles of the motion verbs, the *result* of a completed action. Rather, it is the continuation of a state. It is rare to have an "enduring state" case of a stative verb without some associated marker of continuity, such as *toujours* 'always, still' in 57. For a stative verb in the *passé composé,* the distinction corresponds to that made by Benveniste between the aorist and the perfect, as discussed in section 1 above. Since, as we stated in section 2, the *passé composé* has taken over the *passé simple* (aorist) usages, the "enduring state" cases cannot, then, be excluded from the paradigm of the *composé* tenses. There is no transformation of an action into a state; rather, there is persistence of a state, with neutralization, in this latter case, of whether the focus is on the inception of the state or its current continuation.

Second, we find that the variation between *être* and *avoir* is not confined to the cases of "state terminated in the past." Rather, it exists in both contexts, including that of perduring states, as we see in Table 15-3.

In Montréal French, then, the conjugation with *avoir* is very frequently used when reference is being made to a terminated state. *Avoir* is even used when referring to states perduring through the point of reference, though very much less frequently. *Etre* is more strongly maintained in this latter context.

16. For an interesting parallel, Bickerton in discussing tense and aspect markers in Guyanese Creole says that when a stative verb is not accompanied by any other marker, one presumes that "the state of liking, wanting, knowing or whatever, though it may have commenced in the past, would still be in existence at the present moment" (Bickerton 1975b: 46).

Auxiliary	State terminated in the past		State perduring through the point of reference	
	rester	*demeurer*	*rester*	*demeurer*
avoir	197	64	41	5
être	55	2	45	6
Total	252	66	86	11

TABLE 15-3. Distribution of *avoir* and *être* for stative verbs.

4. SOCIAL DISTRIBUTION OF THE VARIATION

In the previous sections, we have established that:

1) For all verbs, it is possible to establish a distinction between reference to an act or state terminated prior to the point of reference, and reference to a state (in the case of verbs of movement, a state resulting from the act) that perdures through the point of reference.

2) The verbs differ among themselves as to how this distinction affects the use of *avoir* and *être*. For the verbs of motion, reference to an act in the past is analyzed as a *composé* tense in which there is variation between the two auxiliaries, whereas reference to the state that ensues from the act and which perdures through the point of reference is analyzed as COPULA + ADJECTIVE. Here only *être* is possible. These verbs are divided into two subclasses according to whether or not the participle can readily be used adjectivally, a distinction that also corresponds to the possible transitive use of the verbs. Those verbs that can be used transitively, and whose past participles are readily used as adjectives, are much more likely to be conjugated with *avoir* when referring to an act in the past. For stative verbs, there is alternation between *avoir* and *être* in both contexts, although the "perduring state" context seems less hospitable to *avoir*.

We now examine the differences among speakers with regard to the use of the two auxiliaries. Table 15-2 showed that there were differences, since we were able to isolate groups of speakers who seemed more or less willing to use *avoir* with various classes of verbs. In this section, we attempt to investigate just how great are these differences among speakers, and what might explain them.

4.1. Application of the Variable Rule

The variable rule method (cf. section 3 above) enabled us to estimate the tendency of each speaker to use each of the two auxiliaries, taking into account that the verbs themselves show different weightings for *avoir* and *être*.

For each of the 119 speakers who used at least one of these verbs in a *composé* tense, we first evaluated his/her tendency to use *avoir* as a function of his or her situation within the "linguistic market,"[17] as shown in Table 15-4. This table shows that those speakers who figure importantly in the linguistic market (i.e., whose work is somehow language-related: teachers, journalists, lawyers, and so on), whose linguistic production may indeed set standards as to what is considered "legitimate"—these people use *avoir* very little. Thus 83 percent of the 18 speakers with a "linguistic market" index $\geq .76$ have a probability of .33 or less of using *avoir*. Conversely, only 21 percent of speakers with a low linguistic market index ($\leq .33$) have such low probabilities of *avoir* use. More than half of them have a probability of over .67 of using *avoir*.

Insofar as speakers' locations on the linguistic market index are a general indication of their social position, our results show that the higher one is in the social hierarchy, the less likely one is to use *avoir*. We conclude that the alternation between *être* and *avoir* is socially conditioned.

Other aspects of speakers' social position also seem to have an effect on the variation between *avoir* and *être*. More highly educated people (many of whom, of course, are also highly integrated into the linguistic market) tend to use less *avoir*. Men seem to use *avoir* more than women. Holding constant "years of schooling," we find a slight tendency for younger speakers to use more *avoir*, but this tendency doesn't seem strong enough to indicate a real change in progress, especially since young people are spending more and more years in school, an experience that encourages *less* use of *avoir*.

We do not claim that the various components of people's social position are the only things that constrain their use of the two auxiliaries. From what we have already established, it seems that speakers' grammars differ as to the possibility of *avoir* use in the various

---

17. This index was constructed to measure the importance of the mastery of the "legitimate" or standard language (cf. Bourdieu and Boltanski 1975) in the economic life of each person in our sample. It is constructed from an average of the judgments of eight Québec sociolinguists, judgments based on a "work history" for each speaker and his/her family (cf. D. Sankoff and Laberge 1978).

Probability of using *avoir*	"Linguistic market" indices			
	0–.25	.26–.50	.51–.75	.76–1.0
.68–1.00	51%	22%	17%	6%
.34– .67	28%	44%	23%	11%
0– .33	21%	33%	60%	83%
Number of speakers	(53)	(18)	(30)	(18)

TABLE 15-4. The percentage of speakers with high, medium, and low probabilities of using *avoir*, according to their linguistic market indices.

linguistic environments, and that these differences among their grammars are a function of their exposure to the standard language, as well as its importance for them. Nevertheless, it is certainly also the case that people use their grammatical knowledge differently according to the immediate social circumstances. Given that the data for this study come from only one speech situation—an informal interview—we are not able to say much about this social influence on auxiliary production. We did observe two cases where an interviewee appeared to use *être* in direct response to the interviewer's use of *être* in conjugating the same verb in a question, but of course this is difficult to demonstrate conclusively without doing the kind of study especially geared to identifying such influences.

4.2. Speaker Subgroups
Looking more closely at the data from the "past action" or "past state" contexts, we can distinguish three subgroups of speakers:

    i) those who used *avoir* categorically;
    ii) those who used *être* categorically;
    iii) those who used both *avoir* and *être*.

The first two subgroups contain hardly any speakers. Only four speakers were observed to limit themselves to *avoir*, and two of these had so few occurrences that they cannot be treated as significant. As far as *être* is concerned, we found eleven individuals who used only *être*, but only four of them produced enough cases to be considered candidates for categorical *être* users.

Given that the verbs at the two ends of the continuum in Table 15-2 push people very strongly to use *être* (in the case of the verbs on the left) and *avoir* (in the case of the verbs on the right), it is not surprising that there are so few "categorical" speakers. Even a speaker

Number of speakers	*avoir*	*être*
24	+	−
49	+	+
23	−	+

TABLE 15-5. Use of *avoir* and *être* for "action in the past" by the 96 speakers who used the "central" verbs of Table 15-2: (*partir, retourner, descendre, monter, sortir, rentrer*) in *composé* tenses.

with a very strong preference for *avoir*, conjugating a verb like *aller*[18] or *venir*, is hard put not to use *être*. Similarly, those speakers who seem to prefer *être* will still sometimes use *avoir* for a verb like *passer*. If we examine only the six verbs in the middle of Table 15-2 (*partir, retourner, descendre, monter, sortir, rentrer*), however, we still find more "variable" than "categorical" speakers, as shown in Table 15-5.

On the basis of this table, as well as Table 15-2, what should we postulate about the grammars of the various groups of speakers? It would seem that, for the verbs of motion of Table 15-5, the 23 speakers who use only *être* have no markers *in the auxiliary system* to distinguish between action and ensuing state. This is not to say that these people are suffering some cognitive disadvantage, are somehow mentally unable to make the distinction.[19] For them, the aspectual nuance must be expressed by other means. The 24 speakers who use only *avoir* when referring to a past action are different. Their choice between *avoir* and *être* corresponds to the distinction between an action and the ensuing state. They have regularized their auxiliary system such that these *être* verbs of the prescriptive grammars act more like all the other verbs that are regularly conjugated with *avoir*. The largest group of speakers uses *both* auxiliaries in the "action" context, though reserving *être* alone for the "ensuing state." Thus their use of *avoir* is aspectually unambiguous, but their use of *être* can convey either of the two. It is as if they have begun to regularize their auxiliary system, extending the use of *avoir* to more and more verbs in the "action" context, but have not completed the process.

One could speculate about whether the speakers in each pro-

18. Among working class speakers in Montréal, however, the participle *allé* is almost always replaced by *été*, which is conjugated with *avoir*. Thus *je suis allé* is replaced not by *j'ai allé* but by *j'ai été* (cf. D. Sankoff and P. Thibault, in press).

19. Recall that these candidates for "cognitive deficiency" are those people in our sample who had the most education.

gressive "lect" of Table 15-2 actually possess different aspectual categories for the different verbs, since the distinction is often not marked grammatically. The action/ensuing state distinction is not marked morphologically for those speakers who use *être* for both, but what about speakers who begin to use *avoir* with, say, *demeurer, passer, déménager, rester,* and *tomber*? And many speakers vary their usage for the same verb, as we see in the following example, with *partir* being used as a euphemism for dying.

> (47′) Dans un sens quand elle *a parti,* ça m'a fait plus de peine que quand mon père *est parti.* (107.32) 'In a sense when she died, I felt worse than when my father died.'

It seems to us that the aspectual distinction involved can be uncovered elsewhere in the discourse in the vast majority of cases; most speakers do not mark it with their choice of auxiliaries. The more normative the speaker is, the more highly educated and the more highly integrated into the linguistic market, the less likely he or she is to regularize his/her auxiliary system through the extension of *avoir,* thus failing to express morphologically the aspectual distinction that many working class speakers express in this way. The strong social differences we find can be illustrated with the verb *déménager,* which, incidentally, is not considered to require conjugation with *être* in France. Of the 8 people who conjugate *déménager* categorically with *être,* 6 are management personnel or professionals. In contrast, only one of the 7 people who categorically uses *avoir* is not a working class speaker.

For the stative verbs *rester* and *demeurer, avoir* has moved farther, such that even the "perduring state" context sees some use of *avoir.* Extending *avoir* this far would entail the loss of a morphological contrast between completed/noncompleted action or state, the contrast on which the preterit/perfect opposition was formerly based.

5. CONCLUSION

We feel that the use of the auxiliary *avoir* with the verbs we have examined in "action" and "terminated state" contexts represents a tendency toward the regularization of the auxiliary system in French. The small class of verbs for which prescriptive grammars prescribe the exclusive use of *être* seems to us not sufficiently homogeneous nor sufficiently distinct from other verbs to resist this regularization.

The tendency toward the generalization of the auxiliary *avoir* in the *composé* tenses is a process with parallels in many Indo-European languages. Benveniste, in an article on *avoir* and *être,* says "there is no need for two auxiliaries to exist; languages could very well do with only one" (1966: 200). He continues, explaining that in the Indo-European languages with two auxiliaries, an opposition was created between the perfect intransitive with the verb 'to be' and the perfect transitive with 'to have'. The evolution of the perfect transitive in Latin is instructive in this regard. Latin perfect transitive was originally expressed by suffixes on the verb itself. *Esse* 'to be' was the first analytic form to be introduced. The perfect passive underwent an analogous development, but as Benveniste stresses:

> Over time the descriptive form consisting of *past participle* + '*to be*' tended more and more to become the equivalent of a *present* passive, which created conflicts between the form of the perfect active or passive and the expression of a present state with '*to be*' + *verbal adjective*. (1966: 205)

This is, according to Benveniste, the condition which prepared the way for a new expression of the perfect transitive with *habere*. If in Latin, the use of *habere* as an auxiliary allows us to distinguish between examples like "texts that can be found written in such a book" and "texts which were written for such a purpose" (cf. Benveniste 1966: 204), then in French, since the majority of the intransitive verbs are conjugated with *avoir*, it should equally be possible to distinguish between *le livre est brûlé* 'the book is burnt' and *le livre a brûlé* 'the book burned'. However, for the intransitive verbs we examined, most speakers do not systematically use a choice between *être* and *avoir* to mark this distinction. But many of them do seem to have introduced *avoir* for some of the verbs on the right of Table 15-2, which would indeed correspond to the generalization of the grammatical expression of the aspectual distinction, once *être* is abolished from the "preterit" contexts. Whether or not this abolition will take place is not at all certain, given the pressure from the standard language to block the introduction of *avoir*.

Benveniste's discussion clarifies many aspects of the extension of the verb *habere*, but we are not completely in agreement with some of the stronger functionalist implications that seem to derive from his presentation. We would stress that in natural languages, one never finds total correspondence between form and function. Recall that there is no necessity to use auxiliaries to express the aspectual distinction between "action in the past" and "state ensuing from the action." As we have seen, this nuance is often marked by contextual indices other than the auxiliary, and we have identified other cases where it doesn't seem relevant to make the distinction at all.

It is well known that irregularities in language often persist the longest in the most frequent forms. This may help to explain the maintenance of the auxiliary *être* with very common verbs like *aller*, *venir,* and *arriver* (each of these verbs occurs more than 350 times in our data, making them more than twice as frequent in the *composé* tenses as the next runner-up, *partir* with 148). The norm of standard French also contributes to the conservation of *être*. Without claiming that the norm is totally arbitrary, it seems to us obvious that it acts as a brake on the regularization of conjugation through the extension of *avoir* for the small set of verbs we have examined.

Bibliography

ABEL, C. 1977. Missionary lingue franche: Suau. In Wurm, ed. 1977: 971–88.
ABERLE, DAVID. 1960. The influence of linguistics on early culture and personality theory. In G. Dole and R. Carneiro, eds., *Essays in the science of culture*. New York: Crowell, 1–29.
ASHBY, WILLIAM J. 1976. The loss of the negative morpheme *ne* in Parisian French. *Lingua* 39: 119–37.
———. ms., 1977. The status of the negative morpheme *ne* in the French of Tours. Paper read at the Linguistics Society of America annual meeting, 29 December 1977.
BAILEY, BERYL. 1971. Jamaican creole: can dialect boundaries be defined? In Hymes, ed. 1971: 341–48.
BAILEY, CHARLES-JAMES N. 1969–70. Studies in three-dimensional linguistic theory: (1) Some implicational phenomena in dialectology. (2) Implicational scales in diachronic linguistics and dialectology. (3) Lectal groupings in matrices generated with waves defined along the temporal parameter. (4) Mesomodels of linguistic change. University of Hawaii *Working Papers in Linguistics* 1,8: 105–38; 1,10: 245–49; 2,4: 109–24; 2,6: 149–38; 2,8: 1–4.
———. 1970. Building rate into a dynamic theory of linguistic description. University of Hawaii *Working Papers in Linguistics* 2,9: 161–233.
———. 1971. Trying to talk in the new paradigm. University of Hawaii *Working Papers in Linguistics* 3,5: 111–37.
———. 1973. The patterning of language variation. In R. W. Bailey and J. L. Robinson, eds., *Varieties of Present-Day American English*.
BAILEY, CHARLES-JAMES N. and ROGER SHUY, eds. 1973. *New ways of analyzing variation in English*. Washington, D.C.: Georgetown University Press.
BALIBAR, RENEE and DOMINIQUE LAPORTE. 1974. *Le français national: politique et pratique de la langue nationale sous la Révolution*. Paris: Hachette.
BARNES, J. A. 1962. African models in the New Guinea highlands. *Man* 62: 5–9.
BARTON, F. R. 1910. The annual trading expedition to the Papuan Gulf. Chapter 8 of Seligman 1910: 96–120.
BASSO, KEITH, ed. 1979. Portraits of Whitemen. New York. Cambridge University Press.
BEAUMONT, C. H. 1972. New Ireland languages: a review. *Pacific Linguistics* A-35: 1–41.
BEE, DARLENE. 1965. Usarufa distinctive features and phonemes. *Pacific Linguistics* A-6: 39–68.
BENVENISTE, EMILE. 1957–58. La phrase relative, problème de syntaxe générale. *Bulletin de la Société de linguistique de Paris* 53: 39–54. Translated in E. Benveniste, *Problems in General Linguistics,* 1971. Coral Gables: University of Miami Press.
———. 1966. *Problèmes de linguistique générale I*. Paris: Gallimard.

Bibliography

——. 1974. *Problèmes de linguistique générale II*. Paris: Gallimard.
BERLIN, BRENT. 1972. Speculations on the growth of ethnobotanical nomenclature. *Language in Society* 1: 51–86.
BERLIN, BRENT and PAUL KAY. 1969. *Basic color terms: their universality and evolution*. Berkeley and Los Angeles: University of California Press.
BERNDT, CATHERINE H. 1954. Translation problems in three New Guinea Highland languages. *Oceania* 24: 289–317.
BERNDT, R. M. 1962. *Excess and restraint*. Chicago: University of Chicago Press.
BEVER, T. G. 1970. The cognitive basis for linguistic structures. In John R. Hayes, ed., *Cognition and the development of language*. New York: Wiley, 279–352.
BEVER, T. G. and D. T. LANGENDOEN. 1971. A dynamic model of the evolution of language. *Linguistic Inquiry* 2: 433–63.
BICKERTON, DEREK. 1971. Inherent variability and variable rules. *Foundations of Language* 7: 457–92.
——. 1974. Creolization, linguistic universals, natural semantics and the brain. University of Hawaii *Working Papers in Linguistics* 6, 3: 125–41.
——. 1975a. Can English and Pidgin be kept apart? In McElhanon, ed. 1975: 21–27.
——. 1975b. *Dynamics of a creole system*. London: Cambridge University Press.
BLACK, MARY. 1969. Eliciting folk taxonomies in Ojibwa. In S. Tyler, ed. 1969a: 165–89.
BLANCHE, CLAIRE. 1977. L'un chasse l'autre: le domaine des auxiliaires. *In Recherches sur le français parlé*. Groupe aixois de recherche en syntaxe. Aix: Université de Provence, 100–148.
BLOCH, B. 1948. A set of postulates for phonemic analysis. *Language* 24: 3–46.
BLOM, J. P. and J. J. GUMPERZ. 1972. Social meaning in linguistic structures: code-switching in Norway. In J. J. Gumperz and D. Hymes, eds. 1972: 407–34.
BOURDIEU, PIERRE and LUC BOLTANSKI. 1975. Le fétichisme de la langue. *Actes de la Recherche en Sciences Sociales,* juillet, no. 4, 2–32.
BRADSHAW, JOEL. in press. Multilingualism and language mixture among the Numbami. *Kivung* 11.
BRASH, ELTON. 1971. Tok pilai, tok piksa na tok bokis. *Kivung* 4: 1–20.
BROMLEY, MYRON. 1967. The linguistic relationships of Grand Valley Dani: a lexico-statistical classification. *Oceania* 37: 286–308.
BROOKFIELD, H. C. and PAULA BROWN. 1963. *Struggle for land*. Melbourne: Oxford University Press.
BROWN, H. A. 1977. Missionary lingue franche: Toaripi. In Wurm, ed. 1977: 989–99.
BROWN, PAULA and H. C. BROOKFIELD. 1959. Chimbu land and society. *Oceania* 30: 1–75.
BROWN, PENELOPE and STEPHEN LEVINSON. 1978. Universals in language usage: politeness phenomena. In E. Goody, ed., *Questions and politeness*. London: Cambridge University Press, 56–289.
BROWN, R. and A. GILMAN. 1960. The pronouns of power and solidarity. In T. A. Sebeok, ed., *Style in language*. Cambridge, Mass.: The Technology Press, 253–76.

Bibliography

BRUNEL, GILLES. 1970. Le français radiophonique à Montréal. M.A. Thesis, Université de Montréal.

BRUNOT, F. 1922. *La pensée et la langue*. Paris: Masson.

BRUNOT, F. and C. BRUNEAU. 1949. *Précis de grammaire historique de la langue française*. 5th ed. Paris: Masson.

BURKE, KENNETH. 1950. *A rhetoric of motives*. Englewood Cliffs, New Jersey: Prentice-Hall.

BURRIDGE, K. O. L. 1957. The *gagai* in Tangu. *Oceania* 28: 56–72.

CAMDEN, REV. W. G. 1975. Parallels in the structure of lexicon and syntax between New Hebrides Bislama and the South Santo language spoken at Tangoa. Paper read at the 1975 International Conference on Pidgins and Creoles, University of Hawaii, 66 pp.

CANALE, MICHAEL, RAYMOND MOUGEON, and MONIQUE BÉLANGER. 1978. Analogical levelling of the auxiliary *être* in Ontarian French. In Margaret Suñer, ed., *Studies in Romance linguistics*. Washington, D.C.: Georgetown University Press.

CAPELL, ARTHUR. 1949. Two tonal languages of New Guinea. *Bulletin of the Society for Oriental and African Studies* 13: 184–99.

———. 1962. A linguistic survey of the South Western Pacific. *South Pacific Technical Paper* no. 136. Noumea, New Caledonia.

———. 1971. The Austronesian languages of Australian New Guinea. In T. A. Sebeok, ed., *Current trends in linguistics, 8*. The Hague: Mouton, 240–340.

CARROLL, J. D. and J. J. CHANG. 1970. Analysis of individual differences in multidimensional scaling via an N-way generalization of Eckart-Young decomposition. *Psychometrika* 35: 283–319.

CEDERGREN, HENRIETTA. 1972. Interplay of social and linguistic factors in Panama. Ph.D. dissertation, Cornell University.

———. 1973. On the nature of variable constraints. In C. J. Bailey and R. Shuy, eds. 1973: 13–22.

CEDERGREN, H. J. and S. LABERGE. 1972. Les règles variables du *que* explétif dans le français parlé à Montréal. Paper read at the annual meeting of the Canadian Linguistic Association.

CEDERGREN, HENRIETTA and DAVID SANKOFF. 1974. Variable rules: performance as a statistical reflection of competence. *Language* 50: 333–55.

CHOMSKY, N. 1957. *Syntactic structures*. The Hague: Mouton.

CHOWNING, ANN. 1969. The Austronesian languages of New Britain. *Pacific Linguistics* A-21: 17–45.

CHURCHILL, WILLIAM. 1911. Beach-la-Mar, the jargon or trade speech of the Western Pacific. Carnegie Institution of Washington, Publication no. 164.

CLAASSEN, O. R. and K. A. McELHANON. 1970. Languages of the Finisterre Range—New Guinea. *Pacific Linguistics* A-23: 45–78.

CONKLIN, H. C. 1964. Ethnogenealogical method. In Goodenough 1964: 25–55.

COOK, E. A. 1966. Narak: language or dialect? *Journal of the Polynesian Society* 75: 437–44.

CORRIS, PETER. 1973. *Passage, port and plantation. A history of Solomon Islands labour migration 1870–1914*. Melbourne: Melbourne University Press.

D'ANGLEJAN-CHATILLON, A. 1975. Dynamics of second language developments: a search for linguistic regularity. Ph.D. dissertation, McGill University.

DAOUST-BLAIS, DENISE. 1975. L'influence de la négation sur certains indéfinis en français québécois. Ph. D. dissertation, Université de Montréal.

DAY, RICHARD. 1973. Patterns of variation in copula and tense in the Hawaiian post-creole continuum. Ph.D. dissertation, University of Hawaii.

DE CAMP, DAVID. 1971. Toward a generative analysis of a post-creole speech continuum. In Hymes, ed. 1971: 349–70.

———. 1973. What do implicational scales imply? In C. J. Bailey and R. Shuy, eds. 1973: 141–48.

DE CAMP, DAVID and IAN HANCOCK. 1974. Pidgins and Creoles: current trends and prospects. Washington D.C.: Georgetown University Press.

DE LEPERVANCHE, MARIE. 1967–68. Descent, residence and leadership in the New Guinea Highlands. Oceania 38: 134–58, 163–89.

DENISON, N. 1968. Sauris: a trilingual community in diatypic perspective. Man 3 n.s., no. 4: 578–94.

———. 1970. Sociolinguistic aspects of plurilingualism. In International days of sociolinguistics. Rome: Istituto Luigi Sturzo, 255–78.

———. 1971. Some observations on language variety and plurilingualism. In E. Ardener, ed., Social anthropology and language. London: Tavistock, 157–83.

DESSUREAULT-DOBER, DIANE. 1975. Ca fait que: marqueur d'interaction et coordonnant logique. M. A. thesis, Université du Québec.

DI SCIULLO, ANNE-MARIE, A. VAN AMERINGEN, H. CEDERGREN, and P. PUPIER. 1976. Etude de l'interaction verbale chez des Montréalais d'origine italienne. Cahier de linguistique 6, Les Presses de l'Université du Québec, 127–53.

DORIAN, NANCY C. 1973. Grammatical change in a dying dialect. Language 49: 413–38.

———. 1978. The fate of morphological complexity in language death: evidence from East Sutherland Gaelic. Language 54: 590–609.

DURANTI, ALESSANDRO and ELINOR OCHS. 1979. Left-dislocation in Italian conversation. In T. Givón, ed., Syntax and semantics, vol. 12: Discourse and syntax. New York: Academic Press, 377–46.

DU TOIT, B. M. 1962. Structural looseness in New Guinea. Journal of the Polynesian Society 71: 397–99.

DUTTON, T. E. 1969. The peopling of Central Papua: some preliminary observations. Pacific Linguistics B-9.

———. 1970. Informal English in the Torres Straits. In W. S. Ramson, ed., English transported. Canberra: Australian National University Press, 137–60.

———. 1973. Conversational New Guinea Pidgin. Pacific Linguistics D-12.

———. 1976. Austronesian languages: eastern part of South-Eastern mainland Papua. In Wurm, ed. 1976: 321–33.

DUTTON, T. E. and H. A. BROWN. 1977. Hiri Motu: the language itself. In Wurm, ed. 1977: 759–93.

DUTTON, T. E. and C. L. VOORHOEVE. 1974. Beginning Hiri Motu. Pacific Linguistics D-24.

DYEN, I. 1965. A lexicostatistic classification of the Malayo-Polynesian languages. International Journal of American Linguistics, Memoir no. 19, Supplement to I.J.A.L. 31.

Bibliography

ELIOT, DALE, STANLEY LEGUM, and SANDRA A. THOMPSON. 1969. Syntactic variation as linguistic data. R. Binnick et al., eds., *Papers from the Fifth Chicago Regional Meeting*, 52–59.

EMONDS, JOSEPH. 1973. Parenthetical clauses. *Papers from the Comparative Syntax Festival*. Chicago Linguistic Society, 333–47.

ERI, V. S. 1970. *The crocodile*. Milton, Queensland: Jacaranda Press. (2d ed. 1972, Port Moresby: Jacaranda Press.

EPSTEIN, A. L. 1964. Variation and social structure: local organization on the island of Matupit, New Britain. *Oceania* 35: 1–25.

ERVIN-TRIPP, SUSAN. 1972. On sociolinguistic rules: alternation and co-occurrence. In J. J. Gumperz and D. Hymes, eds. 1972: 213–50.

FANON, FRANTZ. 1961. *Les damnés de la terre*. Paris: François Maspero.

FASOLD, RALPH W. 1973. The concept of 'earlier-later': more or less correct. In Bailey and Shuy, eds. 1973: 183–97.

FAUCOUNEAU-DUBUISSON, COLETTE. 1975. Les transformations radicales et preservatrices de structure en français. Ph.D. dissertation, Université de Montréal.

FERGUSON, C. A. 1959. Diglossia. *Word* 15: 325–40.

———. 1971. Absence of copula and the notion of simplicity: a study of normal speech, baby talk, foreigner talk, and pidgins. In Hymes, ed. 1971: 141–50.

FILLMORE, CHARLES. 1972. How to know whether you are coming or going. In Karl Hylgaard-Jensen, ed., *Linguistik 1971*. Frankfort: Athenaum, 369–79.

FIRTH, J. R. 1935. The technique of semantics. *Transactions of the Philological Society*, 36–72. (Reprinted in J. R. Firth, *Papers in Linguistics 1934–51*.)

FISCHER, JOHN L. 1958. Social influence in the choice of a linguistic variant. *Word* 14: 47–56.

FISHMAN, J. 1965. Who speaks what language to whom and when? *La linguistique* 2: 67–88.

FITCH, W. M. 1971. Towards defining the course of evolution: minimum change for a specific tree topology. *Systematic Zoology* 20: 406–16.

FODOR, J., T. G. BEVER, and M. F. GARRETT. 1974. *The psychology of language*. New York: McGraw Hill.

FORTUNE, R. F. 1963. *Sorcerers of Dobu*. New York: Dutton and Co. Revised edition. First published in 1932.

FRAKE, C. O. 1964. Notes on queries in ethnography. *American Anthropologist* 66, no. 3, pt. 2: 132–45.

FRANKLIN, KARL J. 1962. *Tolai language course*. Division of Extension Services, Papua New Guinea, in co-operation with the Summer Institute of Linguistics.

———. 1968. The dialects of Kewa. *Pacific Linguistics* B-10.

FREI, HENRI. 1928. *La grammaire des fautes*. (Reprinted 1971, Geneva, Slatkine.)

FRIEDRICH, PAUL. 1966. Structural implications of Russian pronominal usage. In W. Bright, ed., *Sociolinguistics*. The Hague: Mouton, 214–53.

FRY, E. 1977. Missionary lingue franche: Kuanua. In Wurm, ed. 1977:865–74.

GAATONE, DAVID. 1971. *Etude descriptive du système de la négation en français contemporain*. Genève: Librairie Droz.

Bibliography

GAL, SUSAN. 1978. Variation and change in patterns of speaking: language shift in Austria. In D. Sankoff, ed. 1978: 227–38.

GEERTZ, C. 1960. Linguistic etiquette. Excerpt from *The religion of Java*. (Reprinted in J. Pride and J. Holmes, eds., *Sociolinguistics*. Harmondsworth, Middlesex, England: Penguin, 167–79.)

GEOGHEGAN, W. 1969. The use of marking rules in semantic systems. Working paper number 26, Language behavior research laboratory, Berkeley: University of California.

———. 1971. Information processing systems in culture. In P. Kay, ed., *Explorations in mathematical anthropology*. Cambridge, Mass.: M.I.T. Press, 3–35.

GIACOMI, ALAIN, HENRIETTA CEDERGREN, and MALCAH YAEGER. 1977. "Pi," "et pi," . . . "pi que," à Montréal. In *Recherches sur le français parlé*. Groupe aixois de recherche en syntaxe. Aix: Université de Provence, 87–99.

GIRARD, FRANCOISE. 1957. Quelques plantes alimentaires et rituelles en usage chez les Buang. *Journal d'agriculture tropicale et de botanique appliquée* 4, no. 5–6: 212–27.

———. 1967. Les gens de l'igname. *Journal d'agriculture tropicale et de botanique appliquée* 14, no. 8–9: 287–338.

GIVÓN, T. 1972. Pronoun attraction and subject postposing in Bantu. *Papers from the Relative Clause Festival*. Chicago Linguistic Society, 190–97.

———. 1973. The time-axis phenomenon. *Language* 49: 890–925.

———. 1976. Topic, pronoun and grammatical agreement. In Charles Li, ed., *Subject and topic*. New York: Academic Press, 149–88.

GLADWIN, HUGH and CHRISTINA GLADWIN. 1970. Estimation of market conditions and profit expectations by fish sellers of Cape Coast, Ghana. Paper read at the 1970 annual meeting of the American Anthropological Association, San Diego, Calif.

GLASSE, R. M. 1968. *Huli of Papua: a cognatic descent system. Cahiers de l'homme: ethnologie–géographie–linguistique*. Nouvelle série VIII. Paris: Mouton and Ecole Pratique des Hautes Etudes.

GOFFMAN, E. 1974. *Frame analysis*. New York: Harper and Row.

———. ms., 1975. Calling terms.

GOODENOUGH, WARD. 1964. Introduction. In W. Goodenough, ed., *Explorations in cultural anthropology*. New York: McGraw Hill, 1–24.

———. 1965. Rethinking 'status' and 'role': toward a general model of the cultural organization of social relationships. In M. Barton, ed., *The relevance of models for social anthropology*. A.S.A. Monographs no. 1. London: Tavistock Publications, 1–24.

GOUGENHEIM, GEORGES. 1951. *Grammaire de la langue française du seizième siècle*. Lyon: Edition IAC.

GOUGENHEIM, G., P. RIVENC, R. MICHÉA, and A. SAUVAGEOT. 1967. *L'elaboration du français fondamental (1er degré)*. Paris: Didier.

GRENANDER, U. 1967. Syntax-controlled probabilities. Technical report, Brown University, Division of Applied Mathematics.

GRIMES, JOSEPH E. 1972. Outlines and overlays. *Language* 48: 513–24.

GREVISSE, MAURICE. 1969. *Le bon usage*. 9th ed. Gembloux: Editions Duculot.

GUILLAUME, GUSTAVE. 1970. *Temps et verbe*. Paris: Librairie Honore Champion.

Bibliography

GUMPERZ, JOHN J. 1962. Types of linguistic communities. *Anthropological Linguistics* 4: 28–40.

———. 1964. Linguistic and social interaction in two communities. *American Anthropologist* 66, no. 6, pt. 2: 137–53.

———. 1965. Linguistic repertoires, grammars, and second language instruction. *Monograph Series on Languages and Linguistics* 18: 81–90. Georgetown University.

———. 1968. The speech community. *International encyclopedia of social sciences* 9: 381–86. (Reprinted as chapter 7 of J. J. Gumperz, *Language in social groups*, Stanford University Press, 1971, 114–28.)

———. 1969. Communication in multilingual societies. In S. Tyler, ed., *Cognitive anthropology*. Holt, Rinehart and Winston, 435–49.

GUMPERZ, JOHN J. and E. HERNÁNDEZ-CHAVEZ. 1972. Bilingualism, bidialectalism and classroom interaction. In C. Cazden, V. John, and D. Hymes, eds., *Functions of language in the classroom*. New York: Teachers College Press, 84–108.

GUMPERZ, JOHN J. and DELL HYMES, eds. 1972. *Directions in sociolinguistics*. New York: Holt, Rinehart and Winston.

GUMPERZ, JOHN J. and R. WILSON. 1971. Convergence and creolization: a case from the Indo-Aryan/Dravidian border. In Hymes, ed. 1971: 151–67.

GUY, J. B. M. 1974. Notes on Bichelamar: sound systems and spelling systems. *Kivung* 7: 23–46.

HALL, ROBERT A., JR. 1943. Melanesian pidgin English: grammar, texts, vocabulary. Baltimore: Linguistic Society of America.

———. 1952. The vocabulary of Melanesian pidgin. *American Speech* 18: 192–99.

———. 1955a. Innovations in Melanesian pidgin (Neo-Melanesian.) *Oceania* 26, no. 2: 91–109.

———. 1955b. *Hands off Pidgin English*. Sydney: Pacific Publications.

HALLIDAY, M. A. K. 1964. The users and uses of language. In M. A. K. Halliday, A. McIntosh, and P. Stevens, eds., *The linguistic sciences and language teaching*. London: Longmans.

HARDING, THOMAS G. 1965. The Rai Coast open electorate. In Bettison, Hughes and van der Veur, eds., *The Papua-New Guinea elections 1964*. The Australian National University, Canberra, 194–211.

———. 1967. *Voyagers of the Vitiaz Strait: a study of a New Guinea trade system*. Seattle: University of Washington Press.

HARTIGAN, J. A. 1973. Minimum mutation fits to a given tree. *Biometrics* 29: 53–65.

HAUDRICOURT, A. G. 1961. Richesse en phonèmes et richesse en locuteurs. *L'Homme* 1: 5–10.

HAUGEN, E. 1967. Semicommunication: the language gap in Scandinavia. *International Journal of American Linguistics* 33, no. 4, pt. 2: 152–70.

HEALEY, A. 1964. The Ok language family in New Guinea. Ph. D. dissertation, Australian National University, Canberra.

———. 1976. Austronesian languages: Admiralty Island area. In Wurm, ed. 1976: 349–64.

HICKERSON, H., G. TURNER and N. HICKERSON. 1952. Testing procedures for estimating transfer of information among Iroquois dialects and languages. *International Journal of American Linguistics* 18: 1–8.

HILL, JANE H. 1973. Subordinate clause density and language function. In *Papers from the Comparative Syntax Festival*. Chicago: Chicago Linguistic Society, 33–52.

HOCKETT, CHARLES F. 1950. Age-grading and linguistic continuity. *Language* 26: 449–57.

———. 1963. The problem of universals in language. In J. H. Greenberg, ed., *Universals of language*. Cambridge, Mass.: M.I.T. Press.

HOGBIN, H. I. 1947. Native trade around the Huon Gulf, North-Eastern New Guinea. *Journal of the Polynesian Society* 56: 242–55.

HOGBIN, H. I. and C. H. WEDGWOOD. 1953. Local grouping in Melanesia. *Oceania* 23: 241–76, and 24: 58–86.

HOLLYMAN, J. K. 1962. The lizard and the axe: a study of the effects of European contact on the indigenous languages of Polynesia and Island Melanesia. *Journal of the Polynesian Society* 71: 310–27.

HOOLEY, BRUCE A. 1962. A Buang text. M.A. thesis, University of Pennsylvania.

———. 1964a. A problem in Buang morphology. Linguistic Circle of Canberra publications, Series A–Occasional papers, No. 3.

———. 1964b. The Morobe District–New Guinea. *Oceanic Linguistics* 3: 201–47.

———. 1970. Mapos Buang–Territory of New Guinea. Ph.D. dissertation, University of Pennsylvania.

———. 1971. Austronesian languages of the Morobe District, Papua New Guinea. *Oceanic Linguistics* 10: 79–151.

HOOLEY, B. A. and K. A. MCELHANON. 1970 Languages of the Morobe District—New Guinea. In Wurm and Laycock, eds. 1970: 1065–94.

HORNING, J. J. 1969. A study of grammatical inference. Technical report no. CS 139, Stanford Artificial Intelligence Project, Memo Al–98, Computer Science Department, Stanford University.

HUGHES, COLIN A. and PAUL W. VAN DER VEUR. 1965. The elections: an overview. In Bettison, Hughes, and van der Veur, eds., *The Papua-New Guinea elections 1964*. Canberra: The Australian National University, 388–429.

HYMES, DELL H. 1961a. Functions of speech: an evolutionary approach. In F. C. Gruber, ed., *Anthropology and education*. Philadelphia: University of Pennsylvania Press, 55–83.

———. 1961b. Linguistic aspects of cross-cultural personality study. In B. Kaplan, ed., *Studying personality cross-culturally*. Evanston: Row, Peterson, 313–59.

———. 1961c. On typology of cognitive style in languages. *Anthropological Linguistics* 3, 1: 22–54.

———. 1962. The ethnography of speaking. In T. Gladwin and W. Sturtevant, eds., *Anthropology and human behavior*. Anthropological Society of Washington, 13–53.

———. 1964a. Introduction: toward ethnographies of communication. *American Anthropologist* 66, no. 5, pt. 2: 1–34.

———. 1964b. A perspective for linguistic anthropology. In S. Tax ed., *Horizons of anthropology*. Chicago: Aldine, 92–107.

———. 1964c. Directions in (ethno-)linguistic theory. In A. K. Romney and

Bibliography

R. G. D'Andrade, eds., *Transcultural studies of cognition*. Washington, D.C.: American Anthropological Association, 6–56. (First issued, *American Anthropologist* 66, no. 3, part 2).

———. 1966. Two types of linguistic relativity. In Wm. Bright, ed., *Sociolinguistics*, The Hague: Mouton, 114–65.

———. 1967a. Models of the interaction of language and social setting. *Journal of Social Issues* 23, no. 2: 8–28.

———. 1967b. Why linguistics needs the sociologist. *Social Research* 34(4): 632–47.

———. 1967c. On communicative competence. In *Research Planning Conference on Language Development in Disadvantaged Children*. New York: Yeshiva University, Department of Educational Psychology.

———. 1968. Linguistic problems in defining the concept of 'tribe'. In J. Helm, ed., *Essays on the problem of tribe*. American Ethnological Society, Proceedings of the 1967 Annual Spring Meeting, 23–48.

———. 1970a. Functions of speech and linguistic theory. *International days of sociolinguistics*, Rome: Istituto Luigi Sturzo, 111–44.

———. 1970b. Linguistic method in ethnography. In P. Garvin, ed., *Method and theory in linguistics*. The Hague: Mouton, 249–311.

———. ed., 1971. *Introduction to part III, Pidginization and creolization of languages*. Cambridge: Cambridge University Press.

———. 1972a. Models of the interaction of language and social life. In J. J. Gumperz and D. Hymes, eds. 1972: 35–71.

———. 1972b. Language as culture. Manuscript.

———. 1974. *Foundations in sociolinguistics*. Philadelphia: University of Pennsylvania Press.

———. 1975. Folklore's nature and the sun's myth. *Journal of American Folklore* 88: 345–79.

JACKSON, JEAN. 1972. Marriage and linguistic identity among the Bará Indians of the Vaupés, Colombia. Ph.D. dissertation, Stanford University.

JAKOBSON, R. 1960. Concluding statement: linguistics and poetics. In T. A. Sebeok, ed., *Style in language*. New York: Wiley, 350–73.

JUILLAND, A., D. BRODIN, and C. DAVIDOVITCH. 1970. *Frequency dictionary of French words*. The Hague: Mouton.

KAY, PAUL. 1977. Language evolution and speech style. In Ben G. Blount and Mary Sanches, eds., *Sociocultural dimensions of language change*. New York: Academic Press, 21–33.

KAY, PAUL and GILLIAN SANKOFF. 1974. A language-universals approach to pidgins and creoles. In DeCamp and Hancock, eds. 1974, 61–72.

KEENAN, EDWARD L. 1972. Relative clause formation in Malagasy. In *Papers from the Relative Clause Festival*. Chicago Linguistic Society, 169–89.

KEENAN, EDWARD L. and ROBERT D. HULL. 1973. The logical syntax of direct and indirect questions. *Papers from the Comparative Syntax Festival*. Chicago Linguistic Society, 348–71.

KEMP, WILLIAM. 1978. La variation entre les formes en *ske, kes,* et *kos* dans le français parlé à Montréal. M.A. thesis, Université du Québec à Montréal.

———. 1977. Noun phrase questions and the question of movement rules. *Papers from the tenth regional meeting, Chicago Linguistic Society,* 198–212.

Bibliography

KLEIN, S. 1965. Control of style with a generative grammar. *Language* 41: 619–31.

KROEBER, A. L. and CLYDE KLUCKHOHN. 1952. *Culture: a critical review of concepts and definitions.* Papers of the Peabody Museum of American Archaeology and Ethnology, Harvard University, vol. 47, no. 1. (Reprinted by Random House, New York, 1963.)

KUNO, SUSUMU. 1974. The position of relative clauses and conjunctions. *Linguistic Inquiry* 5: 117–36.

———. 1975. Three perspectives in the functional approach to syntax. In *Papers from the parasession on functionalism.* Chicago Linguistic Society, 276–336.

LABERGE, SUZANNE. 1977. Etude de la variation des pronoms sujets définis et indéfinis dans le français parlé à Montréal. Ph.D. dissertation, Université de Montréal.

———. (in press). The changing distribution of indeterminate pronouns in discourse. In R. W. Shuy and A. Schnukal, eds., *Language use and the uses of language.* Washington D.C.: Georgetown University Press.

——— and MICHÈLE CHIASSON-LAVOIE. 1971. Attitudes face au français parlé à Montréal et degrés de conscience de variables linguistiques. In R. Darnell, ed., *Linguistic diversity in Canadian society.* Edmonton: Linguistic Research, Inc., 89–126.

LABOV, WILLIAM. 1963. The social motivation of a sound change. *Word* 19: 273–309.

———. 1966a. *The social stratification of English in New York City.* Washington D.C.: Center for Applied Linguistics.

———. 1966b. Hypercorrection by the lower middle class as a factor in linguistic change. In Wm. Bright, ed., *Sociolinguistics.* The Hague: Mouton, 84–113.

———. 1969. Contraction, deletion, and inherent variability of the English copula. *Language* 45: 715–62.

———. 1970. The study of language in its social context. *Studium Generale* 23: 30–87.

———. 1971. Methodology. In W. O. Dingwall, ed., *A survey of linguistic science.* Linguistics Program, University of Maryland, 412–97.

———. 1972a. The internal evolution of linguistic rules, In Robert P. Stockwell and R. K. S. Macaulay, eds., *Linguistic change and generative theory.* Bloomington: Indiana University Press, 101–71.

———. 1972b. *Sociolinguistic patterns.* Philadelphia: University of Pennsylvania Press.

———. 1972c. *Language in the inner city: studies in the Black English vernacular.* Philadelphia: University of Pennsylvania Press.

———. 1972d. Where does grammar stop? *Monograph Series on Languages and Linguistics,* no. 25. Georgetown University.

———. 1972e. The linguistic consequences of being a lame. In Labov 1972c: 225–92.

———. 1972f. The transformation of experience in narrative syntax. In Labov 1972c: 354–96.

———. 1972g. The social setting of linguistic change. In Labov 1972b: 260–325.

———. 1973. The boundaries of words and their meanings. In Bailey and Shuy, eds. 1973: 340–73.

———. ms., 1971. On the adequacy of natural languages: I: the development of tense. Draft, mimeographed, University of Pennsylvania.

LABOV, WILLIAM, ANNE BOWER, ELIZABETH DAYTON, DONALD HINDLE, MATTHEW LENNIG, ARVILLA PAYNE, and DEBORAH SCHIFFRIN-SCAVO. 1979. The social determinants of sound change. N.S.F. Project Report on contracts SOC-750024-1 and BNC-76-15421. Philadelphia.

LABOV, WILLIAM, PAUL COHEN, CLARENCE ROBINS, and JOHN LEWIS. 1968. A study of the non-standard English of Negro and Puerto Rican speakers in New York City. Cooperative Research Report 3288.

LABOV, WILLIAM, MALCAH YAEGER, and R. STEINER. 1972. A quantitative study of sound changes in progress. Final report on National Science Foundation contract NSF-3287. Philadelphia, Pa.

LAFERRIERE, MARTHA. 1979. Ethnicity in phonological variation and change. *Language* 55: 603–617.

LANDTMAN, G. 1927. *The Kiwai Papuans of British New Guinea.* London: Macmillan.

LANGENDOEN, D. T. 1969. *The study of syntax.* New York: Holt, Rinehart and Winston.

LANGNESS, L. 1964. Some problems in the conceptualization of Highlands social structure. *American Anthropologist* 66, no. 4, pt. 2: 162–82.

LATTEY, ELSA. 1975. Beyond variable rules. Paper read at the 1975 International Conference on Pidgins and Creoles, University of Hawaii.

LAWRENCE, PETER. 1955. Land tenure among the Garia. Australian National University, Social Science Monographs, no. 4.

LAWTON, RALPH S. 1977. Missionary lingue franche: Dobu. In Wurm, ed. 1977: 907–46.

LAYCOCK, D. C. 1965. The Ndu language family (Sepik district, New Guinea). *Pacific Linguistics* C-1.

———. 1966. Papuans and pidgin: aspects of bilingualism in New Guinea. *Te Reo* 9: 44–51.

———. 1969. Sublanguages in Buin: play, poetry, and preservation. *Pacific Linguistics* A-22: 1–23.

———. 1970a. Materials in New Guinea pidgin (coastal and lowlands). *Pacific Linguistics* D-5.

———. 1970b. Pidgin English in New Guinea. In W. S. Ramson, ed., *English transported: essays on Australasian English.* Canberra: Australian National University Press, 102–22.

———. 1973 (1976). Sissano, Warapu, and Melanesian pidginization. Papers of the first international conference of comparative Austronesian linguistics, 1974. *Oceanic Linguistics* 12: 245–78.

———. 1976. Austronesian languages: Sepik Provinces. In Wurm, ed. 1976: 399–418.

LEFEBVRE, CLAIRE. 1974. Discreteness and the linguistic continuum in Martinique. *Anthropological Linguistics* 16, 2: 47–78.

LEHMANN, W. 1962. *Historical linguistics: an introduction.* New York: Holt, Rinehart and Winston.

LEHRER, A. 1970. Indeterminacy in semantic description. *Glossa* 4: 87–110.

LEVINSON, STEPHEN. ms., 1978. On sociolinguistic universals.

LINCOLN, PETER C. 1976. Austronesian languages: Boungainville Province. In Wurm, ed. 1976: 419–39.

Bibliography

LITHGOW, DAVID R. 1976. Austronesian languages: Milne Bay and adjacent islands (Milne Bay Province). In Wurm, ed. 1976: 441–523.
LOETSCHER, ANDREAS. 1973. On the role of nonrestrictive relative clauses in discourse. *Papers from the Ninth Regional Meeting, Chicago Linguistic Society,* 356–68.
LONDON, JOHN. 1909. Beche de Mer English. *Contemporary Review* no. 525, London, 359–64.
MA, ROXANA, and ELEANOR HERASIMCHUK. 1968. The linguistic dimensions of a bilingual neighborhood. In J. Fishman, R. L. Cooper, R. Ma et al., eds., *Bilingualism in the barrio.* New York: Yeshiva University.
MALINOWSKI, B. 1935. *Coral gardens and their magic.* Vol. 2. London: Allen and Unwin.
———. 1966. *Argonauts of the Western Pacific.* 7th printing. (First published 1922.) London: Routledge and Kegan Paul.
McDAVID, RAVEN. 1948. Postvocalic -r in South Carolina: a social analysis. *American Speech* 23: 194–203.
McELHANON, K. A., ed. 1975. *Tok Pisin igo we.* Kivung Special Publication no. 1. Port Moresby, Papua New Guinea.
McKAUGHAN, HOWARD. 1964. A study of divergence in four New Guinea languages. *American Anthropologist* 66, no. 4, pt. 2: 98–120.
McKAUGHAN, H., ed. 1973. *The languages of the Eastern family of the East New Guinea Highland stock.* Seattle and London: University of Washington Press.
MÉNAGE, GILLES. *Observations de Monsieur Ménage sur la langue françoise.* 2d edition. Paris: C. Barbin, 1975–76.
MIHALIC, REV. F. 1957. *Grammar and dictionary of Neo-Melanesian.* The Mission Press, Westmead, New South Wales, Australia.
———. 1971. *The Jacaranda dictionary and grammar of Melanesian Pidgin.* Port Moresby: Jacaranda Press.
MITCHELL-KERNAN, CLAUDIA. 1971. *Language behavior in a Black urban community.* Monographs of the Language Behavior Research Laboratory, University of California, Berkeley, no. 2.
MORGAN, J. L. 1972. Some aspects of relative clauses in English and Albanian. *Papers from the Relative Clause Festival.* Chicago Linguistic Society, 63–72.
MÜHLHÄUSLER, PETER. 1975a. The influence of the German Administration on New Guinea Pidgin. *Journal of Pacific History* 10: 94–111.
———. 1975b. The functional possibilities of lexical bases in New Guinea Pidgin. Paper read at the 1975 International Conference on Pidgins and Creoles, University of Hawaii.
———. 1976a. Samoan plantation Pidgin English and the origin of New Guinea Pidgin: an introduction. *Journal of Pacific History* 11: 122–25.
———. 1976b. Growth and structure of the lexicon of New Guinea Pidgin. Ph.D. dissertation, Australian National University, Canberra.
———. 1977a. Sociolects in New Guinea Pidgin. In Wurm, ed. 1977: 559–66.
———. 1977b. Creolization of New Guinea Pidgin. In Wurm, ed. 1977: 567–76.
MURPHY, JOHN J. 1966. *The book of Pidgin English.* Revised edition, Brisbane: W. R. Smith and Paterson Pty. Ltd.
NYROP, K. 1930. *Grammaire historique de la langue française. Tome sixième.* Copenhagen: Gyldendalske Boghandel Nordisk Forlag.

Bibliography

OATRIDGE, D. and JENNIFER. 1973. Phonemes of Binumarien. In McKaughan, ed. 1973: 517–22.

OLIVER, D. L. 1949. Human relations and language in a Papuan-speaking tribe of Southern Bougainville, Solomon Islands. *Peabody Museum Papers*, vol. 29. Cambridge: Harvard University Press.

PAWLEY, ANDREW. 1972. On the internal relationships of Eastern Oceanic languages. *Pacific Anthropological Records*. Bernice P. Bishop Museum, Honolulu, no. 13.

———. 1976. Austronesian languages: western part of southeastern mainland Papua. In Wurm, ed. 1976: 301–19.

PAYNE, ARVILLA. 1979. Factors controlling the acquisition of the Philadelphia dialect by out-of-state children. In W. Labov, ed., *Quantitative analysis of linguistic structure*. New York: Academic Press.

PEIZER, D. B. and D. L. OLMSTED. 1969. Modules of grammar acquisition. *Language* 45: 60–96.

PICARD, MARC. 1972. Schwa deletion in function words in Canadian French. Paper read at the annual meeting of the Canadian Linguistic Association.

PIKE, E. V. 1954. Phonetic rank and subordination in consonant patterning and historical change. *Miscellanea Phonetica* 2: 25–41.

POHL, JACQUES. 1968. *Ne* dans le français parlé contemporain: les modalités de son abandon. *Actes due XIe congrès international de linguistique et philologie romanes*. Madrid, 3: 1343–59.

———. 1970. *Ne* et les enfants. *Le langage et l'Homme*, October, 41–43.

———. 1975. L'omission de *ne* dans le français parlé contemporain. *Le français dans le monde*. fév. mars: 17–23.

POPLACK, SHANA. 1978. Quantitative analysis of constraints on code switching. *Centro Working Papers* no. 2. New York: C.U.N.Y.

QUEENSLAND. 1885. *Proceedings of the Legislative Assembly Session*. Royal Commission on Recruiting Polynesian Labourers in New Guinea and Adjacent Islands. Brisbane, Queensland, Australia.

RAPPAPORT, R. 1967. *Pigs for the ancestors*. New Haven: Yale University Press.

RAY, SIDNEY H. 1926. *A comparative study of the Melanesian Island languages*. Cambridge University Press.

READ, K. E. 1965. *The high valley*. New York: Charles Scribner's Sons.

REAY, MARIE. 1959. *The Kuma: freedom and conformity in the New Guinea Highlands*. Melbourne: Melbourne University Press.

———. 1964. Present day politics in the New Guinea Highlands. *American Anthropologist* 66, no. 4, pt. 2: 240–56.

REED, S. W. 1943. *The making of modern New Guinea*. Philadelphia: American Philosophical Society.

REICHENBACH, HANS. 1966. *Elements of symbolic logic*. New York: The Free Press.

RENCK, G. L. 1977a. Missionary lingue franche: Yabêm. In Wurm, ed. 1977: 847–53.

———. 1977b. Missionary lingue franche: Kâte. In Wurm, ed. 1977: 839–846.

RICKFORD, JOHN R. 1973. Long painim as bliong "ia." Paper written for Tok Pisin seminar, Linguistic Institute, University of Michigan.

Bibliography

ROELANDT, ALIN. 1975. *Etude de l'omission de NE dans les phrases négatives en français populaire: des environs de 1750 à 1870.* Mémoire présenté pour l'obtention du grade de licencié en philologie romane. Université Libre de Bruxelles.

ROSS, ALAN S. C. 1954. Linguistic class indicators in present-day English. *Neuphilologische Mitteilungen* 55: 20–56.

ROSS, J. R. 1967. Constraints on variables in syntax. Ph.D. dissertation, M.I.T.

———. 1972. The category squish: endstation Hauptwort. *Papers from the Eighth Chicago Meeting.* Chicago Linguistic Society, 316–28.

———. 1973. A fake NP squish. In Bailey and Shuy, eds. 1973: 96–140.

ROUSSEAU, PASCALE. 1978b. A solution to the problem of grouping speakers. In D. Sankoff, ed. 1978: 97–117.

ROUSSEAU, PASCALE and DAVID SANKOFF. 1978a. Advances in variable rule methodology. In D. Sankoff, ed. 1978: 57–69.

ROWLEY, C. D. 1965. *The New Guinea villager: a retrospect from 1964.* Melbourne: Cheshire.

ROY, ARCHÉLAS. 1960. La grammaire, *Cahiers de l'Académie canadienne-française* no. 5: 107–20.

SACKS, HARVEY and EMANUEL A. SCHEGLOFF. 1979. Two preferences in the organization of reference to persons in conversations, and their interaction. In George Psathas, ed., *Everyday language: studies in ethnomethodology.* New York: Irvington Publishers, pp. 15–21.

SACKS, HARVEY, EMANUEL A. SCHEGLOFF, and GAIL JEFFERSON. 1974. A simplest systematics for the organization of turn-taking for conversation. *Language* 50: 696–735.

SAG, IVAN. 1973. On the state of progress on progressives and statives. In Bailey and Shuy, eds. 1973: 89–95.

SAINT-PIERRE, MADELEINE. 1969. Problèmes de diglossie dans un bourg martiniquais. M.A. thesis, Université de Montréal.

SALISBURY, RICHARD F. 1962. Notes on bilingualism and linguistic change in New Guinea. *Anthropological Linguistics* 4(7): 1–13.

———. 1964. Despotism and Australian administration in the New Guinea Highlands. *American Anthropologist* 66, no. 4, pt. 2: 225–39.

———. 1967. Pidgin's respectable past. *New Guinea* 2(2): 44–8.

———. 1969. *Vunamami: economic transformation in a traditional society.* Berkeley: University of California Press.

SANDFELD, K. 1928. *Syntaxe du français contemporain,* Tome I. Paris, Champion.

SANKOFF, D. 1971a. Branching processes with terminal types: application to context-free grammars. *Journal of Applied Probability* 8: 233–40.

———. 1971b. Dictionary structure and probability measures. *Information and Control* 19: 104–13.

———. 1972a. Context-free grammars and nonnegative matrices. *Linear Algebra and its Applications* 5: 277–81.

———. 1972b. Reconstructing the history and geography of an evolutionary tree. *American Mathematical Monthly* 79: 596–603.

———. ed., 1978. *Linguistic variation: models and methods.* New York: Academic Press.

SANKOFF, D. and H. J. CEDERGREN. 1976. The dimensionality of grammatical variation. *Language* 52: 163–78.

360

Bibliography

SANKOFF, D. and A. DOBSON. 1971. Word replacement, borrowing and the phylogenetics of language families. Montreal: Centre de recherches mathématiques Technical Report 102.

SANKOFF, D. and SUZANNE LABERGE. 1978a. Statistical dependence among successive occurrences of a variable in discourse. In D. Sankoff, ed. 1978: 119-26.

———. 1978b. The linguistic market and the statistical explanation of variability. In D. Sankoff, ed. 1978: 239-50.

SANKOFF, D., REJEAN LESSARD, and NGUYEN BA TRUONG. 1978. Computational linguistics and statistics in the analysis of the Montreal French corpus. *Computers and the Humanities* 11: 185-91.

SANKOFF, D. and G. SANKOFF. 1973. Sample survey methods and computer assisted analysis in the study of grammatical variation. In R. Darnell, ed., *Canadian languages in their social context*. Edmonton: Linguistic Research, Inc., 7-64.

SANKOFF, D. and PIERRETTE THIBAULT. In press. Weak complementarity.

SANKOFF, D., PIERRETTE THIBAULT, and HÉLÈNE BÉRUBÉ. 1978. Semantic field variability. In D. Sankoff, ed. 1978: 23-43.

SANKOFF, GILLIAN. 1968. Social aspects of multilingualism in New Guinea. Ph.D. thesis, McGill University.

———. 1969. *Wok bisnis* and Namasu: a perspective from the village. *New Guinea Research Bulletin* 28: 61-81.

———. 1975. Wanpela lain manmeri ibin kisim Tok Pisin ikamap olosem Tok ples bilong ol. In McElhanon, ed. 1975: 102-7.

———. 1977a. Le parallélisme dans la poésie Buang. *Anthropologica* 19: 27-48.

———. 1977b. Creolization and syntactic change in New Guinea Tok Pisin. In B. Blount and M. Sanches, eds., *Sociocultural dimensions of language change*. London and New York: Academic Press, 119-30.

———. 1979. Review of A. Valdman, ed., *Pidgin and Creole linguistics*. *Language in Society* 8: 137-40.

SANKOFF, G. and HENRIETTA CEDERGREN. 1971. Some results of a sociolinguistic study of Montreal French. In R. Darnell, ed., *Linguistic Diversity in Canadian Society*. Edmonton: Linguistic Research, Inc., 61-87.

SANKOFF, G., ROBERT SARRASIN, and HENRIETTA CEDERGREN. 1971. Quelques considérations sur la distribution de la variable *que* dans le français de Montréal. Paper read at the Congrès de l'Association canadienne-française pour l'Avancement des Sciences.

SANKOFF, GILLIAN, WILLIAM KEMP, and HENRIETTA CEDERGREN. In press. The syntax of *ce que/qu'est-ce que* variation and its social correlates. In R. W. Shuy and J. Firsching, eds., *Dimensions of variability and competence*. Washington, D.C.: Georgetown University Press.

SCHEFFLER, H. W. 1965. *Choiseul island social structure*. Berkeley and Los Angeles: University of California Press.

SCHEGLOFF, E. 1972. Notes on a conversational practice: formulating place. In D. Sudnow, ed., *Studies in Social Interaction*. New York: The Free Press, 75-119.

SCHLESIER, E. VON. 1961. Über die Zweisprachigkeit und die Stellung der Zweisprachigen in Melanesien, besonders auf Neuguinea. In *Beiträge zur Völkerforschung: Hans Damm zum 65. Geburtstag*. Leipzig: Museum für Völkerkunde, vol. 11, 550-76.

361

SCHWARTZ, ARTHUR. 1971. General aspects of relative clause formation. In *Working Papers on Language Universals,* Stanford University, no. 6: 139–71.
SCHWARTZ, THEODORE. 1962. The Paliau movement in the Admirality islands, 1946–1954. American Museum of Natural History, New York, *An thropological Papers* 49(2): 206–421; also 1957 Ph.D. dissertation, University of Pennsylvania.
SEBEOK, T. A. ed. 1971. *Current trends in linguistics.* Vol. 8: *Linguistics in Oceania.* 2 vols. The Hague: Mouton.
SELIGMAN, C. G. 1910. *The Melanesians of British New Guinea.* Cambridge: Cambridge University Press.
SHERZER, JOEL. 1973. On linguistic semantics and linguistic subdisciplines: a review article. *Language in Society* 2: 269–89.
SHIPLEY, E. F. and J. CATLIN. ms. The acquisition of linguistic structure. Technical report V, Grant MH07990. Eastern Pennsylvania Psychiatric Institute. Short-term memory for sentences in children: an exploratory study of temporal aspects of imposing structure.
SHUY, R. 1970. Sociolinguistic research at the Center for Applied Linguistics: the correlation of language and sex. *International days of sociolinguistics,* Istituto Luigi Sturzo, Rome, 849–58.
SHUY, ROGER, WALTER A. WOLFRAM, and WILLIAM K. RILEY. 1968. *Field techniques in an urban language study.* Center for Applied Linguistics, Washington, D.C.
S.I.C.A. n.d. Pijin bulong Solomon. Spelling list. Pamphlet prepared by the pidgin sub-committee of the Solomon Islands Christian Education Committee.
SLOBIN, DAN I. 1977. Language change in childhood and in history. In John Macnamara, ed., *Language learning and thought.* New York: Academic Press, 185–214.
SMEALL, CHRISTOPHER. 1975. A quantitative study of variation: Tok Pisin *i-*. Paper read at the Berkeley Linguistics Society meeting, February 1975.
STRATHERN, ANDREW. 1969. Descent and alliance in the New Guinea highlands: some problems of comparison. *Proceedings of the Royal Anthropological Institute of Great Britain and Ireland for 1968,* 37–52.
———. 1975. Veiled speech in Mount Hagen. In M. Bloch, ed., *Political language and oratory in traditional society.* London and New York: Academic Press, 185–203.
STRATHERN, MARILYN. 1972. *Women in between.* London and New York: Seminar Press.
SUPPES, PATRICK. 1972. Probabilistic grammars for natural languages. In D. Davidson and G. Harmon, eds., *Semantics of natural language.* Dordrecht: Reidel, 741–62.
SWADESH, M. 1950. Salish internal relationships. *International Journal of American Linguistics* 16: 157–67.
SWARTZ, MARC J. 1960. Situational determinants of kinship terminology. *Southwestern Journal of Anthropology* 16: 393–97.
TAYLOR, ANDREW. 1977. Missionary lingue franche: Motu. In Wurm, ed. 1977: 881–91.
THOMPSON, S. 1972. The deep structure of relative clauses. In C. Fillmore and D. T. Langendoen, eds., *Studies in linguistic semantics,* New York: Holt, Rinehart and Winston, 78–94.

Bibliography

TRAUGOTT, ELIZABETH CLOSS. 1973. Some thoughts on natural syntactic processes. In Bailey and Shuy, eds. 1973: 313–22.
———. in press. On the expression of spatio-temporal relations in language. In J. H. Greenberg, C. A. Ferguson, and E. Moravcsik, eds., *Universals of human language*. Stanford: Stanford University Press.
TRUDGILL, PETER. 1972. Sex, covert prestige and linguistic change in the urban British English of Norwich. *Language in Society* 1: 179–95.
———. 1973. Phonological rules and sociolinguistic variation in Norwich English. In Bailey and Shuy, eds. 1973: 149–63.
———. 1976–77. Creolization in reverse: reduction and simplification in the Albanian dialect of Greece. *Transactions of the Philological Society* 1976–77: 32–50.
TYLER, STEPHEN, ed. 1969a. *Cognitive anthropology*. New York: Holt, Rinehart and Winston.
———. 1966b. Contact and variation in Koya kinship terminology. In Tyler, 1969a, 487–503.
WAGNER, ROY. 1967. *The curse of Souw: principles of Daribi clan definition and alliance*. Chicago: University of Chicago Press.
———. 1969. Marriage among the Daribi. In R. M. Glasse and M. J. Meggitt, eds., *Pigs, pearlshells, and women*. Englewood Cliffs, New Jersey: Prentice-Hall, 56–76.
WALLACE. A. F. C. 1961a. On being just complicated enough. *Proceedings of the National Academy of Science* 47: 458–64.
———. 1961b. *Culture and Personality*. New York: Random House.
———. 1961c. The psychic unity of human groups. In B. Kaplan, ed., *Studying personality cross-culturally*. Evanston, Ill.: Row, Peterson, 129–63.
WATSON, J. B. 1965. Loose structure loosely construed: groupless groupings in Gadsup? *Oceania* 35: 267–71.
———. 1970. Society as organized flow: the Tairora case. *Southwestern Journal of Anthropology* 26: 107–24.
WAWN, WM. 1893. *The South Sea islanders and the Queensland labour trade: a record of voyages and experiences in the West Pacific, from 1875 to 1891*. London: Swan Sonnenschein and Co.
WEINREICH, URIEL. 1958. A retrograde sound shift in the guise of a survival: an aspect of Yiddish vowel development. *Estructuralismo e historia, miscelanea homenaje a André Martinet*, 2: 221–68. La Laguna.
WEINREICH, URIEL, WILLIAM LABOV, and MARVIN HERZOG. 1968. Empirical foundations for a theory of language change. In Lehmann and Malkiel, eds., *Directions for historical linguistics*. Austin: University of Texas Press, 97–195.
WOLFRAM, WALTER. 1973. On what basis variable rules? In Bailey and Shuy, eds. 1973: 1–22.
WOLFRAM, WALTER A. 1969. Detroit Negro speech. Center for Applied Linguistics, Washington, D.C.
WOOLFORD, ELLEN. 1975. Variation and change in the *i* predicate marker of New Guinea Tok Pisin. Paper prepared for the 1975 International Conference on Pidgins and Creoles.
———. 1977. Aspects of Tok Pisin grammar. Ph.D. dissertation, Duke University.
WURM, S. A. 1960. The changing linguistic picture of New Guinea. *Oceania* 31: 121–36.

———. 1961. Language map of the eastern, western and southern highlands, territory of Papua New Guinea. *Pacific Linguistics* D-4.

———. 1964. Australian New Guinea highlands languages and the distribution of their typological features. *American Anthropologist* 66, no. 4, pt. 2: 77–97.

———. 1966. Languages and literacy. In E. K. Fisk, ed., *New Guinea on the threshold*. Canberra: Australian National University Press, 135–48.

———. 1966–67. Papua-New Guinea nationhood: the problem of a national language. *Journal of the Papua New Guinea Society* 1(1): 7–19.

———. 1969. English, pidgin and what else? *New Guinea* 4(2): 1971: 30–42.

———. 1971a. The Papuan linguistic situation. In Sebeok, ed. 1971: 541–657.

———. 1971b. New Guinea highlands pidgin: course materials. *Pacific Linguistics* D-3.

———. 1971c. Pidgins, creoles and lingue franche. In Sebeok, ed. 1971: 999–1021.

———, ed. 1975. New Guinea area languages and language study, vol. 1; Papuan languages and the New Guinea linguistic scene. *Pacific Linguistics* C-38.

———, ed. 1976. New Guinea area languages and language study, vol. 2; Austronesian languages. *Pacific Linguistics* C-39.

———, ed. 1977. New Guinea area languages and language study, vol. 3: language, culture, society, and the modern world. *Pacific Linguistics* C-40.

WURM, S. A. and J. B. HARRIS. 1963. Police Motu: an introduction to the trade language of Papua (New Guinea), for anthropologists and other field-workers. *Pacific Linguistics* B-1.

WURM, S. A. and D. C. LAYCOCK. 1961. The question of language and dialect in New Guinea. *Oceania* 32: 128–43.

WURM, S. A. and D. C. LAYCOCK., eds, 1970. Pacific linguistic studies in honour of Arthur Capell. *Pacific Linguistics* C-13.

WURM, S. A., ed., with P. MÜHLHÄUSLER, D. C. LAYCOCK, and T. E. DUTTON. 1979. Handbook of New Guinea pidgin. *Pacific Linguistics* C-48, in press.

Z'GRAGGEN, J. A. 1971. Classificatory and typological studies in languages of the Madang District. *Pacific Linguistics* C-19.

———. 1976. Austronesian languages: Madang Province. In Wurm, ed. 1976: 285–99.

Author Index

Subject Index

Subject Index

constraints (*cont.*)
80, 289–90; contextual, 84, 154,
172; discourse, 82, 269; grammatical, 37, 84; linguistic, 55, 73, 78, 92,
214, 287; pragmatic, 285, 287; sequential, 279, 289–92; social, 84, 92,
171; syntactic, 83, 87, 217, 239, 278,
285
contact: language, linguistic, 7, 116,
141, 257
context, xviii, xx n, 31; linguistic,
58–59; sequential, 247; social, xvii,
82, 165, 188
continuum, 32, 44–45, 63, 77, 127,
165–66, 175, 177, 185; creole, 26,
64–65, 72
copula, contraction, 59; *être,* 312,
316–18, 320–22, 334–35, 337, 339
creole, 197–98; Guyanese, 64–65,
338 n
creolization, xx, 193, 197–98, 251,
254, 258, 267, 329

deixis, xxi n, 211, 221–23, 238
deletion: copula, 59; coreferential NP
(Equi-NP), 214–15, 217, 246, 251–
52; *i,* 269; *l,* 55–58, 62–64;
phonological, 269; *ne,* 295, 300–301;
que, 66–68, 85, 88–89
determinacy, 82
dgwa, 155–90
dialect(s), 5, 8–10, 12, 48, 57–58, 62,
72, 74–75, 101, 104–5, 134, 285; atlas, 76; boundary (*see* boundary,
linguistic); Buang, 34–35, 110,
113–15, 135–41, 153; chain, 3, 72,
110–11; French, 296; Kewa, 112;
Koiari, 111; leveling, 10, 257;
Narak, 112–13
diffusion, 143, 147–50
diglossia, 32–33, 43 n
discourse, xxi, 56, 160, 164, 171, 188,
211–55, 281, 289, 323; sequencing,
230, 320–21
Districts, Papua New Guinea. *See*
Papua New Guinea Provinces

elaboration, grammatical, xxi, 11,
193; lexical, 11; phonological, 11;
stylistic, 6
English, 23–26, 35, 39, 57, 65, 120,

122–29, 131, 196, 200, 212 n, 222–
23, 245 n, 247, 264; American, 14;
Black, 33, 52, 59; dialect, 32;
nonstandard, 7; "pidgin," 125 n
equivalence, 271, 288–89, 293; partial,
278
être. See auxiliary
Ewe, 212 n
exchange, silent, 117; verbal, xviii
existential sentence, 248, 265

feature, xviii, 37, 48, 54, 73, 76;
grammatical, 66; phonological, 66;
prestige, 16; probabilistic weights,
93; stigmatized, 14
France, 69, 76, 295, 300, 343. *See also*
French
free variation, 33, 55
French, 6, 64, 82, 138; Belgian, 295;
Canadian, 15; eighteenth century,
296; modern, 296, 314; Montréal,
52–53, 55–57, 61–62, 66, 82, 90–92,
193, 271–93, 295–345; nineteenth
century, 314; Parisian, 7, 300, 303
n; popular, 315; Québec, 15, 296;
seventeenth century, 295–96, 313;
sixteenth century, 295, 313; standard, 85, 92, 304, 345; of Tours, 295
frozen form, 297, 299
function, deictic, 222; discourse, 211,
260, 267, 270; grammatical, 200,
203, 314; language, linguistic, xxi,
30, 196, 258, 344; lexical, 314;
metalinguistic, 283; referential, xxi;
social, xxi, 39, 46, 198; of speech,
xvii n, 29, 48, 259

German, 5, 7–8, 20, 35, 128 n, 196,
199
grammar, xviii, xxi, 3, 11, 48, 50, 64,
72, 74, 78, 81–82, 85, 197, 262, 271,
341; French, 89–90; generative, 58,
60; phrase structure, 93; prescriptive, 314, 334, 342–43
grammaticalization, 193, 260, 269

Hiri Motu, 20, 35, 101, 120, 122–24,
126–29, 131
hypercorrection, 64, 73–74
i, 261–69
ia, 193, 212–55; deictic, 221–31, 253–